Population, Modernization,
and Social Structure

Population, Modernization, and Social Structure

CALVIN GOLDSCHEIDER

University of California, Berkeley

LITTLE, BROWN AND COMPANY *Boston*

LIBRARY OF CONGRESS CATALOG CARD NO. 74-165756

FIRST PRINTING: SEPTEMBER 1971

Printed simultaneously in Canada by
Little, Brown & Company (Canada) Limited

PRINTED IN THE UNITED STATES OF AMERICA

IN HONOR OF MY MOTHER
and
IN MEMORY OF MY FATHER

Preface

This book is a preliminary statement about the sociology of demographic processes. It represents part of the continuing search for the ways in which population and social systems can be articulated within more general theoretical models. I have attempted to identify and analyze, clearly and systematically, critical areas of convergence in sociological and demographic inquiries and to locate and clarify the theoretical issues, methodological dilemmas, and empirical problems associated with sociological demography. My intention has been to convey the intellectual excitement and fruitfulness of investigating the junctures of social and demographic systems, to raise challenging and critical questions about the sociological approach to population phenomena, and to provide analytic blueprints for future sociological studies of population processes.

The analysis focuses neither on all of sociology nor on all of demography; rather, specific gray areas of overlap and intersection have been selected to demonstrate the many ways in which our understanding of human society is improved through sociological analyses of demographic patterns. Two major substantive themes are emphasized: the role of population processes in the modernization of societies and the relationships between social differentiation and population processes. By carefully reconstructing historical and comparative evidence on social and population processes, we are able to find critical links between the major aspects of societal transformations encompassed by modernization and changes in fertility, mortality, and migration. From societal transformations the analysis shifts to the connections between population processes and social differentiation. Evidence on the social inequalities of death, religion and fertility, and social integration and migration is analyzed within consistent sociological frameworks.

Modernization and social differentiation are core areas of analytic concern to sociologists and demographers and are, in my view, the most conducive themes for sociological demography. To be sure, sociology and demography converge in other areas of inquiry and substantive spheres of research. However, these two themes are broad, flexible frameworks within which a comprehensive and systematic portrait may be sketched. Together with theoretical and methodological guidelines, the analysis provides beginning solutions to the challenge of sociological demography.

I have elected to concentrate on the theoretical and methodological side of sociological demography, although the empirical issues and evidence are by no means neglected. Nevertheless, measurement problems, procedures and techniques, and the general quantitative and statistical thrust of formal and descriptive demography have been kept to the bare minimum. Although a wide range of studies and data is reviewed, reflecting comparative and historical research strategies, the materials presented and the evidence cited are only illustrative of general patterns. I have attempted to avoid the dull, often boring, descriptions of demography that border on abstracted empiricism, and have refrained from the temptations of grand theory. My search has been toward the middle — shuttling between theory and research — to display sociological demography as a complex, interesting, and profound science. The only prerequisite for understanding the arguments and evaluating the data is a critical, inquisitive quest for comprehending human society.

Three elementary questions have guided the analysis: First, in what ways are population processes basic to the structure and functioning of human society? Second, how do we explain alterations, variations, continuities, and discontinuities in population processes within a systematic sociological framework? Third, what are the consequences of population dynamics for social change, social structure, and social process? If I have not succeeded in answering these questions fully, it is because my objective was to provide some direction toward their resolution and stimulate others to think creatively and to research systematically the issues posed by sociological demography. The results of the analysis presented in this book are therefore incomplete, suggestive, and largely prologue. The effort will have been worthwhile only if others fill in the gaps, revise tentative conclusions, qualify generalizations, sharpen the arguments, and add to our cumulative efforts in sociological demography.

Hundreds of researchers, sociologists, and demographers have contributed bits and pieces to this work. Their painstaking descriptions and detailed research have formed the heart of this book. Although emphasis has been placed on going beyond the descriptive toward the analytic, no one could proceed very far without the enormous amount of hard elementary labor upon which the theoretical foundations rest. Their contributions are inadequately acknowledged in the form of footnotes and references.

It is difficult to reconstruct or to trace the intellectual influences on my thinking about sociology and demography. Several scholars, however, shaped and guided my work directly and indirectly. My first exposure to sociology and demography was in a series of courses and conversations I had as an undergraduate at Yeshiva University under the tutelage of Professor Nathan Goldberg. Only in retrospect do I realize the richness of the experience and the greatness of the man. As an undergraduate I had never fully realized that demography and sociology were distinct areas of inquiry because they were always treated as parts of one general system. If this book argues successfully for their reintegration, it largely reflects the spirit of inquiry pursued by Nathan Goldberg.

As a graduate student, I had the good fortune of becoming an apprentice to Professor Sidney Goldstein of Brown University. His grasp of demographic materials, methodology, and research enlarged my appreciation of the unique contribution of demography to sociological inquiry. His demand for systemic and careful research and his uncompromising standards of scholarship have been of enormous help in guiding my work. More important, his friendship, encouragement, and concern for me as a colleague can never be thanked adequately or repaid fully. It is a great joy and inspiration to see humanistic and scientific qualities blend so harmoniously in one man. He took time out of his hectic schedule to carefully read and critically evaluate an earlier version of this book. Although I was unable to enlarge on all his creative suggestions for revision, his insights and keen sense of judgment are sincerely appreciated.

No one who writes about the sociology of demographic processes can neglect the important contributions of Kingsley Davis. More than anyone, he has argued convincingly and forcefully for the integration of sociology and demography. His ideas and research in sociological demography have inspired the orientation of the analysis presented in this book. Neil Smelser, Reinhard Bendix, and Arthur Stinchcombe, colleagues at the University of California, Berkeley, influenced my general sociological perspective through their published research and in personal discussions. In general, the stimulating intellectual atmosphere in the Department of Sociology at Berkeley provided an exciting setting for thinking about and researching sociological and demographic problems.

Most material presented in this book has not been published before. A draft of sections of Chapters Two and Three was circulated in preliminary form, and Arthur Stinchcombe, Sidney Goldstein, and Ruth Dixon kindly provided constructive criticisms. The section in Chapter Three outlining the migration system was presented at the general conference of the International Union for the Scientific Study of Population, London, September 1969. Parts of Chapter Ten represent an expansion and revision of materials that first appeared in an article entitled "Fertility of the Jews," *Demography*, 4, 1967, and were expanded in "Minority Group Status and Fertility," *American Journal of Sociology*, 74, 1969 (coauthored with Peter Uhlenberg). The basic data presented in parts of Chapter Eleven derive from a larger study directed by Georges Sabagh and Maurice D. Van Arsdol, Jr., and were described in the two papers cited in that chapter. But the arguments have been totally reorganized and enlarged, and I accept sole responsibility for the interpretations presented here. I am grateful for the opportunity to have collaborated closely with these scholars. In a seminar I offered in the sociology of human migration, David Laitan, a graduate student in political science at Berkeley, brought to my attention the importance of examining African migrations. Discussions with him led me to consider the possibility of converting what I had thought was the unique into the illustrative. The results, presented in Chapter Seven, owe much to his initial stimulation.

Writing requires, in addition to stimulating colleagues and students, time to think and engage in research. I was fortunate to receive a University of California faculty fellowship in the summer of 1968 which provided me time to begin systematically organizing the materials for this book. Some of the analysis presented in Part 2 and the final touches to the manuscript were completed during my stay in Jerusalem, Israel, for the academic year 1969–1970. I would like to thank the University of California, Berkeley, and its Department of Sociology for granting me a partial sabbatical and leave of absence to work on these and other materials. The Department of Demography at the Hebrew University of Jerusalem, its staff and students, provided a stimulating atmosphere for my work and an opportunity to sound out some of my ideas.

The chores of typing, proofreading, and living with me during the completion of this book fell upon my wife, Barbara. As on previous occasions, she did a masterful job. Her positive response to my work encouraged me to overcome the many periods of frustration and depression. She is neither a demographer nor a sociologist and in general is disinterested in both areas of inquiry. Nevertheless, she read through the manuscript with patience and care and found some of the materials readable and exciting. What more can I ask of my "Woman of Valor"?

C. G.

Contents

Part 1
SOCIOLOGY AND DEMOGRAPHY

Part 2
MODERNIZATION AND POPULATION PROCESSES

Part 3

SOCIAL DIFFERENTIATION
AND POPULATION PROCESSES

*Population, Modernization,
and Social Structure*

Part
1

Sociology
and Demography

Chapter One

SOCIOLOGICAL DEMOGRAPHY: THE CHALLENGE

Population events are conspicuous and regular occurrences in the lives of persons, families, and societies. The birth of a baby, the death of a relative or friend, the relocation of a family are clearly occasions of personal and social relevance. If we judge from the secular and religious rituals surrounding population events and from the social and personal meanings attached to them, it becomes clear that birth, death, and movement are neither trivial nor insignificant. By extension, the cumulative processes of population events and the resultant implications for the size, distribution, and composition of populations are fundamental to the structure and functioning of human societies. People are the stuff from which families, groups, societies, and nations are constructed; the processes of population are the building blocks shaping the form and content of social units. In turn, the individual and personal aspects of population phenomena are conditioned and affected by the power of social forces; what appears on the surface to represent biological and idiosyncratic events are by their nature social as well.

In a time when "ecology" has become a social movement and the "population explosion" a household phrase, it is almost unnecessary to emphasize the societal and social problems generated by population growth, size, and distribution. The size, growth, density, concentration, and dispersal of population, birth and death rates, cityward and suburbanward migrations, have become social issues for many reasons and in various social contexts, but mainly because population processes affect and are affected by the organization and anatomy of society. The quantity of population shapes the quality of social life. The reverse is

3

equally true: the quality and fabric of social life shape the quantity and character of population processes.

THE SCIENCE OF DEMOGRAPHY

Demography is the systematic scientific study of population events in individual and aggregate forms. Several distinct but interconnected layers of emphasis form the science of demography, so it is necessary to establish from the outset the thrust of our approach. In its most narrow, mundane, and descriptive form, demography is the collection, organization, and presentation of the statistics of population; the technical, statistical manipulation of demographic data; the development of quantitative measures of population phenomena; and the description of national, subnational, and local populations in terms of demographic data. No analysis of population processes can neglect the data, techniques, measurements, and descriptions of demography. Yet, to view these exercises as ends in themselves is to whet the appetite and neglect the soul.

Building upon this elementary layer of social or demographic bookkeeping are two divergent trends. One emphasizes formal statistical models of population patterns. Analyzing the patterns of population size, structure, composition, and distribution that emerge from relationships among demographic variables is often called *formal demography*. Certain regularities, for example, are observable in the aggregate between age and death in every society; population size is a function solely of the cumulative patterned relationships between levels of births, deaths, and net movements; systematic interconnections may be charted between levels of births and deaths over time within societies. In short, given a relatively limited number of population variables in interaction, fixed and varied forms of demographic models may be constructed and analyzed. These models may summarize empirical evidence, often quantified and mathematical, or evaluate and/or reconstruct demographic data, or provide the foundation for extrapolating past demographic patterns into the future. Formal models are often statistically elegant and have been of great practical utility; however, they seldom provide insight into social scientific questions associated with the "whys" of population patterns and processes.

To unravel these "whys" of population processes we must turn to the second trend within demography, which is based on cumulative demographic analyses and descriptions. *Sociological demography* [1] is a clearly

[1] The emphasis on the connections between population phenomena and social variables, with some variation, has also been referred to as "population studies" (in contrast to demographic analysis), "social demography," and "demographic sociology." See Philip Hauser and Otis D. Duncan (eds.), *The Study of Population* (Chi-

distinct theme in the science of demography, and its goals are to identify, illustrate, and analyze systematically and rigorously the junctures of social and demographic processes. In contrast to the emphasis on population descriptions, demographic measurement and techniques, the statistical manipulation of population data, and demographic modelbuilding (where the objective is analyzing the variables of the population system per se), sociological demography shuttles between the population and the social system, utilizing the cumulative theories, methodologies, and evidence available from sociology and demography to resolve one fundamental question: How do we improve our understanding of human society through the analysis of population processes? Demographic data, measurement, techniques, and models are necessary means but they are only part of the analytic picture; not only must population processes be unraveled but the social processes that are the determinants and consequences of population phenomena must be analyzed as well. The sociological approach to demography argues on theoretical, methodological, and empirical grounds that social scientists cannot understand fully the nature of human society without a clear comprehension of the integral role played by population processes in the dynamics of social life. In turn, demographers cannot hope to understand population dynamics without comprehending the social processes within which population changes occur.

This book takes up the challenge of sociological demography — a challenge espoused by many but pursued by few. What emerges is not a new demography but a selective synthesis of perspectives about population phenomena and a fresh critical approach to placing population processes in the mainstream of sociological analyses. To be effective, this synthesis requires consolidation, expansion, experimentation, reconceptualization, and establishing creative guidelines for future inquiries. What will be offered perhaps are too many interesting and provocative questions with too few firm and convincing answers. Those who read through the analyses expecting that solutions will be proposed to the complex and perplexing problems posed by the sociological analysis of population processes will surely be disappointed. Instead, the lesson to be learned is that much work is yet to be done, and that there are no simple or obvious solutions. We hope to convey some sense of direction in the systematic sociological analysis of demographic processes; we want to reroute the questions of population research to offer beginning solutions to problems of population analysis. A critical reading of the population

cago: University of Chicago Press, 1959), pp. 2–3; Kingsley Davis, "Social Demography," in *The Behavioral Sciences*, ed. Bernard Berelson (New York: Basic Books, 1963), chap. 17; Pitirim Sorokin, *Contemporary Sociological Theories* (New York: Harper and Row, Harper Torchbook edition, 1964), chap. 7.

literature suggests, at least to me, that demographers have rarely provided sound sociological answers to population problems because they have rarely asked the right sociological questions.

The emphasis on sociological demography will be combined with a deemphasis on quantification and techniques. The prestige of quantification has become so great in the social sciences that the value of population studies has often been viewed almost exclusively in terms of their data, measurement, and techniques. Hence, many social scientists, unfamiliar in large part with the special tools of demography, tend to view population phenomena as tangential or inconsequential in the analysis of society. Most demographers tend to reinforce this view by their own parochialism. Overwhelmed in part by the regular and massive outpouring of population information, demographers have directed their major attention to the technical and descriptive side of demography. Consequently, when social scientists utilize demographic data they often trivialize the empirical complexities; when demographers attempt to explain refined population data, they often trivialize the theoretical complexities.

Almost without exception, and quite properly, population analyses emphasize safeguards against inadequate statistics and common data pitfalls. Rarely, if ever, are warnings given against an equally prevalent malady — conceptual and theoretical pitfalls. Sources, problems, techniques, measurements, and descriptions of data have regularly been presented, but it is rare to find a systematic discussion of the theoretical or methodological issues emerging from the social scientific analyses of demographic patterns.

Demographic data and techniques have such obvious practical uses that to focus on description and learn the technical tricks of the trade without understanding the sociological significance of population patterns or the analytic value of demographic information is not entirely without merit. However, when the social scientist wants to investigate the role of population processes in the structure and functioning of human society, he must know the conceptual foundations of population analysis and evaluate them critically. Despite the many practical applications of demography, which are still being explored, its chief value for our purposes rests with its meaning for the understanding of human society.

Because this book seeks to systematically analyze the interconnections between population and social systems, it cannot provide instruction in the technical construction of demographic measures except as they relate to this objective. Hence, no discussion of how to calculate demographic rates will be presented nor will we set forth the formal construction of life tables, nor cohort fertility measures, nor the various procedures for estimating migration ratios, nor for that matter any technical paraphernalia of demographic measurement. Materials and manuals on population techniques, from the elementary to the mathematically sophisticated, are readily available as are books and pamphlets on how to utilize population data and how to avoid the common errors of population statistics. But our objective is to exhibit population processes as an integral part of social, economic, political, and cultural life; to examine population materials not as isolated items of interest but as both cause and effect of social life and its institutional structure. When a tree has been bent so much in one direction, it is not possible to merely straighten it out. To have the tree grow erectly once again, it has to be bent in the extreme opposite direction. Demography has been bent toward the technical, descriptive, and statistical; as a balance, we shall stress the theoretical and methodological side of population processes in sociological perspective. Hopefully, the end result of both tendencies will be more fruitful intellectual development. Generally, an essential feature of a science for the vast majority is that it is profound. Whatever else a science might be, it must represent a body of theoretical, methodological, and empirical materials tied together systematically so that the finished product is not trivial.[2] One way toward this goal in the science of demography is the sociological analysis of population processes.

THE POPULATION SYSTEM

The first step toward locating the junctures of population and social processes is to clarify the essential features of the population system. The systematic sociological analysis of the determinants and consequences of population processes must be formulated on the answers to three logically prior questions: (1) What are the basic elements of the population system? (2) How do these elements combine to engender changes in the system? (3) How are the elements related to each other? Only after the elements of the population system are identified, correlated, and analyzed can we shift attention to the interaction of the population system with other subsystems of human society.[3]

[2] For a general discussion of this notion in sociology, see Allan Mazur, "The Littlest Science," *The American Sociologist*, 3 (August 1968), pp. 195–200. For a critique of the tendency toward triviality in the social sciences, see Barrington Moore, Jr., *Political Power and Social Theory* (New York: Harper and Row, 1965), pp. 138–139.

[3] The same argument is made by Kingsley Davis, "The Sociology of Demographic Behavior," in *Sociology Today*, ed. Robert Merton et al. (New York: Basic Books, 1959), p. 326.

Population Elements and Change

There are only two basic processes in every population system — the number of people who enter and the number of people who leave that population. The size of a population at any point in time and changes in population size over time are determined exclusively by these cumulative processes.[4] Persons may enter a population through birth, which we call *fertility*, or through moving into it, which, when the nation is the unit of investigation, is referred to as *immigration;* when some unit smaller than a nation is the unit of investigation (e.g., state, region, neighborhood), we refer to moving as *in-migration.* Exiting may occur through death, which we call *mortality*, or through moving out of the population, *emigration* or *out-migration* depending on whether the nation or a unit smaller than a nation is defined as the focus of investigation.

Entering and exiting thus entail three elements of the population system: fertility, mortality, and migration. Unlike fertility and mortality, migration involves *both* entering and exiting processes. When the analysis unit is the "world population system" or when a smaller sociogeographic unit is defined as the population system *and* that unit does not experience any substantial immigration (or in-migration) or emigration (or out-migration), only two elements must be considered: fertility and mortality. These two components are often referred to as *vital elements,* not because they are more crucial than migration but simply because they refer to the biologically related processes of birth and death and are universal. At times, for various analytic purposes, it is desirable to "think away" the migration component of the population system and to treat the population under investigation *as if* it were "closed," i.e., closed to migration.

At least three additional factors are often included as integral elements of the population system: (1) population structure, i.e., age and sex distribution; (2) population composition, i.e., a wide range of sociodemographic "characteristics" of populations, including such items as

---

[4] The centrality of "entering" and "exiting" in population processes parallels in interesting and significant ways entering and exiting in other social processes. For example, entering and exiting are critical processes in family formation (marriage, family building, divorce), social mobility (entering and exiting social class strata, inter- and intrageneration mobility), educational processes (entrance, dropping out, graduation), organizational changes, religious membership (religious intermarriages and conversions), among many others. In one sense, entering and exiting phenomena are integral to general social processes, and population processes may represent but one specific example. For a different view of the population system see Norman Ryder, "Notes on the Concept of a Population," *American Journal of Sociology,* 69 (March 1964), pp. 447–463.

marital status, income, race, education, occupation, or religion; (3) population distribution, i.e., the spread and location of a population over a
given territory.[5] These three factors will be treated extensively in later
sections of the book. Population structure, composition, and distribution
provide the beginning clues for analyzing the determinants and consequences of mortality, fertility, and migration; as such, we shall treat these
factors as part of the social context of population analysis. In one sense,
the structure, composition, and distribution of a population may be
viewed as intermediate "connectors" between population and social systems, rather than as elements of the population system narrowly defined.

The entering and exiting processes associated with fertility, mortality, and migration are the most elementary components of the population system. We must examine how they affect population size and
how these elements relate to one another.

We may start with a simple proposition: Between any two time
periods population size may either increase, decrease, or remain stable.
If we view the population system as "closed" to migration, three models
of population change based on the interaction of vital elements emerge:
(1) population size can increase only when fertility is higher than mortality; (2) population size can decrease only when mortality is higher
than fertility; and (3) when fertility and mortality are equal, population
size remains stable.

When we move beyond the interaction of vital elements in a closed
population and "open up" the population system, the *net* contribution of
migration to population size must be added. Net movements may result
in a positive addition of numbers, a negative subtraction of numbers, or
no net change. If the analysis unit is a nation, these three patterns of net
movement are the result of *international migrations;* when it is any
geographic unit smaller than a nation, net movement is the result of
internal or *international migration.*

When we combine these three types of net movements with the
patterns of population change flowing from the interaction of fertility
and mortality, thirteen models of population change may be identified
(see Table 1.1).

[5] For a broader inclusive delineation of demography, see Hauser and Duncan,
The Study of Population, chap. 1. Other social processes have been included within
population studies, for example, marriage and family patterns. But again these
processes are more appropriately viewed as social correlates of population processes
rather than as elements of the population system. Wrigley includes marriage and family patterns as basic elements in demographic behavior but he neglects issues of
integral importance, in particular migration. See E. A. Wrigley, *Population and
History* (London: Weidenfeld and Nicolson, World University Library, 1969), pp.
8–14.

Sociology and Demography

Table 1.1. Models of Population Change in Terms
of Population Components

	Net migration		
	Positive	*Negative*	*Zero ("closed")*
Mortality higher than fertility	I.D.S.	D	D
Mortality lower than fertility	I	I.D.S.	I
Mortality same as fertility	I	D	S

Note: I = Population increase; D = Population decrease; S = Population stability.

Population *increase* may result when:

   1. mortality is higher than fertility but net positive migration compensates for *vital* losses;
   2. mortality is lower than fertility whether there is net positive migration, or
   3. no net migration, or
   4. where net negative migration is not large enough to offset fertility gains;
   5. mortality is the same as fertility and there is net positive migration.

Population *decrease* may result when:

   6. mortality is higher than fertility whether there is net negative migration, or
   7. no net migration, or
   8. when net positive migration does not compensate for population losses due to higher mortality;
   9. mortality is lower than fertility and net negative migration is large enough to erase the gains flowing from the balance of vital elements;
  10. mortality and fertility are equal and net migration is negative.

Population size *will not change* when:

  11. mortality is higher than fertility and net positive migration restores the loss due to excess mortality;
  12. mortality is lower than fertility and net negative migration compensates for the gain due to excess fertility;
  13. mortality and fertility are equal and there is no net migration.

The original three models of demographic change in a closed population are identical to the patterns obtained when no net migration occurs. Most importantly, the thirteen population change models represent

the range of *all* possibilities of population size changes in terms of the
three elementary processes that compose the population system.

Of course, this is only a minimum and elementary picture of the
population system. The first difficulty with these population models
emerges from discussing migration in terms of *net* gains, *net* losses, or no
net changes. Net gains through migration or net positive migration may
result from either the one-way movement of persons into a population
with no countermovement out of the same population, *or* movements into
or out of a population where the former exceeds the latter. Similarly,
net negative migration or losses may result from one-way movements out
of a population with no counterflows into that population *or* from two-
way movements into and out of a population where there is greater out-
movement than in-movement. Finally, no net migration may result from
an equal flow into and out of a population *or* no movements in either
direction. When "net" migration patterns are subdivided into these
dichotomous alternatives, the total number of population change models
based on the interaction of population components doubles to twenty-six.

The importance of subdividing net migration into these alternative
possibilities is of more than passing significance. With respect to population growth. i.e., treating migration as an element of the population system, the subdivision is not of particular relevance because attention is
directed to the contribution of *net* migration changes to population size
changes. Yet, in subsequent analysis, when the interrelationships of
population and social systems are examined and, in turn, migration is
reconceptualized as an independent social process, the elements of the
migration system must be examined in detail.[6] For example, if we are
interested not only in the role of migration in rural population change
but also in *why* people move out of rural areas, we must consider various
migration streams, including rural out-migration, rural in-migration, and
return migration (i.e., previous out-migrants who return to their rural
homes). Thus, we will have to locate elements of *in-* and *out-*movement
and not be content solely with *net* movement. Similarly, the sociologist is
often interested in *movers* rather than *net movement*. If, for a given year,
3,000 persons move to a country and 2,500 persons move out of a country, the *net* migration gain is 500 persons. When our focus is on the role
of migration in population size changes, this net figure of 500 is relevant.
However, when we are concerned with *movers*, we will have to account
for the movement of 5,500 persons. That is, when the analysis unit is the
moving individual, the total number of movers is the relevant item.
Under some conditions, even when the analysis unit is the community,
subdividing net migration into its component parts is significant, par-

[6] See the outline of the migration system in Chapter 3, this book.

ticularly in some types of comparisons. For example, two metropolitan
areas may have experienced no *net* migration during a specified interval.
Suppose, however, that in one metropolitan area *heavy but equal* migratory flows into and out of the area result in no net migration, although
the absence of net migration in the second metropolitan area is a result
of no movements into or out of the area. The social, economic, political,
demographic, and cultural impact of the heavy but equal migratory
flows in the first metropolitan area may be substantially different than
the total lack of movement in the second metropolitan area, *despite* that
no overall net population change due to migration has occurred in either
area. This would also hold if we were dealing with international migration with the nation as the analysis unit. Thus, whenever we move beyond the narrow question of the role of migration in population size
changes we must analyze carefully the elements involved within the migration process.

In these elementary models of population change, population increases, decreases, and stability were treated without regard to the overall character of demographic conditions. A second set of complicating
issues relates, therefore, to the *level* of population processes that affect
population size changes. In general, population size may change under
two extreme ideal-typical situations: under conditions when the vital elements are "high" or "uncontrolled," and under conditions when the vital
elements are "low" or "controlled." Thus, for example, population growth
in a closed system may occur when fertility is higher than mortality
when both elements are relatively high or when both elements are relatively low.[7] The same is true for population decrease and stability. In
short, population size and change in a closed system reflect the balance
of fertility and mortality under the two ideal-typical conditions of control
or noncontrol. It is also possible, and quite common in historical and
comparative contexts, that one of the vital elements might be more controlled while the other less controlled. The basic pattern is still applicable, although the result is accentuated changes in population size.

Separating the vital components of population into high or low
ideal types is important precisely when we must identify sources of
potential changes and not only describe past changes. As will become
clear, it is essential to note not only whether population is growing but
the general *demographic* conditions under which population growth occurs. Because our concern is with future changes, particularly the interaction of population and other elements of the social system, it becomes
necessary to distinguish at least between those demographic situations

---

[7] It is difficult to posit ideal-typical models of control or noncontrol for migration. For a discussion of the general complexities of migration, see Chapter 3; an
illustrative analysis of migration changes in the modernization process is presented in
Chapter 7.

where fertility and mortality are not controlled and when they are controlled. The introduction of the control-noncontrol distinction in the relationship between fertility and mortality doubles once again the models of population change.

Finally, for purposes of illustration, the extent of population changes has been simplified. Underlying the presentation of population models rests an implicit assumption of unilinearity and unidirectionality: between any two time periods population size may increase, decrease, or remain stable. In its most simple form, that is essentially correct. However, a little reflection suggests that *in between* two time periods population size and the elements of the population system may vary in direction and zig-zag in pattern. For example, if by comparing population processes and sizes in 1960 and 1970 we discover that the population of a particular country has increased as a result of a combination of net positive migration (one-directional) and higher fertility than mortality (under "controlled" conditions). However, it is possible and likely that population growth was not uniform *during* this decade nor may it be assumed that population elements and population size changed in the same direction throughout this period. Population size may have declined during the first several years of the decade and increased sufficiently in the latter half of the decade to yield an overall growth rate for the entire decade; or population size may have increased throughout the decade but the *pace* of growth may have been more rapid at various points within the arbitrary selected period. Moreover, changes in one element may have been a more significant factor in population increase during selected periods within the decade. In short, the overall view of population growth in terms of population elements *between* two time periods may obscure fluctuations and variations in population processes and size *during* two time periods and says little about the pace of change.

Hence we must exercise caution in choosing time periods and attempt to locate continuities as well as discontinuities in the patterns of population change and in the elementary component processes of that change. Indeed, the zig-zags of population changes, fluctuations and variations in population processes often provide important clues for analyzing overall population changes. Further, for introductory purposes, it is sufficient to refer to "increase" or "decrease" in population size and to suggest the ways in which population elements interact to produce these changes. However, in the detailed subsequent analysis particularly close attention will be focused on the *pace* of population changes and on the relative contribution of the three elements of the population system in affecting those changes.

At this point, two connected principles emerge: (1) only through the combined effects of mortality, fertility, and migration can the size of populations change; (2) any analysis of changes in population size as a first step must identify the component structure of those changes. Together, these principles provide a major premise for our subsequent inquiry: If we are to find links between population and social systems, our analysis must focus on the elementary processes of the population system — fertility, mortality, and migration — separately and in combination. Stated in negative form: Analyzing the relationship between population size changes — growth or decline — and alterations in the social system is not likely to yield fruitful conclusions when population size changes are treated in abstraction from the three elements that shape its form.

The various *possibilities* of population change models in no way imply that some models are not more prevalent in the demographic history of societies than others. Indeed, a significant theme in demography centers on "demographic transition theory," which posits that under preindustrial conditions population growth is relatively low due to the relative balance of vital rates at high levels. In modern industrialized societies, population growth is also relatively slow due to a relative balance of fertility and mortality at low levels. In the transition from traditional to modern, from agricultural to industrial, from rural to urban societies, population growth is rapid due to sharper and swifter declines in mortality than in fertility. The various and cogent criticisms of demographic transition theory and the implicit assumptions underlying its formulation will evolve as we focus in subsequent analysis on modernization and population processes. Suffice it to say that despite the general temptation of viewing demographic history through the lens of demographic transition theory, the theoretical, methodological, and empirical inadequacies associated with these hypothesized relationships render the theory virtually useless analytically. Two points are important in the present context: First, the theory is a statement largely about the population system as such; hence, it provides but minimum interest to the social scientist concerned with the determinants and consequences of population transformations. Second, even as a statement confined to the population system, the theory omits one major factor in population growth, migration. It fails as well to specify the interrelationships among the elements of the population system.

THE INTERDEPENDENCE
OF POPULATION COMPONENTS

The various ways the elements of population systems combine to affect population size and change bring us to the third aspect of the population system, i.e., the interdependence of the population elements.

It should be clear that the interaction of fertility, mortality, and migration determines the size of a population; whenever one of these elements changes, some change in population size *or* in one of the other elements is inevitable. If, for example, net positive migration increases, population size must increase unless fertility decreases or mortality increases to balance gains brought about by migration. The dynamics of the population system suggest further that population size and change may *affect* fertility, mortality, and migration. The relationship between the elements of population and population change therefore must be viewed as two-directional: changes in population size are both resultants and determinants of mortality, fertility, and migration.

Moreover, the interaction and interdependence of these population system elements may be analyzed irrespective of their relationship to changes in population size. Each element may be viewed as a determinant and as a consequence of the other elements: Fertility may be treated as an "independent" demographic process that may affect mortality and migration processes; fertility may also be conceptualized as a "dependent" process that results from particular patterns of mortality and migration. Similarly, mortality and migration may be viewed as independent and dependent demographic processes. At times, it will not be possible analytically to isolate whether a particular element is an independent or dependent process — all we will know is that the elements are *correlative*. When viewed in some time perspective, the population system elements tend to have a chain reaction, each becoming a determinant and subsequently a consequent of the other. To illustrate the interdependence of the population components and the possible consequences of population growth for migration, fertility, and mortality changes, we shall examine two hypothetical cases.

First, let us imagine a traditional agricultural village. Most people who live in "Agriville" were born there, marry others from Agriville, and will die there. There is no movement in and out of Agriville, and it is relatively isolated from other communities in this imaginary country. Family size in Agriville is fairly large on the average, and children are viewed as assets for farm labor. Most people marry and at early ages, have their babies soon after marriage, and continue having children until they are no longer able biologically to reproduce. Medicine and medical services are nonexistent except for various folk remedies. Most people do not live to very old age and many babies die before they are a year old. These patterns of high fertility, high mortality, and little or no net migration result in population stability as well as social stability for the population of Agriville.

Let us now suppose that the government of the "traditional" country within which Agriville is located decides to accept the offer of an international health organization to curb its high mortality. Public health programs designed to rid the rural countryside of malaria and other communicable diseases are instituted, and these major causes of death are eliminated effectively and inexpensively. The people of Agriville are inoculated, their crops are sprayed, and death rates decline drastically in a short period. Although the people of Agriville have done nothing themselves, the external influence that brought about swift mortality declines may have some drastic demographic consequences independent of population growth changes.

The decrease in mortality may result in an increase in fertility. Adult men and women in the prime reproductive ages who might have died from communicable diseases have been "spared" and their fertility span may increase. The general increase in health levels may affect positively the ability to produce more and healthier babies. Children who would have died at an earlier age and those who would not have survived their first year are now able to live to reproduce others. The total effect of the mortality reduction may result in increases in aggregate and individual fertility, in the number of conceptions resulting in gestation, in the number of children born who remain alive, in the number of children who grow up to have children of their own, and in the length of time the married couple may spend during their reproductive years before one spouse dies.

The stable balance in population size maintained for centuries in Agriville has now been upset. Population growth results directly from the disequilibrium, externally induced, of mortality decline and indirectly by increases in fertility. A now greater population size occupies the same territory as before. The increasing population limits the ability of the agricultural, subsistence-based economy to sustain an ever increasing population; the hardest hit are those who previously were at subsistence levels – the great majority. Without adequate food and opportunity, a selected number of young persons may begin to leave Agriville for other communities to seek means of sustenance and some chance to share in life's opportunity. In short, mortality declines have led to fertility increases and selected out-migration. Under subsistence conditions, if the population increase is not "neutralized" by either fertility reduction, out-migration, major increases in agricultural yields, or the external importation of food supplies, mortality levels have to increase. Over time, a population has to maintain some balance with food supplies; if the challenge of population growth brought about by mortality reduction does not engender a response in terms of "positive" changes, mortality will increase to a level consistent with the food supply.

Let us take a different starting point and examine the impact of out-migration on demographic processes. Let us note that for some reason a significant number of young adults leave Agriville. (This may be the result of mortality declines, or the opening up of a nearby government factory, or offers of land in other parts of the country, or any one of many factors. The initiation of the change at this point is not relevant.) This out-migration of young persons may have dramatic repercussions for the two other demographic processes — fertility and mortality — and population size. Given a significant stream of selective out-migration, let us say of young adults, it is likely that the aggregate fertility of Agriville will decrease. Because many young persons who are in their prime reproductive years leave, marriages and births will decline. This will occur whether the young adults who migrate out are primarily of one sex, leaving an imbalance in the sex ratio (the number of males to females), or whether there is no sex selectivity but an equal out-movement of men and women, reducing the overall reproductive potential of Agriville. Individual fertility responses also may result from out-migration. Delays in family formation, reduction in the fertility of the migrants, or increases in native fertility may follow from heavy out-migration of selective groups.

In a similar way out-migration of young adults may affect the mortality of Agriville. If many young adults leave Agriville, the age composition of the remaining population in Agriville will be more heavily weighted toward older persons, whose death rates are higher. Thus, *areal* mortality or the overall death rate of Agriville will increase. Furthermore, the mortality of the migrants may increase (if the hardship of moving is high) or decrease (if the areas of destination have better medical and health facilities). In sum, when out-migration is viewed as the independent process, changes in fertility and mortality result.

Let us now take a third starting point and imagine that fertility in Agriville increases. Again, it is not our immediate concern why this occurs, whether because of mortality declines, or reduced venereal disease, or improved living conditions, or any other factor. If fertility increases, one possible consequence is increases in selected types of mortality — particularly those associated with childbearing. We might expect that maternal mortality, i.e., mortality of women as a result of childbearing, will increase, not only in its total incidence in Agriville but particularly for women of high parity (women with a large number of pregnancies). Moreover, with fertility increases, assuming a stable but subsistence economy, the total number of persons to feed increases and overall mortality, but especially among children, might increase. Along similar lines, when fertility increases and the subsistence economy remains the same, some pressure toward out-migration might develop.

Thus, any change in one population element in Agriville tends to affect the other elements. If mortality levels decrease, fertility or out-migration or both may increase; if out-migration of the young increases, areal fertility as well as individual fertility may decrease and areal mortality may increase, although individual mortality may increase or decrease; if fertility increases, selective mortality may increase and out-migration may result. Most important, this illustrates the chainlike characteristics of population elements that result in each element becoming in turn an independent and dependent demographic process. Mortality declines may result in fertility increases, which in turn may increase out-migration, and, in turn, may change mortality levels.

This illustration may create the impression that the interdependence of population elements is limited to traditional, rural areas with sustained high vital rates and geographic isolation. To dispel this erroneous conclusion, let us consider briefly another illustration in which the analysis unit changes from a rural area within a country to a modern nation-state, "Modland," where vital rates are low, and a substantial amount of movement is a regular feature.

Let us imagine that for various "external" reasons (for example, war, excessive air pollution, natural disasters, economic depressions, or urban riots), mortality rates increase in Modland. As a consequence of increases in mortality, delayed fertility, family formation changes, and family size might be affected. If the mortality increase operates selectively, as is most likely, and reduces the number of young adult males, as in war, fertility declines may occur. As a consequence of such selective mortality, labor shortages may result and additional persons may be needed to occupy jobs vacated by males. Consequently, immigration may increase either in response to "economic opportunities" created by labor demands resulting from mortality changes or as part of a government recruitment program. Internal migration may also increase.

If we now start with the immigration of young adults, we may expect the fertility level of the country to increase and, depending on the areas of origins of the immigrants, fertility of the migrants may increase or decrease. We might also expect that the immigration of a large number of persons in selective ages would alter the age composition of Modland and areal mortality would decrease. The mortality of migrants might increase (hardship of travel, overcrowded urban living conditions), or decrease (exposure to better health and medical facilities and services), and the mortality of natives of Modland might increase as a result of the specific new diseases brought by newcomers.

Finally, let us imagine that, in Modland, new or improved contraceptive devices are developed and diffused throughout the population and fertility declines. With declines in the fertility level the need for space and larger housing units declines and suburbanization decreases. We might also expect that part of maternal mortality associated with higher parity women would also decline as might deaths from abortion following the decline in "unwanted" children with the use of more efficient contraception. Again, as in the case of Agriville, population elements in Modland exhibit chainlike characteristics.

The various types of interdependence among the population components that emerge from these illustrations only suggest possibilities and do not imply any necessary pattern of change. However, mortality, fertility, and migration may be treated as both independent and dependent demographic processes in all societies, whether the analysis unit is an area within a country or the country itself, and whether the area is "traditional" or "modern." Moreover, any change in one population element may affect changes in other components of the population system irrespective of and/or in conjunction with its impact on changes in population size. The interdependence of population elements implies a chainlike reaction among fertility, mortality, and migration processes. Hence, over time, these processes may be viewed as correlative. In addition, changes may occur more or less simultaneously in two of the elements engendering alterations in the third component. Increases in fertility and mortality reduction may result in out-migration through the impact of population growth on food supplies; fertility reduction and out-migration may bring about increases in areal mortality through changes in the age structure; declines in mortality and in-migration may result in reductions in levels of fertility through changes in marriage rates or economic conditions.

Up to this point, the population system has been treated as a total system more or less independent of external nondemographic influences. The isolation of the elements of the population system and the brief examination of their relationship to population growth and to each other are but preliminaries to identifying and analyzing the interactions of population and social systems. Upon the elementary layer of the population system we may begin constructing the analytic apparatus of sociological demography. Essentially we want to know what happens when the elements of the population system and their various configurations are reconceptualized as a subsystem of the broader society. In what ways are the processes of population structure and change shaped and affected by the contours of the social system, and how do population processes condition and determine the other elements or subsystems of society? Indeed, what roles do population phenomena play as consequences and determinants of the economy, polity, family, and culture in human society?

Before turning to these substantive issues and problems, general theoretical and methodological guidelines must be reviewed. The sociological analysis of demographic phenomena involves assumptions and preconceptions about both social and demographic analysis. Often these logically prior issues have been ignored in demographic research or have been treated inadequately or inaccurately. Sociological demography cannot proceed very far unless these issues are identified and clarified.

Chapter Two

DILEMMAS IN
SOCIOLOGICAL DEMOGRAPHY

It is generally accepted that natural and social science is guided by the search for comprehensive theories and systematic explanations about reliable, empirically observed evidence. All the advances that may be made in data collection, observation methods, measurement techniques, concept specification, refinements of variables, and descriptions of empirical correlations are necessary adjuncts to and indispensable, perhaps prerequisites, for sound theory construction. In no way, however, can these critical dimensions of the scientific enterprise be substituted for theoretical analysis and methodical explanation. Indeed, all empirical research *implicates* theory, but some studies focus on theory explicitly, formally, and deliberately, whereas others treat theory more casually, informally, and implicitly.[1] From the other side, building theories and fashioning explanations in an empirical vacuum are empty exercises. The scientific framework demands a constant interplay between theory and research, explanation and observation, the collection, measurement, organization, analysis, and conceptualization of empirical evidence, the systematic explanation of relationships uncovered between variables, and the linking of hypotheses that have been confirmed by reliable data into broader generalizations. Presenting the case for sociology, Blau argues convincingly that

> the aim of sociological studies is always theoretical — to contribute
> to the development of valid generalizations that explain observable
> social facts. But the only scientific criterion of the probable validity

[1] Walter Wallace (ed.), *Sociological Theory* (Chicago: Aldine, 1969), p. viii.

21

of a generalization is that its implications are confirmed in empirical research. Hence all sociological inquiry worthy of the name is both theoretical and empirical — theoretical in its ultimate aim, yet oriented to empirical research. . . .[2]

To be sure, this scientific credo applies to the sociological analysis of demographic processes. The goal, and the challenge, of sociological demography is to maximize the most advanced features characteristic of both disciplines — extracting the systematic theories of sociology to analyze and interpret the sophisticated, reliable data of demography. Often, however, when sociology and demography are combined, neither the sociological reasoning nor the demographic evidence is cogent and convincing. Unfortunately, the results of all too many attempts at sociological demography have been unacceptable sociology and poor demography. In part, this state of affairs may be attributed to the emphasis in demography on techniques, measurement, procedures, descriptions, and the general *quantitative* thrust of formal demography, which the social scientist defines as bookkeeping rather than as analysis and which he has mastered only in barest outline. Moreover, the preoccupation of sociologists with explaining data they have examined only superficially results at times in loosely connected, ad hoc verbal generalizations, of which the demographer is properly suspicious.[3] However, the apparent hiatus between sociology and demography is much deeper, more fundamental, and complex. The acceptance of the scientific credo in the reciprocal relations between theory and research is, as Merton notes, "suspiciously irreproachable" and hence needs to be "specified" and "concretely exemplified."[4]

The premise of this chapter and our subsequent analysis is twofold: First, connections between sociology and demography are neither fortuitous nor an historical academic accident.[5] Obviously, not all of demography is of interest or relevance to sociology and not all of sociology is applicable to population analysis. Both disciplines encompass a wide

[2] Peter Blau, "Objectives of Sociology," in *A Design for Sociology: Scope, Objectives, and Methods,* ed. Robert Bierstedt (Philadelphia: The American Academy of Political and Social Science, 1969), p. 45.

[3] This is in part the argument that Kingsley Davis makes in "The Sociology of Demographic Behavior," in *Sociology Today,* ed. Robert Merton et al. (New York: Basic Books, 1959), pp. 311–314.

[4] Robert Merton, *Social Theory and Social Structure,* rev. ed. (Glencoe, Ill.: The Free Press, 1957), p. 4.

[5] The "accidental" connection between sociology and demography is argued by Philip Hauser, "Demography in Relation to Sociology," *American Journal of Sociology,* 65 (September 1959), pp. 169–173; cf. Philip Hauser and Otis D. Duncan (eds.), *The Study of Population* (Chicago: University of Chicago Press, 1959), chaps. 1–5 and chap. 33 by Wilbert Moore on "Sociology and Demography"; N. B. Ryder, "Notes on the Concept of a Population," *American Journal of Sociology,* 69 (March 1964), pp. 447–463; Davis, "The Sociology of Demographic Behavior," pp. 309–311.

range of substantive materials, frameworks, methodologies, and data, and to restrict either is counterproductive. The circles of sociological and demographic inquiry are large and not identical. Yet, there are substantial areas of convergence in which interpenetration strengthens both sociology and demography, and at this intersection the disciplinary focus of each becomes mutually indispensable. It is these gray areas of overlap that must be identified and where we shall search for the junctures of social and demographic processes.

From this premise, a second element emerges: Many apparent difficulties associated with sociological demography stem from some critical theoretical assumptions in the sociological analysis of demographic phenomena. The development of sociological demography has been stymied by the general reluctance of demographers to enter into the theoretical arena, by fragmentation in the sociological analysis of population processes, and by the view from both sides that sociological and demographic inquiries are largely independent of and tangential to one another. We contend, however, that the time has come, as a result of advances in systematic sociological theory and method and in the development of cumulative demographic research, for a major breakthrough in sociological demography. A precondition of that potential breakthrough is the prior solution of theoretical issues, assumptions, and dilemmas of sociological demography. Hence, as background and guideline for the analytic tasks, we shall review some of the major theoretical pitfalls in sociological demography and discuss selected caveats that have not been heeded in past attempts at developing the sociology of population processes. Indeed, unless the connections between theory and research are specified and illustrated, unless the theoretical issues posed by sociological demography are exposed and clarified, few advances will be made in identifying, understanding, and explaining the junctures of population and social systems.

The theoretical issues associated with sociological demography may be subdivided conveniently into two major areas. First, some issues revolve around the question of what is to be observed; second, some problems are associated with the types of explanations brought to bear on these observations. To be sure, both issues are only separable analytically, because there is a mutual dependence of observation and explanation: observation is influenced by the scope and statement, implicitly or explicitly, of the analytic problem and the general categories or relationships that are to be extracted from the observations; explanations are, in turn, conditioned by the evidence that has been observed and interrelated. Nevertheless, it is convenient and useful to consider separately the theoretical issues associated with observation and explanation, at least at this preliminary stage.

PROBLEMS OF OBSERVATION

A strong tendency in the sociological analysis of demographic processes is to treat population items as dependent variables to be explained
and social processes as independent variables that are called upon to
explain the patterns of population. Basically nothing is wrong with this
approach except that it focuses artificially on only one side of the relationship. Although it is often *argued* that social and demographic processes are related to each other as determinants *and* consequences,
research rarely has been oriented directly toward unraveling the two-way
interaction. For example, a great many observations have been made on
the decline in mortality in Western societies and the connections these
patterns have to socioeconomic development. In large part, the analytic
question has been, What are the mortality consequences of modernization processes? Or more simply, What were the historical causes of the
reduction in mortality levels? However, the reverse relationship, the impact of mortality levels on the modernization of societies, has almost
never been investigated. Both sets of analytic issues are integral to sociological demography.[6]

Similarly, substantial research has been undertaken on the relationship between religion, religiosity and fertility behavior, norms, and attitudes. Almost without exception, these studies treat fertility as the
dependent variable and religion and religiosity as part of the explanation
of fertility variation. The question posed is, what effect do religion and
religiosity have on fertility? But on theoretical, methodological, and empirical grounds the sociologist must inquire as well into the impact of
fertility on patterns of religion and religiosity.[7] A considerable literature
has appeared on the influence of political and legal systems on migratory
patterns. However, only scattered evidence or research has been directed
to the important issue of the effects of migration on political and legal
processes.[8] The argument that population factors influence social processes does not imply that demographic variables are necessarily dominant or determining; rather it suggests that the variables of the population
system are an integral part of the larger complex of factors influencing social processes.

It is not necessary or even desirable for all research to focus simultaneously on both sides of particular relationships. However, in an overall

---

[6] Cf. the discussion in Chapter 5, this book.

[7] Cf. the discussion of the impact of religion on fertility in Chapter 10. For
a preliminary attempt to examine, theoretically and empirically, the impact of fertility
on religiosity, see Calvin Goldscheider, "Childlessness and Religiosity: An Exploratory
Analysis" (paper presented at the Fifth World Congress of Jewish Studies, Jerusalem,
1969).

[8] Cf. the discussion in Chapter 7, this book.

view, we must be able to interrelate findings, evaluate their theoretical significance, and locate research gaps and neglected relationships that require systematic investigation. Most importantly, it is necessary to know exactly where limited research foci fit into a broader, more comprehensive portrait of the relationships between social and demographic processes. The overemphasis on one side of the relationship to the neglect or exclusion of the other is unacceptable theoretically, methodologically, and empirically. It is likely that to understand the "causes" of demographic processes, information on the "consequences" of population patterns is necessary; to analyze the consequences of social and demographic processes we must also know the causes of the phenomena we investigate.[9]

The error of viewing relationships between population and social processes in only one direction results at times in making rigorous observations on only one part of the relationship. Demographers have tended to examine their dependent variables (population items) systematically and carefully, whereas the independent sociological variables are not analyzed rigorously and poor explanations, even of the one-way relationship, result. Sociologists throw demographic variables into their analytic picture haphazardly and more often than not treat demographic variables as "given." It is clear, therefore, that to avoid the one-way error in sociological demography, systematic and rigorous observations must be attempted for both sociological and demographic variables. If population and social systems are to be interrelated systematically, comprehensive observations must be collected for both systems and the two-way interrelationship must be recognized explicitly.

Perhaps the most fundamental dilemma of observation is in variations in the observation unit and the heterogeneous content of observations. The primary units of social life range from the individual to families, social relationships, groups, communities, associations and organizations, population aggregates, and total societies.[10] Although there is a range of emphasis in sociological demography in the units selected

[9] On the general point, see Stanislav Andreski, *The Uses of Comparative Sociology* (Berkeley: University of California Press, 1965), p. 15; with respect to fertility, see Ronald Freedman, "The Sociology of Human Fertility," *Current Sociology*, 10/11 (1961–1962), p. 42; on migration, see Calvin Goldscheider, "An Outline of the Migration System" (paper presented at the International Union for the Scientific Study of Population, General Conference, London, 1969), p. 5; Gino Germani, "Migration and Acculturation," in *Handbook for Social Research in Urban Areas*, ed. Philip Hauser (Paris: UNESCO, 1964), p. 159; an overall review is presented in United Nations, *The Determinants and Consequences of Population Trends* (New York, 1953).

[10] See Alex Inkeles, *What Is Sociology? An Introduction to the Discipline and Profession* (Englewood Cliffs, N.J.: Prentice-Hall, 1964), p. 12; Freedman, "The Sociology of Human Fertility," p. 37.

for observation, the extremes, or ideal types, may best be represented by the micro-macro continuum: the micro end focuses on the individual; the macro end focuses on societies. Related to this distinction are the types of observations that may be made — micro or macro. For example, we may observe attitudes toward death, ideals about family size, motivations for migration, or we may shift emphasis to fertility patterns, mortality levels, and migration trends. The first group of observations relates to the subjective, individual, social-psychological, and normative microlevel; the second observes the objective, behavioral, structural, societal, macro-level.

The following analytic questions illustrate different emphases in relating economic and fertility patterns:

1. What is the relationship between economic development and fertility levels?
2. In what ways does maintaining high fertility affect economic growth in preindustrial societies?
3. What is the relationship between social class aspirations and family size norms?
4. How do attitudes toward family size influence economic motivation?

The first two questions deal with observable, objective patterns of social and demographic processes at the macrolevel; the latter two questions focus on microlevel subjective elements in social and demographic patterns.

Macro- and microlevel questions must be separated to define precisely the type of observations that the analytic problem requires. Moreover, the focus on different units of observation affects the inferences and causal factors to be analyzed. When individuals are analysis units, the behavior and attitudes of individuals and their relationship to social conditions that affect these individuals may be investigated. However, it is impossible to examine variations in social structure and their determinants when the focus is on the individual actor. To investigate social structural patterns, to compare structures with different characteristics, and to search for variations in the antecedents that produce structural differences, some unit larger than the individual must be observed. Hence, to analyze the determinants and consequences of social structure, organized collectivities must be treated as the study unit.[11]

Similarly, the criteria of relative success in explanation differ when different observation units are used. If individuals or micro units are the basis for observation, then success is measured by explaining variation

[11] On this point, see Blau, "Objectives of Sociology," pp. 51–52.

among individuals; if macro units are the basis for observation, then success is measured by explaining variation among groups or societies.[12]

Another distinction that must be considered is in the differences between cross-sectional and longitudinal observations, or between synchronic and diachronic dimensions of social life.[13] Usually this distinction refers to methodological problems of how we might proceed to gather evidence on particular analytic questions. The methodological side of this issue will be dealt with in later chapters. Here we need to stress the importance of differentiating between questions that relate to the functional interdependence of parts of the social system (synchronic) and questions of historical sequences and patterns (diachronic). Obviously, synchronic and diachronic dimensions of social life are intertwined, but analytic problems related to the maintenance and stability of social and demographic patterns require a different set of observations than analytic problems related to the genesis and alteration of social and demographic processes.

When the analytic question focuses on cross-sectional or synchronic patterns of functional interdependence, we look for uniform patterns throughout groups or other units and also investigate differences and conflicts between groups. Similarly, examining social-demographic changes must be combined with observing the continuities and stability of patterns through time. In short, whether synchronic or diachronic observations are made, continuities and discontinuities must be examined.[14]

SOCIOLOGICAL EXPLANATION

Undoubtedly, the major theoretical problems in sociological demography are explaining and analyzing population patterns. An elementary and deceptively simple question is, What are the determinants of fertility? As suggested in Chapter 1, both mortality and migration may be treated as "determinants" of fertility. No doubt, empirical connections and theoretical arguments may be made to demonstrate the relationship between mortality, migration, and fertility. However, other demographic processes are not the only determinants of fertility.

Sociological questions about population processes move out of the narrow boundaries of the population system and conceptualize population processes as elements of the broader social system. Sociological questions deal with the determinants and consequences of population processes as these represent part of the social fabric. But there are many

[12] See Ryder, "Notes on the Concept of a Population," pp. 456–457.
[13] Blau, "Objectives of Sociology," pp. 63–77.
[14] Ibid., p. 63.

ways to respond to questions about the determinants and consequences of population processes. We should be able, even at this early stage, to think of long lists of fertility determinants. For example, it seems reasonable to argue on logical (and empirical) grounds that the availability of contraceptives and the extent of their use, the amount of celibacy, the education level, the attitudes of persons and groups toward family size and fertility control, the extent of social mobility, economic development levels, biological aspects of reproductive potential, norms and values associated with sex, marriage, and family life, along with demographic aspects of mortality, age structure, and migration are among the possible factors that determine fertility patterns.

However, this casual list is not very helpful in *organizing* systematically the factors influencing fertility. Hence, the question remains, How do we understand and organize these diverse elements into some sort of framework or conceptual scheme? At this point, we are not concerned directly with the specific determinants of fertility, because those will emerge out of our later theoretical and empirical inquiries. But which potential hypothesized determinants are more fruitful to study and which are addressed to different types of analytic inquiries? Indeed, what are the right sociological questions to ask so that we may arrive at some sound sociological answers?

When it is argued that one determinant of fertility is the pattern of mortality, we have neither a complete nor a satisfactory answer because it leaves unspecified several critical and fundamental issues. First, it does not specify how the level of mortality affects decision-making processes associated with fertility behavior, i.e., the connections between mortality and fertility are largely at the macrolevel of analysis and ignore the microlevel component of sociological inquiry. But even more serious is that the mechanisms of connection between mortality and fertility, even at the macrolevel, are left unspecified; we must know the connecting links between mortality and fertility levels. How are mortality patterns related to the norms of family size? How are patterns of mortality related to contraceptive usage, biological aspects of fecundity, and age at marriage? How are mortality levels connected to social organization, social structure, and social change? In short, we need to "fit" this specific determinant of fertility into some system of interconnected variables so that we can test the connecting lines between mortality and fertility within the context of the social system. Unless we know the social mechanisms connecting mortality and fertility, unless we can identify the general factors influencing mortality, and unless we fit mortality levels and changes into a total social systems scheme, we are unable to move beyond description, mechanical correlations, and one-variable relationships.

Levels of Fertility Analysis

Fortunately, we have available a beginning framework that helps organize some factors involved in determining fertility patterns.[15] Some basic social processes surrounding the physiological processes of sexual intercourse, conception, and gestation directly affect fertility patterns. Factors affecting exposure to intercourse include: age of entry into sexual unions, extent of celibacy, length of the reproductive period spent after or between sexual unions, abstinence (voluntary and involuntary) within sexual unions, and coital frequency. Not all sexual intercourse results in conception. The factors governing exposure to conception include the extent of fecundity (the biological ability to reproduce) as determined by voluntary and involuntary causes and the use or nonuse of contraception. When sexual intercourse results in conception, factors affecting gestation and successful parturition become important. These include fetal mortality from voluntary and involuntary causes. These three sets of factors are always present in society and often are unintended, that is, they may develop for reasons other than fertility regulation; each factor can have a negative or positive effect on fertility; and the fertility level of a society or group is a function of the combined operation of all these variables. Most important, these variables are *intermediate* between the organization of society on the one hand and fertility on the other.[16] Although it is reasonable to argue that the fertility level of society is a function solely of the specific combination of intermediate variables, the sociological question moves to a different level of abstraction by inquiring about those aspects of social organization that determine fertility *via* the intermediate variables. Thus, if late age at marriage, combined with the efficient use of contraception and abortion, results in low or controlled fertility within society, the sociological question becomes: What aspects of social organization influence these intermediate variables and thereby fertility? One response rests with the particularistic norms about family size and about the intermediate variables, that is, variation in fertility is a function of the intermediate variables that are shaped by particular norms. Now the question shifts once again: What are the determinants of these norms? Do aspects of social organization necessarily operate through the particularized norma-

[15] The basic framework was developed by Kingsley Davis and Judith Blake, "Social Structure and Fertility: An Analytic Framework," *Economic Development and Cultural Change*, 4 (April 1956), pp. 211–235; cf. the discussion in Freedman, "The Sociology of Human Fertility," pp. 38–43.

[16] For a somewhat dissenting view, see David Yaukey, "On Theorizing About Fertility," *The American Sociologist*, 4 (May 1969), pp. 100–104. Cf. our discussion in Chapter 6.

tive system or do they directly affect the intermediate variables of fertility, bypassing the normative system?

Through this "funnel" strategy we move from the narrow end and work back from observed fertility patterns to the intermediate variables, through (or bypassing) particularized norms about family size and about the intermediate variables and arrive at the wider, less definite, more abstract area of social organization. Abstracting to higher levels of generalities now requires us to specify the wide range of elements encompassed by the general construct "social organization." Although we shall deal more specifically with this question in Chapters 6 and 10, here we shall note the need to separate levels of factors within the social organizational framework, including demographic factors (e.g., mortality and migration), social structural and institutional arrangements (e.g., family, economic, and political systems — included in the latter are formal fertility policies), cultural and normative variables (generalized values and norms as opposed to specific and particular fertility norms), and social-psychological and personality components. The sociological question, therefore, deals with structural (demographic and social), social-psychological, and cultural components of the social system to discover the determinants of fertility patterns.

In formal terms, the broad, poorly defined area of social organizational fertility determinants encompasses a wide range of macro and micro elements; hence, the explanation of fertility involves different levels of analysis. Just as we must distinguish between macro and micro observations, so we must separate macro and micro explanations. Returning to the question of how mortality may be viewed as a determinant of fertility, we should now (1) connect mortality to other types of social organizational determinants; (2) connect this total picture to particular norms about family size and the intermediate variables; or bypass these particular norms and proceed directly to (3) the intermediate variables themselves and finally to (4) fertility.

The importance of step 1 is critical in avoiding the tendency to establish empirical generalizations between selected variables and fertility one at a time. For example, mortality, industrialization, kinship structure, political policies, generalized values, and role patterns among other variables have been related to fertility behavior and attitudes. But we must not stop at this point. To go beyond low-level generalizations, we must further abstract common elements from these single relationships. We must ask what in specific social organizational variables tie them to fertility? Unless we can identify at a more general and abstract level the common elements involved in individual correlations and generalizations we shall have to be content with mechanical, ad hoc relationships, low-level theories, and descriptions that are not cumulative. The fertility framework puts our empirical observations into some organized perspective but represents only the beginning task for connecting theory and research, explanation and observation, in fertility analysis.

This framework relates to the determinants of fertility. It is clear that sociological demography must handle the question of the social consequences of fertility as well. Two general points must be emphasized: First, fertility patterns not only result from the specific stages of intermediate variables, particular norms, and levels of social organization but may affect these elements as well. The arrows connecting these sets of items and fertility must flow both ways. Second, the theoretical problems of abstraction levels, explanation levels, and intermediate mechanisms connecting analytic variables are as significant when discussing the consequences of fertility as when considering the determinants of fertility.

A final comment on this framework relates to its general macro orientation. The construction of the analytic framework focusing on intermediate variables and social organization was formulated to help explain comparative fertility levels in developed and underdeveloped societies. Hence, the analytic question relates to "societal" fertility and not to the motivational complex of decision making by individual couples.[17] Both micro- and macrolevels of observation and interpretation must be separated for preliminary analysis but ultimately must be reintegrated to provide a comprehensive sociological picture.

Some have argued for the need to keep levels of analysis separate and investigate problems at *either* the macroanalytic or microanalytic level.[18] Others have criticized explanations directed at one level of analysis for not offering explanations at other levels.[19] We reject both notions: ultimately we cannot justify an "either-or" argument, nor can we expect macrotheories to focus on microexplanations and vice versa. Although in general it is invalid to transform micropropositions into macropropositions or convert ecological correlations into individual relationships,[20] there are elementary reasons to shuttle between macro- and microlevels within both the observational sphere and the area of explanation.[21] When we make macro-observations and employ macro-

[17] See the original analytic problem posed by Davis and Blake, "Social Structure and Fertility," p. 211.

[18] Although recognizing that explanation can be formulated at various levels and that different theories offer alternative perspectives on population variation and change, Hauser and Duncan argue against the social-psychological approach and apparently do not see the need for reintegration. See Hauser and Duncan, *The Study of Population*, pp. 101–102.

[19] See, for example, Rupert Vance, "The Development and Status of American Demography," in *The Study of Population*, ed. Hauser and Duncan, pp. 299–302.

[20] On this see Ryder, "Notes on the Concept of a Population," p. 457.

[21] For this general argument, see the important article by C. Wright Mills, "Two Styles of Research in Current Social Studies," *Philosophy of Science*, 20 (1953),

explanations, we often fail to make empirical connections between what is observed and the interpretation of those observations; when observations and explanations remain at the microlevel, we often fail to note the larger implications of our analysis; when macro-observations are tied to microexplanation, we often end up unduly stretching an index; when micro-observations and macroexplanations are combined, we often falsely concretize our concepts. When the level of observation is different from the level of explanation, we also fail to establish logical connections between what we observe and how it is explained. As Mills notes:

> Only by moving grandly on the macroscopic level can we satisfy our intellectual and human curiosities. But only by moving minutely on the molecular level can our observations and explanations be adequately connected. So, if we would have our cake and eat it too, we must shuttle between macroscopic and molecular levels in instituting the problem *and* in explaining it — developing the molecular index structure of general concepts and the general conceptual implications of molecular variables. . . . The sociological enterprise requires macroscopic researchers to imagine more technically, as well as with scope and insight; it requires technicians to go about their work with more imaginative concern for macroscopic meaning, as well as with technical ingenuity.[22]

Therefore, scientific conceptualization and theories imply, among other things, looking at the same phenomena from different points of view and different levels of observation, abstraction, and analysis. They also imply the need for the systematic integration of different perspectives and the cumulation of a wide range of evidence.

In analyzing fertility, we had some ready-made analytic guidance for theoretical organization that is not available for either mortality or migration. In general, the macro-micro problem and the issues associated with analysis levels are less severe with respect to mortality. Fertility and migration may be analyzed at the microindividual level because both often involve decision making and norms, attitudes, motivations, and ideals that fit more easily into normative and sociopsychological analyses of behavioral patterns. However, mortality is largely unmotivated, except for selected types like suicide, and in general, norms and values supporting longer life are widespread although by no means universal. Important microlevel issues in mortality analysis include decisions to seek a positive state of health; motivations to obtain health and medical aid; the impact of political, social, cultural, and economic factors on these

pp. 265–275, reprinted in *Power, Politics and People: The Collected Essays of C. Wright Mills*, ed. Irving Louis Horowitz (New York: Ballantine, 1963), pp. 553–567.
[22] Ibid., pp. 563, 566 of the Horowitz volume.

motivations and decisions; and personal consequences of mortality variation. Nevertheless, the general analysis of the determinants and consequences of mortality processes can proceed quite far without resorting to microlevel explanations and without involving normative considerations.

Levels of Migration Analysis

In contrast, the levels problem is critical for an analysis of migration. There are various conceptual approaches to the systematic study of the determinants and consequences of migration. In general, three strategies have been used most often: (1) *categorization* of the diverse factors that lead to or result from migration; (2) the construction of *typologies*, focusing mainly on types of movement and referring indirectly to the causes and resultants of various forms of movement; (3) *model building*, usually based on "push" and "pull" factors engendering migration along with intervening obstacles that impede or facilitate movement. All these approaches have merit, individually and in combination, and there is no point in arguing which is the "best" analytic strategy. Rather, each strategy, along with others, has been plagued by the failure to separate analysis levels. A review of selected examples of these general approaches provides some insight into the levels problem.

One approach to migration research has been through ad hoc categorization. Often in reviewing the migration literature, the major factors that cause or result from migration have been categorized. For example, as an aid to Bogue's summary of existing knowledge about internal migration, fifty "determinants" of migration were identified.[23] These determinants were organized under three general headings: "migration-stimulating situation for persons," "factors in choosing a destination," and "socioeconomic conditions affecting migration." Among twenty-five diverse situations stimulating migration included in the first category are restlessness and wanderlust urges, oppression and discrimination, forced movement resulting from legal enactments, community disasters, marriage or lack of an offer of marriage, offers of good or better employment. Among the fifteen factors in choosing a destination are sex ratios, hearsay information, physical attractiveness of the community, and moving costs. Within the third category, defined as the "objective situation which the individual migrant experiences as a subjective migrating-stimulating experience," Bogue lists technological changes, degree of intergroup tolerance, business recessions or depressions, provi-

[23] Donald Bogue, "Internal Migration," in *The Study of Population*, ed. Hauser and Duncan, pp. 499–501.

sions among a population for retirement, medical care, insurance for dependents, and several others.[24]

As a general rule, any such categorization will not exhaust the range of migration determinants; nor will the items included be mutually exclusive. Because scientific categorization involves two basic principles — categories must be mutually exclusive and the items must exhaust the range of possibilities — the lists of determinants available for migration do not meet minimum scientific standards. Perhaps, it may be argued, these lists are intended as "illustrative." Yet, within these categories of determinants, a heterogeneous array of factors at different analytic levels are lumped together. The mixture of social-psychological (restlessness), demographic (sex ratio), economic (business recessions), political (oppression), legal (legal enactments), cultural (degree of intergroup tolerance), social (marriage patterns), and environmental (natural disasters) factors is neither justifiable analytically nor profitable scientifically as a means to understanding migration processes within a coherent and consistent framework. Examining migration as a process of change involves analyzing changes in the relationship of persons or groups to the society or community at areas of origin and destination as well as alterations in the structure of these areas. However, these types of changes must be separated analytically to identify the various changes that operate at different analysis levels, independently of one another and as interdependent elements. Categorization that does not make the distinction between levels of analysis is more confusing than instructive. Furthermore, unless categorization provides clues to the priority of factors involved, we often end up with the notion that "everything" is linked to migration processes, which is neither very helpful nor enlightening.

The conceptual confusion that results from mixing analytic levels may also be illustrated in the typological approach. One of the most sophisticated migration typologies available has been developed by Petersen,[25] several aspects of which relate to the levels problem. As part of his orientation to migration analysis, and as a basis for part of his typology, Petersen distinguishes between migration as a means of achieving the new, which he calls "innovating," and migration as a means of retaining the status quo in response to alterations in conditions, which he terms "conservative." Further, he suggests, when migration is forced

---

[24] Along similar lines a decade later Bogue developed another list of factors organized into "push" and "pull" categories. The same criticism of his earlier list applies with equal force to his latest attempt. Donald Bogue, *Principles of Demography* (New York: Wiley, 1969), pp. 753–754.

[25] William Petersen, "A General Typology of Migration," *American Sociological Review,* 23 (June 1958), pp. 256–266.

or when migrants play a passive role, migration is innovative or conservative depending on how it is defined by the activating agency. The
activating agency includes "ecological pressure" or the state as well as
the individual migrant's choice.

Hence, we judge the consequences of migration as innovative or
conservative in terms of the situation defined by either the migrant or the
activating agency. The question remains, innovative or conservative for
whom? Or for what? Surely, migration may be innovative irrespective
of, and sometimes contrary to, the motives of the migrants or the activating agents. Moreover, migration may be innovative in terms of changes in
economic, demographic, political, and social structures, or in terms of cultural and personal changes, or both. Indeed, these various consequences
may result from intermediate structural alterations that stem directly
from selective movement. For example, selective out-migration of males
may affect sex ratios at areas of origin and destination, which, in turn,
may affect changes in marriage patterns, labor force rates, kinship interaction, demographic processes, and so on. Similarly, the redistribution of
population from rural to urban areas may have a series of "innovative"
consequences independent of any individual motivations involved. Suburbanization, which under some conditions results from the desire of
persons to retain their status quo in the face of "invading" ethnic or racial
minorities or because of deteriorating housing conditions, has had major
innovative consequences in the structure of the modern metropolis as
well as in the relationships of persons to the social structure. International migrations following ethnic or religious persecutions or political
oppression will affect the ethnic and religious composition of sending
and receiving countries independent of the personal or social consequences for the migrants and irrespective of the motivations of the
activating agencies.

Another modification Petersen makes to the migration literature
relates to the causes rather than the consequences of migration. He
notes correctly that the "push" factors in migration comprise a heterogeneous array of causes and thus distinctions must be made among
underlying causes, facilitating environments, precipitants, and migration
motives. Hence, he argues, that without distinguishing between the
motives of migrants and the social causes of migration, the analysis of
migration lacks logical clarity.[26] Including the migrants' levels of aspiration within schemes of migration is an important first step. Once recognized, the issue becomes, Where do personal aspirations and individual
motivations fit into the total migration picture? For which analytic
problems are motivations of key significance in unraveling processes of

[26] Ibid., pp. 258–259.

migration? More directly, what types of migration research questions require the inclusion of the motivational dimension and which can be answered by examining the "social causes" of migration? In neither Petersen's typology nor his discussion of migration are these critical questions about analysis levels addressed.

The final illustration of the levels problem in migration research relates to a common pattern of model-building. Underlying a great deal of migration research is a simple notion of push-pull factors along with intervening obstacles. One of the best summaries of this approach is contained in Lee's migration "theory." [27] He identifies four elements that enter into the decision to migrate and the migration process: (1) factors associated with areas of origin, (2) factors associated with areas of destination, (3) intervening obstacles, and (4) personal factors. Identifying these four elements, however, does not tell us which types of "factors" are involved — demographic, social, cultural, technological, economic, environmental, legal, political, etc. — nor about the interaction of "personal" factors with what may be presumed to be objective (nonpersonal?) factors. Lee suggests that "it is not so much the actual factors at origin and destination as the perception of these factors which results in migration." But of course that depends at which level of analysis one chooses to operate. Ironically, Lee's own excellent research betrays his theoretical argument. At the level of abstraction to which his research is directed — at the structural, social, economic, and demographic systems level — there is little need for social-psychological reductionism.[28]

Inherent in the push-pull model as exemplified by Lee's presentation is the failure to separate decisions to move at the individual level from migration processes at the systems level. Consequently, there is little recognition of the various levels of abstraction that are involved in accounting for population movement. None of the propositions that Lee deduces from his scheme includes "personal factors." Because personal factors have been included as all-encompassing, nondefined, nebulous predispositions, any deviation from the "rational" model of calculating advantages and disadvantages at areas of origin and destination can be attributed to "personal factors." As a catchall concept it obscures rather than clarifies. Whenever migration does not take place it may be argued that the perception of positive factors did not outweigh the negative factors, or that the intervening obstacles were too great, or that personal factors were involved. As presently formulated, Lee's scheme cannot be tested empirically and is not helpful for theoretical or empirical analysis.

To organize the factors involved in migration analysis, we need to

[27] Everett Lee, "A Theory of Migration," *Demography*, 3:1 (1966), pp. 49–52.
[28] See, for example, Everett Lee et al., *Population Redistribution and Economic Growth, United States 1870–1950*, vol. 1 (Philadelphia: The American Philosophical Society, 1957).

stress three important interrelated distinctions. First, it is fruitful to separate questions about the causes of migration and those that relate to the motives of migrants. We may argue, for example, that "motives" are the immediate subjective forces influencing migration whereas "causes" reflect objective conditions that operate by arousing motivations for movement.[29] The analytic problem of why population movement occurs has a different focus than problems associated with why people move. Moreover, when we insist, correctly, on examining the motivational linkages between migratory behavior and the social causes of migration, it is not necessary to revert to psychological reductionism or attitudinal responses to "why did you move?" Analysis focusing on attitudinal questions about migratory behavior or intentions assumes that people understand their own complex behavior patterns — an assumption which is probably unsound. Reasons offered by migrants tell us what factors went into a decision to migrate, not why people move.[30] One way to uncover the motivational linkages is to *infer* them from migration selectivity and from the social correlates of migration rather than reporting or describing in vacuum the selectivity or correlation.

This conclusion leads us into another distinction in analysis levels. Just as we argued the need to integrate findings of particular one-variable relationships in fertility research, so we need to both analyze and synthesize the specific social relationships found in migration research. Although we must distinguish between social-personal, structural, and cultural elements in the causes and consequences of migration, we must ultimately integrate these levels of analysis. "Economic opportunity," measured objectively, might constitute an important cause of population movement but the subjective evaluation of alternatives, including the migrant's level of aspiration, affects the degree to which persons selectively respond to that opportunity. At one level, migration involves social behavior, including decision-making processes of individuals. At another level, migration is a collective group process. These separable analytic levels must, however, be reintegrated for a comprehensive portrait of migration processes.[31]

[29] See Henry Pratt Fairchild, *Immigration* (New York: Macmillan, 1925), p. 8. See also Robert Park, "Human Migration and the Marginal Man," *American Journal of Sociology*, 33 (May 1928), pp. 881–893.

[30] Hawley notes that too often the search for causes of migration becomes a matter of ascertaining the motives of migrants, though the announced motives may not have any connection with factors of change attending the migration. The important question is therefore not why migrants think they move but what are the conditions common to instances of migration and lacking in instances where no migration takes place. Amos Hawley, *Human Ecology* (New York: Ronald, 1950), p. 328. See also Bogue, *Principles of Population*, p. 754.

[31] For a helpful discussion of the integration of objective, normative, and psychosocial migration levels, see Germani, "Migration and Acculturation," pp. 160–161; for an attempt to focus empirically on social psychological, demographic, and

Finally, as we move between analysis levels and shift to higher levels of abstraction and generality, we must bear in mind the distinction between direct and facilitating factors involved in migration processes. We do not have a set of "intermediate" variables for migration as we have for fertility, mainly because migration does not have a biological component.[32] But migration analysis should consider some factors that facilitate or impede migration rather than determine migration directly. National policies concerning migration are among the clearest examples of facilitating or impeding factors. At one extreme, laws prohibiting movement impede mobility directly. On the other hand, the absence of legal barriers to mobility facilitates movement, i.e., it is a necessary factor in potential migration but not a sufficient condition for its occurrence. Similar facilitating or impeding factors are associated with levels of technology, physical and social barriers, housing availability, etc.

Emerging Guidelines

What emerging principles may be abstracted from our discussion of theoretical problems and dilemmas of sociological demography? Several important guidelines need to be emphasized.

Sociological demography is an empirical and theoretical science searching for data and explanations, evidence and interpretations, and observations and generalizations so that the nature of human society might better be understood. The ties between theory and research in the sociological analysis of population processes have been blurred by the general neglect of theory and the absence of overall guidelines and frameworks for collecting relevant observations. Theories and theoretical perspectives implied in much demographic data and descriptions provide explanation, interpretation, blueprints for hypothesis testing, guidance for collecting data necessary for systematic analyses, organization of findings, integration, and cumulation of what is generally known and what are generally held interpretations. In its most basic form, "theory puts things known into a system" and attempts "to make sense of what would otherwise be inscrutable or unmeaning empirical findings."[33] But theories must do more. Although if theory is to be sound, it must be

---

ecological perspectives in intrametropolitan mobility, see Edgar Butler et al., "Demographic and Social Psychological Factors in Residential Mobility," *Sociology and Social Research,* 48 (January 1964), pp. 139–154; cf. Georges Sabagh et al., "Some Determinants of Metropolitan Residential Mobility," *Social Forces,* 48 (September 1969), pp. 88–98.

[32] The greater complexity of migration is discussed in Chapter 3, this book.

[33] Abraham Kaplan, *The Conduct of Inquiry* (San Francisco: Chandler, 1964), p. 302.

based on empirical evidence, we need not conclude that no theories or explanations should be put forth unless they are substantiated fully by the research data available. To await such time is to condemn sociological demography to sterility. Ideally, the construction of sociological theories must be grounded in comprehensive data; during construction, however, theories must *outrun* available observations.[34] Ironically, in most of the population literature, data outrun theories.

As a guideline to theoretical and empirical analyses, several important theoretical issues have been specified and various conceptual distinctions offered. In terms of observation, we noted distinctions between different units of observation, macro and micro problems, and the need to incorporate these distinctions within the two-way interaction of social and demographic processes. Although we shall be concerned with the modes of interrelationships between these conceptual distinctions, it should be clear that types of analytic questions appropriate for one level may not provide the observations required for other levels.

The most important caveats for the sociological explanation of demographic processes are in the level of abstraction and the level of analyses desired in sociological demography. In part, explanations are statements that satisfy the curiosity of the person who raised the analytic question. The problem of explanation is deciding what kinds of explanations should be accepted.[35] The sociological analysis of population processes can be handled at various levels of abstraction. All explanations are *intermediate,* in the sense that every explanation offered is subject in turn to being explained.[36] Hence, explanations are steps toward higher levels of abstraction and generalization. Once theoretical propositions, explanations, and hypotheses are demonstrated to be true empirically, they lose their theoretical status and become empirical correlations that require more abstract levels of explanation. Empirically confirmed correlations are not explanations of empirical observations. Converting theoretical propositions into confirmed empirical generalizations demands that we move on to higher levels of abstraction and generality for theoretical analysis.[37]

Just as we separate macro- and micro-observations, so we need to distinguish between micro- and macrolevels of explanations. The separation of observation and explanation problems and the distinction between macro and micro issues within each are somewhat artificial. Levels are continuous rather than dichotomous, and observations and explanations

[34] Andreski, *The Uses of Comparative Sociology*, p. 44.
[35] Ibid., p. 47.
[36] Cf. Kaplan, *The Conduct of Inquiry*, p. 354. For other characteristics of explanations, see pp. 351–355 in Kaplan's book.
[37] See Blau, "Objectives of Sociology," p. 46.

are but segments of the gestalt of the scientific enterprise. Nevertheless, the failure to separate analysis levels results in a host of logical and methodological problems. Ultimately we are required to integrate macro- and micro-observations and macro- and microexplanations. This integration is not achieved by mixing levels between the data and the interpretation; synthesis can only result from preliminary separation of micro- and macroanalysis and their eventual reintegration. We must not remain satisfied with mechanistic and descriptive correlations in sociological demography. Our goal is to move beyond description into analysis, beyond post facto and ad hoc generalization into theories that embrace a greater complex of phenomena.

Once we move out of the population system to locate the connections between population processes and the social system, it is not likely that a grand, sociologically oriented population theory can be developed. In part, this is because demographic processes involve more than the aggregate concepts of population growth, structure, change, and distribution. Even when we disaggregate the population system and analyze its elementary components, it becomes clear that fertility, mortality, and migration are fundamentally different despite some commonalities. Moreover, relationships between aggregate growth and social processes operate through many social, political, economic, cultural, and personal subsystems, and neither logical nor empirical grounds exist for postulating that these subsystems will react in the same way under all conditions to aggregate population changes.[38]

In addition, we should not overlook the reality that a comprehensive sociological theory of anything has not yet been developed. Competing theories, frameworks, strategies, and assumptions are still being debated and discussed in sociology despite advances in systematic theory construction. Hence, although it has not been possible, or perhaps desirable, to construct a unified elaborate sociological theory of population, we should not totally despair. The choice is not between unified grand theory on the one hand and description, mechanistic empiricism on the other. There is of course a middle ground. We shall neither pursue overall theories nor focus exclusively on describing the facts of population that may have sociological relevance. To move sociological demography toward the analytic at a level lower than grand theory, often referred to as "middle-range," we shall seek to place the empirical findings of population processes, trends, structure, and change into various suitable sociological frameworks. We shall aim for theories intermediate to

[38] For a specific example, see Gayl D. Ness, "Population Growth and Economic Development," *American Sociological Review*, 27 (August 1962), pp. 552–553.

working hypotheses and all-inclusive speculations comprising a master conceptual scheme.[39] In working toward theoretical explanations and interpretations of population phenomena, the significance of the search shall be stressed rather than the importance of any definitive end product. Although we are far from formulating a sociological theory of population, we are able to aim more realistically at suggesting theoretical orientations and sociological considerations for the empirical world of demographic analysis.[40]

SOCIOLOGICAL CONTEXTS OF DEMOGRAPHIC ANALYSIS

The overall clarification of theoretical issues in sociological demography places in perspective questions about the sociological contexts of population analysis. Population processes have been investigated within several major sociological contexts or general frameworks. By identifying these general contexts and evaluating their strengths and weaknesses, the essential elements of a framework that represent a comprehensive, systematic, and fruitful guideline for our analytic inquiries will emerge.

Population and Social Problems

The most conspicuous context within which the convergence of population and social processes has been examined is the social problems framework. In its most common form, emphasis is placed on the social problems generated by population growth, and, in particular, the consequences of the population "explosion" for human societies.

The sociological analysis of population problems has several layers of argument.[41] First, and most often discussed, is the increase in the number of people in the world. Starting from about the mid-seventeenth century and an estimated world population of about 550 million, the size and rate of population growth have increased, slowly at first and then more dramatically during the twentieth century. In 1750, for example, world population was around 730 million, doubling by 1900, increasing to over 2 billion by 1930, and pushing over the 3½-billion mark in 1970. The rapid increase in numbers and the consequence of increasing growth rates on space, food, resources, quality, and what is subsumed under the

[39] See Merton, *Social Theory and Social Structure*, pp. 5–6, 87–89.

[40] For a similar goal in another area of sociological inquiry, see Peter Blau and Otis D. Duncan, *The American Occupational Structure* (New York: Wiley, 1967).

[41] Cf. Kingsley Davis, "The World's Population Crisis," in *Contemporary Social Problems*, ed. Robert Merton and Robert Nisbet (New York: Harcourt, Brace and World, 1966), pp. 374–408.

catchall category "ecology," rank population size and growth among the major social problems of the world. Given the finiteness of the universe in terms of space and the *potential* unlimited growth of population, Malthusian "standing room only" problems have been conjured. In terms of ultimate, long-range patterns, mechanisms for reduced or zero population growth are inevitable.

A second layer to the world population problem emphasizes disparities in growth rates between poorer, developing countries and the richer, industrialized nations. For the poorer regions the population problem of growing numbers is essentially treated in the context of potential socioeconomic development or modernization. The argument is often made that the relatively high rate of population growth and related problems of age structure and distribution in underdeveloped countries thwart economic growth, block social progress, impede socioeconomic change, frustrate social and economic aspirations, and perpetuate poverty and misery. The population problems of developed nations revolve around issues less direct than hunger, subsistence, and socioeconomic growth and more around the quality of life, space for leisure and recreation, and specific problems of group conflict. In general, questions of population problems relate to shifts in population growth rates (largely through changes in migration patterns or fertility, e.g., the "baby boom") but more so in terms of the concentration and dispersal of population.

In most discussions of population problems, either of the world or of developed and underdeveloped nations, population aggregate processes (growth, size, structure, distribution) are emphasized as the independent variables affecting or generating social problems. Another layer of analytic concern has been in the relationship between specific population processes (fertility, mortality, and migration) and social problems. Generally, this takes the form of relating fertility, mortality, and migration to the social problems noted previously as well as to other problems, e.g., fertility as a determinant of social mobility or stability; migration as a determinant of social disorganization and ethnic conflict; mortality as a generator of personal-family problems.

The social problems framework of population analysis accentuates a tendency noted earlier toward a truncated view of the complex interrelationships between population and social processes. For example, it was suggested that fertility, mortality, and migration must be treated as dependent, independent, and correlative processes within the population system (in relationship to each other and to population growth and structure) and within the social system (as cause and effect of social processes). However, most analyses of population and social problems omit this two-way relationship by stressing the social consequences of population patterns and de-emphasizing the demographic consequences of social problems. The impact of family disorganization on fertility; the role of violence and war on mortality; the effects of mental illness on migration, crime on population dispersal, race relations on population distribution, and economic problems on population structure — have rarely been investigated systematically.

Most literature on population problems concentrates on macrolevel aggregate issues — population growth, structure, and distribution; microlevel problems have been treated only occasionally and unsystematically. Although several attempts have been made to link population problems to microsocial problems, empirical connections have not been handled convincingly. In short, the emphasis on the consequences of population patterns for social problems must be paralleled by research into the consequences of social problems for population processes; the emphasis on macrolevel connections must be supplemented by microlevel analysis of population and social problems.

Finally, it has become somewhat fashionable to link every social problem or social failure to population growth — from traffic congestion and overcrowding, to air and water pollution, juvenile delinquency, slums and ghettos, racial tensions, student unrest, drugs, etc.[42] Clearly, if population patterns and general features of social disorganization have commonalities, they are rather indirect. At best, one might argue that population patterns facilitate or impede, accentuate or ease, the conflicts, tensions, and problems of modern society. Whatever the case may be, analysis of the relationship between social and demographic problems must identify the mechanisms of correlation and not remain satisfied with mechanistic and spurious relationships.

Most attempts at treating population processes in a social problems context have not used a comprehensive framework. To do so would involve at a minimum the following considerations: First, population processes may generate social problems. Within "population processes," treated as an independent variable, we include not only population growth, structure, and distribution but also the specific elementary components of the population system. Thus, fertility, mortality, and migration patterns may generate or accentuate social problems. Second, the relationship between social problems and population processes is two-way: we need to include demographic consequences of social problems within a systematic social problems framework. This other side of the analytic coin includes the ways in which selected social problems

---

[42] The most popular exponent of this view is Paul Ehrlich. See his *The Population Bomb* (New York: Ballantine, 1968). Arguments against this trend are presented in Ansley Coale, "Should the United States Start a Campaign for Fewer Births?" *Population Index*, 34 (October–December 1968), pp. 467–472.

may influence aggregate population patterns (growth, structure, and distribution) and the population processes of fertility, mortality, and migration.

Third, no matter whether we examine the effects of population on social problems or the effects of social problems on population patterns, a distinction must be made between macro- and microquestions and explanations. Social problems relate to the structure of society and to the lives of groups and individuals. Hence, the relationship between population and social problems must include macro- and microlevel considerations.

In addition, we must exercise caution in linking population to every social problem and be prepared to examine the specific mechanisms that relate social problems to population processes. Not every social problem is a function of population processes and not every process of population is affected by social problems. We should, as in other analytic inquiries, uncover the mechanisms of connection and isolate intervening, indirect, and facilitating processes.

Finally, the social problems context in general is a limited perspective in sociology. Not all sociological inquiry involves questions of social problems. Similarly, it is much too narrow to restrict the search for the junctures of social and demographic processes within a social problems framework. In large part, the sociologist must uncover the causes of social problems, seek their determining contexts, and find their relationships to other areas of social behavior.[43] By analyzing the determinants and consequences of problems, alternative solutions can be extracted and evaluated. Similarly, by understanding the sociological determinants and consequences of demographic problems, alternative policies for solving these problems will emerge and may then be evaluated.

Beyond the Social Problems Framework

A natural context for sociological demography is the social action framework, the focus of which has usually been on demographic behavior and its social determinants, i.e., the analytic question focuses on fertility and migration as social behavior that requires explanation. Mortality, because it ordinarily does not involve decision making, is usually not treated within this context, and migration has rarely been examined within a social action or behavioral framework.[44]

[43] See Robert Nisbet, "Introduction: The Study of Social Problems," in *Contemporary Social Problems*, ed. Merton and Nisbet, pp. 16–18.
[44] Cf. Peter Rossi, *Why Families Move* (Glencoe, Ill.: The Free Press, 1955); also see the discussion and references in Chapter 11, this book.

There is little agreement on the elements that may be involved in an analysis of fertility and migration as social behavior; the tendency nevertheless is to work at microlevels. Roles, interpersonal relations, interaction, communication, and also the institutional context of population patterns (religious, family, political, economic, etc.) have usually been emphasized.[45] Concentrating on the motivational linkages between social and demographic processes is an important corrective to the longstanding neglect of motivational elements in demographic behavior. However, not all population issues involve motivational components, and in some ways population factors are unintended.[46] This applies to fertility and migration patterns as well as to mortality.

Moreover, motivational analysis and, in general, social and psychological considerations in demographic analysis have often been combined with a neglect of the structural constraints of behavior and the societal contexts of action, and have ignored the larger implications of microlevel analysis. Again, both social structural (macro) and social psychological (micro) approaches must be treated as independent and interacting variables influencing the flow of social and demographic processes. This is not an argument for reductionism of one approach to the other but for the articulation of the two for certain purposes and under specific conditions as part of a general model of analysis.[47]

The social action framework emphasizes only part of the total population system and almost completely focuses on the determinants of demographic behavior. This one-way error is as common within the social action framework (in emphasizing the determinants of demographic behavior) as within the social problems framework (in emphasizing the consequences of population processes).

These limitations of the social action framework suggest two conclusions: First, whatever framework is used for sociological demography, it must recognize explicitly the motivational and behavioral dimensions of population analysis and attempt to locate where microlevel analysis fits into a broader scheme. Second, the social action or behavioral framework is an incomplete and restrictive sociological context precisely because it does not cover major areas of intersection between social and demographic processes and cannot identify the gray areas of overlap between sociological and demographic inquiries.

The elementary population processes have also been utilized as

---

[45] See the brief discussion in Thomas Ford and Gordon De Jong (eds.), *Social Demography* (Englewood Cliffs, N.J.: Prentice-Hall, 1970), pp. 9–13.

[46] See Davis, "Social Demography," pp. 204–207.

[47] See the discussion by Alex Inkeles, "Personality and Social Structure," in *Knowledge and Society*, ed. Talcott Parsons (Washington, D.C.: U.S. Information Agency, Voice of America Forum Lectures, 1968), pp. 13–16.

indicators of the broader social processes of which they represent one part. We have already emphasized that population factors may be viewed analytically as consequences and determinants of social processes. Over time, therefore, population processes may be viewed as *integral* elements in the unfolding of major social processes, and may be utilized as general indicators of these processes. Three major analytic conditions illustrate how this procedure operates.

First, we may know empirically or hypothesize theoretically that particular social and demographic variables are interdependent, i.e., sometimes social processes may be viewed as independent variables and sometimes demographic processes may be viewed as independent variables. For example,[48] let us suppose that the relationship between mortality and socioeconomic modernization is interdependent, i.e., changes in modernization affect mortality levels and changes in mortality levels affect modernization. If we are able to demonstrate this relationship empirically, we can subsequently use mortality levels and changes as one indicator of relative modernization.

This example assumes that we know the cause-effect relationship and that over time that relationship is interdependent. However, it may not be possible to determine, theoretically or empirically, whether demographic variables cause or effect sociological variables. All we can establish is that specific population and social processes usually appear together or that they change in some systematic way together, i.e., they are correlated. We may establish, for example, that an integral part of industrialization processes is migration from rural-agricultural areas to urban-industrial areas. It may not be clear, however, which is cause and which is effect, i.e., we cannot tell whether industrialization generated migration or whether migration stimulated industrialization. Both appear to be integral to each other, which allows us to utilize one as an indicator of the other. Similarly, we may observe that high fertility is correlated with extended family structure whereas low fertility is correlated with nuclear family structure, but it may not be clear whether high fertility is the determinant or consequence of family structure. We may still be able to use one as an indicator of the other.

We may locate instances where population and social processes are commonly found in a particular relationship but are "caused" by a third set of factors. For example, differentially higher mortality is usually found among deprived social groups (e.g., lower classes) and both mortality differentials and class deprivation result from class discrimination and the unequal distribution of goods and services. In this case, mor-

[48] These hypothetical examples will be more fully explored in Chapters 5 and 9.

tality may be viewed as an indicator of class position or of class discrimination.

Because demographic variables are often easily quantifiable and are more readily available in government and administrative records, the temptation to use demographic indices for social research is great. Such a procedure has two major drawbacks, however. First, to utilize demographic variables as indicators, we must know that real interrelation occurs from *both* sides. For example, we may observe that whenever industrialization occurs urbanward migration takes place. Before using migration as an indicator of industrialization, we must also observe the reverse: whenever urbanward migration takes place, industrialization occurs as well. Before using mortality as an indicator of inequality we must observe whether inequality may manifest itself without mortality differentiation. Before using fertility as an indicator of family structure we must observe whether nuclear family structure "fits" with high (as well as low) fertility and extended family structure "fits" with low (as well as high) fertility. In short, we must avoid the danger of substituting indicators for analysis.

Reductionism is another danger in using demographic processes as indicators of and references for the broader social process of which they are a part. Using indicators often results in reducing the "whole" to the "sum of its parts." [49] Mortality patterns may be a reliable indicator of socioeconomic modernization at the macrolevel and of social inequality at the microlevel, but neither modernization nor inequality may be reduced to variations in mortality.

In the search for a framework or context within which to analyze the junctures of social and demographic processes, we need to bear in mind the critical points raised in connection with the social problems framework, the action perspective, and the use of demographic variables as social indicators. It does not appear that we shall in the immediate future locate the definitive sociological framework best suited for demographic analysis. Rather we shall be forced to employ a pluralistic sociological approach to encompass these contexts and frameworks and go beyond them as well.

[49] Kaplan, *The Conduct of Inquiry*, p. 81.

Chapter Three

THEORETICAL ISSUES IN
MIGRATION RESEARCH

Human migration is interrelated systematically with population changes in general, and with fertility and mortality in particular. When each population component is conceptualized as an independent process and connections are established between it and broader social processes, fundamental similarities may be discerned in analyzing all three population elements. Thus, the general theoretical and methodological issues outlined in Chapter 2 relate as much to migration analysis as to the investigation and interpretation of fertility and mortality. Yet migration processes have some distinctive qualities that differentiate them from processes associated with either fertility or mortality, which cause distinct theoretical and methodological problems. The objectives of this chapter are to isolate the distinctive qualities of migration processes, to identify and elucidate methodological and theoretical issues that result from these special features of migration, and to illustrate some complexities of migration analysis.

THE UNIQUENESS OF MIGRATION

Several general features of migration distinguish it from fertility and mortality. First and foremost, birth and death are biological processes that may be viewed as distinct, uniform, discrete events. Birth is limited biologically to one sex and certain ages, and there are biological restraints on the amount of fertility (the reproductive potential of women or fecundity) and mortality (no one dies more than once). At the societal level, rates of fertility have an upper limit owing to the impact of fer-

48

tility on the age distribution, although it is difficult to fix that upper limit empirically. Over time, mortality levels cannot be zero but have the "potential" of being so high so as to destroy a total society. In sharp contrast, migration has neither a biological referent nor uniform processes. Migration is not restricted biologically to one sex or to an age span, although it may be so restricted socially. Further, migration appears to have no upper limit, hence the total migration of communities or societies would not imply their demise but their removal to another location. Most important, migration processes are not uniform: movements within local neighborhoods differ from international migration; movements of children accompanying parents involve different social processes than the frontier movements of male adventurers. As a result of the uniform biological processes associated with reproduction and death, questions of "definition" and "types" are rarely raised and of little social scientific relevance. But the definition and types of migration raise several issues, e.g., whether to include all spatial moves within the migration concept, which movers to consider migrants, and what various types of migration to investigate.

Second, moving always involves exiting from one population and entering another population, but fertility and mortality relate to only one population process, either entering or exiting. This quality of migration implies a requirement to examine analytically the determinants and consequences of migration in two populations, the area of origin and the area of destination. Furthermore, migration involves a move from one area to another area selected from among other possible destinations. Given population movement between two places, that is, entering and exiting processes, the question of selective destination must be raised, i.e., why one destination is selected over another. Thus, migration analysis requires an investigation into various migratory flows. In microlevel context, we argued that migration and fertility may involve decision-making processes. Yet, the content of those decisions may differ. The decisions in fertility, at any point in time, may be whether to have a child or not, and over time, when and how many to have; the choice in migration usually will not involve the planning for the total number of lifetime moves but may involve whether or not to move, when to move, where to move, and for how long. One specific consequence of the "where to move" factor is the need to examine the movement of persons between two places in the context of potential other destinations that might have been selected but were not. The question of "for how long," or in an objective context, "duration of residence," relates to another methodological issue: How "permanent" does a move have to be to be included in the migration concept?

Finally, mortality and fertility are *societal universals*, i.e., human societies, if they are to survive, require reproduction and some control over the inevitability of death, which is not true of migration. Just as migration has no fixed upper limit, so it has no necessary lower limit, i.e., societies may be characterized by the absence of migration. At the individual level, migration is similar to fertility but differs from mortality in that it is not an inevitable event occurring to everyone, and it is repeatable and reversible. Consequently, the study of migration must involve not only the mobile segment of the population but also the stable sector; return as well as repeated movements must be included.

These general differences between migration and the other two demographic components have been noted in the literature in many contexts.[1] However, these differences rarely have been related systematically to special theoretical or methodological issues associated with migration analysis. Most demographers conclude that the special qualities of migration processes result in greater analytic complexity. Our concern at this point is to examine systematically the various complex conceptualization problems that flow from these unique features of migration processes.

The specific theoretical and methodological issues associated with migration, in conjunction with the more general issues discussed in Chapter 2, are fundamental to the sociology of human migration. These issues are fundamental because, first, all research concerned with human migration must deal with them either by solving them, explicitly or implicitly, or by ignoring them through exclusion; second, all other theoretical issues and all migration theories depend on their prior solution.

THE STABILITY COMPONENT

Whether migration is conceptualized as sociodemographic behavior or as sociodemographic process, we must account not only for decisions to move but also for decisions not to move; not only for rates of population movement but also for general population stability. The need to examine the stability component in migration research is in one sense not unique to this inquiry. For example, in fertility studies, childlessness (voluntary and involuntary) is examined; couples deciding to have a third or fourth child are compared to those deciding against additional children. In mortality research, some analytic questions require comparing character-

[1] See, for example, Dennis Wrong, *Population and Society*, 3rd ed. (New York: Random House, 1967), pp. 82–83; William Petersen, *Population*, 2nd ed. (New York: Macmillan, 1969), pp. 253–254; Donald Bogue, *Principles of Demography* (New York: Wiley, 1969), p. 753; Norman Ryder, "Notes on the Concept of a Population," *American Journal of Sociology*, 69 (March 1964), pp. 447–463.

istics of those who die and those who remain alive. Nor is this problem restricted to substantive demographic research. Social scientists in general need to make similar types of comparisons: for example, studies of voting behavior will compare voters and nonvoters; research in deviance may involve the comparison of criminals with noncriminals. Thus, in terms of analysis, nonmovers are a significant comparative-contrast population in migration research.

The need to examine stability as well as mobility characterizes macrodemographic and microdemographic analysis levels. At the macrolevel, sometimes the basic question is why population movement does not occur. For example, why are traditional societies usually characterized by geographic stability? More specifically, given a set of powerful push and pull factors, why did American Negroes not migrate out of the South in large numbers before World War I? [2] Examples of nonmovement can be multiplied. At the microlevel, many individual ideal types may be identified, ranging from persons who spend their entire lives from birth to death in the same dwelling unit or in the same community to those, like nomads, who are constantly on the move and where mobility is an institutionalized life style. In contemporary societies, developed and underdeveloped, the nomad has often been typed the "repeat" mover or the "floating" migrant. Examining repeat migration is significant for analyzing an extreme pattern of movement at the microlevel, but also for comprehending and interpreting overall migration rates and the adjustment of societies to the permanent instability of a select number of its inhabitants. [3]

Between the extremes of nonmobility and repeated mobility, various culturally determined situations involve movement, such as moves associated with setting up independent nuclear households as a result of marriage, moves associated with marital dissolution and disruption, life-cycle changes involving moves, and selected job-career patterns combining social and residential mobility. [4] To type the United States or any

---

[2] See William Petersen, "A General Typology of Migration," *American Sociological Review*, 23 (June 1958), p. 258; William Petersen, *Planned Migration* (Berkeley: University of California Press, 1955), chap. 3.

[3] Sidney Goldstein, "Repeated Migration as a Factor in High Mobility Rates," *American Sociological Review*, 19 (October 1954), pp. 536–541; Sidney Goldstein, "The Extent of Repeated Migration: An Analysis Based on the Danish Population Register," *Journal of the American Statistical Association*, 59 (December 1964), pp. 1121–1132; M. B. Deshmukh, "A Study of Floating Migration," in UNESCO, *Social Implications of Industrialization and Urbanization in Africa South of the Sahara* (Paris: UNESCO, 1956), pp. ix, 143 ff.; Jose Alvarez, *Return Migration to Puerto Rico*, Institute of International Studies, Population Monograph Series no. 1 (Berkeley: University of California, 1967), pp. 40–41. Cf. Chapters 7 and 11, this book.

[4] See, in general, Everett Lee, "A Theory of Migration," *Demography*, 3:1 (1966), pp. 51–52; Petersen, "A General Typology of Migration," pp. 258–259;

other country as a "nation of nomads" because of high total mobility rates evidenced by cross-sectional census data on net lifetime mobility or on a five-year question[5] is imprecise and incomplete. It fails to account for the impact of repeated mobility on total migration rates, the large stable segments of populations, and for the overwhelming majority of total moves that are life-cycle related and culturally determined.

The importance of considering stability is most clearly evident in explanations of migration patterns, that is, in relating migration to social, demographic, and economic processes. Not everyone moves at the same rate in a migration stream. Young adults may move more than older people, occupational and educational groupings are characterized by differential migratory selectivity, sex differentials exist in migration, and so on. Yet, although young adults may move more than older persons, not all young adults are mobile and not all older persons are nonmovers. To examine why young adults predominate among movers we need to investigate the general stability of the older population plus two additional, often neglected, components — why some young adults do not move, and why some older persons move. The same would be true of other differentials.[6]

TYPES OF MIGRATORY FLOWS

To understand the movement of population in one direction from an area of origin to an area of destination, three alternative, complementary types of migration patterns must be considered: (1) reverse or counterstream flows; (2) first-time moves separated from return moves; and (3) movement to and from alternative origins and destinations.

The need to examine counterstream flows and return movement

Ashish Bose, "Migration Streams in India," in International Union for the Scientific Study of Population, *Contributed Papers* (Sydney Conference, 1967), pp. 598–599, observes that "marriage migrations" in India or "associational migration" are greater than the economic causes that are "relatively unimportant." On the relationship between geographic mobility and career patterns in the United States, see Jack Ladinsky, "Occupational Determinants of Geographic Mobility Among Professional Workers," *American Sociological Review*, 32 (April 1967), pp. 257–264; Jack Ladinsky, "Sources of Geographic Mobility Among Professional Workers: A Multivariate Analysis," *Demography*, 4:1 (1967), pp. 293–309; Gerald Leslie and Arthur Richardson, "Life Cycle, Career Pattern, and the Decision to Move," *American Sociological Review*, 26 (December 1961), pp. 894–902. Cf. Chapter 11, this book.

[5] As have, for example, William Petersen, "Internal Migration and Economic Development," in *The Politics of Population*, ed. William Petersen (New York: Doubleday, Anchor Books, 1965), pp. 291–300; Everett Lee, "The Turner Thesis Reexamined," *The American Quarterly* (Spring 1961), pp. 77–83; Ralph Thomlinson, *Population Dynamics* (New York: Random House, 1965), p. 214.

[6] Cf. Chapter 11, this book.

hardly needs elaboration or justification. Nevertheless, these two types of movement are not necessarily synonymous. At times, the counterflow movement is composed solely of return migrants. For example, in parts of Africa most urban migrants return to spend the greater part of their lives in their rural areas of origin. Counterflow migrations from the United States to Italy or to Puerto Rico have been composed largely, if not totally, of return migrants.[7] However, counterstream migratory flows may contain only a small proportion of return migrants or none at all, as appears to be the case with the large interurban and intermetropolitan movements in contemporary America. Thus, as Ravenstein and, more recently, Lee, argue,[8] if for every major stream of migration, a counterstream develops, *both* stream and counterstream must be subdivided into first-time movement and return migration components. The inclusion of both elements is significant because of their independent analytic value, and also because these components are integral to the explanation of migration between two places. In simple terms, it is inadequate to argue that "economic opportunity" determines migration; it fails to account not only for the larger stability component and for selective movement, but also neglects the separation of those moving for the first time to new opportunities from those returning either because of family, kinship, or community ties or because prior mobility and adjustment have been unsuccessful. Moreover, if people are moving from areas of "lesser" to areas of "greater" opportunity, one must also account for first-time and return movements to areas of lesser opportunity, if they exist. At a minimum, our migration scheme must include the possibility of such alternative flows.

The omission in migration research of the stability component and counterstream and return migratory flows is often combined with a truncated view of migration streams between two places. Most migration analysis is based on a push-pull model: certain factors at the area of origin "push" people out and certain factors at the area of destination "pull" or attract movers.[9] To understand the determinants and consequences of migration between any two places, however, it is necessary to fit the specific migratory stream into a broader systems framework. We cannot begin to account for population movement between any two areas before considering the interchange of movements between specific areas of origin and destination and other areas of origin and destination.

---

[7] Cf. Chapter 7, this book.

[8] See Lee's discussion, which reviews Ravenstein, in "A Theory of Migration," pp. 47–48, 55.

[9] Cf. Lee "A Theory of Migration"; Donald Bogue, "Internal Migration," in *The Study of Population,* ed. Philip Hauser and Otis D. Duncan (Chicago: University of Chicago Press, 1959), pp. 486–509.

Similarly, to measure the integration and assimilation of migrants from an area of origin in an area of destination, comparisons must be made with migrants from other areas of origin to the same area of destination. Furthermore, unless specific migration streams are examined in broader systems perspective, differential replacement of population at both areas of origin and destination cannot be gauged adequately.

AN OUTLINE OF THE MIGRATION SYSTEM

When the stable sector of the population is included, when the distinction between first-time and return migrants is made for both stream and counterstream, and when migration streams between areas of origin and destination are treated in broader societal system perspective, a complex scheme of the migration process emerges. The following are the skeletal components of the migration system (see also Table 3.1).

I. Movers from an area of origin (X) to an area of destination (Y), subdivided into first-time movers (Ia) and return movers (Ib).

II. The population within the area of origin (X), subdivided into movers *within* the area of origin (IIa) and nonmovers within the area of origin (IIb).

III. Movers from the area of origin (X) to all areas of destination (Z) excluding area (Y), subdivided into first-time movers (IIIa) and return movers (IIIb).

IV. The population within the area of destination (Y), subdivided into movers *within* the area of destination (IVa) and nonmovers within the area of destination (IVb).

V. Movers from the area of destination (Y) to the area of origin (X), i.e., counterstream migrants, subdivided into first-time movers (Va) and return movers (Vb).

VI. Movers from the area of destination (Y) to all areas of destination (Z) excluding the area of origin (X), subdivided into first-time movers (VIa) and return movers (VIb).

VII. Movers from all areas (Z) excluding the area of origin (X) to the area of destination (Y), subdivided into first-time movers (VIIa) and return movers (VIIb).

VIII. Movers from all areas (Z) excluding the area of destination (Y) to the area of origin (X), subdivided into first-time movers (VIIIa) and return movers (VIIIb).

IX. The population of all areas (Z) excluding the area of origin (X) and the area of destination (Y), subdivided into movers between and within area Z (IXa) and nonmovers within area Z (IXb).

Table 3.1. The Migration System

Origin	Area Y	Destination Area X	Area Z
AREA X	Ia/Ib	IIa/IIb	IIIa/IIIb
AREA Y	IVa/IVb	Va/Vb	VIa/VIb
AREA Z	VIIa/VIIb	VIIIa/VIIIb	IXa/IXb

Ia.	First-time movers X to Y	Vb.	Return movers Y to X
Ib.	Return movers X to Y	VIa.	First-time movers Y to Z
IIa.	Movers within X	VIb.	Return movers Y to Z
IIb.	Nonmovers within X	VIIa.	First-time movers Z to Y
IIIa.	First-time movers X to Z	VIIb.	Return movers Z to Y
IIIb.	Return movers X to Z	VIIIa.	First-time movers Z to X
IVa.	Movers within Y	VIIIb.	Return movers Z to X
IVb.	Nonmovers within Y	IXa.	Movers within Z
Va.	First-time movers Y to X	IXb.	Nonmovers within Z

Migration research that does not explicitly deal with return versus first-time movers would exclude subdivisions within I, III, V, VI, VII, and VIII; research excluding the stable component omits II, IV, and IX; failure to integrate mobility from one area of origin to one area of destination into broader societal perspective results in the exclusion of III, VI, VII, VIII, and IX.

To illustrate the complexity of this outline and its utility, we can examine a comprehensive study of migration during a specified period, from rural areas of a country to the largest urban center. All rural areas may be designated X; the largest urban center may be designated Y; and all urban areas exclusive of the largest urban center may be designated Z. Note that for this simple illustration, external migration is not included, although where appropriate movement outside of a country could be incorporated within the scheme. Also, designating rural areas as X and other urban areas as Z allows for a comparative analysis of local movement *within* rural areas (and *within* other urban areas) and movements *between* rural areas (and *between* other urban areas). The nine categories of migration-stability groupings include: (1) first-time and return movers from rural areas to the largest urban area; (2) movers within and between rural areas and nonmovers within rural areas; (3) first-time and return movers from rural areas to all other urban areas exclusive of the largest urban center; (4) residents of the largest urban center including local movers and nonmovers; (5) first-time and return counterstream movers from the largest urban center to rural areas; (6) first-time and return movers from the largest urban center to other urban areas; (7) first-time and return movers from other urban areas to the largest urban area;

(8) first-time and return movers from other urban areas to rural areas;
(9) movers within and between other urban areas and nonmovers within
other urban areas.

In a general and preliminary way, each of the eight elements (II–
IX) in combination with the specific migratory stream between one area
of origin and one area of destination (I) provides the following essential
relationships:

1. *Selectivity* of out-migrants from an area of origin in terms of
those not moving out of the area of origin and in terms of those moving
within, but not out of, the area of the origin (I and II).

2. *Uniqueness* of the move from the area of origin to the area of
destination in terms of movers to other areas of destination (I and III).

3. *Assimilation and integration* of migrants from the area of origin
in the area of destination relative to the native population in the area of
destination (I and IV).

4. *Efficiency* of the migration stream between the area of origin
and the area of destination in terms of the amount of counterflow movement (I and V).

5. *Impact* of movement into the area of destination from the area of
origin on the movement out of the area of destination (I and VI).

6. *Relative assimilation* and integration of migrants from the area
of origin in the area of destination in terms of other migrants in the
area of destination (I and VII).

7. *Replacement* of population who left the area of origin with others
coming to the area of origin (I and VIII).

8. *Comparison* of the movers from the area of origin to the area of
destination with those in other areas who did not move (I and IX).

Numerous other comparisons may be made depending on the
analytic problem being investigated. We may want to compare the
movement out of the area of destination (Y) to other areas (Z) with
counterstream movement from Y to X (VI and V); or compare the replacement of population at the area of origin (moves between Z and X)
to the native population in the area of origin (VIII and II).

Whatever the multitude of comparisons may entail within the migration system, identifying these migration-stability groupings is only the
first step. Further complicating the picture would be the substance of
information required, i.e., social, economic, and demographic characteristics of places and persons; details on distance and direction moved;
measures of permanence and duration of residence; comparisons over
time; attitudinal data for survey studies, and more.

To illustrate the consequences of omitting some of these relationships we can examine a survey of migration to greater Santiago (Chile),[10] which was concerned with "demographic and social aspects of the migrant as contrasted with the non-migrant population." However, non-migrants are defined with respect to residents of Santiago (area of destination) rather than nonmigrants at areas of origin. The key items included in the survey to obtain the determinants of mobility are the characteristics and motivations of movers to Santiago, particularly "reasons for movement" and "employment" at the place of previous residence. But we know only the employment conditions and attitudes of *migrants* from the area of origin and of nonmigrants at the area of destination. We know nothing of the employment conditions of nonmigrants at areas of origin or of migrants from the areas of origin to other places excluding Santiago. Thus, we are limited in dealing fully with the differential characteristics and motivations of migrants because of the absence of an appropriate contrast-comparative population at areas of origin. Moreover, if the analysis of migrant assimilation in Santiago, which is the primary research objective of the study, is related to why people moved to Santiago, our inability to examine the determinants comprehensively inhibits our understanding of the consequences.[11] Furthermore, the truncated view of migration (between one area of origin and destination) that this study exemplifies leaves out, among others, questions of alternative destinations from rural areas; the impact of in-migration to Santiago on the mobility of the native population of the area; and return and first-time movers.

It may not be feasible to include all these migration-stability items in every migration study due to the lack of necessary data or because of the desire to examine selected aspects of the migration process. However, at a minimum, it is important to know exactly where limited research foci fit into a broader, comprehensive portrait of the migration process. Without a perspective on migration that includes stability as well as mobility and that fits specific migratory streams into a systems approach, we are not able to see how migration is interrelated with more generalized social processes, nor are we able to interpret adequately the

[10] Many studies might have served equally well. The Santiago study was selected because it is recent, quite comprehensive, a model for similar studies in Lima (Peru) and greater Buenos Aires, and was based on survey data that presumably allowed for greater flexibility in research design than census studies. Juan C. Elizaga, "A Study of Migration to Greater Santiago (Chile)," *Demography*, 3:2 (1966), pp. 352–377.

[11] Germani correctly notes that "the study of assimilation would require a knowledge and an understanding of the whole process of migration, including the process which occurs in the place of origin, the outcome of which is the decision to emigrate and the actual physical transfer to the city." Gino Germani, "Migration and Acculturation," in *Handbook for Social Research in Urban Areas*, ed. Philip Hauser (Paris: UNESCO, 1964), p. 159.

determinants and consequences of mobility. Most important, migration research will not be cumulative.

Essentially we are arguing that a logically prior step before constructing theories of human migration involves identifying the skeletal components of the migration system. Only after the requisite elements necessary for a comprehensive portrait of the migration process are isolated and interrelated can we locate the junctures of migration and social, demographic, and economic processes, which is generally true for population processes as well.[12] Although our conceptualization of the migration system is often geared to the types of information available, it seems clear that specific relationships, based often on limited data, cannot be understood fully or integrated with other findings unless the total migration system is outlined. Needless to say, a comprehensive scheme of migration is indispensable for the systematic design of survey studies focusing on migration patterns.

An outline of the migration system, however complete, is not in any way a substitute for theory construction. Nevertheless, theories or empirical research that attempt to correlate migration processes and social, economic, and demographic processes will not be adequate unless the elements of the migration system are identified and interrelated. Unless the types of migratory flows are isolated, unless we can account for stability as well as mobility, fitting specific migratory streams into broader systems perspective, and, in turn, unless we identify the types of comparative groupings that a systematic examination of migration requires, we will have to be content with descriptions of migration patterns that may be incomplete and that may or may not be relevant sociologically. Migration is too significant a social and demographic process to permit us to be satisfied with the Ravenstein style of empirical generalization or with the current style of migration research.

DEFINITIONS AND TYPES OF MIGRATION

Up to this point, we have implicitly assumed a definition of migration. Although we have identified types of migratory flows, we have not described various migration types. Migration always involves a move from one location to another, but we must identify what is implied by this general statement and locate the composition of migration streams.

It is usually quite clear under most conditions and to most persons when birth and death occur. Each involves a recognizable discrete, biological event. In a social scientific sense birth and death are self-defining. Although there are technical or medical difficulties in defining the small number of marginal instances where an infant is technically alive for

---

[12] See Chapter 1, this book.

only a short period of time or in identifying the medical or legal signs of deaths, defining birth and death represents no real problem for social scientific analysis. To be sure, some issues are associated with the measurement of fertility and mortality, the accuracy of information, and the completeness of data. But these are general problems, not specifically related to definitional issues or to demographic materials and will be discussed in other contexts. Questions about the definition of migration are of a different type. How to define "migration" and what should be included within the concept "migrant" have been problematic. The solutions to issues that have been raised, explicitly or implicitly, in connection with the definition of migration are fundamental to the sociological analysis of human migration.

If someone moves across the street, or around the corner, or from one apartment to another within the same dwelling unit, is he a migrant? How do we classify "migrant" workers, commuters, nomads, travelers, students at colleges away from home, tourists? Should frontier movements within countries be categorized along with mass movements between countries, movements within neighborhoods, return movements, refugee movements, urban renewal relocations, and population transfers? Some of these questions relate to the general problem of defining "migrant" and "migration"; others examine the types of movement that are included in the migration concept. Social scientists who have been concerned with migration theory and research, as well as agencies responsible for collecting and organizing migration information, have been confronted with these "definitional" questions. Although solutions that have been suggested are often arbitrary and contradictory, these questions must be answered before any systematic analysis begins.

These definitional issues may be viewed as part of two basic and interrelated questions: First, is there an identifiable "minimum" end of the migration continuum, i.e., are there spatial moves that should not be considered migration, and are there movers who should not be defined as migrants? Second, can some types of migration be distinguished analytically? The second question may be organized into three parts: (1) Is the conventional separation of migration within countries (intranational or internal) from migration between countries (international or external) justifiable? (2) Can other types of migration be distinguished by boundary changes? (3) Are there other criteria by which migration types may be distinguished?

The Minimum Question

Identifying the minimum end of the migration continuum has only two logical possibilities: all residential changes should be included within the migration concept; or some moves, either because of the short distance involved, or the temporariness of the move, or the minimum degree of change implied by the residential change, or for other reasons, should be excluded. The latter position does not imply that the exclusions are insignificant or inappropriate for analysis but rather that they are not relevant for *migration* research.

Identifying the minimum end of the migration continuum has often been arbitrary. For example, Shryock notes that "there seems to be no obvious cutting point on the basis of demographic theory for determining what part of internal movement shall be called internal migration. Indeed, practices among demographers have differed. . . . In demographic theory, it is not clear whether the typical move to the suburbs qualifies as migration." [13] Our concern at this point is not to employ arbitrary limits to the definition of migration but to consider the justifications for imposing limits. If indeed moves from urban to suburban areas are not included as "migration" in demographic theories, we must explore and evaluate the underlying reasoning behind this exclusion, and in turn accept, revise, or reject such theories. Similarly, migration research may be somewhat limited by the definitions imposed by data collection agencies. Nevertheless, we must inquire into the rationale behind these definitions and decide whether to accept or revise them, or use other research strategies (such as sample surveys) to gather more adequate migration information.

Adherents may be found on all sides of the "minimum" migration question. Smith argues the most inclusive definition, following the first alternative: "the term migration seems generally to be employed to refer to all movements in physical space with the assumption more or less implicit that a change of residence or domicile is involved." [14] Others take an intermediate position. Everett Lee, for example, incorporates into the definition of migration all moves of a permanent or semipermanent change of residence with no restrictions placed on distance moved or whether forced or voluntary: "Thus, a move across the hall from one apartment to another is counted as just as much an act of migration as a move from Bombay, India, to Cedar Rapids, Iowa. . . ." [15] The only categories of movers excluded from his definition of migration, without providing some justification, are temporary movers (e.g., vacationers, tourists) or continual movers (e.g., migrant workers, nomads).

In contrast to these more or less inclusive definitions, others have

[13] Henry Shryock, *Population Mobility Within the United States* (Chicago: Community and Family Study Center, University of Chicago, 1964), pp. 8–9.

[14] T. Lynn Smith, *Fundamentals of Population Study* (Philadelphia: Lippincott, 1960), p. 420; cf. United Nations, *The Determinants and Consequences of Population Trends* (New York, 1953), p. 98.

[15] Lee, "A Theory of Migration," p. 49.

been much more restrictive. Bogue, for example, suggests that, "Theoretically, the term 'migration' is reserved for those changes of residence that involve a complete change and readjustment of the community affiliations of the individual." [16] Similarly, Thomlinson states, "Not all people who change their geographical positions are migrants. . . . In order to be considered a migrant, one must make a move of some consequence. Demographers thus define a person as a migrant if he changes his place of normal habitation for a substantial period of time, crossing a political boundary in the process." [17]

The basis for delimiting the concept "migration" seems to fall into one or more categories: (1) exclusions based directly on the limited consequences of some moves; (2) exclusions based on the type of boundary crossed; (3) exclusion of continual movers; or (4) exclusions based on some notion of "time" or "permanence." Within the last three categories is often an *implicit* notion that the changes involved in particular types of moves are minimal, or that the types of changes involved have unique qualities that justify their exclusions. That is, movement that does not involve crossing an administrative or political boundary, moves of short duration, temporary movement, or continual movement involve small or different changes when compared to what may be involved in "migration."

The first category of exclusions relates directly to the potential consequences of some moves. But limiting the definition of migration to movements that involve "a complete change and readjustment" or to moves "of some consequence" is unnecessarily restrictive, unjustifiable theoretically, and unworkable empirically. To exclude some movement because it involves minimum consequences is to omit some of the very relationships that require systematic investigation, i.e., whether different types of geographic movement result in a range of varying degrees and forms of change. Moreover, it does not seem appropriate analytically to limit migration to moves that generate changes in the "community affiliations of individuals," because this excludes significant types of population movement that do not necessarily result in individual changes but have major social structural consequences. Large population movements between homogeneous metropolitan areas will have major economic, political, and social structural consequences independent of changes in the

[16] Bogue, "Internal Migration," p. 489. A somewhat different approach may be found in his *Principles of Demography*, pp. 752–753. Hawley defines migration as "nonrecurrent movement which requires the readjustment of the population in a modified or entirely new structure of relationships." Amos Hawley, *Human Ecology* (New York: Ronald, 1950), p. 327. See also Robert Park, "Human Migration and the Marginal Man," *American Journal of Sociology*, 33 (May 1928), pp. 886–887.

[17] Thomlinson, *Population Dynamics*, p. 211.

relationships of persons to their communities. As discussed earlier, macro-
and microlevels must be separated. Most important, how can we determine whether a particular type of movement will result in macro- or
microlevel changes unless it is included as part of our analysis? Underlying the attempt to limit the definition of migration in terms of consequences may rest an implicit notion of "change" that is inadequate.
Change is often viewed as dichotomous — note Bogue's use of the word
"complete" — rather than continuous, i.e., we should conceptualize change
in terms of degrees (as well as types) rather than in terms of "no change"
versus "complete change."

Because all movement implies changes in other social subsystems,
most demographers who restrict the definition of migration, therefore, do
so on arbitrary grounds in terms of boundary crossings. Following United
States census practice, "migration" is typically limited to crossing a
county boundary, whereas within-county movement is termed "mobility."
One implicit assumption underlying this arbitrary definition is that crossing an administrative or political boundary will involve greater changes
of all types than movement within administrative units. But it is quite
clear that this is not necessarily the case. As an extreme example, movement between two neighborhoods of different class or ethnic composition
within the same county (as a move around the corner from a Puerto
Rican lower class neighborhood to the upper class area of Park Avenue
in Manhattan, or the typical move to the suburbs from the urban area
in one county) will involve changes of greater magnitude and of various
types far beyond what might be involved in a cross-country move from
one neighborhood of a major metropolitan center (e.g., Boston) to another (e.g., San Francisco) with the same social and economic characteristics. Although administrative units may be useful as general, albeit
crude, guides to distinguish analytically *among* migration types, the arbitrariness of the specific unit selected and the implications that change is
at a minimum when movement takes place within that specified unit,
make crossing political or administrative boundaries a poor criterion for
delimiting migration.

Distance and heterogeneity are related to using boundary changes
to delimit migration. Certain moves within specified boundaries may be
shorter and involve less areal heterogeneity than movement between
boundaries; therefore, "local" movement should be excluded. Again, distance and heterogeneity factors (as with the general question of boundary changes) may best be viewed as criteria for distinguishing *among*
migration types rather than for delimiting migration.

Excluding those movements that are part of an institutionalized
life style, such as nomadic wandering or "migratory" laborers, is again
arbitrary, or justified on the grounds that social change is at a minimum.
The exclusion of continual movers in the migration definition is un-

justified: first, even under these conditions the individuals involved must adjust to new or constantly varying physical, social, and economic environments; second, the types of institutional consequences of migration when it is a way of life are significant for social scientific inquiry, not only for the groups involved but for the broader society of which these groups are but one segment.[18] Most important, continual movements represent the opposite extreme from stability; just as we need to include the stable sector of the population, we need also to include the extreme nonstable sector for comparative analysis.

Another basis for delimiting migration, noted in some definitions cited and implicit in others, is the question of permanence. Migration is usually defined as a move that involves a "substantial" period of time or one that is "permanent" or "semipermanent." But what about "permanence" is relevant? What of seasonal movers? or labor movements? or return movers? Who defines the lower limits of "permanence" or "temporariness"? We have several options: we may use subjective definitions of the "intentions" of the mover, or the legal or social definition that others place on the mover; or we may establish an objective criterion of some residence duration to define permanence, however arbitrary; or some combination of subjective and objective criteria.

When we invoke either subjective or objective criteria, or some combination of the two, a degree of arbitrariness is involved. If we accept the self-definition and intentions of the mover, he may define himself as a long-term mover but his stay may be short or, in reverse, he may define himself as a short-term mover but stay longer. If we, therefore, use some arbitrary but objective length of time, for example, at least a year, some consequences of movement will vary if the migrant or the community defines the migrant as a "resident" or a transient sojourner. Even if we combine extremes of objective and subjective criteria for defining migrants, we run into difficulty. Let us say that those people, who define themselves and who are defined legally or socially as temporary residents and who also stay a short period of time, should not be classified "migrants." This indeed may be the circumstances of seasonal moves and movers who intend to "return" to their place of origin. But this would exclude such major migratory streams as the post-World War II movement of Mexicans and Puerto Ricans to the United States, some Italian migration to the United States before World War I, rural-urban movements in parts of Africa, labor movements from Italy to Switzerland and France, and many more. All these movements involved, in part, the "temporary" movement of persons based on subjective and objective criteria. Yet these types of seasonal, temporary movements demonstrate the im-

---

[18] Cf. Smith, *Fundamentals of Population Study*, p. 418; Petersen, "A General Typology of Human Migration."

pact of moving on the lives of people and the structure of communities at areas of origin and destination. It, therefore, seems unwise to exclude them a priori or automatically from the concept migration.

Yet, on the other hand, we may argue intuitively that some quality of permanence should be employed to separate this type of temporary migrant from such "movers" as tourists, travelers, visitors, commuters, and the like. Movement that is "permanent" involves a sense of shifting for some period of time social structural attachments and activities from one locality to another.[19] Even when the move is for a short duration, or when the mover defines himself as transient or as "just passing through," the total round of activities are reorganized in the new location. Tourism, visiting, commuting, and similar moving processes, however, do not imply this minimum detachment from a *total round of activity*. Thus, they are qualitatively and analytically distinguishable from migration, although they might be incorporated as part of the broader concept of "residential or community experience." Permanence, therefore, does not necessarily relate to an arbitrary self-definition or an objective residence duration, but rather to detachment and reorganization of activities. In this sense the migration processes of "entering" and "exiting" go beyond the physical and mechanical into the social and structural.

In sum, defining the minimum that has to be involved for a move to qualify for inclusion in the migration concept is not as simple as it first appears. The exclusion of moves from migration cannot be justified on the grounds of potential minimum consequences, or in terms of political boundaries, or on the basis of time elements defined subjectively or objectively. Nor does it appear necessary to exclude continual, nomadic movements that involve "institutionalized" wandering. At this point, we will include within the concept of migration all residence changes — from one domicile to another. The only exclusions will be these moves (traveling, touring, and commuting) that do not involve detachments from the organization of activities at one place and the movement of the total round of activities to another place.

Internal-External Dichotomy

The greater the inclusiveness of the migration concept, the greater the need to specify and categorize the types of internal heterogeneity. To help identify and clarify types of movement, let us examine the relevance

[19] I am indebted to Arthur Stinchcombe for this distinction. It is important to note at this point that we reject the notion suggested by Lacroix that there are no criteria to distinguish between migrants and travelers. Cited in Petersen, *Population*, p. 41.

of distinguishing between migration within countries (internal or intra-national) and migration between countries (external or international).

Some have argued that the distinction between internal and external migration is "chiefly a matter of convenience" [20] or that "it is not necessarily of theoretical significance." [21] On the other hand, some have suggested that movements between countries are "qualitatively" different from movement within countries and usually involve greater distances.[22] Others argue that internal and international migrations have similar causes and consequences, yet they qualify this position by enumerating key differences. For example, Thomlinson argues: "Internal and international migration causes are similar, with the qualifications that international moves generally involve greater distances, cultural and linguistic barriers, legislative hindrances, and political barricades." [23] Similarly, Wrong states: "Internal movements do not differ greatly from international movements in their causation and motivation. In-migrants, however, are less likely to face acute problems of acculturation than immigrants with the result that personal, noneconomic motives play a larger part in internal than in international migrations." [24] These latter arguments are simply non sequiturs. The qualifications that Thomlinson and Wrong suggest imply that separating internal from international migration is an empirical and theoretical necessity. Because these general forms of movement potentially involve differential consequences for the individual and society, because they may involve differential motivations and social causes and may be facilitated or impeded in different ways, it follows that there is every reason for their analytic separation.

To illustrate the problems that arise when internal-external distinction is not made, let us examine one hypothesis that has been suggested in the literature. In developing what Everett Lee calls "a theory of migration," he notes that the "initiation and consequences" of internal and international migration are "vastly different." [25] His definition of migration cited earlier includes moves "around the corner" as well as between countries. However, the propositions about migration he discusses do not take into account his qualified distinction between internal and international movements, and generally deny the need for such distinctions. Indeed, a careful examination of his propositions points strongly to the inadequacy of generating hypothesis without differentiating in-

[20] George Barclay, *Techniques of Demographic Analysis* (New York: Wiley, 1958), p. 245; Bogue, "Internal Migration," p. 486.

[21] Petersen, "A General Typology of Migration," p. 264. For a more modified position see his *Population*, pp. 41–42.

[22] Shryock, *Population Mobility Within the United States*, p. 10.

[23] Thomlinson, *Population Dynamics*, p. 223.

[24] Wrong, *Population and Society*, p. 95.

[25] Lee, "A Theory of Migration," p. 49.

ternal from external migration. For example, Lee argues, "Unless severe checks are imposed, both volume and rate of migration tend to increase with time." [26] This seems to be a reasonable hypothesis for international migration (under some conditions), but is not at all accurate for internal migration in the United States for the last several decades. Indeed, Lee has prepared estimates that indicate internal migration rates in the United States have been *high and stable for over a century*, and no checks (severe or otherwise) have been imposed on internal movement.[27]

Of course, national boundaries are arbitrary administrative units. Yet, it is not the national boundary crossed that separates internal from international migration but rather the amount and type of change that these movements may differentially involve. The amount and type of change are a function of three primary conditions usually associated with the internal-external distinction: (1) distance covered, (2) impeding factors, and (3) heterogeneity between the area of origin and the area of destination. International migration usually, but not always, involves greater distances, greater legal and political controls, and greater diversity between areas of origin and destination when compared to internal movements. In turn, distance, barriers, and heterogeneity are linked in important ways to the degrees and types of change involved in migration. Therefore, on a continuum of change, the *probabilities* of greater and more diverse changes associated with migration, as determinants and consequences, are higher when migration is international than when it is internal.

To be sure, exceptions to the general association of greater and more diverse change with international movement may be cited. Changes involved with international movement may be less now than a hundred years ago, and vary with the degree of homogeneity of the countries involved and the social location of persons within countries. In short, internal and external migration may overlap with respect to the distance, barriers, and heterogeneity criteria; nevertheless, these migrations are not identical. The exceptions are primarily in those instances where international migration has taken on the characteristics and qualities of internal movements of short distances, between social-cultural homogeneous areas, with few legal barriers, or where internal movement involves greater distances, some political-administrative control, or movement between social-cultural heterogeneous areas within countries. For most historical circumstances, the association of greater changes in degree and

---

[26] Ibid., p. 53.

[27] Everett Lee, "Internal Migration and Population Redistribution in the United States," in *Population: The Vital Revolution*, ed. Ronald Freedman (New York: Doubleday, Anchor Books), p. 127; see also Shryock, *Population Mobility Within the United States*, p. 411 and chap. 5.

kind with external movement is sustained. The distinction between internal and external movement must be made analytically if only to identify, isolate, and analyze the conditions under which the internal-external dichotomy does not coincide with distance, political-legal-administrative barriers, and heterogeneity factors and, in turn, does not relate to variations in the degree and type of changes. Surely lumping together internal and international migration cannot be justified on a priori theoretical grounds or on the basis of empirical evidence now available.

Other Migration Types

The argument that internal migration should be separated analytically from external migration raises additional questions. First, are there other migration types that may be identified according to the boundary crossed? Second, do these migration types relate to the distance, barriers, and heterogeneity criteria? Third, what other criteria may be useful to differentiate types of migration that do not relate to geographic units?

Migration may involve crossing administrative or political boundaries other than the boundaries of total nations, as in the internal-external dichotomy. Neighborhoods, districts, communities, cities, counties, states, provinces, and regions are among many boundaries that may be involved. Although these boundaries are drawn arbitrarily and are designed for administrative purposes, they may help distinguish types of migration. But to utilize these convenient administrative units to distinguish migration types, we need to inquire into the implications or meanings of these boundaries for migration. In short, if these or other boundaries have no meaning other than their administrative designation, it would not be justifiable to use them as a basis for migration types. Some empirical evidence indicates that administrative units may be helpful in distinguishing migration types. Various research studies, usually based on census information, have pointed to the differences in the determinants, consequences, and selectivity of migration when different administrative units are utilized. For example, let us say that we want to find out whether nonwhites migrate more than whites, or whether males migrate more than females, or whether "economic" factors are more important than "family" factors as determinants of migration. It will be impossible to discover general patterns that hold true of all types of migration. Indeed, we cannot inquire systematically into these research questions without at the very minimum subdividing internal movement by the type of boundary crossed.[28] The evidence reveals, for example, that in the United

---

[28] Of course, we must also place any such analysis in social, economic, political, and cultural contexts. See Chapter 7, this book.

States, nonwhites tend to have higher intracounty migration rates than whites, although whites have higher intercounty migration rates; males have slightly higher intercounty migration rates than females but there is little sex differentiation in the movement within counties; job or employment factors loom larger in intercounty migration, whereas housing and family factors are more important in local migration.[29] Hence, the relationship between race, sex, employment, and family factors and migration cannot be clarified unless elementary distinctions among boundary units are made.

Given that the types of boundaries crossed within countries are significant because of the possible differential determinants, consequences, and relationships involved, the question remains, Why? Surely no magical relationship exists between crossing administrative boundaries and the types of relationships involved. Crossing boundary lines may best be viewed as an *indicator,* however crude and incomplete, of the three general processes in the internal-external dichotomy: distance, economic and social barriers, and heterogeneity. It is not the boundary lines that are crossed which distinguish mechanically and automatically types of internal migration, but rather it is the implications of these boundary crossings for the criteria of distance, economic and social barriers, and areal heterogeneity that are significant. In turn, these three criteria relate directly to the causes and effects of migration.

As a basic hypothesis we would argue that distance moved, all other things equal, is related to the degree and type of change in other subsystems of society. The importance of distance moved may be observed most clearly in family-community ties.[30] We can imagine, for example, what occurs to family and kinship relationships when one family member moves a great distance. Suppose that intense personal relationships developed between an individual and his family and kin before the move. He then moves out of the local community to another community a considerable distance away. No doubt his relationships with family and kin, of necessity the frequency of personal interaction, will decline as a consequence of the distance involved. Personal interaction may be replaced by increases in the frequency of other relationships, e.g.,

---

[29] See data presented in Shryock, *Population Mobility Within the United States,* pp. 400–401.

[30] Goode argues that one crucial pressure from industrialization on traditional family structure is the physical movement from one locality to another. Movement over long distances decreases the frequency and particularly the intimacy or quality of contact among members of a kin network. At later stages of industrialization this may be partly counteracted by greater ease and different forms of contact. See William Goode, *World Revolution and Family Patterns* (New York: The Free Press, 1963), p. 369; also, Eugene Litwak, "Extended Kin Relations in an Industrial Democratic Society," in *Social Structure and the Family,* ed. Ethel Shannas and Gordon Streib (Englewood Cliffs, N.J.: Prentice-Hall, 1965), pp. 290–323.

telephoning, writing, visiting, etc. Nevertheless, one consequence of a long-distance move will involve changes in personal interaction with family and kin, unless, of course, family and kin move as well. At times, we may not be able to measure the distance factor directly. Indirectly, we may be able to test this general hypothesis relating distance and family interaction by comparing the consequences of intracounty and intercounty migration, *assuming* that these geographic units are rough indicators of what is at the basis of the relationship — distance.

Distance may also be important in accounting for differential movement. We may compare, for example, the intracounty and intercounty migration rates of private physicians and research physicians. Our reasoning might be that private physicians build up a clientele from a local community and their migration patterns will be more or less limited within a circumscribed distance. On the other hand, research physicians may be more likely to move greater distances, to other states and regions, because their jobs are not dependent on extensive community ties. Thus, we might utilize boundary changes as an *indicator* of the distance factor because the distance and community-occupation relationship serve as the underlying theory. People in the labor force cannot migrate from New Jersey to North Dakota without switching job locations in the process.[31]

We usually consider "barriers" as impeding factors in international migration but not in internal migration. But barriers consist not only of legal restrictions, immigration quotas, entrance and exit permits, etc., but are also social and economic. In this latter sense social and economic barriers relate to both the distance moved and the boundary crossed within countries. As Lee notes, "between every two points there stands a set of intervening obstacles which may be slight in some instances and insurmountable in others." [32] Among some barriers that may be associated with movement we might include moving costs, knowledge about other communities, and, under some conditions, such physical barriers as rivers, mountains, and deserts. Again, let us take an extreme example. Movement between two areas assumes some degree of accessibility. If between two areas such physical barriers as large rivers or hazardous environmental conditions exist, and the means to overcome them have not been developed, large migration to these areas is not likely to take place. Frontier movements within countries are composed initially of selected persons who attempt to overcome the physical barriers involved. Only after access routes are evolved and mapped and only after transportation facilities are developed does any large-scale frontier movement materialize. Just as international movements from Europe to the United

[31] For a documented analysis see Ladinsky, "Occupational Determinants of Geographic Mobility Among Professional Workers," pp. 257–264. See also Chapter 11, this book.

[32] Lee, "A Theory of Migration," p. 51.

States did not gain momentum until the physical barrier of the Atlantic Ocean was overcome, so the movement to the West coast of the United States was restricted until access routes and transportation facilities were developed.

Similar arguments appear relevant for studying heterogeneity. As with distance and "obstacles," crossing boundary lines is a crude indicator of the heterogeneity involved. Movement within administratively defined units involves greater homogeneity than movement between different types of units. For example, movement between homogeneous areas (e.g., urban to urban, or rural to rural, or within community units) will involve fewer and different types of changes than movement between areas of cultural or socioeconomic diversity (e.g., rural to urban, urban to suburban, or frontier movement). Again, we justify separating different types of boundary crossings because of their implications for heterogeneity.

"Homogeneity" and "heterogeneity" involve various components. Two areas may be defined as homogeneous in terms of "economic" criteria but as heterogeneous culturally, linguistically, or politically. Moreover, identifying the various types of heterogeneity at the areal or structural level should be supplemented by evidence on the social location of persons within areas. Movement between two urban areas with similar structural and cultural features may occur, but part of the movement may be of persons who move from one slum area to another slum area whereas another segment of the migrating population move from one slum area to a middle-class neighborhood. The reverse may also happen: movement may take place between two very dissimilar areas (e.g., rural to urban) but the location of movers within the area of destination may be quite similar to their social location within the area of origin. Thus, the elements of heterogeneity must be defined with respect to the broad structural features of areas as well as with respect to the social location of movers within areas.

In brief, boundary changes, in and of themselves, are not the basis of migration types but rather the implication of these boundary crossings for distance, social and economic barriers, and heterogeneity. In turn, distance, barriers, and heterogeneity have implications vis-a-vis the types and degrees of change associated with migration; these factors have a systematic interrelationship. Most migration analysis will take the distance factor into consideration either directly or by emphasizing boundary changes. Often, however, little attempt is made to take into account the heterogeneity factor or, at most, to limit heterogeneity to broad structural characteristics. Failure to note the importance of "heterogeneity" of places and persons in some migration research has led to overgeneralization and imprecise analysis. To illustrate, Lee argues that a high degree of areal diversity results in high rates of migration,[33] which seems to be accurate for some types of movement (e.g., rural to urban migration or frontier settlement), under some conditions (e.g., the early stages of industrialization). However, the opposite proposition is equally true, i.e., a high degree of similarity of areas results in high rates of migration. The evidence available points to high rates of interurban and intersuburban movement in the United States. Even in such underdeveloped countries as Chile, India, and parts of Africa, migrations among urban areas and among rural areas are significant, and often are the dominant migration patterns.[34] Moreover, because Lee's proposition focuses solely on "areal" characteristics, variation within broadly homogeneous units is not considered. The type of rural-to-urban migration that at times results in establishing rural enclaves, cultural areas, or segregated ghettos within the urban core, in developed and underdeveloped countries, is thus omitted. Hence, homogeneity or heterogeneity must be conceptualized for varying structural or areal features as well as the social location of persons within areas.

Up to this point we have discussed the definition and types of migration in terms of geographically defined analysis units. We thus made some observations about the minimum end of the migration continuum and the types of migration based on boundary crossings. Some theoretical and empirical justifications for such distinctions were highlighted. However, another basis for distinguishing migration types is the migrating unit itself. Whether we are dealing with local moves or international moves, short or long distance moves, moves between heterogeneous or homogeneous areas, migration streams must be separated by (1) moves of individuals or groups of individuals; (2) family movement — whether the mover is an unattached individual or part of a moving conjugal or extended family unit, and whether the mover is a wife accompanying her husband or a child accompanying parents; (3) "chainlike" movers — where the move may involve initially an individual who later sends for family, kin or community, thus combining elements of (1) and (2) in longitudinal perspective; or (4) mass migration — where substantial parts of communities migrate.[35] These various movements have differential implications for assimilation and integration at macro- and micro-

[33] Ibid., p. 52.

[34] See, for example, Shryock, *Population Mobility Within the United States;* Elizaga, "A Study of Migration to Greater Santiago (Chile)," pp. 358–359; Bose, "Migration Streams in India," p. 600; Joginder Kumar, "The Pattern of Internal Migration in India During 1951–61," in International Union for the Scientific Study of Population, *Contributed Papers* (Sydney Conference, 1967), pp. 623–628. On Africa, see Chapter 7, this book.

[35] Cf. Petersen, "A General Typology of Migration," pp. 256–265. On the importance of chainlike migration, see the discussion in Chapter 7, this book.

levels of analysis and are differentially determined as well. Over an extended period these migration types, under some conditions, may occur in sequence, starting from the movement of individuals to family-kin movement to chainlike community patterns and finally to mass movement. Such mass movements as immigration to the United States beginning toward the end of the nineteenth century, or general movements from rural to urban areas, urban to suburban areas, and frontier settlements are important illustrations of this process. Thus, we will need to separate the nature of the migration stream *within* each type of migration geographically defined.

Usually migration is viewed in its *instantaneous* form as a detachment from one location and starting anew in another location. Another perspective treats migration in its *cumulative* aspect, i.e., the way the lives of persons are subdivided into time segments spent in different locations — the *biographical* aspect of migration.[36] Migration is not only an immediate change in the life situation of persons and one aspect of the net redistribution of population; also, the sum of migratory decisions constitutes a life-cycle of social attachments. At a certain age, or under some family situations, or with some types of career mobility, the appropriate solution for a person in that life-cycle stage is to go somewhere else, perhaps to eventually come back or return. The migration of college students, of soldiers, or of physicians in underdeveloped countries who spend two years in local villages, of older persons to retirement communities, or of persons when they marry, are as much part of a life plan as they are the restructuring of social attachments. Migration for some may be a matter of starting a new biography at the place of destination, whereas for others migration may be a continuation of the old biography. Moving to a retirement community is not so much changing one's social relations because of migration as it is carrying out the changes of social relations made appropriate by the fact of retirement. Moves associated with marriage and setting up independent nuclear residences or moves associated with family formation, expansion, and dissolution are changes that may be viewed in cumulative rather than instantaneous perspective, as can the "temporary" migration of Puerto Ricans to the United States or "seasonal" rural-to-urban movement in Africa.

SOME THEORETICAL IMPLICATIONS

Several implications emerge from the clarification of issues associated with defining migration and identifying migration types that paral-

[36] This concept and its description were suggested to me by Arthur Stinchcombe.

lel some general theoretical issues in demographic analysis discussed earlier.

First and foremost, migration always involves changes in other subsystems of society. Movement in space must either be determined by some changes, or result in changes, or be a concomitant of changes — the latter implying that migration may often be viewed as a link in the process of change, neither clearly as a determinant nor as a consequence. A decision, voluntary or involuntary, to move around the block or even within the same apartment house must have been precipitated by some alteration in the status quo. This is not to argue that man is naturally stable but rather that some change must occur to precipitate a disruption of stability. Moreover, once mobility occurs, other subsystems are usually altered.

The relationship between migration and economic development illustrates the various ways population mobility and processes of change may be viewed at the macrolevel of analysis. Under some conditions, for example in the early stage of industrialization, when rural-urban migration or international movement takes place, population movement may stimulate economic development in areas of destination. In these cases, migration may be viewed analytically as the *independent* variable and economic growth as the *dependent* variable. Under other conditions, for example, movement between metropolitan areas in mature or developed stages of industrialization, migration may be a response to economic growth and labor demands. Therefore, migration in these situations may be viewed as a *consequence* of economic growth. Moreover, it is likely that the particular role of migration as a determinant or as a consequence of economic changes is unclear empirically. In fact, migration may be viewed as an integral part and a necessary condition for economic developmental processes, that is, migration and population redistribution are important components in the evolution of industrial societies. Its particular cause-effect relationship may be impossible to isolate empirically and unrealistic to predict theoretically. In broadest perspective, migration and economic development should be treated as a circular interdependent probability process wherein mobility changes may stimulate economic growth, which in turn may further stimulate mobility, and so on.[37] From this perspective it would follow that analyses of the determinants and consequences of migration should at a minimum interrelate and scrutinize the interactional character of causes on effects and vice versa.

[37] Cf. Simon Kuznets, "Introduction: Population Redistribution, Migration, and Economic Growth," in *Population Redistribution and Economic Growth, United States 1870–1950*, vol. 3, ed. Hope Eldridge and Dorothy Thomas (Philadelphia: American Philosophical Society, 1964), pp. xxiii–xxxv.

Ideally, our conceptualization of migration processes should be based on the notion that migration is an integral part of change processes.[38]

The same basic pattern characterizes microlevels of analysis. For example, migration may result in income changes and income changes may lead to migration. Moreover, social mobility (of which income changes may be one element) and geographic mobility usually are correlated, i.e., these two social processes are integral to one another. Persons may move because of changes in social status, and changes in social status may result from geographic mobility.

If we argue that migration is inextricably interrelated in processes of change, a distinction must be made between *degrees* and *types* of change. Essentially, we will want to know how much change and of what kind. Some types of migration may involve lesser cultural changes whereas others may involve greater cultural changes; some migration may involve few cultural or linguistic changes but radical changes in personal interaction with kin or broader demographic or economic changes.

Given this general orientation, it is clear why exclusions of moves from the concept "migration" based on potential minimum consequences is unjustifiable analytically. The only moves that may be excluded are those that do not involve the "migration" process – i.e., detachment and reorganization of activities and structures. Because detachment and reorganization always imply correlative changes, the analytic task is to identify the range and form of changes associated with differing types of migration.

The contradictions noted in the literature with respect to the inclusiveness of the migration concept and the types of migration that may be distinguished are partly a function of ad hoc and arbitrary considerations resulting from inadequate and imprecise conceptualization. We have insisted on conceptual or theoretical justification when examining the definition of migration or when deciding on a basis for separating migration types. Mechanical, automatic, or arbitrary procedures may be easier, but less convincing. Moreover, we noted various types of conceptual abstractions involved in identifying the implications of various axes in the development of migration types. For example, boundary crossings have implications for the criteria of distance, heterogeneity, and socioeconomic barriers; in turn, these criteria for various reasons have

---

[38] From another point of view Hawley argues "Change without movement is impossible. In organic life changeability is the measure of adaptive capacity, and mobility is the mechanism of change. . . . Migration is both the means by which change is effected and the most accessible evidence of change." *Human Ecology*, pp. 324, 326.

meaning vis-a-vis the degree and type of change associated with migration.

We also identified two general bases for typing migration. The first is based on the migration process itself, often defined in terms of geographic units. We can separate analytically short or long distance moves, moves between heterogeneous and homogeneous areas (variously defined), or moves facilitated or impeded by social and economic barriers. Migration types may also be based on the composition of the migrant group — whether individual, family, chainlike, or mass migration. Thus, the type of research focus varies when the *unit* of analysis varies.

The impression created at the onset of our discussion of migration definitions and types may have been that the issues were trivial, elementary, or arbitrary. However, these issues are quite complex and are relevant theoretically and empirically. The issues and problems associated with delimiting the migration concept and identifying migration types are a basic introduction to any analysis of migration processes. Of equal importance, solutions to these issues parallel the general theoretical problems discussed in Chapter 2. Involved in dissecting the migration concept and types are issues associated with levels of analyses, levels of abstraction, units of analysis, and static and dynamic perspectives. Indeed, one objective of this excursion into definitions and types of migration was to convey the importance and relevance of these complex problems and propose some alternative solutions. Identifying and analyzing these issues are only preliminary — but necessary — steps to isolating the determinants and consequences of migration. Plunging into migration analysis without systematic clarification of these fundamental issues is hazardous analytically and unacceptable methodologically.

Part
2

Modernization and Population Processes

Chapter Four

MODERNIZATION AND POPULATION CHANGE

Population processes do not operate in a social vacuum. Births, deaths, and movement are integral to the functioning of human society, responsive to the patterns of social structure, and affect the character of social life. Concomitantly, changes in fertility, mortality, and migration reflect more general changes in society and, as well, shape, accelerate, or impede alterations in other elements of the social system. Examining the alternating roles of population processes as determinants and consequences of social structure and social change forms the basis for the sociological analysis of demographic phenomena.

Identifying the junctures of population and social systems requires, therefore, a critical examination of population elements in the context of the dynamics of human society. One way to uncover these major interconnections and linkages is to investigate how fertility, mortality, and migration have varied between societies over time, weaving together variation and change in population and social variables. To achieve this objective systematically and rigorously, we need to locate a persistent, inclusive process of change, a dynamic social force that has transformed and reshaped human societies. The broad social change process that most closely meets these criteria is the *modernization of human societies*. The inescapable and complex reality of social modernization has become the master theme of social scientific inquiry and the common thread linking the theoretical, methodological, and empirical preoccupation of classical and contemporary scientists of human society. Modernization is not synonymous with all social change; it does, however, cover the most visible, large-scale structural and cultural social changes that have engulfed significant segments of the world. The major revolutions that have occurred during the past several centuries, and continue unabated in some areas — including agricultural, industrial, urban, technological, family, political, and demographic revolutions — and that are beginning to appear in the underdeveloped two-thirds of the world are integral processes of modernization.

It would be untenable logically and sociologically if population elements were not responsive to the massive social changes associated with modernization and were not themselves partly responsible for the course and pace of modernization. Hence, no study of the determinants and consequences of population processes can proceed very far without analyzing systematically and in detail the links to modernization; no investigation of modernization can be complete without analyzing demographic variables.

The complexity of modernization, its multidimensionality and inclusiveness, has analytic advantages and disadvantages. On one hand, it allows population transformations to be linked to other major social changes and integrates population studies within a general sociological framework. However, because modernization includes an enormous range of changes — social, economic, political, cultural, and personal — we must be wary not to end up connecting every change to demographic processes. Nor would it be very illuminating to conclude that fertility is reduced and "controlled" as modernization proceeds, or that migration from rural areas to urban locations increases during modernization, or that mortality levels decline and population growth rates change with concomitant modernization, *without* specifying the particular features of modernization that are operative and the mechanisms that connect population changes to specific elements of modernization. Indeed, the major emphasis in the next several chapters will be to select from the labyrinth of interconnected processes comprising modernization those major changes that affect the components of population — mortality, fertility, and migration — most directly and critically. In turn, consideration will be given to the analysis of how population changes affect the patterns of modernization. However, a general overview of the broader issues is needed to provide an analytic setting within which the subsequent materials will be examined. Toward this goal, we shall discuss in this chapter three sets of introductory questions: (1) What are the general and specific objectives of linking population processes to modernization? Why is it so essential to analyze population changes as part of the processes of modernization? (2) How do we proceed to link these two processes? What types of analytic comparisons should be made in relating changes in the population elements to the social, economic, political, cultural, and personal changes associated with modernization? (3) What is meant by modernization? What are some critical processes of modernization that are interrelated with demographic changes?

LINKING POPULATION PROCESSES TO MODERNIZATION

Why Population Changes

When we link population variables to the broader social changes associated with modernization, we have in mind several implicit objectives. First, we must uncover the determinants of population changes. During modernization, basic alterations in population elements occur in a systematic and patterned way. Our task is to identify and document, fully and rigorously, the nature of those population changes. Describing population changes is complicated by the further requirement of understanding why population processes change. By linking population changes to general social and economic modernization, we can work toward resolving this question.

To illustrate, a casual glance at the demography of countries around the world [1] reveals major national differences in fertility levels, mortality patterns, migration processes, and population growth rates. The most dramatic and striking national demographic differences are between those societies that may be called "modern-industrial" states and other "traditional-agricultural" countries. Confronted with detailed empirical documentation of the specific facts of population differences, the social scientist naturally asks what the heterogeneous countries lumped together in the "modern" category have in common which results in such a clear-cut pattern of demographic differentiation when compared to countries in the nonmodern or less-modern category. Obviously these categories have many differences — social, economic, political, and cultural. To illustrate, let us suggest that one social characteristic, among many, which separates "modern" from "non-modern" countries is the education level: The populations of modern nations are generally characterized by higher levels of formal educational attainment than the populations of nonmodern nations. Because both education levels and population variables are related clearly to the differentiation between modern and nonmodern states, we shall hypothesize tentatively that the two processes are interrelated. More specifically, the educational level of a society, as an element of modernity, seems related somehow to demographic variation.

[1] The beginning point was selected arbitrarily, and the order of analytic questions used in this illustration has no particular significance. The choice of an inductive rather than deductive strategy is by personal preference and does not imply that other approaches are not as cogent.

On further investigation, we may note that there are demographic differences among modern and nonmodern countries. Moreover, these dichotomized groupings have correlative educational heterogeneity and variation. Hence, our hypothesis is extended: Does the relationship between educational level and demographic variables found in the gross classification of modern and nonmodern countries obtain as well in the internal variation *within* these categories of nations? Are those nations that are "more modern," defined in terms of higher levels of educational attainment, characterized by systematic demographic variation? Are those nations which are "more traditional," defined in terms of lower levels of educational attainment, characterized by the reverse demographic pattern? Assuming for the sake of argument that these hypotheses are supported fully by the evidence, i.e., educational variation between and within modern and nonmodern categories of nations is related systematically to demographic variation, our analysis may be extended further. It may be argued that the type of demographic pattern identified in contemporary modern societies is relatively new historically. In many respects, population processes in currently nonmodern nations parallel the general demographic picture of the so-called modern states in the eighteenth and nineteenth centuries. Moreover, the same seems to be true for patterns of formal educational attainment levels. Thus, a third set of questions may be posed: What happened in the social history of modern nations that resulted in marked changes in demographic and educational levels? Indeed, is there any relationship between these changes? Did increases in educational levels during modernization result in systematic changes in the rates of demographic variables? Are the nations that were in the forefront of demographic population changes also those in which modernization (as indicated by changes in educational attainment) began early and proceeded rapidly? Conversely, is the lack of demographic change associated with the absence of change in education?

Let us assume that the cross-sectional comparative evidence, between and among modern and nonmodern countries, concerning the relationship between the educational component of modernization and population changes, is reinforced and supported empirically by historical analysis. Pushing our analysis further, we may turn to yet another set of related hypotheses to add weight to our conclusions. Does the relationship between educational changes in modernization and population factors operate *within* societal units, historically and comparatively? Are the more educated subgroupings within society characterized by the same demographic pattern as the more educated nations? Does this internal pattern hold for both modern and nonmodern nations? Did the more educated segments have earlier demographic changes in historical perspective? If, for all these various tests, the same pattern of relationship between educational attainment and population changes emerges, it is relatively safe to conclude that at least one major determinant of demographic processes has been identified, i.e., educational attainment. Thus, by analyzing variations and changes in population patterns in the context of modernization, a critical independent variable affecting population processes has been located.

It should be clear that the pattern of analysis has been greatly oversimplified for illustrative purposes. In reality, however, the nature of human social systems is such that anything close to "full" confirmation is not likely. In our illustration, for example, it is almost certain that we would only be able to obtain the grossest confirmation of the relationship. Most important, we should recognize that there are many other social, political, economic, and cultural differences between and within modern and traditional societies, as well as other major transformations that have taken place in the historical trend toward modernization, independent of and in addition to changes in educational attainment. Unless we could demonstrate that the relationship between changes in education and demographic variables was not spurious (i.e., was not a function of other variables related both to education and population processes), and unless we had negative evidence on the relationship between other social changes associated with modernization and population processes (i.e., evidence that demonstrated clearly that other social changes did not operate in the same way with population variables as educational attainment), our conclusions would have to remain quite tentative, even if correct empirically.

A related point about identifying and locating population determinants by analyzing social changes associated with modernization must be clarified. Assuming that all the evidence available points convincingly to the role of educational changes as the key component of modernization in the analysis of population changes and that the relationship is not spurious and other evidence is available to reject equally significant alternative hypotheses, our analytic inquiry must further untangle the *mechanisms* that link educational attainment to fertility, mortality, migration, and population growth. Surely, the relationships between education and population processes are neither automatic, nor magical, nor mechanical. Isolating educational attainment as one determinant of population patterns is only an elementary starting point for theoretical analysis. The more difficult next step would be to investigate what about educational changes represents the causative mechanisms in population changes. Do changes in education levels imply "rationality" in social and demographic behavior, or changes in the kinship-reward system, or alterations in social mobility and social stratification, or technological changes, or new directions for personal aspirations, or a dozen other factors that define education and connect it to population changes? The multi-faceted nature of any one specific change, its interconnection with other parts of the changing social system in the process of modernization, demands that we disentangle the web of connections to understand the direct mechanisms determining population processes.

We have assumed in this illustration that changes in population processes are uniform and unidirectional over time and that population processes have a simple interrelationship, i.e., as one population element changes, the other variables of the population system change. These assumptions are neither realistic nor reasonable. Moreover, there is no a priori reason to postulate that the same causal mechanism linking education to one population element operates as the key mechanism for other population variables. The links between changes in educational attainment (or any other variable) and demographic transformations must be analyzed separately for each component of the population system. Thus, the probability of locating one social process associated with modernization as the key determinant of *all* demographic change is low on both empirical and theoretical grounds.

Despite all the caveats of our simple illustration, the general point should not be obscured: One major objective of linking population variables to modernization processes is to help us analyze the determinants of population changes.

Prediction and Control

An interrelated yet analytically distinct objective of investigating demographic changes in the modernization process is to help predict and control population changes for nonmodern and less-modern nations and areas. Moreover, we should be able to extrapolate from the nations that have experienced demographic changes more fully to those nations that have lower rates and levels of demographic change. To continue with our oversimplified example, if changes in the educational level are related unexceptionally to population transformations, then as the nonmodern and less-modern nations of the world increase the educational levels of their populations, basic alterations in demographic processes may be expected. Moreover, once the mechanisms that link educational and population changes during modernization are identified, we should be able to anticipate the type and pace of demographic changes before they occur.

Beyond the analytic advantage of projection and prediction (along with other practical advantages), linking population variables to modernization processes is of critical importance in developing population control policies. Assume, for example, that the government of a non-modern, preindustrial, rural society recognizes the disadvantages of high population growth rates for economic development. If that government desires to reduce population growth rates by encouraging lower fertility levels, an analysis of how fertility levels were reduced in modernization of modern nations may provide important clues for government intervention and policy. Assuming that educational advancement turns out to be the key to the "natural" reduction of fertility in modern societies, emphasis of government policy might be placed on increasing educational opportunities and facilities. The same type of reasoning would be involved in government planning efforts to increase population size through encouraging increased fertility. If we know why couples restrict their family size, various measures may be taken to alter socioeconomic conditions so that family size would increase.

When we go beyond the mechanical relationship of modernization elements and population processes and isolate the specific mechanisms engendering population change, we may be able to bypass some difficult social structural changes to affect and control population processes directly. Let us assume, for example, that the key factor in the relationship between education and fertility reduction during modernization is acquiring contraceptive knowledge. (It isn't, but it makes for a simplified and interesting argument.) In lieu of the difficult and major task of restructuring educational systems and opportunities, an alternative policy, of hypothesized direct fertility consequences, would be to provide channels for disseminating contraceptive knowledge.[2]

The most important analytic danger in the prediction and control objective of linking population to modernization processes is the implicit evolutionary bias. The foundation of prediction and control, as previously discussed, assumes that currently nonmodern nations will follow similar patterns of demographic development experienced by currently modern nations, and that specific relationships between social, economic, political, and cultural variables on one hand and population variables on the other will be the same in the modernization process of developing societies as they were in the historical experience of developed societies. For varying reasons, to be discussed in a subsequent section, the demographic histories of developing countries probably will not exactly replay population changes that have occurred in developed areas.[3]

The inadequacies of the evolutionary model of demographic development do not necessarily invalidate the prediction and control objective of linking population to modernization. Although we shall argue for

[2] For a fuller discussion, see Chapter 6, this book.
[3] In addition to pp. 97–101, see specific discussions in Chapters 5–7.

a pluralistic model of demographic change, analyzing the critical links between population processes and modernization, along with identifying the mechanisms of change, takes us quite far toward understanding future demographic history and appreciating the complexities of population control.

Consequences of Population Changes

The third major set of objectives in connecting population and modernization processes is based on the premise that population changes are *integral* elements in modernization, which means that no society can enter into the societal processes associated with modernization unless certain demographic changes are visible. As such, the analysis of population changes in the process of modernization enables using population transformations, which are readily identifiable and quantifiable, as indicators of the broader processes of which they are a part. Again, we must exercise caution in using population changes as indicators of broader modernization processes because not *all* population changes reflect modernization. As we shall examine in detail in subsequent chapters, urbanization, mortality reduction, and to a lesser extent fertility changes may occur without concomitant modernization. However, the reverse is generally not the case: modernization almost always in its initial stages, and always in advanced stages, implies migration from rural to urban areas, reduction in mortality levels, and declines in fertility rates.

A more important implication is that population factors may be treated as both dependent and independent variables. Up to this point, the major emphasis has been on population changes as responses to the processes associated with modernization, i.e., as dependent variables. Hence, we pointed out that connecting population patterns to modernization processes would uncover the determinants of population changes, and, in turn, form the basis for prediction and control. When we use population processes as indicators of modernization, assuming that the relationship between population variables and modernization processes are *correlative*, then neither of these processes is treated necessarily as cause or effect. But population changes often operate as determinants of the shape, speed, and character of modernization.

Let us take a simple example of the impact of population growth on per capita income. Assume that two countries start out with the same yearly per capita income level, $100, and that total income doubles thereafter every twenty years. However, in one country population patterns are such that population size doubles every twenty years, although in the second country population size doubles every fifty years. After forty years, per capita income remains at the same level, $100, in the first country but will have more than doubled to $230 in the second country.[4] In short, the level of economic modernization, as measured crudely by per capita income, is influenced directly by the population growth rate, which, of course, is a function of the combined effects of fertility, mortality, and migration levels.

Another example of the possible role of population processes as determinants of modernization relates to educational attainment and changes. In the illustration presented earlier it was assumed that the relationship between educational attainment and population processes was causal in that educational attainment was the independent variable and population changes were the resultants or dependent variables. However, over time, and under some conditions, it is reasonable to examine the reverse: population processes as determinants of educational changes. For example, fertility reduction through delayed marriage may facilitate spending a longer time in educational institutions; family size reduction may permit couples to send their children to school for a longer period without economic hardships. Similarly, reduction in child and adult mortality may facilitate increases in educational attainment. Spending a dozen or more years in formal educational activity may not be very sensible or realistic when average life expectancy is short and the conditions of life precarious. Migration, when interrelated with kinship breakdown and tied to economic opportunity, may also affect changes in educational levels. Finally, at the macrolevel, reductions in population growth rates may channel economic investment into educational institutions rather than into other areas of economic necessity required to accommodate growing numbers of people. In short, the relationship between educational attainment and population changes should be viewed in both directions: (1) educational changes as determinants of population changes; (2) changes in demographic processes as determinants of educational changes. The potential two-way relationship between these processes should caution us in reaching conclusions on but half the interaction.

THE SCOPE OF COMPARISONS

How do we proceed methodologically to uncover the links between population processes and modernization? Comparison is the essential methodological ingredient in the shift beyond description toward analy-

---

[4] This illustration is discussed in greater detail in Gavin W. Jones, *The Economic Effect of Declining Fertility in Less Developed Countries* (New York: The Population Council, Occasional Paper, 1969).

sis; comparing nations to one another is an elementary step toward understanding modernization.

To note that comparisons allow us to examine population variables in modernization processes takes us to the next logical step: specifying the range and scope of comparisons and identifying general categories and major types of comparisons that should be made. In a narrow and specific sense, particular cases that are potentially available for comparisons are limitless; even if finite, the range of comparisons is all-inclusive and the number is exceedingly large. The actual comparisons that have been made in social scientific research cover long spans of historical time and encompass a tremendous range of societies. Comparisons have been limited only by the availability of evidence and the creative imagination of social scientists. Nevertheless, whatever comparisons may be made, we are able to categorize them within some general types ("general" to include the many specific cases that have been compared and that are potentially available for comparison). Grouping comparisons into categories, however general, is useful conceptually because it organizes diverse research, pinpoints methodological limitations and problems, and directs attention to particular gaps in our knowledge.

Categories of comparisons vary along two major axes: time and social location. Differences between comparison types depend on whether time or social location is variable or controlled. We shall illustrate the major categories of comparisons as they relate to demographic processes and focus largely on societal units.[5] Each comparison category parallels parts of the classical experimental design: before and after situations, with and without control groups, with some analytically isolated "stimulus." In large part, social scientific comparisons reflect more or less systematic attempts to reach analytic conclusions by simulating, imperfectly and illustratively, the laboratory controlled conditions of the experimental design.

Types of Comparisons

In the pure *historical* comparison model, time varies and social location is controlled. Historical comparisons in demographic research trace population changes over time, or between two or more specific time periods, within one social unit. For example, we may examine changes in the population size of the United States between 1770 and 1970; fertility rates in industrialized nations may be compared before and after World War II; mortality patterns of underdeveloped countries may be examined

[5] In Part 3, we discuss intrasocietal units. See the introductory arguments in Chapter 8.

in 1920 and 1950; the pace of migration in Africa may be analyzed from the colonial to the postcolonial period. In all these examples, among many others, time, defined in several ways, varies; a single unit, also variously defined, is used for analysis.

In formal methodological terms, the historical model of comparison represents a "before-after" situation, with the "stimulus" represented by some change in a social situation or some social event or process that is thought to affect the demographic variable under investigation. Hence, in the examples presented, population size may be related to nation-building, fertility patterns to war, mortality to technological diffusion of medical care and public health services, or migration to political-social conditions. The historical model omits the "control" group, i.e., it does not consider evidence on before-after conditions where the stimulus is not present. It is also "culture-bound" because it concentrates on changes within only one unit.

In *comparative* analysis, population processes between two or more social units are compared holding time constant. The pure comparative model examines variations in population phenomena between societal units around the same general time. Included within this category are studies of fertility differences between and among industrialized and nonindustrialized nations in the post-World War II era, investigations into mortality differences between France and Switzerland in the eighteenth century, research comparing immigration patterns into Canada and the United States during the 1920's, and analyses of nineteenth-century population growth in Japan and China.

In methodological terms, comparative analysis between societies at the same point in time represents either two "after" situations, in which one or more social units was exposed to a "stimulus" and the second was not (for example, the fertility comparison of industrialized and nonindustrialized nations where the former have been exposed to industrialization and the latter have not), or two "before" situations, which contrast differences in initial conditions to account for subsequent but assumed differences (for example, comparing China and Japan in the nineteenth century provides clues to their differential demographic history). At times, the cases chosen for comparison have been similarly exposed to some stimulus or have similar subsequent demographic histories. If we compare the post-World War II upswing in fertility in several industrialized countries, without any negative cases of fertility stability or decline at the same time in other industrialized nations, we have two "after" situations with added, but not necessarily confirmatory, evidence of a general pattern.

A *hybrid* type of comparison retains partial features of comparative analysis (comparison of two or more units) and partial features of historical analysis (time varies but not within each unit). For example, demographic conditions in preindustrial Western European countries may be compared to currently nonindustrial Latin American or Asian nations to determine what in the European situation engendered its subsequent demographic development or to determine the possible future demographic course of underdeveloped nations. The hybrid comparative type is parallel to comparing the before (or after) of the experimental group to the after (or before) of the control group, along with some implicit assumptions about the missing cells.

A logical extension of this is combining the pure historical and comparative types. Instead of making assumptions about the missing cells as in the hybrid comparison, these comparisons are an explicit part of the model. Comparisons that involve variation in both time and social location are referred to as *historical-comparative* or *comparative-historical*. For example, some studies focus on population changes in two or more societal units, or differences in population processes among societal units over time, such as research on mortality trends in developed and underdeveloped areas from 1900 to 1960; studies of fertility changes in Japan and Germany from the prewar through the postwar periods; internal migration patterns in England and Sweden from the eighteenth to the nineteenth century; and population growth differences between Chile and Argentina during the twentieth century.

These examples combine the strong points of both historical and comparative types — examining before and after conditions with control groups. In their more elegant form, historical comparisons parallel closely the classical experimental design. The most convincing comparative-historical analysis uses negative and positive comparisons.[6] In positive comparisons using the historical-comparative strategy, population processes in several countries are traced over time, identifying similarities associated with common outcomes. For example, what general features do Western industrialized societies share that resulted historically in reducing fertility levels? Supplementing this historical comparison, we need to determine whether the specific changes in Western industrial nations did not occur in other countries where fertility levels did not fall. Hence, we use a negative comparative strategy, i.e., the identification of conditions associated with divergent outcomes. If, for example, economic changes associated with industrialization are the key factors in fertility reduction, then we would expect to find that as countries industrialize, fertility levels fall and also that no country that failed to industrialize experienced fertility reduction.

[6] For a discussion of positive and negative strategies as applied to economic activity, see Neil Smelser, *Essays in Sociological Explanation* (Englewood Cliffs, N.J.: Prentice-Hall, 1968), pp. 69–73.

When both positive and negative comparisons are made in historical and comparative contexts, we can best isolate the essential dimensions of the relationships between population and social processes. As such, we can obtain insights into the convergence or divergence of population patterns and note similarities and differences in the paths to demographic development. In short, comparative-historical research strategies form the basis of modern demographic theory, in general, and are the essential methodological foundation of linking demographic changes to modernization processes.

A final category, *differential analysis*, involves a comparison between certain types of social units when both time and social location are controlled. In its cross-sectional form (it may also involve comparative and historical strategies [7]) differential analysis focuses on differences between social categories and social groupings within the same society at one point in time, for example, fertility differences between religious groups, age differentials in migration, and social class variation in mortality, when such comparisons are intrasocietal. Because of the special nature of this type of comparison, involving different units of analysis and different methodological and theoretical issues, we shall treat it separately, and in detail, in Part 3. Our focus here is on societal analysis.

Obviously, because comparison is the key to analysis, examining society in cross-section is not analytic unless it analyzes differences within society. Research that concentrates on describing a demographic case study of one society, at one point in time, may be of great value in uncovering new variables or illustrating possible leads for some historical or comparative analysis.[8] At best, demographic case studies may allow for inferences about the "fit" between demographic patterns and social structure. Demographic case studies may allow us to argue, for example, that high fertility and mortality "fit" with major aspects of the social structure of premodern communities or that certain types of geographic mobility are correlated with aspects of the economic structure of modern societies. However, without some comparisons, static cross-sectional studies do not in and of themselves yield analytic conclusions.

Three critical elements in categorizing types of comparisons are time, the nature of the social unit, and the type of stimulus. These elements cannot be specified without going into particulars and those depend on the specific problem under investigation. Time may be defined in years (1950, 1951, 1952 . . . 1970) or in centuries (eighteenth century),

---

[7] See the discussion in Chapter 8, this book.
[8] Cf. the discussion of case studies in sociology, Smelser, *Essays in Sociological Explanation*, p. 19.

or in terms of general periods (preindustrial, economic depression, World War II, traditional societies). The societal unit may be a nation, groups of nations, regions, or areas defined culturally (Western nations), politically (totalitarian countries), ethnically (Asian areas), economically (industrialized or developed regions), or religiously (Moslem or Catholic countries). But whatever social unit or time period is selected, the objective remains to search for the links between population processes and social changes, social structures, and social processes.

The element that links population and social processes is the so-called stimulus. Our focus will be on the social processes associated with the "stimulus" modernization.

THE MEANINGS OF MODERNIZATION

In the discussion of linking population variables to modernization processes and the types of comparisons that such a linkage entails, we assumed an implicit general understanding of the overall processes encompassed by "modernization." However — whether population changes are treated as independent, dependent, or correlative elements in modernization processes; whether the objective is to analyze the consequences of population changes for modernization or uncover the specific processes of modernization that determine demographic transformations; which methodological strategies are selected to locate the junctures of demographic and modernization processes — an overall clarification of the meanings of modernization is required.

We have already reviewed the elements of the population system and their relationships to each other and to population growth.[9] The meanings of fertility, mortality, and migration will be further specified in subsequent analyses.

It is difficult to define modernization and do even minimum justice to the vast, comprehensive, but yet incomplete, social scientific literature that has attempted to come to grips with the complexities of the issues involved. Taken as a whole, the empirical materials available do not allow for uniform conclusions. In this regard, it has been noted that sources of variation in modernization processes "render it virtually impossible to establish hard and fast empirical generalizations concerning the evolution of social structures during economic and social development."[10] Moreover, divergent interpretations of the evidence combined

[9] See Chapter 1, this book.
[10] Smelser, *Essays in Sociological Explanation*, pp. 128–129; see also Wilbert Moore, *The Impact of Industry* (Englewood Cliffs, N.J.: Prentice-Hall, 1965), p. 12; Neil Smelser, *The Sociology of Economic Life* (Englewood Cliffs, N.J.: Prentice-Hall, 1963), p. 106; Herbert Blumer, "Early Industrialization and the Laboring Class," *Sociological Quarterly*, 1 (January 1960), pp. 5–14.

with different perspectives, viewpoints, and frameworks of analysis obscure rather than clarify the meanings of modernization. Nevertheless, despite empirical and theoretical difficulties, general guidelines for analysis are necessary. We require at this point not a detailed examination of the specifics of modernization but a general understanding of the major processes that form the essence of modernization.

Structural and Cultural Dimensions

The key to understanding modernization begins with the process of *structural differentiation*,[11] which involves the evolution of specialized role structures from multifunctional structures. In a formal sense, structural differentiation may be defined as "a process whereby one social role or organization differentiates into two or more roles or organizations . . . structurally distinct from each other, but taken together are functionally equivalent to the original unit."[12] During modernization, differentiation of major social structures, roles, and organizations occurs, including specialization and separation of economic, family, religious, political, and stratification systems. As an integral part of differentiation-segregation processes, the daily social, economic, political, and cultural spheres of the members of societies expand. The small local rural (and urban) units wherein members of a given society take care of most needs within relatively narrow and confined communities weaken.[13] In short, modernization involves increased division of labor, specialization, differentiation of institutions and structures, and social expansion.

To illustrate these major processes we may note the dominance of kinship groupings in premodern societies.[14] Prior to modernization, economic production, exchange, and consumption occur largely within family and kinship groupings and are located typically in local community settings. Subsistence farming and supplementary small-scale industry are attached to local villages and are controlled by extended family units. Economic activities are, therefore, relatively undifferentiated from kinship groupings. Furthermore, occupational position is established by extended kin, perhaps caste, as is status and rank. Ascrip-

[11] The formulation and development of the concept of structural differentiation owes much to the work of Neil Smelser. See especially *Social Change in the Industrial Revolution* (Chicago: University of Chicago Press, 1959); *The Sociology of Economic Life;* and various chapters in *Essays in Sociological Explanation.* See also Robert Marsh, *Comparative Sociology* (New York: Harcourt, Brace and World, 1967).

[12] Smelser, *Essays in Sociological Explanation,* p. 129.

[13] S. N. Eisenstadt, *Modernization: Protest and Change* (Englewood Cliffs, N.J.: Prentice-Hall, 1966), pp. 7–10.

[14] For other illustrations and the details and literature review with respect to this illustration, see Smelser, *Essays in Sociological Explanation,* pp. 130–140.

tion, inherited privilege, political, and religious positions are intertwined with kinship position and confined spatially to the local village or community. Moreover, the educational-socialization function takes place under the aegis of the kinship group either directly through the family or indirectly through kinship-dominated religious institutions. The dominance and multifunctionality of kinship units result in the expression of loyalty and identification through kin and the investment of political and social control within the localized kin group, clan, or tribe. In short, rewards and sanctions, survival and growth, social structure and process are dependent on, controlled by, and located in local kinship groups.

If the general feature of premodern societies is kinship dominance and relatively undifferentiated structures, roles, and institutions, the major processes of modernization are associated with the separation, segregation, and specialization of structures, roles, and institutions. In modernization, economic activities, following increases in the division of labor, move from kinship to more specialized organizations; economic roles shift from the local family setting to large nonfamilial institutions. The family no longer is the production unit nor are occupational positions kinship-controlled as agriculture expands and industry develops. The loss of the economic function of the family unit to more specialized agencies typically involves socioeconomic mobilization — the physical movement of household and community members, often as individuals, in search for employment in labor markets.[15]

Along with the shift from the family-kinship group, the family ceases to be the primary economic unit of production. In turn, family apprenticeship declines, and other economic and social training functions previously performed by family units are established in separate specialized institutions. Apprenticeship is impersonalized and nonfamilial; formal educational systems develop to substitute for and expand kinship programs. Similarly, once kinship groups are unable to assign occupational positions and status is conferred by other systems, the political power exercised by the family system shifts to informal specialized political parties. The separation of family, economic, and political roles engenders the breakdown of traditional ascriptive criteria, the development of more flexible and variegated social strata, and the upsurge of social mobility.[16] Moreover, social identification and sociopolitical loyalties are realigned toward other units beyond the family and larger than the local village. Once the rewards and sanctions are no longer tied to family and kin, social control is exercised by larger specialized institutions.

[15] On social mobilization, see Eisenstadt, *Modernization: Protest and Change*, pp. 2–3; Karl Deutsch, "Social Mobilization and Political Development," *American Political Science Review*, 55 (September 1961), pp. 494–495.

[16] Eisenstadt, *Modernization: Protest and Change*, p. 11.

The overall processes of differentiation of social structures, increased division of labor, specialization, and role segregation touch every sphere of organized social life. The break-up of family-kinship dominance brings about an emphasis toward individualism; the expansion of village-tribal control results in the replacement of localism with nationalism.[17] Hence, the transformation from the social-economic isolation of the village to the social isolation of modern man. As the familial, economic, political, and cultural universe begins to crumble, the urban man stands alone and his survival depends on the new emerging social system.[18]

The impression one receives from an emphasis on structural differentiation and the disorganization and dislocation that are basic parts of modernization processes must be balanced by the simultaneity of growing interconnectedness of the developing new social system. The specialization and segregation of roles and structures is only half the picture; the integration of differentiated structures on a new basis is the other half.[19] As Durkheim, among others, noted, one concomitant of a growing division of labor is an increase in integrative mechanisms for social coordination and for bringing different groups into a common bond.[20]

As long as there is little differentiation between economic and family roles, the kinship and community structures serve as integrative forces of diverse but unspecialized activities. Concomitant with the separation of roles and organizations, new institutions and organizations emerge that themselves specialize in integration. As Smelser notes: "Development proceeds as a contrapuntal interplay between differentiation (which is divisive of established society) and integration (which unites differentiated structures on a new basis). Paradoxically, however, the course of integration itself produces more *differentiated* structures."[21] The new society thus represents a new balance and integration along different lines that are more complex, diverse, and heterogeneous. Coordination and integration are as much a part of modernization as are fragmentation and differentiation.

Concomitant with structural differentiation and reintegration are personal and cultural changes. Perhaps above all, modernization means changes in values, alterations in ideals, and the reorientation of aspira-

[17] For an analysis of the role of nationalism in modernization, see Kingsley Davis, "Social and Demographic Aspects of Economic Development in India," in *Economic Growth: Brazil, India and Japan*, ed. Simon Kuznets, W. E. Moore, and J. J. Spengler (Durham, N.C.: Duke University Press, 1955).

[18] See William McCord, *The Springtime of Freedom: Evolution of Developing Societies* (New York: Oxford University Press, 1965), pp. 22–37.

[19] Smelser, *Essays in Sociological Explanation*, pp. 137–140.

[20] Ibid., p. 137; Emile Durkheim, *The Division of Labor in Society* (Glencoe, Ill.: The Free Press, 1949), chaps. 3–8; Eisenstadt, *Modernization: Protest and Change*, p. 20.

[21] Smelser, *Essays in Sociological Explanation*, p. 138.

tions. It means developing "rationality" and new ways of thinking and their infusion into every sphere of human social activity. Modernization means, of course, dynamic changes but its implications include not only the breakdown of traditionalism, the absence of the fear of change, but the *striving* to bring changes about.[22]

Modernization therefore encompasses two broad dimensions: First, the development of social structures characterized by differentiation, diversification, and separation — the general transformation of social systems and their reintegration around a matrix of different structures. Second, modernization involves the development of institutional structures to deal with continual change and sustained modernization, including sets of organized values, attitudes, aspirations, and goals — personal and social, and general patterned ways of thinking and acting that set into motion or are shaped by the dynamics of social structural changes.[23]

Hence, social structural processes of modernization — differentiation of roles and organizations, social mobilization, and reintegration of differentiated structures — are linked and combined with personal and cultural dimensions. The social structural changes of modernization *and* the values or aspirations toward modernity together are the most overwhelming and penetrating features of the contemporary scene.[24] It is probably fruitless to engage in arguments about the priority of social structural and personal-cultural forces in modernization or their specific sequence.[25] Certain attitudes and values are preconditions to social structural changes in modernization, types of thinking that lead man to behave in "modern" ways. Conversely, appropriate attitudes and behavior flow from structural opportunities and incentives that accentuate real possibilities for social change. Whatever the priority of social forces or their sequence, social structural and personal-cultural dimensions operate jointly to generate the specific processes of modernization.

Process and Transition

Often the dramatic and dynamic transformations associated with modernization have not been viewed in the context of "process" but in the context of "transition" from wholly traditional to wholly modern. The

22 E. Shils, *Political Development in the New States* (New York: Humanities Press, 1964), pp. 7–8.

23 Eisenstadt, *Modernization: Protest and Change*, p. 43.

24 Ibid., p. 1.

25 Myron Weiner, "Introduction," in *Modernization: The Dynamics of Growth*, ed. Myron Weiner (New York: Basic Books, 1966), pp. 5–6; Alex Inkeles, "Making Men Modern: On the Causes and Consequences of Individual Change in Six Developing Countries," *American Journal of Sociology*, 75 (September 1969), pp. 208–225.

emphasis on traditional and modern as mutually exclusive, and at times static, societies, the analysis of traditional societies as if they represented isolated social systems, and the ahistorical view of modern societies obscure several important elements in transformation processes.[26]

Continuity is often neglected in analyses of modernization. Elements of modernity may be observed within traditional societies and traditional patterns persist within modern social systems. Therefore, it is more accurate to postulate that traditional societies have differential degrees and types of "modernness" within their social structures and value systems and that there will be some carry-over of traditional elements in modern societies.[27] Treating societies as either traditional or transitional or modern obscures the interpenetration of elements.

Variation also is not emphasized when societies are viewed "in transition." The sources of variation in modernization are many: for example, variations in premodern conditions, in the impetus to change, in the paths toward modernization, in the advanced stages of modernization, and in the content and timing of dramatic events during modernization.[28] The societies lumped together within traditional and modern categories are heterogeneous and the paths to modernization vary greatly. Moreover, change is not solely a characteristic of modern societies. Although changes in the long history of premodern societies have been slow, discontinuous, and more particularized, change is an intrinsic feature of all societies.[29] The way things are now reflect how they came to be, which, in turn, shapes the paths to what they will be in the future. Societies differ not only in the degree but in the kind of modernity as well.[30] The variety of starting points of modernization, which greatly influences the specific contours of development, and variations in the internal and external forces, which give impetus to modernization, further reduces the utility of the transition model.[31]

When modernization is viewed as a transition from traditional to modern societies, the *timing* and *sequence* of modernity are often neglected. Historical and comparative evidence reveals clearly that mod-

[26] Cf. the discussion in Wilbert Moore, "Social Aspects of Economic Development," in *Handbook of Modern Sociology*, ed. Robert Faris (Chicago: Rand McNally, 1964), chap. 23.

[27] See Reinhard Bendix, "Tradition and Modernity Reconsidered," *Comparative Studies in Society and History*, 9 (April 1967), pp. 313–314, 326–327; Weiner, "Introduction," p. 5.

[28] See Smelser, *Essays in Sociological Explanation*, pp. 127–128.

[29] Moore, *The Impact of Industry*, p. 15; Wilbert Moore, *Social Change* (Englewood Cliffs, N.J.: Prentice-Hall, 1963).

[30] Moore, *The Impact of Industry*, p. 15: Bendix, "Tradition and Modernity Reconsidered," pp. 312–314.

[31] Eisenstadt, *Modernization: Protest and Change*, pp. 1–2, 46.

ernization cannot occur twice in the same way.[32] Variation in timing and sequence may be influenced, for example, by government initiative and planning, by emulation and imitation, by nationalism, and by cultural and ideological diffusion.[33] The transition model often implies incorrectly that change once initiated must follow the lines indicated by some preexisting, usually "Western" model and that in the transition to modernity all aspects of social structure change in a more or less simultaneous and integrated fashion. However, the timing and sequence of modernization are critical not only for its success or failure but for its pace and pattern.[34] The outcome of modernization processes and the specific pattern that emerges are functions of premodern conditions, the forces which give impetus to modernization, and the specific historical period when modernization occurs.

The emphasis on pluralism in modernization, on continuity and variability, and on differences in timing and sequences of modernization appears at first glance to deny the fruitfulness of a search for commonalities in the meanings of modernization. Indeed, two general themes in modernization research may be identified.[35] The first emphasizes commonalities in modernization processes, noting similarities and convergences. From observed similarities of modern nations follow, implicitly or explicitly, arguments of the evolutionary trend to be experienced by nonmodern areas. Organizational and institutional requirements imposed by a modern-industrial system constrain the outcome of modernization processes wherever and whenever they occur.

In contrast, a second theme emphasizes pluralism in modernization, noting premodern differences, differential rates and routes of change, and variations in the timing and agents of change. Generalization is confined to broad processes of change rather than to precise forms of social organization, and the tendency is to limit generalization to less than all societies but usually to more than one.[36]

Of course, both themes have elements of truth and neither is usually argued in extreme form. In part, differences between evolutionary

[32] This is a major theme in Bendix, "Tradition and Modernity Reconsidered," pp. 310–311. See also his "The Comparative Analysis of Historical Change," in *Social Theory and Economic Change*, ed. T. Burns and S. B. Saul (London: Tavistock Publications, 1967), pp. 67–86.

[33] Bendix, "Tradition and Modernity Reconsidered," pp. 308–309.

[34] Ibid., pp. 310–311; see also Wolfram Eberhard, "Problems of Historical Sociology," in *State and Society*, ed. Reinhard Bendix et al. (Boston: Little, Brown, 1968), pp. 16–27; Kingsley Davis, "Problems and Solutions in International Comparison for Social Scientific Purposes," originally appeared in Spanish in *America Latina* (January–March 1965), pp. 61–75, translated in Institute of International Studies, Population Reprint Series no. 273 (Berkeley: University of California, n.d.).

[35] See Moore, *The Impact of Industry*, pp. 10–14.

[36] Bendix, "The Comparative Analysis of Historical Change," pp. 76–83.

and pluralistic themes reflect degrees of emphasis. It seems reasonable to search for general similarities and commonalities in modernization processes, because modernization does indeed have patterned preconditions and consequences. At the same time, analyzing variation, continuity, and timing should help to identify the range of commonalities, the complexities of reality, and the specific features of individual patterns. However, simple evolutionary schemes, extrapolations from the past experience of modern nations to the future possibilities of nonmodern nations, are neither analytically justifiable nor theoretically cogent.

IMPLICATIONS FOR POPULATION ANALYSIS

In the next three chapters, the relationships between socioeconomic modernization and mortality, fertility, and migration will be investigated in detail. The methodological and theoretical issues outlined in this chapter provide the background for that analysis. In particular, the following points require emphasis:

First, no one single methodological strategy can be utilized in uncovering the interconnections of population variables and modernization. Rather, various comparison strategies — historical, comparative, and historical-comparative — will be blended to provide a broad foundation for drawing generalizations, with particular emphasis on historical comparisons using positive and negative forms. Where appropriate and possible, an attempt will be made to find variations in population processes between societies that have similar key variables so that we can better isolate the influence of other variables which account for the differences to be explained.[37] For each population process we shall provide a multiplicity of observations to increase confidence in the generality of particular findings. At times, for various reasons, we shall be confined to analyzing the "fit" between social structure and social process, on the one hand, and population patterns, on the other. Moreover, after repeated unsuccessful attempts to employ an historical-comparative strategy for migration analysis, a weaker form of illustrative detailed historical case study was selected with some supplementary comparative observations. (Perhaps the difficulties of the comparative analyses of historical migration trends stem from special theoretical and methodological problems of migration analysis.) For all the subsequent analysis, our objective was to heed the advice to proceed with logic of scientific inquiry and the art of asking "why." [38]

[37] For the discussion of this general strategy, see Smelser, *Essays in Sociological Explanation*, pp. 71–72.
[38] Reinhard Bendix, "Introduction," in *State and Society*, pp. 3–5.

The analyses that follow emphasize identifying the determinants of population changes during modernization. Nevertheless, systematic consideration has also been given to linking population variables to modernization. We shall deal specifically with the consequences of mortality and migration for modernization processes, with somewhat less attention on the consequences of fertility. The analysis of the prediction and control of demographic processes attempts to avoid evolutionary biases, and the assumption that particular relationships between social and demographic variables in the past will also characterize those relationships in the developmental processes of the future.

In the search for the determinants of population changes and variations, a concerted effort shall be made to go beyond simple mechanistic correlations to identify the specifics of modernization processes that are most critical and to isolate the mechanisms relating social and population processes. By selecting among many variables and clarifying the operative mechanisms, we hope to avoid the pitfall of relating "everything" to population transformations. Attention will be directed to specifying those aspects of structural differentiation, reintegration, and value changes associated with modernization that most clearly shape and affect population changes and variation.

The general overview of modernization processes pointed to the need to analyze continuities and variations in premodern conditions, in the impetus to change, in the path to change, in the timing of change, and in the need to pay close attention to government initiative and planning, emulation and imitation, nationalism, and cultural-technological diffusion. These same analytic requirements apply as well to the specifics of population processes. Except in its most general and often sterile form, evolutionary assumptions of population transformations find little theoretical or empirical support. *Demographic pluralism* emerges from systematic comparative and historical analyses.

A significant part of the literature on the "population revolution" and on "demographic transitions" has failed to consider all three components of the population system in their interaction with each other and in their connections to the social system as both cause and effect. In large part, demographic research has not specified the particular processes of modernization that are interrelated with population changes and has not identified the mechanisms that connect population and social processes. The concentrated effort to develop "a theory of demographic transition" has tended to ignore or to consider inconsequential variations and fluctuations in population changes before, after, and during the transition, and has rarely treated the question of continuity in population patterns. Only during the last two decades or so have demographers considered the significance of historical timing of demographic changes and examined the role of "external" influences on population changes around the world. The extensive search for universal empirical generalizations about the demographic transition as an end in itself, rather than as a preliminary to comparative explanation, has resulted in an exaggerated preoccupation with the empirical universality or nonuniversality of one type of Western demographic change sequence. Although some findings in these research efforts are quite valuable, the nature of the analytic questions that have been raised has provided little in the way of systematic specification and clarification of factors associated with demographic variation and change.[39]

In contrast, our premise is that any theory of demographic change, transition, or transformation must integrally involve the following: (1) an analysis of all three population components — fertility, mortality, and migration, as dependent and independent variables within population and social systems; (2) the specification of modernization processes that are related to population changes and the identification of the particular mechanisms connecting population and social processes; (3) the investigation of variations and fluctuations in population variables before, after, and during the shift from traditional to modern patterns; (4) the identification of the extent of demographic continuity, in particular, examining the ways in which the modernization of population processes represents "new" patterns or extended forms of older patterns; (5) the explicit recognition of the importance of historical timing of population transformations and the role of such "external" influences as cultural and technological diffusion, emulation and imitation, nationalism, and government planning in shaping the contours of past, present, and future demographic changes.

Our examination of population change patterns during modernization is not geared to the discovery of empirical universals but rather toward the systematic explanation of population change patterns. It shall become clear that we have not attained that goal. But we have moved closer to its attainment and uncovered more fruitful paths toward the systematic comparative analysis of historical population changes.

[39] For parallel arguments about the limitations of searching for empirical universals in the relationship between the urban-industrial complex and the isolated nuclear family, see Smelser, *Essays in Sociological Explanation*, pp. 74–75.

Chapter Five

THE MORTALITY
REVOLUTION

Historically, mortality levels have been reduced so radically that high life expectancy, low infant mortality, and the control of the lethal consequences of infectious diseases and epidemics are conspicuous demographic features of modern societies. Comparatively, not all countries have participated equally or at the same pace in the "mortality revolution," and international variations in the extent of mortality control persist. Examining historical and comparative mortality patterns allows for the isolation and identification of the causative mechanisms involved in the transformation from high and uncontrolled mortality to low and controlled mortality; it also permits linking the mortality revolution to other long-run social processes. Moreover, a revolution in the extent and character of a vital and intimate event such as death must have major repercussions not only for those institutions of human society that have developed to cope specifically and directly with mortality, but also for those features of social organization that are shaped by, and depend indirectly on, the length of human life.

The two major issues in analyzing historical and comparative changes in mortality are (1) the relationship between modernization and mortality, and (2) the consequences of the mortality revolution for the nature of human society. These two issues in turn focus on several general questions. First, what is the substantive nature of the mortality revolution, and what are the causal connections between mortality reductions and social revolutions associated with agriculture, industry, urbanization, and technology? More specifically, to what extent are low death rates restricted to "modern" societies; that is, how new or recent is this societal characteristic? If mortality was high in premodern societies, what social forces may be linked systematically and empirically to its reduction? Is low mortality a function of "modernity" or "contemporarity"; that is, does low mortality characterize only modern, industrialized nations of the contemporary world or is it a feature of most or all societies in the post-World War II era? Have imported, low-cost, mass medical and public health projects in underdeveloped countries reduced or eliminated mortality discrepancies between the developed and developing areas of the world? To what degree are mortality changes integral to the modernization of Western societies over time and to levels of socioeconomic development in the contemporary world? We must go beyond any mechanical correlation to specify those elements that connect modernization and mortality.

Second, we must determine the impact and implications of the mortality revolution. Whether or not the reduction of mortality levels is a function of modernization in sociohistorical and socioeconomic contexts, the question remains, What relevance do differing levels of mortality have for the nature of human society? Irrespective of the relative newness or pervasiveness of low death rates, "controlled" mortality is a unique feature of modern society. What are the implications of this uniqueness for economic, political, cultural, and social institutions? How do sociocultural responses to death vary under conditions of high and low mortality? In what ways are ideologies and explanations of death sensitive to the changing quantity and distribution of deaths within society? If mortality reduction is integral to modernization processes, how do declines in mortality facilitate social and economic development and under what conditions is controlled mortality an impediment to modernization?

MODERNIZATION AND MORTALITY REDUCTION

To specify the features of modernization that are linked systematically to mortality changes, some general empirical evidence on historical patterns of mortality processes and comparative contemporary levels of mortality is needed. Thus, the first task in analyzing the relationship between modernization and mortality reduction is to raise and solve the basic *empirical* issues. First, what were the patterns of mortality before the onset of the Industrial Revolution?[1] If we are to relate changes in

---

[1] In this context, the Industrial Revolution is a shorthand expression for the whole process of industrial, agricultural, and urbanization changes. Although distinct analytically, modernization and industrialization will be used synonymously in this chapter.

mortality to industrialization specifically, or to modernization generally, some overall indication of mortality levels and patterns in preindustrial and premodern societies is necessary. Although this question seems straightforward, it specifies neither how far back into the vast expanse of the preindustrial era we need to venture nor in what areas of the world we should look.

As a corollary, the logical follow-up question is: How did mortality change during industrialization and modernization? Again, this question is not as specific as it might seem. Industrialization is not a uniform process, confined to one time period with discrete starting and ending points. Thus, we should not be surprised if the pace of mortality changes varied between and within countries and related differently to various stages of industrial development. Indeed, we should be skeptical if the evidence showed uniform changes.

These first two general questions focus primarily on the socio-historical context of "Western" industrialized nations — Europe and North America. A third empirical question considers the relationship between socioeconomic development and mortality levels in the contemporary post-World War II era. Are there general uniformities in mortality levels among contemporary nations, irrespective of their pattern of socioeconomic development or their pace of industrialization? Obviously, to test the hypothesis of mortality "convergence" among contemporary nations or examine the diffusion of mortality control, we need to specify the different types of comparative populations: we may compare nineteenth-century and post-World War II mortality patterns and uncover certain convergences, although different results may be obtained by comparing pre- and post-World War II mortality rates.

Preindustrial Mortality

Mortality conditions before the Industrial Revolution were terrible. But were they high uniformly throughout this long period of human history, in all areas and for all populations? Indeed, how "high" were mortality levels and how accurate are the records from which the evidence is derived? If we were to require a rigorous, scientific, quantitative answer to these questions, we should have to abandon the search ·and indicate simply that such an objective is impossible, because the *systematic* collection of detailed information — about mortality as well as other social data — is as unique to modern society as is low mortality. Thus, any attempt to document the pattern of mortality in the preindustrial world must rely on fragmentary evidence for local areas, of sometimes unknown completeness, of uneven quality and detail, using methodologies of estimation that are more in line with the canons of the historian-detective than the scientist-demographer. The scientist will surely err (although to an unknown degree) if in reconstructing mortality patterns in the preindustrial world, the data of historians and anthropologists are presented uncritically. It seems equally unwise to apply modern sophisticated measurement techniques to such information. Evidence on preindustrial mortality presented in tabular form often conveys the impression of exactitude and definitiveness, which may be unjustifiable methodologically.

If data on mortality patterns in fifteenth- or sixteenth-century Europe are scarce and if available data are of uneven, and often unknown, quality, a fortiori mortality records of the ancient and early medieval world are limited. Nor does it appear necessary for us to travel back into ancient history. Except for the sheer joy of such intellectual exercises, such an undertaking has little scientific or analytic merit. Fifteenth-through eighteenth-century evidence may in large part be generalized to the more distant past. Attempts at the demographic reconstruction of primitive populations, of prehistoric man, and of the Egyptian, Greek, and Roman populations, may be important for historians or anthropologists or archaeologists but are of little direct value to social scientists interested in analytic demography. For our purposes, the evidence on preindustrial populations will be selected from materials of more recent historical periods, but there is no reason to suspect that these findings cannot be extended to cover the longer history of man before the modern era.

Thus, in our inquiry into mortality conditions of the preindustrial world, we essentially require a "feeling" for the situation, a general portrait pieced together from various sources to form a coherent pattern. The available evidence, particularly of the painstaking research on family reconstruction carried out by historian-demographers in France and England in the 1960's, points to the following general arguments, which, without too much error, may be taken as the overall preindustrial mortality pattern. Preindustrial mortality — that is, mortality throughout the world before about the eighteenth century — was in large part *uncontrolled directly*. By this we mean that *mortality levels were high but not uniformly high; the extent of mortality fluctuation over time within the preindustrial world depended on social, economic, political, and environmental conditions in local areas that affected the response of populations to climatic conditions, food shortages, famines, diseases, epidemics, and sociopolitical disturbances; these same societal forces resulted as well in mortality variation between different areas, and for different subpopulations within areas, at any point in time.* Premodern patterns of mortality were therefore by-products of the general social, economic, political, and cultural conditions in preindustrial societies. Although mortality was "uncontrolled," these general social and cultural conditions were not; hence, mortality patterns were not haphazard. After reviewing evidence on historical fluctuations in preindustrial mortality, Wrigley concludes:

> Some of the most important influences on mortality were altogether outside the control of pre-industrial societies. . . . [But] the inability of preindustrial societies to protect themselves against disease by medicine and public health measures does not mean that mortality levels were not greatly influenced by social and economic conditions. On the contrary the level of real income enjoyed by a population played a great part in determining its death rate. Abundant food, good clothing and warm dwellings can cause a vast improvement in mortality even when medical knowledge is slight, while conversely those who face the rigours of winter in rags, those who live with their families in damp and chilly hovels or have no shelter at all, are much more likely to fall victim to disease and, having done so, to succumb.[2]

Indeed, social, political, economic, and environmental situations may have played a more decisive role in determining patterns of mortality under conditions of "non-control" than under modern conditions of the medical revolution and its mass public health application. We will return to this argument in a subsequent section.

Preindustrial mortality thus involved three important ingredients: mortality was high, fluctuated over short periods, and varied widely at any point in time between areas and subpopulations. To convey a "feeling" for these three features of preindustrial mortality, we use selected illustrations that are neither exhaustive of the available, and increasing, evidence nor "random samples" of the existing data. Rather, in large part they represent major mortality features under preindustrial conditions so that comparisons can be made with subsequent changes in mortality patterns during industrialization. These illustrations focus first on presenting a general picture of the fluctuating high levels of mortality in "normal" preindustrial periods; subsequently, mortality variations as a result of famines and epidemics will be illustrated. The period covers the thirteenth through the eighteenth centuries, but concentrates on the sixteenth to the eighteenth centuries, and mostly refers to Europe.

Overall levels of preindustrial mortality may be obtained by examining estimates of life expectancy at birth for European populations. Al-

---

[2] E. A. Wrigley, *Population and History* (London: Weidenfeld and Nicolson, World University Library, 1969), pp. 127, 129.

though it is rare to have accurate information of this sort, because it requires knowledge of the distribution of population and deaths by age, enough material exists to show that mortality levels in preindustrial Europe were high and varied substantially. Based on a review of several studies, the United Nations estimated that between the thirteenth and seventeenth centuries, life expectancy at birth in Europe ranged from twenty to forty years; during the eighteenth century the range was between thirty-three and forty years for Europe and the United States.[3] In seventeenth-century England, life expectancy at birth averaged thirty years,[4] but some local areas enjoyed much more favorable conditions. For example, life expectancy at birth in one small urban parish in England from the sixteenth through the eighteenth centuries is estimated to have been as high as forty-six years and only as low as thirty-five years.[5] Similarly, mortality tables for France in the late eighteenth century show a life expectancy at birth of less than thirty years, whereas in the cities of France and other European countries it was seldom over twenty years.[6] Whereas estimates of life expectancy at birth in Spain and Italy in the eighteenth and nineteenth centuries are below thirty years,[7] in the early days of settlement in Plymouth Colony in New England life expectancy at birth was probably as high as fifty years in some localities.[8]

Another measure of mortality, considered by many to be the most sensitive indicator of social, economic, and environmental conditions, is the infant mortality rate — the proportion of babies born who die in their first year. Infant mortality among the British aristocracy, which in all likelihood had more favorable mortality patterns than the general population, fluctuated around 20 per cent of all births during the sixteenth and seventeenth centuries, dropping to 16 per cent during the first half of the eighteenth century.[9] Similarly, fully one-fourth of the babies born in one wealthy urban parish in England in the late sixteenth century and in rural villages of seventeenth- and eighteenth-century France died be-

[3] United Nations, *The Determinants and Consequences of Population Trends* (New York, 1953), pp. 50–51; Louis Dublin et al., *Length of Life* (New York: Ronald, 1949), p. 41.
[4] Peter Laslett, *The World We Have Lost: England Before the Industrial Age* (New York: Scribner's, 1965), p. 93.
[5] E. A. Wrigley, "Mortality in Pre-Industrial England," *Daedalus*, 97 (Spring 1968), p. 574, table 17.
[6] Wrigley, *Population and History*, p. 131; Dublin et al., *Length of Life*, pp. 35–36.
[7] Massimo Livi-Bacci, "Fertility and Population Growth in Spain in the Eighteenth and Nineteenth Centuries," *Daedalus*, 97 (Spring 1968), pp. 527–529.
[8] Wrigley, *Population and History*, p. 131.
[9] Wrigley, "Mortality in Pre-Industrial England," pp. 570–571, table 16; cf. T. H. Hollingsworth, *The Demography of the British Peerage*, Supplement to *Population Studies*, 18 (1964), p. 67, table 52.

fore their first birthday.[10] Other areas may have had lower or higher rates of infant deaths: Colyton, a small urban English parish, is estimated to have had an infant mortality rate of only 120 to 140 per 1,000 live births during the sixteenth and seventeenth centuries.[11] In some areas of France where the registration of infant births and death appears to have been unusually complete, infant mortality ranged at high levels of 24 to 29 per cent during the eighteenth century. In other areas of France at the same time the range was from 15 to 20 per cent. In Brittany, France, half the children did not survive to the tenth year, and there was no noticeable improvement during the eighteenth century. In Southwest France conditions were better: two out of three children survived to age ten. Indeed, within France, infant mortality through the eighteenth century varied more between regions than between time periods.[12]

If variation and fluctuation around high levels of mortality were the rule for "normal" times in preindustrial societies, periods of crisis — food shortages, famines, disease, epidemics, wars, etc. — accentuated these patterns of diversity. Thus, although the small English parish of Colyton seems to have had favorable mortality levels relative to other areas of England from the sixteenth through the eighteenth centuries (life expectancy at birth of thirty-five to forty-five years and infant mortality between 12 and 14 per cent), it too had severe setbacks. For example, in the twelve months beginning November 1645, the plague outbreak reduced the population of Colyton by about a fifth.[13]

In crisis years, local populations throughout Europe experienced crude death rates as high as 200, 300, and even 400 per 1,000 population. National populations and often all of Europe were subject to mortality levels in given years that are hard to imagine. In the fourteenth century plague is estimated to have killed 25 million persons, one-fourth to one-third of the population of Europe.[14] The population of Denmark fell by more than 20 per cent in the decade starting in 1650, and in the year 1696–1697, Finland may have lost over one-fourth of its population.[15] In the 1690's, a succession of poor harvests created a "crises of subsistence" throughout Europe; some regions of Sweden experienced death rates around 160 per 1,000 population.[16] In Norway, the number of

[10] Wrigley, "Mortality in Pre-Industrial England," pp. 571–572; Laslett, *The World We Have Lost*, p. 124.

[11] Wrigley, "Mortality in Pre-Industrial England," pp. 557–560; see his revised estimates, p. 570.

[12] Pierre Goubert, "Legitimate Fecundity and Infant Mortality in France During the Eighteenth Century: A Comparison," *Daedalus*, 97 (Spring 1968), pp. 598–601.

[13] Wrigley, *Population and History*, p. 82.

[14] Ibid., pp. 62–63; United Nations, *The Determinants and Consequences of Population Trends*, p. 52.

[15] Wrigley, *Population and History*, p. 63.

[16] Cited in William Petersen, *Population* (New York: Macmillan, 1969), p. 387.

deaths in 1741 was three times as high as in the prior four-year period.[17] Moreover, many periods of high mortality were local in their incidence, caused by a local harvest failure, or by an outbreak of an epidemic disease in a circumscribed geographic area, which most likely was never documented fully.

Although local and regional variation in mortality, as a result of harvest failures or epidemics, is difficult to document empirically, a reconstruction of the pattern of the plague epidemic in France, 1720–1722, may be instructive.[18] The evidence on the last important epidemic of the plague in Western Europe suggests that localities were not affected at random; rather, patterns followed communication routes. Moreover, the concentration of population appears to have been decisive in spreading the lethal plague; the larger the population, the more it was affected. All French cities over 10,000 population were affected, although a large number of small areas escaped any mortality consequences. In Marseilles, for example, 44 per cent of the population (estimated at 90,000 before the plague) died, 30 per cent of Aubagne (population 77,000) died, 51 per cent of Toulon (population 27,000) died, but small isolated French areas had few deaths. Similarly, whereas the epidemic of 1665 killed about 15 per cent of London's population, whole quarters of the city remained untouched.[19] In part, village or areal isolation may have been a safeguard during periods of epidemics but may have resulted in disaster in times of food shortages.

These illustrations of preindustrial mortality picture fluctuating overall national death rates revolving around fairly high levels. Mortality in local areas may have fluctuated even more. If these patterns were plotted on a chart, for almost any time period and for nations as well as local populations, we would end up with the zig-zags of mortality variation over which people had virtually no direct control. Folk medicine does not appear to have been effective and prayers for health and agricultural prosperity must have often been answered in the negative. Because preindustrial mortality patterns were not controlled directly but rather were responsive to social, economic, political, and environmental conditions, it follows that when these conditions were altered, mortality patterns would change as well. Therefore, the impact of the agricultural, industrial, technological, and urban revolutions on mortality must be considered.

[17] United Nations, *The Determinants and Consequences of Population Trends,* p. 51; cf. H. Gille, "The Demographic History of Northern European Countries in the Eighteenth Century," *Population Studies,* 3 (June 1949), pp. 3–70.

[18] Jean-Noel Biraben, "Certain Demographic Characteristics of the Plague Epidemic in France, 1720–1722," *Daedalus,* 97 (Spring 1968), pp. 536–545.

[19] Ibid., p. 545, fn. 6. On epidemics in France, see also J. Meuvret, "Demographic Crises in France from the Sixteenth to the Eighteenth Century," in *Population in History,* ed. D. V. Glass and D. Eversley (Chicago: Aldine, 1965), chap. 21.

Industrialization and Mortality

These preindustrial mortality patterns, so long characteristic of human society, began to change in some areas of Europe as early as the mid-eighteenth century, and followed in most of Europe throughout the nineteenth century. By 1840, the population in the most advanced European countries had a life expectancy of over forty years slowly increasing to forty-five years by 1880, to fifty-one years by the turn of the twentieth century, to over sixty years by 1930, and to over seventy years by the 1950's.[20] The changes in life expectancy and infant mortality for Great Britain from the mid-nineteenth century to the contemporary period are representative.[21] In mid-nineteenth century England and Wales, life expectancy at birth was around forty years for males and forty-two years for females. By 1910, life expectancy at birth had increased eight years for males and ten years for females; continued medical and socioeconomic improvements raised life expectancies for males and females to fifty-nine and sixty-three years, respectively, by the 1930's. In the mid-1960's, life expectation for a newborn was, on the average, sixty-eight years for males and seventy-four years for females. Thus, in a little over a century, life expectancy at birth had improved by 70 per cent for males and by 76 per cent for females. Similarly, from the mid-nineteenth century to the beginning of the twentieth century, infant mortality in Great Britain fluctuated around 150 per 1,000 live births. After 1900, a period of continuous and steady reduction in infant mortality occurred through the 1960's. In the late 1930's the rate had fallen to around 55 per 1,000 live births; immediately after World War II only 3.2 per cent of all babies born died in their first year; by the mid-1960's, the proportion had been reduced below 2 per cent. The quality of information in Great Britain allows for a subdivision of infant mortality into neonatal (death during the first month of life) and postneonatal (death during the first to the eleventh month) during the twentieth century. The evidence shows that the neonatal mortality had been reduced in the 1960's by 60 per cent of its early twentieth century level, whereas the postneonatal deaths, reflecting genuine social and economic improvements, were reduced by over 90 per cent during the same period.

Several important features of this sketch of mortality distinguish it from death patterns in the preindustrial period. First, and foremost, is the level of mortality. During the Industrial Revolution, particularly be-

---

[20] United Nations, *The Situation and Recent Trends of Mortality in the World,* Population Bulletin no. 6 (1963), table IV.1.

[21] Data from R. K. Kelsall, *Population* (London: Longmans, Green, 1967), pp. 24–26.

ginning in the nineteenth century, mortality reached low levels that were unknown, as far as evidence is available, in prior human history. Although some local areas or short time periods may have had preindustrial mortality levels as low or lower than in the early stages of the Industrial Revolution, never was there such a *continuous* period of lowered mortality levels inching its way downward. In Norway, for example, the crude death rate was steady at about 20 per 1,000 from 1815 to 1850 before falling below 20. In several earlier periods between 1740 and 1815 in Norway, crude death rates were not far above 20 per 1,000 but the pattern was erratic. In 1745, the crude death rate in Norway was 20 per 1,000, but it had fallen from a high of over 50 per 1,000 in 1742–1743 and rose to almost 35 per 1,000 in 1747. So went most of the period before 1815 in Norway. However, after maintaining the steady level of mortality from 1815 to 1850, crude death rates in Norway declined from 20 to 12 per 1,000 by the 1920's.[22] Similarly, infant mortality in Sweden fluctuated around 200 per 1,000 live births from 1750 to 1810, occasionally dipping below 200 only to increase again. But after 1810, the level of infant mortality fell below 200 per 1,000, never to go that high again. Not until the late nineteenth century, however, were fluctuations converted into a steady and precipitous decline.[23]

Thus, along with the decline in the mortality level, a second related feature of the modern period is the virtual elimination of the enormous mortality fluctuations that characterized the preindustrial world. This was the result of the almost complete absence of crises associated with harvest failures and epidemic disease. With the outstanding exception of Ireland, where famines began in 1845, such European countries as France starting in the mid-eighteenth century, and most other industrializing nations beginning in the early nineteenth century, did not experience the mortality devastations that famines and epidemics brought. This virtual disappearance followed the improvements in communications and transportation that facilitated transferring harvest surpluses to deficient areas. In addition, the beginning of the agricultural revolution broadened the variety of crops available. People began to overcome systematically the natural forces of harvest failures and were better able to ward off severe sickness.[24]

Although the modern period effectively reduced the large mortality fluctuations that resulted from food shortages and epidemics, wars continued to have major demographic consequences in general, and mortality consequences in particular. Mortality patterns in the Russian

[22] Data from Wrigley, *Population and History*, fig. 5–2, pp. 162–163.
[23] Data from Donald Bogue, *Principles of Demography* (New York: Wiley, 1969), fig. 16–4, p. 562.
[24] Wrigley, *Population and History*, pp. 165–169.

Empire and the Soviet Union from 1861 to 1965 are extreme but instructive.[25] Crude death rates fluctuated around 35 per 1,000, beginning a slow descent in the last decade of the nineteenth century. By 1917, crude death rates were around 25 per 1,000. But the downward trend was interrupted by both world wars; in 1919 and 1941 the crude death rate was estimated at over 50 per 1,000. After World War II, crude death rates again resumed their downward trend, at an accelerated pace, remaining at below 10 per 1,000 from 1950 to 1965.

But aside from wars and local sociopolitical disturbances, nineteenth-century Europe experienced reductions in mortality levels and controlled significantly the fluctuations of the preindustrial era. Most mortality changes in Europe during the initial period did not result from medical breakthroughs or public health applications, which were not causal to any degree in reducing mortality until the end of the nineteenth century, when mortality had already begun to decline. As a result, the third feature of mortality reduction in Europe was its greater initial impact on children above age one and on adults, rather than on infants below age one or on the older population. Infant mortality, as noted earlier, did not visibly decline in England and Wales until the late nineteenth century, whereas overall mortality began to fall earlier. The same pattern is true of France.[26] Knowledge of the causes of infant deaths and effective countermeasures came later than the improvement in standards of living and food supplies. Thus, the initial decline in mortality appears to have been the result of better food, housing, and "rising living standards," whereas public health measures and the control of infant mortality were clearly slower and later developments.[27]

Changes in mortality in Europe, because they initially reflected improved living standards, were neither swift nor spectacular. Rather they mirrored the steady but slow spread of many improvements in private and public hygiene and in the variety and quality of obtainable foods.[28]

[25] For data and discussion, see Jean-Noel Biraben, "Essai sur L'evolution demographique de l'U.R.S.S.," *Population*, 2A (June 1958), pp. 41–44; David Heer, "The Demographic Transition in the Russian Empire and the Soviet Union," *Journal of Social History*, 1 (Spring 1968), pp. 193–240; D. Peter Mazur, "Expectancy of Life at Birth in 36 Nationalities of the Soviet Union," *Population Studies*, 23 (July 1969), pp. 225–246.

[26] E. A. Wrigley, *Industrial Growth and Population Change* (Cambridge, Eng.: Cambridge University Press, 1961), p. 101, table 24.

[27] Wrigley, *Population and History*, pp. 169–172; Thomas McKeown and R. G. Brown, "Medical Evidence Related to English Population Changes in the Eighteenth Century," in *Population in History*, ed. Glass and Eversley, pp. 285–307; T. McKeown and R. G. Record, "Reasons for the Decline of Mortality in England and Wales During the Nineteenth Century," *Population Studies*, 16 (November 1962), pp. 94–122; cf. P. E. Razzell, "Population Change in Eighteenth Century England," *The Economic History Review*, 28 (August 1965), pp. 312–332.

[28] Wrigley, *Population and History*, p. 170.

Preindustrial mortality patterns varied among areas as a result of local responses to food shortages, famines, diseases, epidemics, and the like. During the early periods of industrialization, mortality variations were accentuated, but for different reasons. Obviously, all European nations and all areas and subpopulations within nations did not have equally improved living standards. For example, in the last years of the nineteenth century, infant mortality in the poorest areas of England affected one out of four babies born, two and one-half times the level of infant deaths among the wealthy. Life expectancy at birth was as low as twenty-four years in some areas of nineteenth-century England and as high as fifty-one years in other areas, although it was forty-one years nationally.[29] Hence, most initial "depths of misery" commonly associated with the early stages of Western industrialization are more appropriately viewed as the result of early urbanization and differential gains in living standards. Late nineteenth-century popular, reformist, and scholarly literature portrays vividly the poor mortality conditions of the slums. Yet, overall mortality declined and, in time, medical advances, public health programs, and improved sanitation along with the continuing rise in living standards reduced urban mortality levels considerably. Thus, the poorer mortality conditions in urban areas of Europe and the United States during their early industrialization should not obscure the overall relationship between industrialization and mortality reduction. As Wrigley notes:

> The literature of all the industrializing countries of Western Europe is full of novels examining the depths of misery into which people sank in the worst of the new slums and the immense toll of life exacted at all ages. Yet it would be as dangerous to base an assessment of the effect of the industrial revolution upon mortality on these facts and impressions as it would be to assume that the conditions which occurred in pre-industrial Europe during the periodic demographic crises were typical of pre-industrial times generally, for what was then concentrated into certain short periods of time was later concentrated into certain restricted areas.[30]

Although, in the short run, urbanization brought a concentrated number of people into closer contact, which helped spread communicable diseases, and although urban areas were unprepared in housing, sanitation, and minimum health and environmental levels for the influx of rural migrants, urbanization within the industrializing nations of the late nineteenth and early twentieth centuries was part of social and economic modernization. Hence, over time, improved living conditions and in-

[29] Ibid., p. 173.
[30] Ibid., pp. 173–174.

creased health and wealth in cities conspired to bring mortality under control.

The transformation of European mortality patterns from conditions of noncontrol to societal control, from high fluctuating rates to low steady rates, must be understood therefore in the context of the social, economic, and political revolutions that transformed European society. In the initial stages of the agricultural and industrial revolutions, mortality improved as living standards improved. The causitive mechanisms were largely the same in nineteenth-century Europe as in preindustrial periods. The difference in mortality levels between the periods reflected economic and social developmental differences: as economic and social conditions became better, mortality levels were reduced. But beginning in the late nineteenth century another intermediate force began to obscure the clear-cut relationship between socioeconomic modernization and mortality reduction. The developing science and technology of medicine began to revolutionize mortality patterns even further. Once the causes of death were uncovered and preventive public health measures were applied, a diffusion of direct mortality control occurred not only within Europe but throughout the world. Thus, the slowness and regularity of mortality declines characteristic of nineteenth-century Europe reflected the slowness and regularity of economic and social development. But the applications of medical discoveries and the development of medical and public health technologies, which were themselves by-products of the Industrial Revolution, affected the pace and sharpness of mortality reduction directly, *independent of developmental levels*.

The Spread and Pace of Mortality Control

The fall in mortality within the industrializing world after the turn of the twentieth century, particularly infant mortality, was swifter than previous periods. Moreover, countries outside of the industrialized nations, without undergoing any dramatic alterations or even slight improvements in their social and economic development, around 1930 began to import medical and public health technologies that had developed slowly in Europe. The technological diffusion model of mortality decline, in contrast to the socioeconomic developmental model, may be observed in the mortality pattern of almost every underdeveloped, nonindustrialized country. For example, life tables for Latin American countries show an expectation of life at birth below thirty years before the twentieth century, which reflected poor social and economic circumstances. These conditions in nineteenth-century Latin America were worse than in eighteenth-century Europe; hence the higher mortality rates in Latin America. Between 1900 and 1930 some Latin American countries experienced social and economic improvements; standards of living increased and mortality levels were reduced slowly as a result. But after 1930, mortality levels not only decreased much more sharply in Latin America than they had previously and faster than in nineteenth-century Europe, but did so irrespective of social and economic changes. Between 1930 and 1950, expectation of life at birth increased to thirty-seven years, on the average, for Latin America and jumped another fourteen years in the next decade. Between 1930 and 1960, for selected Latin American countries, about three-fourths of a year were added *annually* to life expectancy at birth, a pace three times as rapid as that between 1910 and 1930 and five times as rapid as that between 1860 and 1910.[31]

Although only a small island in the Indian Ocean, mortality changes in Mauritius may also illustrate the swiftness of mortality reduction without major economic or social development. Mauritius had a fairly constant crude death rate in the first four decades of the twentieth century — over 35 per 1,000. Between 1941 and 1947, the crude death rate declined from 36 per 1,000 to 20 per 1,000; by 1961 the rate had fallen to 10 per 1,000. Infant mortality declined from 155 per 1,000 live births, 1944–1948, to 62 per 1,000 live births in 1961; life expectancy at birth was around thirty-two years, 1942–1946, and reached close to sixty years by the 1960's. These mortality changes in Mauritius can in no way reflect major social or economic revolutions.[32] Not only was the pace in mortality reduction dramatic but, relative to the experience of European nations, unprecedented. Within the eight-year period following World War II, Mauritius raised its average life expectancy from thirty-three to fifty-one years, a gain that took Sweden a century and a quarter to achieve.[33]

This impressive accelerated pace of mortality decline in developing countries during the twentieth century, when compared to the experience of the industrializing nations of the world during the 1800's, is further illustrated in comparing mortality changes in Sweden with several other developing nations. Infant mortality began to fall regularly in Sweden around the turn of the nineteenth century; it took about a hundred years

[31] For historical trends in mortality in Latin America, see Eduardo Arriaga and Kingsley Davis, "The Pattern of Mortality Change in Latin America," *Demography* (August 1969), pp. 223–242. The pattern of declining mortality and socio-economic development in nineteenth-century South Asian populations is discussed in Gunnar Myrdal, *Asian Drama: An Inquiry into the Poverty of Nations*, vol. 3 (New York: Pantheon, 1968), pp. 1557–1559.
[32] Population Reference Bureau, "The Story of Mauritius: From the Dodo to the Stork," *Population Bulletin*, 18 (August 1962), pp. 93–115; cf. R. M. Titmuss and B. Abel-Smith, *Social Policies and Population Growth in Mauritius* (London: Methuen, 1960).
[33] Kingsley Davis, "Population," *Scientific American*, 209 (September 1963), p. 69.

before the rate fell by 50 per cent to below 100 per 1,000 live births. But Chile took less than three decades to achieve this decline starting with the mid-1930's.[34] Similarly, the increase in life expectation at birth in Ceylon between 1946 and 1954 required half a century in Sweden; for the decade beginning in 1946, Barbados experienced increases in life expectancies that took Sweden four times as long beginning in 1890. In 1921, Jamaica had the same life expectancy at birth that Sweden had in 1780; by 1951, Jamaica had the same life expectancy at birth that Sweden had in 1910, i.e., what it took Sweden one hundred and thirty years to accomplish was completed in three decades in Jamaica.[35]

These examples could be multiplied by substituting other developed and underdeveloped areas. Mortality declines, particularly since the 1930's, have accelerated and have been compressed. This acceleration has taken place independent of economic and social development and may be understood only as a result of the diffusion of direct mortality control techniques from the developed to the underdeveloped world. Even within the industrialized world, the clear-cut one-to-one relationship between socioeconomic improvements and mortality reductions is no longer observable during the twentieth century, particularly since the 1930's.

The swift mortality decline after the 1930's may be observed as well with measures of infant mortality. For the 1936–1938 period, infant mortality rates for over forty countries have been compiled by the United Nations.[36] Of course, some countries with the highest rates were omitted, e.g., India, China, and almost all of Africa, due to an absence of reliable information; but a sufficient range of countries and rates are represented to illustrate pre-World War II patterns. Of forty-three countries, 1936–1938, twenty-three had infant mortality rates over 10 per cent of all births (a bare minimum because Asian and African countries not listed because of poor data had rates at least that high). Of the twenty countries with rates below 10 per cent only three (Netherlands, Australia, and New Zealand) had rates below 4 per cent. Comparison of these same countries in the mid-1960's shows that only one country out of the forty-three had a rate over 10 per cent (Chile), despite the fact that Chile's infant mor-

---

[34] Basic data derived from materials presented by Bogue, *Principles of Demography*, fig. 16–4, p. 562; table 16–9, p. 586.

[35] United Nations, *The Situation and Recent Trends of Mortality in the World*, p. 50. For other comparisons see Arriaga and Davis, "The Pattern of Mortality Change in Latin America"; George Stolnitz, "Comparison Between Some Recent Mortality Trends in Underdeveloped Areas and Historical Trends in the West," in *Trends and Differentials in Mortality* (New York: Milbank Memorial Fund, 1956), pp. 26–34.

[36] United Nations, *The Situation and Recent Trends of Mortality in the World*, table IV.8, reproduced with additions from the U.N. *Demographic Yearbook* in Bogue, *Principles of Demography*, p. 586, table 16–9.

tality rate had declined 55 per cent in the thirty-year period. Fully twenty-two countries had rates below 3 per cent. The pace of the decline during these three decades varied. Most countries cut their infant mortality rates by over 60 per cent; only one country (New Zealand) reduced its rate by less than 40 per cent — but it had the lowest recorded rate in the 1930's. The most impressive declines in infant deaths for this period occurred in the Soviet Union (from 184 to 31 per 1,000), Singapore (from 162 to 28 per 1,000), Japan (from 113 to 23 per 1,000), Taiwan (from 145 to 26 per 1,000) and Czechoslovakia (from 115 to 22 per 1,000).

Changes in specific causes of death also illustrate these new unprecedented patterns of mortality reduction through the use of swift, inexpensive, and mass public health applications. This is particularly the case for malaria control and declines in tuberculosis. Ceylon is a favorite demographic example, although it is clearly an extreme case. The overall death rate in Ceylon fell from 20 to 14 per 1,000 in 1946–1947 following DDT spraying, which virtually wiped out the malarial mosquito, a major cause of death. Such a fall in death rates took seventy years in England and Wales.[37] In Guatemala, the deaths due to malaria dropped from 6,238 to 124 in 1958–1959; India's annual incidence of malaria ranged upward to over 100 million before World War II, but dropped in 1966 to fewer than 50,000; in the United States malaria caused 200,000 to 400,000 deaths annually before 1946 and has since been eliminated entirely.[38] In 1945, malaria caused 3,534 deaths in Mauritius, 25 per cent of all deaths; by 1955 only three people died of it.[39] Among the Maori population, the decline in the crude death rate due to reduction in tuberculosis was about 50 per cent for males and 43 per cent for females (1945–1956).[40]

Mortality Convergence

These spectacular and amazing mortality declines throughout the world, but most impressively in the underdeveloped countries without concomitant industrialization, raise the question of the general convergence of mortality around the world. Are mortality patterns among countries in various stages of development so similar that few systematic differences remain? Have mortality levels among the nonindustrialized

[37] Political and Economic Planning (PEP), *World Population and Resources* (London: George Allen and Unwin, 1955), p. 12.
[38] Cited in Petersen, *Population*, pp. 562–563.
[39] Population Reference Bureau, "The Story of Mauritius," p. 101.
[40] D. I. Pool, "Post-War Trends in Maori Population Growth," *Population Studies*, 21 (September 1967), pp. 87–98.

countries been reduced so rapidly by diffused public health and medical technologies that the general relationship between modernization and mortality has been eliminated entirely? The question on mortality convergence cannot be fully answered. Some mortality measures show world-wide convergence, whereas others do not; comparisons between some countries show convergence, other comparisons show a widening of mortality differences, and still other comparisons show no change in the relative mortality discrepancy between countries. Moreover, the patterns of some mortality convergences should not obscure the very real differences in mortality levels that still characterize contemporary nations.

Comparatively, mortality levels between countries at any point in time may be significant. Mortality comparisons over time for the same country must be supplemented by comparisons between countries at the same point in time. Moreover, historical comparisons of mortality between countries may yield conflicting answers to the convergence question when differing starting points are selected. For example, if accurate mortality data were available for the sixteenth century, no doubt we would observe greater mortality homogeneity between nations then compared to the mid-twentieth century. If the starting point for comparison was the late nineteenth or early twentieth century, we might draw the conclusion of mortality convergence. Hence, we must take great care in drawing any meaningful conclusions. Perhaps the long-range view points to a curvilinear pattern of mortality from homogeneity to heterogeneity to homogeneity for the period of the premodern era to the contemporary world.[41]

Another difficulty is measurement. If we examine crude death rates (number of deaths per 1,000 population), some overall mortality convergence may be observed by the late 1960's. Countries with very different levels of economic development had very low crude death rates. For example, among the forty countries with crude death rates of 10 per 1,000 or less in the late 1960's are the United States, Canada, Japan, Chile, Mexico, Barbados, South Yemen, and others. But among these countries with low crude death rates, six had *infant mortality* rates over 70 per 1,000 live births, while nine had infant mortality rates below 20. Because the crude death rate does not take into account age differences within populations, it is not the best measure to be used for comparative analysis. Nevertheless, the range in crude death rates in the late 1960's around the world is large — from 5 per 1,000 in Hong Kong and Singapore to 35 in Upper Volta and Guinea and probably higher in some

---

[41] This is consistent with the basic outline of demographic transition theory (see Chapter 1, this book). For a similar hypothesis about differential mortality, see Chapter 9.

other African nations. Infant mortality ranges from a low of 13 per 1,000 live births in Sweden to over 250 per 1,000 for some African nations; contemporary life expectancy at birth ranges from the late twenties to early thirties for African areas to the late sixties and early seventies for Scandinavian countries, Western Europe, and North America.[42]

Although some convergence in mortality may be observed with crude mortality measures, infant mortality rates are more complex.[43] If we examine the data on infant mortality for over forty countries in the pre- and post-World War II periods, different country comparisons yield divergent results. For example, if we compare Chile and Sweden, infant mortality appears to have widened between the countries despite major reductions. In 1936–1938, Chile had an infant mortality rate of 243 per 1,000 live births; by 1963–1964 this had been reduced by more than half to 111 per 1,000 live births. Sweden's 1963–1964 infant mortality rate was the lowest in the world, about 15 per 1,000 births, a reduction of two-thirds its pre-World War II level. Hence, despite the impressive declines in Chile and Sweden, the infant mortality gap between these countries widened. In 1936–1938, Chile's infant mortality rate was five and one-half times higher than Sweden; in the 1960's, it was almost seven and one-half times higher.

But this is not the whole picture. Absolute levels of infant mortality are converging from pre- to post-World War II periods. Moreover, if we had compared New Zealand and Mauritius, the results would have indicated a narrowing of the infant mortality gap. In the late 1930's, infant mortality in Mauritius was five times higher than the rate in New Zealand; by 1963–1964 it was less than three times higher. Similarly, some existing infant mortality differences in the 1930's were eliminated completely in three decades. Japan, Czechoslovakia, Singapore, and Taiwan had infant mortality rates about twice as high as the United States, Scotland, Canada, and France in the 1930's. By 1963–1964 all eight countries had about the same rate.

In sum, mortality convergence depends on the periods compared, the measures utilized, and the specific national comparisons made. Nevertheless, mortality reduction is no longer necessarily dependent on social and economic development. Yet national differences in the level of mortality remain, and some features of mortality are not unrelated to developmental levels. Contemporary mortality levels in Africa, for example, largely resemble preindustrial mortality patterns, and are consistent with its backward level of social and economic modernization. Although the mortality level in contemporary African nations is not known with

[42] Data derived from United Nations, *Demographic Yearbook*, 1966.
[43] Data derived from official materials organized in Bogue, *Principles of Demography*, table 16–9, p. 586.

any accuracy, and historical patterns can only be approximated by guess-work, mortality estimates prepared by the United Nations are reveal-ing.[44] Two features in particular, common to populations that have not yet experienced any mortality control, are noteworthy: first, mortality rates in Africa are high, but not as fluctuating as in preindustrial Europe; second, wide variation in mortality levels characterizes areas within Africa with different levels of social and economic progress and with different types of environmental conditions. Estimated crude death rates range from around 20 per 1,000 population in Morocco, Kenya, Uganda, and Zambia (lower rates characterize some island populations, e.g., Mauritius had a crude death rate of 9 per 1,000, roughly comparable to many industrialized nations; the same is true for the white popula-tions of South Africa and Southern Rhodesia) to rates that probably ex-ceed 35 or 40 per 1,000 estimated for Upper Volta, Guinea, Mali, and Angola. Thus, the lowest levels outside the island and white populations in Africa are roughly twice as high as for most developed areas.

More dramatic evidence on the persistence of high mortality rates in Africa can be illustrated with estimates of infant deaths. Of the thirty-five African countries (excluding South Africa and Southern Rhodesia) for which the United Nations has estimated infant mortality rates, twenty countries have rates over 175 per 1,000 live births, and in eleven countries over 20 per cent of all babies born die in their first year of life. In no African country — other than the island populations, South Africa, and Southern Rhodesia — is infant mortality less than 10 per cent; in Mali, West Africa, 35 out of every 100 babies born do not live long enough to celebrate their first birthday. Similar patterns of high mor-tality and variation in mortality level may be observed by life expectancy rates, which range from around fifty years for parts of North Africa (e.g., Morocco, the United Arab Republic) and the island populations of East Africa (e.g., Mauritius), to twenty-six to twenty-eight years in Mali, Angola, and Guinea.

Continued wide national variation in mortality may be observed for Latin America. Expectation of life at birth in Latin America is much more similar to the industrialized nations of Europe, North America, and Japan than it is to African populations. Yet, evidence for the mid-1960's (1960–1965) points to wide variation within Latin America. United Na-tions estimates [45] reveal a range in life expectancy at birth among Latin

[44] Data for Africa were derived from Ranjan K. Som, "Mortality Levels in Africa" (paper presented to the General Assembly, International Union for the Sci-entific Study of Population, London, 1969), table 1.

[45] Data adapted from Jorge L. Somoza, "Mortality in Latin America: Present Level and Projections" (paper presented to the General Assembly, International Union for the Scientific Study of Population, London, 1969), table 1.

American populations of about twenty-five years: estimated life expectancies at birth in Nicaragua, Honduras, and Bolivia are less than forty-five years at birth, whereas populations in Argentina, Uruguay, and Costa Rica have a life expectancy at birth of sixty-two to sixty-five years.

A major persistent difference in mortality patterns between developed and underdeveloped countries is the distribution of deaths by age, reflecting, in part, infant mortality differentials. A comparison of age-specific death rates in India and Sweden in 1961 shows that India has excessive high rates for children compared to Sweden: the rate for children under one year of age was 165 per 1,000 in India and 15 per 1,000 in Sweden; for children one to four years of age, India had a rate of 23 per 1,000 compared to only 1 per 1,000 in Sweden. Another way of looking at the same data shows that, in Sweden, 92 per cent of all deaths in 1961 were among adults *over* age forty-five; in India, 72 per cent of all deaths were among the population *below* age forty-five.[46]

Similarly, national differentials in the distribution of mortality may be illustrated by a special study of mortality patterns in Ghana and Hungary.[47] By no means do these countries represent extremes in terms of underdeveloped and developed areas. Nevertheless, the distribution of deaths by age and cause in these populations are revealing. In 1966, over one-fifth of all deaths in urban areas of Ghana were of children less than one year of age and another one-fourth were of children from one to four years old. By comparison, only 5 per cent of the deaths in 1966 in Hungary were of children less than one year of age and .5 per cent were of children from one to four. Infective and parasitic diseases accounted for one-fourth of all causes of death in Ghana, ten times the rate in Hungary, whereas the major causes of death peculiar to older age groups are conspicuously rare in Ghana.

Comparing age-specific death rates in Peru and the United States shows the significant differential distribution of death by age.[48] Although the crude death rates of Peru and the United States are fairly close, the rate of infant deaths below age one is six times higher in Peru as in the United States, and the death rate for children one to four years of age is seventeen times higher in Peru as in the United States.

The rapid introduction of medicines and public health measures in underdeveloped countries may have affected not only the more rapid

[46] Basic data are presented in Bogue, *Principles of Demography*, table 16–1, p. 552.

[47] K. Miltenyi, "Mortality Pattern in Ghana" (paper presented to the General Assembly, International Union for the Scientific Study of Population, London, 1969), tables 1 and 3.

[48] See data compiled by David Heer, *Society and Population* (Englewood Cliffs, N.J.: Prentice-Hall, 1968), table 4–1, p. 35.

pace of mortality reduction in these areas relative to the slow and regular improvements in Western nations, but may have resulted in differential diffusion patterns within countries. We noted earlier that in the initial stages of nineteenth-century mortality reduction within Europe, higher mortality plagued the urban areas. In time, the urban-rural mortality differential was eliminated as effective public-health programs, sewage, sanitation systems, and major changes in factory environments improved urban conditions. In the technological diffusion of mortality control to underdeveloped areas, the public health targets were urban areas, where larger population concentrations yielded more immediate and dramatic results. Contrary to the European experience, urban populations in many developing nations have more favorable mortality patterns than rural populations.[49] This "reverse" pattern may complicate already severe problems of urban growth generated by large-scale migration from the countryside and sustained high fertility. This mortality pattern may also have important implications for economic and social modernization.

Two Models of Mortality Reduction

What general relationships between socioeconomic development and mortality may be deduced from these comparative and historical mortality patterns? First, and most important, no evidence, historically or comparatively, appears to invalidate the general positive relationship between socioeconomic development and mortality reduction. Every country that has moved from lower to higher levels of social and economic modernization has also experienced significant, and often dramatic, increases in length of life, which is not surprising because social and economic modernization implies increases in general living standards; improvements in the quantity and quality of food; changes in the amount and quality of health care; applications of public health standards in sanitation, sewage, and general control of the seriousness of diseases; and improvements in distributing these benefits throughout society. But the general relationship between modernization and mortality must be qualified in at least two ways: the relationship is "long run," rather than step-by-step; and it is not a "necessary" relationship. It cannot be argued from the evidence that every step in improving social and economic conditions leads to a noticeable increase in length of life. Nor is mortality reduction brought about only through social and economic development.

[49] See, for example, Frederick C. Shorter, "Information on Fertility, Mortality, and Population Growth in Turkey," *Population Index*, 34 (January–March 1968), pp. 3–21; on Ghana, see Chapter 7, this book.

In the long run, improvements in social and economic conditions will result in mortality improvements, but other factors may intervene to speed up the pace of mortality reduction or to slow it down. Once mortality reduction occurs, it appears to gain momentum on its own and moves to lower levels without dependence on social and economic gains. Moreover, there is a limit to the reduction in mortality, at least until the degenerative diseases of heart and cancer are brought under direct control.

In addition, modernization may be a *sufficient* condition for mortality reduction but it is surely not a *necessary* condition. The alternative and supplement to modernization, followed by most underdeveloped areas, has been the importation of medical and public health technologies from the Western world. Without visible social and economic development, and, significantly, without changes in the values and attitudes of populations, length of life can be increased, often swiftly and inexpensively. The diffusion of medical and public health technologies from the developed to the underdeveloped areas of the world, and the subsequent reduction in mortality in nonindustrialized nations, must be viewed not as evidence to dismiss the relationship between modernization and mortality decline but to qualify it. It is true that mortality reductions have been swifter in underdeveloped areas than in the experience of industrialized nations and, thus, mortality declines in underdeveloped nations have no real precedent in world history; furthermore, mortality in developing countries is lower that it was in industrialized countries at the same stage of economic development. Nevertheless, in lieu of rejecting the modernization theory of mortality reduction, it is more appropriate to posit an alternative causal model.

It is evident, therefore, that there are two models of mortality reduction in comparative historical perspective. The "modernization" model suggests that the pre-eighteenth-century pattern of high, fluctuating, noncontrolled mortality in Europe was brought under "control" to steady low death rates, slowly but precipitously, as part of the general revolution in agriculture and industry. As part of these general social revolutions that transformed European societies, new medical and public health technologies were developed, which in turn accelerated the pace of mortality decline into the twentieth century. The "technological-diffusion" model points to alternative mechanisms for mortality reduction, independent of the slow and painful process of social and economic modernization. Starting with levels of mortality that may have exceeded eighteenth-century European experience, underdeveloped nations, particularly after World War II, brought their mortality levels down not as a result of social and economic revolutions but through the direct application of medical, public health, and agricultural technologies imported from the industrialized world. Once the techniques of direct mortality control through mass public health and medical technology had been developed in Europe, as a by-product of modernization, they could be applied to any area. The pattern of mortality reduction, once it had occurred in Europe, precluded by its very nature repetition in other areas of the world.

Although the diffusion model is an essential qualification to the historical model of mortality reduction through social and economic development, the modernization model is not merely of historical interest. Some forms of mortality cannot be easily sprayed away or inoculated against. Such sensitive indicators of social, economic, and environmental conditions as infant and maternal mortality have not been reduced dramatically in those areas where some social and economic modernization has not occurred. Thus, infant and maternal mortality rates, and to a lesser extent overall death rates, continue to be related to the living standards of national populations.[50] Similarly, whereas dramatic reductions in those causes of death that have been more easily controlled through mass medical and public health measures are evident, such mortality declines may be more dramatic but less permanent in the long run, unless some increase in standards of living and real changes in social, economic, and environmental conditions take place.[51] Finally, although epidemic diseases and famines are past history in industrialized nations, it is not uncommon to read of selected areas of famines in underdeveloped countries or of outbreaks of cholera, smallpox, or other diseases. In short, the technological-diffusion model is a qualifier of the necessary role of modernization in mortality control, but should not obscure the very real differences in patterns of mortality that persist in differentiating modern from "transitional" and traditional societies.

MORTALITY AND SOCIETY

The historic and comparative pattern of mortality reduction, the general outline of causative factors involved, and the persistence of mortality differentials among contemporary nations of the world are for

[50] See, for example, Edward G. Stockwell, "The Measurement of Economic Development," *Economic Development and Cultural Change,* 7 (July 1960), pt. 1, pp. 419–432; David Simpson, "The Dimensions of World Poverty," *Scientific American,* 219 (November 1968), pp. 27–35. Simpson states, "Perhaps the most useful single index of the health conditions prevailing in a community is the infant death rate . . . [which] reflects a multitude of diseases and the entire spectrum of social and economic conditions" (p. 32).

[51] See Jean Bourgeois-Pichat and Chia-Lin Pan, "Trends and Determinants of Mortality in Underdeveloped Areas," in *Trends and Differentials in Mortality* (New York: Milbank Memorial Fund, 1956), pp. 11–25.

the most part known in broad outline among students of population. The context or framework within which the mortality revolution is analyzed may differ somewhat between the demographer and the sociologist; the former might stress the role of mortality in the demographic revolution, whereas the latter may emphasize the broader context of social and economic modernization. In analyzing the general patterns of mortality reduction and its determinants, these contexts overlap substantially, and differences between the demographic and sociological contexts largely reflect differences of emphasis. However, when connections between mortality reduction and social change are examined, i.e., when the focus is on the consequences of death control for the nature of human society, the population analyst often reverts to demographic parochialism. In most discussions of the "consequences" of the mortality revolution, analyses are restricted to the impact of mortality changes and variations on population growth, age structure, fertility, and to a lesser extent, on migration. If the "social" consequences of mortality changes are discussed at all, it is usually in the context of by-product results that flow *indirectly* from the impact of mortality on population dynamics. Notwithstanding the very important relationships between mortality and other population processes, and the significance of mortality reduction as a generator of social problems through its association with population growth under some conditions,[52] mortality levels and changes have *direct* social structural implications.

Because the role of mortality as a dependent variable has been so often emphasized, it is useful to explore the complementary side of the relationship — the impact of mortality changes on modernization. It is reasonably clear that mortality reduction is *integral* to the complex changes associated with modernization, that is, modernization is unthinkable without major alterations in the level and pattern of death. Obviously, social, economic, and technological changes that are manifestations of modernization operate as powerful agents for the control of mortality, but it is also equally significant, and often overlooked, that mortality control *facilitates* in important ways social and economic development. The use of the word *facilitates* rather than *causes* is important for two reasons: First, in analyzing the consequences of mortality reduction for social and economic development it is often impossible, theoretically or empirically, to isolate the causal chain, although we know that the two processes are correlated. This is due to the constant interaction of these processes, the complexity of modernization, and the likelihood that intervening factors connect mortality reduction to modernization. Second, even where the connections are less obscure, mortality changes set up

[52] See Chapter 2, this book.

potentialities for elements of modernization, in the sense that low mortality is a *necessary* but surely not a *sufficient* condition for social and economic development.

One illustration of the consequences of mortality reduction for social and economic modernization examines the impact of changing patterns and levels of death on key social institutions: family and kinship, socioeconomic, and religiocultural systems. For analysis it is helpful first to construct ideal-typical models of the mortality structure under the extremes of "non-control" and "control." We may extract four key interrelated features of mortality under extreme noncontrolled conditions. First, mortality levels are high — crude death rates are around 50 per 1,000; life expectancy at birth is less than thirty years, and infant mortality rates are at least 35 per cent of all births. These levels of mortality mean *an ever-presence of death* within society. Second, mortality levels fluctuate widely over short periods of time. When harvests are poor or when epidemics are rampant, not infrequent occurrences, mortality takes a heavy toll of the total society. Combined with the generally high mortality levels, such fluctuations imply *great uncertainties about length of life* over time. A third feature of mortality under noncontrolled conditions is the *mystery of death*. Mortality patterns in these circumstances are by definition uncontrolled; when death occurs it cannot be explained in terms of scientific or "rational" causal sequences, because these are in large part unknown, but rather must be "explained away" by nonrational, sometimes mystical, reasoning. Fourth, mortality under noncontrolled conditions is not randomly distributed throughout all ages but takes extraordinary large numbers of the very young. The timing of death is thus *accentuated in the early few years of life*. In short, life under extreme conditions of the noncontrol of mortality is precariously short, death is ever-present, shrouded in mystery and uncertainty, and is concentrated among the very young.

At the opposite extreme is the ideal-typical condition of death where mortality is controlled. The level of mortality is low — crude death rates are below 10 per 1,000; life expectancy is over seventy years, and only about 1 per cent of all babies born die in their first year. Death rarely interrupts the daily activities of societies, and when it occurs it is largely to older persons dying in institutions from degenerative diseases. The quantity of life is discussed not in terms of uncertainties but as "probabilities," and death is explained largely in rational, scientific vocabularies. These two ideal-typical models have been abstracted from reality and presented in extreme form for analytic purposes, but they are not far removed from the real world. Noncontrolled mortality conditions, as discussed earlier, are in large part characteristic of the preindustrial world of Europe and North America before the seventeenth or eighteenth centuries, and of Latin America before the 1930's. With qualification, preindustrial, noncontrolled mortality continues to characterize parts of Asia and significant sectors of Africa in the 1960's. In contrast, controlled mortality, in its more accentuated but not in its "final" form, is typical only of the most socially and economically developed areas of the contemporary world, i.e., Europe, North America, Japan, and some selected smaller populations.

Mortality and Socioeconomic Development

If uncontrolled mortality is characteristic of traditional societies and controlled mortality is a feature of modern societies, we can begin to link other key features of traditional and modern societies to mortality. In traditional societies, kinship units are the primary sources of identification and power; they dominate the allocation of status to individuals, the distribution of goods, and the exercise of power. The emphasis on kinship "fits" well with facts of uncontrolled mortality. Emphasis on individual merit or the nuclear family in isolation would be difficult to sustain given the precariousness and shortness of life. Societal organization and social identification must be formed around some unit that is more permanent and less likely to be eradicated in brief periods. It is therefore not surprising that the wider kin group or even larger clan or tribe unit is invested with such power. In contrast, one feature of modern societies is the breakdown of kin dominance through structural differentiation and the assignment of social identification through the nuclear family. Combined with the emphasis on "individualism," the small nuclear family is *possible* only by extending life and reducing infant deaths. Although individualism and nuclear family structure vary somewhat between modern societies and are determined by many complex features of modernization processes, the *potential* emergence of the nuclear family as *the* social unit and the emphasis on individual worth are limited to conditions where the length of human life is relatively long.

Another characteristic of traditional societies is large family size. As we will discuss in detail in Chapter 6, the number of babies born to a family in traditional societies was high. One conditioning factor for high fertility is high mortality, particularly of infants. For societies to survive under high mortality conditions, that is, to have two or three children survive to adulthood to have children of their own, a much larger number of babies has to be conceived. The institutionalized emphasis on high fertility in high mortality societies results, in part, from the fact that replacement of the family unit is circumscribed by the extent of mortality. Only after mortality is reduced can families have a smaller number of children in confidence that two or three will survive to adulthood. But we should take care in viewing the causal relationship only as one way, that is, that reduced mortality leads to reduced fertility. It is equally valid to argue, and some scattered evidence supports this, that reduced family size may have resulted in lower mortality. Nevertheless, it is inconceivable that an average family size of two or three children could for very long characterize a society with uncontrolled mortality without resulting in demographic suicide. Controlled mortality thus is one of many complex factors that sets up the potential for the emergence of the small family system. Although approximating a "necessary" condition for lower fertility, reduced mortality is by no means a "sufficient" condition.

Several other features of family structure, family formation, and family life are related to changing mortality levels,[53] four of which have special interest in historical and comparative contexts. First, a common pattern in many traditional and preindustrial societies is for marriages to be arranged either by the parents of the prospective bride and groom, or through some relative, or through a formal intermediary. In modern societies, "romantic love" replaces arranged marriages, and individuals usually select their own marriage partners. It is likely that one basis shaping this transformation is increased length of life. Choosing a marriage partner requires at least time for exploration, particularly when that decision involves emotional and romantic components. Entering into the game of marriage selection, seeking and searching for a partner, is less likely to occur under precarious mortality conditions than when time is not a major consideration. Similarly, the higher mortality among the young in traditional societies reduces the probability of strong emotional involvements and investments between parent and child. Where child mortality is low, greater emotional attachments between parent and children are more likely to be institutionalized. A third family feature that has changed over time is the increased potential for longer marriages and, as well, for several changes in marriage partners within the life span. Whether individual marriages remain intact longer depends on many complex factors; but both the possibility of longer marriages and the option for "serial monogamy," or divorces and remarriages, are shaped by the average length of human life. Finally, due to the high mortality of traditional societies a large proportion of the population consists of orphans or widowed persons.[54] Moreover, the widowed are more likely to be younger in traditional communities. Such is not the case, in

---

[53] See the brief discussion in Heer, *Society and Population*, pp. 43–45.
[54] See Laslett, *The World We Have Lost*, pp. 95–96.

large part, for modern societies. The conspicuousness of bereavement as reflected in the proportion of widowed and orphaned has declined sharply as mortality patterns become concentrated among the elderly.

Along with major alterations in family-kinship systems in modernization, major changes in socioeconomic institutions occurred. In general, the revolutionary changes in mortality set up the conditions under which socioeconomic modernization takes shape. Under conditions of constant sickness, and early death, men in traditional societies had neither time nor energy to improve very much upon subsistence conditions or acquire the knowledge necessary to plan for its improvement. A description of morbidity and mortality conditions in contemporary Africa is revealing.

> In the African social drama sickness has a strong claim to being the arch-villain. It is bad enough that a man should be ignorant, for this cuts him off from the commerce of other men's minds. It is perhaps worse that a man should be poor, for this condemns him to a life of stint and scheming. . . . But what surely is worst is that a man should be unwell, for this prevents his doing anything much about either his poverty or his ignorance.[55]

In more general terms, modernization implies the need for occupational specialization, fluid labor markets, career preparation, social mobility, and others, which require training and skill circumscribed by time factors. Moreover, modern economies require social and personal planning and rational calculations. Such planning requires time. People under preindustrial mortality conditions lived in a "moving present" and "short-term prospects occupied most of their attention. Even the seven fat and seven lean years of scripture cover a longer span than would have entered the calculations of most men." [56]

An interrelated feature of kinship and stratification systems in pre-modern communities is the emphasis on ascription, and the relative absence of major intergenerational or intragenerational social mobility. In contrast, achievement is emphasized in modern societies and, in turn, social mobility is fostered. Again, these changing patterns fit the mortality picture of these ideal-typical societies. It is unthinkable that men should acquire the knowledge and skills based on long-term training when mortality is high and life is precarious. Spending a dozen or more years in formal education and training is absurd, when life is short and uncertain.[57] Similarly, the processes of socioeconomic mobility depend not

[55] George Kimble, *Tropical Africa*, vol. 2 (Garden City, N.Y.: Doubleday, Anchor Books, 1962), p. 156; cf. William McCord, *The Springtime of Freedom: Evolution of Developing Societies* (New York: Oxford University Press, 1965).

[56] Wrigley, *Population and History*, pp. 77–78.

[57] See Holger R. Stub, "Education, the Professions, and Long Life," *British Journal of Sociology*, 20 (June 1969), pp. 177–189.

only on time per se, but on a *Weltanschauung* that includes planning ahead, saving, and deferred gratification, all of which are difficult conceptions of self when people live in the moving present.

Mortality and Religiocultural Systems

Most of the indirect impact of mortality levels on social institutions and social processes depends on time factors that are shaped by mortality. If the transformation from high to low death rates has facilitated social and economic changes tied indirectly to the length of human life, it should be expected that those social institutions that are concerned directly with mortality will be responsive to its structure and frequency. In particular, we should expect that the dominance of death in premodern societies would influence both the social relevance and content of institutions organized around death.[58]

In every society — traditional and modern — man must explain and understand the meaning of life and death and has to cope with his own mortality and that of his family and friends. The press for explanation must be greater under conditions where death is open, frequent, and conspicuous on a regular basis. In the preindustrial world the society was "inured to bereavement and the shortness of life. It clearly had to be." [59] In a description of village life in India, McCord notes:

> How long one can live is the primary preoccupation of every villager. For in Khampur, (Uttar Pradesh, India) where half of the children die before they are ten and rats carry the bubonic plague and every adult has at times experienced malarial fever, death cannot be hidden.[60]

In sharp contrast, the low level of death in modern society and its segregation from the ongoing social system reduce regular confrontations with the mortality of man. When death is confined largely to the elderly — those retired from work, finished with direct parental responsibilities — and handled within specialized bureaucracies, mortality becomes removed from the daily business of social life. The constant presence of death in traditional societies means that society has to incorporate its regularity within the ongoing system of life. The "nonpresence" of death in modern societies physically and socially removes the death of man from the life of society.

An important feature of traditional societies is the emphasis on,

[58] Cf. Robert Blauner, "Death and Social Structure," *Psychiatry*, 29 (1966), pp. 378–394, reprinted in Rose Coser (ed.), *Life Cycle and Achievement in America* (New York: Harper Torchbook, 1969), pp. 223–260.
[59] Laslett, *The World We Have Lost*, p. 96.
[60] McCord, *The Springtime of Freedom*, p. 22.

and dominance of, religious institutions. The decline of religion and the emergence of secularism is, in part, tied to the changing needs that religion can satisfy. When life is precarious, when death is frequent and mysterious, social institutions are needed to explain death. With the decline in mortality, its removal from daily concern, and its concentration among the elderly, the pressing need for social reinforcement in times of bereavement is considerably reduced. Moreover, the decline of "fate" or "God's will" as explanatory concepts and fatalism as a dominant religious theme are, in part, related to the extension of the length of life and the concomitant changes in the timing of death.[61]

Therefore, religious institutions must redefine the content of their message, or at least place different emphasis within that content, if they are to remain vital in the modern world. Indeed, it is not surprising that, along with the decline in mortality, shifts occur from an emphasis on "other-world" orientations to "this-world" matters, in both general values and in the context of religious institutions. Rewards for religious adherence are no longer placed in other worlds or other lives but in the quality of life in this world.[62] In premodern societies, people live in the present but, paradoxically, are other-world oriented. In modern societies, people plan for the future and are this-world oriented. Both patterns fit the facts of mortality and its meaning in these different types of society. The current emphasis among religious institutions and their philosophers on social theologies of the quality of life could hardly attract the attention of persons surrounded by the quantitative shortness of life. Conversely, emphasizing cities of God seems too far removed from the long span of time people have to live in the cities of man.

Some have gone so far as to suggest that the stress on religion in general and on ghosts and communities of the dead in particular may be attributed to the nearness and frequency of deaths in premodern societies. Hence, the absence of stress on ghosts and extrahuman forces in modern society is not simply the routing of superstition by science and rational thought but "reflects the disengaged social situation of the majority of the deceased."[63] The removal of death from everyday life in modern society and the bureaucratized control of death further disengage the ongoing society from concern and interest in death. Mortality in modern society rarely interrupts the business of life.[64] If the revolution in mortal-

---

[61] Ibid., p. 22; Stub, "Education, the Professions and Long Life," p. 183. On India, see Kingsley Davis, *The Population of India and Pakistan* (Princeton: Princeton University Press, 1950), p. 64.

[62] On this point, see Heer, *Society and Population*, p. 44.

[63] Blauner, "Death and Social Structure," in *Life Cycle and Achievement in America*, pp. 232–235.

[64] Ibid., p. 228; cf. David Sudnow, *Passing On: The Social Organization of Dying* (Englewood Cliffs, N.J.: Prentice-Hall, 1967); Barney Glazer and Anselm Strauss, *Awareness of Dying* (Chicago: Aldine, 1965).

ity has not influenced directly the shift from religiousness to secularism, it surely has played an integral, supporting role.

In sum, the decline in mortality and its changing character and distribution has had major implications, direct and indirect, on the functioning of social systems and the nature of social institutions. Modern society in all its social, economic, and cultural dimensions is inconceivable under conditions of high mortality. The integral role of the mortality revolution in the transformation from traditional to modern is beyond dispute, because mortality processes are responsive directly to modernization and also because mortality reduction shapes the potential for socioeconomic development. The former reason has almost always been stressed; the latter argument is by no means less important. As Heer suggests: "It is possible that the dramatic decline in mortality since the end of the nineteenth century has evoked more changes in social structure than any other single development of the period." [65] In this sense, social scientists concerned with modernization cannot neglect mortality.

Some Theoretical Observations

The "fit" between low, controlled mortality and socioeconomic modernization, particularly mortality decline as a facilitating factor in developmental processes, balances the accentuated and dramatized focus on the consequences of reduced mortality for the population growth problems of underdeveloped nations. The argument is usually made, and in its skeletal form the reasoning is cogent, that reduced mortality among the nonindustrialized areas of the world, as a result of the technological diffusion of medical and public health measures, has led to unprecedented population growth. In turn, this growth from sustained high fertility (or increased fertility) and low and falling mortality impedes major social and economic modernization and engenders varying social, economic, political, and population problems. The role of mortality reduction as an impediment to socioeconomic development appears, on the surface, to challenge arguments, pointing to the contribution of low mortality as a facilitating factor to developmental processes. How can we argue that mortality reduction sets up the potential for the emergence of major social and economic changes, when at the same time we note that mortality control, through its population growth consequences, inhibits modernization? These relationships conflict only if they are treated mechanically, in isolation from their societal contexts, and if the two-way interaction between mortality and modernization is ignored.

Within the historical context of mortality reduction in Western

[65] Heer, *Society and Population*, p. 43.

industrialized countries, as well as within the context of mortality declines in contemporary nonindustrialized nations, fertility levels exceeded mortality sufficiently to generate continuous population growth. But several critical differences between the historical Western experience and the contemporary post-World War II experience of the emerging nations are strategically significant. First, the level of population growth, following sharper reductions in mortality than in fertility, in Western nations was probably lower than in the nonindustrialized Third World. This is partly a function of differences in the level of fertility in this initial demographic stage — because of marriage and socioeconomic patterns, fertility in preindustrial Western nations was lower in general than fertility in contemporary, preindustrial, non-Western nations; it is also a function of the differential pace of mortality reduction — mortality declined slower in Western nations than it did in post-World War II non-Western nations. Second, international migration may have operated historically as a developmental safety valve for some Western nations, although contemporary developing nations cannot obtain relief from population growth in this way.

A more significant, and in the present context the most critical, factor differentiating the historical experience of the West with that of the developing nations of Asia, Africa, and Latin America, is the societal context of mortality changes. The mortality experience of industrialized countries was shaped by social and economic development; mortality reduction was an integral element in modernization. Mortality levels were responsive to socioeconomic changes, and, in turn, paved the way for further socioeconomic alterations. In contrast, declines in mortality in underdeveloped countries took place independent of internal social and economic processes. Whereas the *potential* for social and economic change is established by the extension of life in every societal context, it remains potential in nonmodernized countries until other major social revolutions emerge. In short, the consequences of death control for social and economic evolution vary when the mortality revolution is the result of simple "technological diffusion" or when it flows from internal developmental processes. The *interaction* of "cause" and "effect" clearly emerges.

Indeed, this general reasoning led to our earlier conclusion that population growth per se, isolated from the social underpinnings of that growth and without specifying the demographic components defining that growth, cannot have uniform relationships with social and economic development.[66] In short, it is reasonable to postulate that social and economic development alone is *sufficient* for mortality reduction, and low,

[66] See Chapter 1, this book.

controlled mortality is *necessary* for the emergence of social and economic modernization. But mortality reduction by itself is not *sufficient* for social and economic development nor is modernization a *necessary* prerequisite for mortality reduction. Only when we appreciate analytically the distinction between "necessary" and "sufficient" conditions can we begin to unravel the complex relationships between modernization and the mortality revolution.

Chapter Six

FERTILITY IN COMPARATIVE AND HISTORICAL PERSPECTIVE

Several analytic threads connect the interlocking web of mortality and fertility.[1] First, the balance of vital processes — mortality and fertility — determine population growth in a closed population. Given the dramatic reduction in mortality levels, historically and comparatively, it is natural to consider fertility levels. Did they decline before, or after, or at the same time as mortality? Was the pace of reduction in fertility faster, slower, or similar to that of mortality? Are sequences in mortality and fertility changes discernible from preindustrial to industrial conditions or from traditional to modern societies? Indeed, is there empirical support for the postulate of demographic transition "theory" — that a particular sequence of change in the vital processes occurs as social and economic modernization proceeds, i.e., that mortality declines precede alterations in fertility?

A second connection between mortality and fertility is based on the *interaction* between these changes. Social scientists have been tempted to view the declines in mortality and fertility, when fertility follows regularly the pace of mortality reduction, not as two population processes responding independently to a broad set of social and economic factors, or as two correlated processes, but rather as a *causal* sequence. Hence, we must ascertain how much fertility levels are determined by increased population after sharp mortality declines, or the degree to

[1] See the discussion in Chapter 1 on the interrelationship among the population components.

which mortality conditions set up demographic circumstances conducive to fertility changes.

At a different level, the relationship between modernization and fertility processes must, in part, be combined with the analysis of modernization and mortality reduction. The investigation of fertility changes over time and fertility differences between various societies may involve a similar theoretical framework as our inquiry into the factors associated with historical and comparative mortality patterns. Are the broader social, economic, political, and technological factors linked to the mortality revolution equally at work to shape the decline in fertility? Moreover, does the emergence of public health measures that circumvent modernization in mortality reduction have parallels in the use of public health technology, e.g., efficient contraceptive technology, to lower fertility before social and economic modernization takes place in the emerging nations?

These possible connections between mortality and fertility — that there are sequential patterns of decline in the vital processes and, in particular, that fertility reduction follows the pace set by mortality; that mortality levels are a major determinant of the level of fertility; and that historical and comparative analogies may be made between the general determinants of mortality and fertility — have been argued in one form or another in the demographic literature. Each argument, if correct, suggests that the analytic study of fertility flows from a careful examination of mortality patterns. However, as we shall demonstrate in this chapter, specific interconnections between mortality and fertility analysis are often tenuous and spurious. In particular, these postulates are based on three assumptions that are in part fallacious. The first partial fallacy is empirical. Contrary to the premise of demographic transition theory, fertility appears to have fallen *before* mortality in several industrialized countries, and, in others, fertility increased when mortality began its slow descent. Thus, the sequence of change in vital processes will have to be reformulated. The simple leap from the correlation of mortality and fertility to a causal model, positing that mortality "determines" fertility, must be taken with caution or abandoned entirely.

A second inadequacy is methodological, consisting of two parts. If we are to interrelate mortality and fertility changes, at a minimum the relationship must be viewed as a potential two-way process; mortality may be related to fertility as both an independent and dependent variable. Most importantly, any relationship between mortality and fertility must operate within the context of social structure and organization. Not only should we identify and analyze the intervening mechanisms linking mortality to fertility, but we need as well to examine the interaction between these vital processes and the broader shape and character of social change. In this sense, mortality conditions may *facilitate* or *impede* changes in fertility but cannot be linked causally to fertility without considering additional social forces.

The third fallacy relates to the mechanistic analogy between the broader determinants of mortality and fertility. These processes share certain basic demographic features: both focus on one population process — entering or exiting, each has a biological component, and both are societal universals. Fertility, however, in contrast to mortality, is intimately connected with particularistic norms about family size, norms surrounding the means acceptable to control fertility, and more general norms and values that connect fertility to other human goals and aspirations.[2] In large measure, it is not directly relevant to analyze whether or how attitudes toward death changed with modernization to account for the mortality revolution. Although universal norms and values for long life may not be taken as given, improvements in living standards and conditions, sanitation, nutrition, and public health programs, inoculations, and spraying fields chemically do not depend on complex mortality norms and values that must be altered directly or indirectly. Thus, it would be absurd to search for clues to high mortality in traditional societies in the attitudes and social values that encourage high death rates.

Similarly, the decline in mortality throughout the world can be analyzed successfully without recourse to the dissection of changes in individual planning. We did not argue that mortality in contemporary Africa or in pre-twentieth-century Latin America was high because these populations valued deaths whereas twentieth-century European or Western populations valued life. In a similar way, we would not want to argue that fertility in one society is high because its members value large families whereas in another society fertility is low because its members value small families.[3] That provides little explanation and only rephrases the question. Nevertheless, explanations of the social structural conditions underlying changes in fertility must attempt to link these conditions to the mechanisms by which individuals and groups absorb, translate, and interpret broader social structural changes into goals that include family size control. In short, fertility involves a different type of social complexity when compared to mortality that makes mechanistic analogies between the two vital processes inadequate theoretically and hazardous intellectually.

Investigating fertility involves more complex analytic problems than mortality analyses, and it is reasonable to tackle less complex issues first.

---

[2] See Chapter 2, this book; Ronald Freedman, "The Sociology of Human Fertility," *Current Sociology,* 10/11 (1961–1962), pp. 38–42.

[3] See Kingsley Davis, "The Theory of Change and Response in Modern Demographic History," *Population Index* (October 1963), pp. 345–366, particularly p. 362.

Indeed, our discussion of population processes in historical and comparative perspective will conclude with an analysis of modernization and migration (see Chapter 7), which may be viewed as a further step toward additional analytic complexity. Migration is neither a societal universal, nor does it have a biological referent, and involves both entering and exiting processes.[4]

We can promise no startling revelations in this chapter. A great deal of research has been undertaken in this area of demographic inquiry; much more is being completed now. The next decade will probably witness an increasing flow of historical and comparative materials to confirm, correct, and qualify what will be presented herein. Indeed, no chapter or book could do full justice to the wealth of descriptive and sometime analytic materials now available, not to mention the important technical and sophisticated statistical analyses of fertility data.

MODERNIZATION AND FERTILITY: THE OVERALL PATTERN

To unravel the complex interrelationships between modernization and fertility processes, the analytic problem must be clear. In particular, the *specific mechanisms* directly affecting fertility trends and variations must be distinguished from the *social organizational determinants* of fertility, which are linked to it by way of these specific intermediate mechanisms. Whatever changes may be observed in fertility patterns over time and whatever societal fertility differences that may be located at any point in time must be a direct function of variations associated with sexual intercourse, conception, and gestation. The balance of these "intermediate" variables directly determines the level, trend, and variation in fertility. But these variables are "intermediate" between fertility levels on one hand, and the organization of society, social structure, on the other.[5] We will not examine variation in a series of intermediate mechanisms but rather the relationship between modernization and fertility. If increased contraceptive usage has been the primary mechanism of fertility control in the United States, if abortion has been largely

[4] For a review of some theoretical issues emerging from the greater complexity of migration processes, see Chapter 3, this book.

[5] For an outline of the intermediate variables, see Kingsley Davis and Judith Blake, "Social Structure and Fertility: An Analytic Framework," *Economic Development and Cultural Change*, 4 (April 1956), pp. 211–235; cf. the discussion by Freedman, "The Sociology of Human Fertility," pp. 38–42; also by Ronald Freedman, "The Transition from High to Low Fertility: Challenge to Demographers," *Population Index*, 31 (October 1965), pp. 417–430; "Worldwide Fertility Trends" Moderator's statement, United Nations, World Population Conference (Belgrade, Yugoslavia, August 1965). Compare the discussion in Chapter 2, this book.

responsible for the rapid reduction in the birth rate of Japan and selected Eastern European countries, if delayed marriage and celibacy have been important means of fertility control in Ireland and elsewhere in Western Europe, and if sterilization has become the key intermediate variable in fertility declines in Puerto Rico during the 1960's, our question remains, Why? And the question is not directed to why the *specific* response or choice of mechanism, or why and how such mechanisms relate to fertility; rather our concern is why these societies responded at all! In short, it is not the relationship between modernization and particular intermediate mechanisms (e.g., the relationship between economic development and age at marriage), nor the relationship between the intermediate mechanisms and fertility (e.g., the relationship between abortion rates and marital fertility), but rather the general relationship between social organizational changes and fertility changes [6] that we must study.

When we focus on the links between social structural changes and fertility, we must not overlook *particularistic* norms about family size and about the intermediate mechanisms themselves. Changes in these particularistic norms may be important in understanding fertility responses and which mechanisms of fertility control have been utilized. However, changes in particularistic norms are shaped by social structural alterations; analyzing those aspects of social organization that are the underpinnings of particularistic norms provides the most intellectually profitable framework for fertility research. Our view does not necessarily imply that norms are always dependent variables. It is not our task here to enter into what appears to be an unsolvable intellectual controversy: whether norms are determinants of or responses to social structural changes. Rather we must *locate those aspects of social structural changes, of which the cultural subsystem is one integral part, that are linked most clearly to fertility changes either via particularistic norms about family size and/or via particularistic norms about the intermediate variables, but always through the intermediate variables themselves.*

Preindustrial Fertility

Notwithstanding the fluctuations over time in preindustrial fertility patterns, the significant fertility variations among preindustrial populations, and the enormous social, economic, political, and cultural com-

---

[6] Our approach emphasizes that the "intermediate variables" are *intermediate;* they are not viewed separately as independent variables (affecting fertility) and as dependent variables (consequences of social structure). For a different approach, see David Yaukey, "On Theorizing about Fertility," *The American Sociologist*, 4 (May 1969), pp. 100–104.

plexities within which premodern fertility processes operate, fertility levels in traditional, preindustrial societies are relatively high. It would be untenable sociologically if this fact were not consistent with the general societal features of preindustrial states. Further, despite variations and complexities, these societal contexts may be abstracted from their specifics and analyzed at a general level. Therefore, what general societal features do preindustrial, traditional societies have in common that result in, or are correlated with, high fertility levels? Against this background, we can identify the reasons underlying the historical changes in fertility, analyze the implications of fertility variation in traditional and modern societies, and discuss prospects for fertility changes in contemporary underdeveloped areas.

There is some consensus among social scientists that the following macro- and microlevel factors conspire to produce high levels of fertility under premodern conditions. For systematic and concise analysis, we will focus in sequence on demographic, social, economic, and cultural subsystems; of course, the simultaneity and coincidence of societal patterns shape fertility behavior.

The first and most often cited reason for high fertility levels in premodern societies is the conditioning role of premodern high mortality patterns. With the precariousness and shortness of life, particularly the heavy tolls taken by infant losses, such societies could not survive unless fertility levels were also high. Hence, from a macrosocietal point of view, high fertility represents a functional adjustment to high death rates.[7] It is likely that some societies did not make that adjustment, and, as a result of combined low fertility and high mortality, failed to survive. It is also likely that fertility fluctuations over time and fertility variations among preindustrial societies represented in part adjustments to parallel mortality variations and fluctuations, which themselves were responsive to variations and fluctuations in socioeconomic conditions. Hence, it is not clear whether fertility variations were direct results of mortality fluctuations, or indirect reflections of similar socioeconomic changes. Moreover, high fertility might have influenced mortality levels. Some scattered evidence indicates that large family size and short spacing between children result in higher levels of infant and maternal mortality. When fertility was higher than mortality, population increase either had to be absorbed by preindustrial economies or, if that were not possible, mortality would have had to increase. Over time, the demographic adjustment to popu-

---

[7] Freedman, "The Sociology of Human Fertility," p. 48; Davis, "The Theory of Change and Response in Modern Demographic History"; Kingsley Davis, "Institutional Patterns Favoring High Fertility in Underdeveloped Areas," *Eugenics Quarterly*, 2 (March 1955), pp. 33–39.

lation increase might involve fertility reduction as well as out-migration or both.[8]

Perhaps the critical factor in the relationship between mortality and fertility in preindustrial societies is not so much the level of mortality but the precariousness of uncontrolled mortality. This precariousness helped shape pressures toward having children early before death removed one spouse, and may have led to having "extra" children as a safeguard against infant and child losses.[9] However, we must not infer from the behavioral patterns of high birth rates a necessary connection to large family size norms. Families may have desired and wanted "several" children but had "many" children so that "several" would survive. The discrepancy between existential family size and the total number of children born may have been large. Nevertheless, there are, as we shall see, other indications of large family size norms in traditional populations. But fertility and mortality patterns in traditional societies "fit" together, and "fit in" with the social and economic features of these societies; the precise causal nature of this relationship is still open to question.

A dominant feature of premodern societies is the centrality of kinship and family structures. Preindustrial communities are generally organized around families, groups of families, clans, tribes, and general kinship units. As noted in Chapter 5, this emphasis on supraindividual social units may have been shaped by prevailing preindustrial mortality conditions. In this sense, the relationship between mortality and fertility may be mediated through the institutional structure of society. In the present context it may be argued that mortality patterns set up the conditions for kinship emphasis, which, in turn, had certain consequences for the nature of fertility patterns. Nevertheless, whatever forces shaped the emergence of kinship units as the central focus of traditional societies, kinship dominance generally had a pronatalist consequence.[10]

---

[8] E. A. Wrigley, *Population and History* (London: Weidenfeld and Nicolson, World University Library, 1969), p. 180; Davis, "The Theory of Change and Response in Modern Demographic History"; Dov Friedlander, "Demographic Responses and Population Change," *Demography, 6* (November 1969), pp. 359–381. For empirical evidence on the possible impact of fertility on mortality, see John Knodel, "Infant Mortality in Three Bavarian Villages: An Analysis of Family Histories from the 19th Century," *Population Studies, 22* (November 1968), pp. 297–318; David Heer and Dean Smith, "Mortality Level and Desired Family Size," in *International Union for the Scientific Study of Population, Contributed Papers* (Sydney Conference, 1967), pp. 26–36.

[9] See Davis and Blake, "Social Structure and Fertility," pp. 215–220; Freedman, "The Sociology of Human Fertility," p. 48.

[10] Cf. Davis, "Institutional Patterns Favoring High Fertility in Underdeveloped Areas," pp. 34–36; Freedman, "The Sociology of Human Fertility," pp. 48–49.

From the macroperspective, children were viewed by the community as valuable assets that assured kinship and, hence, group survival. The social strength of the kinship system relied on its size; that size was less determined by extra-kin recruitment than by high reproduction levels. The centrality of kinship implies more than kin importance; it signifies pervasiveness as well. The kin group determined who was who, who got what, and why. In short, kinship groupings were central in political, economic, social, and cultural systems. What and who you were had less importance than to what family or kin group you belonged. Under such a social system, children enhanced the ability of families and kin to achieve socially valued goals.

The reproducing couple, therefore, found built-in rewards for large families. Equally important, the burdens of a large family, involving economic and social costs, social and personal care, and the like were shared and controlled by the larger kinship-family structure. Parents not only had personal rewards for having large families but they could escape from direct responsibilities of their many children.

The value placed on children within kinship structures was thus translated into direct motivation for having large families. Thus norms of early and universal marriages were probably widespread in premodern communities. Young wives were urged to have children early; husbands, desiring the prestige and status associated with large families, were equally motivated.

Another important aspect of kinship systems under premodern conditions was sex-role segregation. Although the family, including women, may have been a working unit, the role and status of women was tied to the society through childbearing. The most direct and often the only way for a woman to obtain prestige and other socioeconomic rewards and benefits was contributing to the survival of the group by bearing healthy children. The general pressures from kinship centrality led to high fertility values at both macro- and microlevels.

The underlying assumption of this argument is that high birth rates fit into the social goals of kinship-based, preindustrial societies. It follows that, under some conditions where high fertility interfered or conflicted with kin-group objectives, some pressure toward reduced fertility may also have developed. This might have taken the form of delayed marriages, nonmarriages, intercourse restrictions, infanticide, abortion, the use of *coitus interruptus,* and fertility controls. Among preindustrial societies, pressures toward high fertility to ensure at least a minimum number of children often faced counterpressures to minimize or eliminate the surplus of children under difficult subsistence conditions.[11] On the

[11] Freedman, "The Sociology of Human Fertility," p. 49; Davis and Blake, "Social Structure and Fertility."

whole, the former pressures exceeded the latter. In this sense, relatively high fertility was a "rational" response to kinship and mortality conditions, just as variation and fluctuations in preindustrial fertility were adjustments to changing social and demographic conditions.

Because of this important role of family and kinship within premodern societies, combined with the precariousness of life, the reproduction of children, as a source of protection and prestige, takes on unusual significance. Thus, for example, one traditionally greets the bride in India with the incantation, "May you be blessed with sixteen children." [12] Variations of "be fruitful and multiply" may be found in the mores of other premodern communities.

The social and demographic assets of large family size in traditional societies is complemented by the productive assets of children in familial-based economies. The economy of traditional agricultural societies required a quantitative labor flow rather than a quality of workers. For the kin group, children represented economic and sustenance continuity. Because human labor produced the only means of sustenance and wealth, the larger the labor supply through reproduction, the greater the potential for maintaining or increasing the holdings of the kinship group. Similarly, direct economic benefits accrued to the parents of large families. The more offspring, the more workers within the family; the larger the family, the greater the potential that someone would sustain parents in their old age. Children represented to their parents one type of old age insurance. Conversely, to control family size to the point of bearing only several children ran the demographic hazards of group and family suicide, the social risks of group weakness, and the economic risks of an inadequate labor supply. Within a kinship-dominated system, the chances of social mobility were too minimal, the level of aspirations too low, the probability of recognizable increases in living standards too negative to result in social and personal gains from family size reduction or to offset demographic and social pressures for high fertility. With everything to gain and little to lose, it is not difficult to appreciate why preindustrial families were relatively large. As long as things worth having in a society depend mainly on local kinship-based institutions, fertility is likely to remain high.[13]

Over time within premodern societies, these demographic, social, familial, and economic conditions resulted in institutionalizing high fertility within the cultural system.[14] Fertility in traditional communities

---

[12] William McCord, *The Springtime of Freedom: Evolution of Developing Societies* (New York: Oxford University Press, 1965), p. 23.

[13] Freedman, "The Transition From High to Low Fertility," p. 418.

[14] Davis, "Institutional Patterns Favoring High Fertility in Underdeveloped Areas," pp. 33–39.

was high not only because such communities valued large families; that may have been true because of general social structural pressures. More important, because high fertility represented one mechanism for the achievement of general goals and values, various aspects of the cultural-religious life of preindustrial communities were organized around the reinforcement of values and attitudes conducive to large family size. Some values and attitudes may have related to particularistic norms around "ideal family size" or particularistic norms surrounding the utilization or nonutilization of fertility controls. In short, social goals were translated into high fertility values and, in turn, to high fertility behavior.

To illustrate the interacting roles of kinship, mortality, and economic subsistence shaping the institutionalization of fertility, and as an example of how high fertility fit with the mechanical solidarity of premodern communities, we can review briefly the results of a demographic research project in Western New Guinea.[15] The study notes that the family, the small kinship group, or small local groupings are central to the social structure of Western New Guinea. Given the antagonisms between local groups, the rivalry between small kinship units, the significance of the family as a working unit, and the marginal economic and social conditions that threaten these groups with extinction, the research project notes:

> A failure to maintain an adequate fertility rate would soon lead to the collapse of the group. In this context it is noteworthy that in the ceremonial religious life of several groups acts which are connected with the continued existence, the welfare, and the fertility of the group occupy a central position.[16]

The institutionalization of high fertility values and the social structural conditions surrounding fertility must be viewed against countervailing forces that depress fertility below maximum levels. Among these forces the New Guinea study includes: First, women are charged with extremely difficult tasks of providing food for the family. Too close a succession of births is considered undesirable in many parts of New Guinea because it would aggravate the tasks of women. Hence, such fertility controls as abortions, infanticide, drinking "roots" to prevent conception, and intercourse taboos during lactation are used to both lower birth rates and influence the survival chances of children. Because a rapid succession of births might mean higher infant losses, these control practices are more favorable to the ultimate numbers of the group.

[15] K. Groenewegen and D. J. van de Kaa, *Results of the Demographic Research Project, Western New Guinea,* Part I, *New Guinea as an Area for Demographic Research* (The Hague: Government Printing and Publishing Office, 1964).
[16] Ibid., p. 111.

Second, chronic or periodic food shortages make it necessary to abandon the old and physically ill, and infanticide and birth control techniques are employed. Under extreme conditions, groups object to the departure from agricultural labor of pregnant women or women who could be married off to another group. Hence, direct fertility control is complemented by changes in marriage.

Third, the marginal economic conditions and periodic food crises of these premodern communities affect the form of marriage. In some areas older or physically weaker men have more than one wife for prestige and economic motives — and because women attend to the food supply. If the first wife is old, a younger wife may be obtained; these arrangements may, in turn, affect fertility. The general dowry system forces some men to lead "a lengthy bachelor existence," as older men often use their accumulated wealth to take younger wives. In short, various intermediate mechanisms affect short-run fluctuations around high fertility levels. Many other examples may be found in the literature to illustrate the general patterns of high fertility in premodern societies and the general fit between fertility processes and the overall social organization of these communities.

The Fertility Transition

Against this background of preindustrial fertility levels, we can begin to appreciate the revolutionary nature of fertility reduction. The patterns of fertility change during modernization may be illustrated by data on fertility trends in England and Wales. If we hold in abeyance questions with respect to variations in the onset and pace of the fertility decline, and with respect to the initial level from which the fall in fertility began, the pattern of fertility decline in England and Wales is not atypical.[17]

Around the turn of the nineteenth century, fertility in England and Wales was fairly high: the crude birth rate in 1800 has been estimated at over 38 live births per 1,000 population. From 1800 to 1870 very few changes occurred in the crude birth rate that would signify a downward trend. However, starting in 1870, with a crude birth rate of 36 per 1,000, a steady uninterrupted decline may be observed in England and Wales through the 1930's. In 1900, the crude birth rate was 28 per 1,000, and by the 1930's it fell below 15 per 1,000 — an almost 60 per cent decline in six decades. These same changes may be observed with more refined fertility measures as well. For example, the number of live births per 1,000 women in the reproductive ages (15–44) fell at about the same

[17] Data on England and Wales are presented in Wrigley, *Population and History*, tables 5–15, 5–17, and 5–18; for estimates of the crude birth rates around 1800, see Friedlander, "Demographic Responses and Population Change," table 4.

pace as the crude birth rate: from 154 per 1,000 women, 15 to 44 years of age in 1871–1880, to less than 61 per 1,000 women in the reproductive ages for the period 1936–1940. Further, marital fertility (legitimate live births per 1,000 married women in the reproductive ages, 15 to 44) in England and Wales declined smoothly and uninterruptedly from the 1870's through the early 1940's: from 296 to 105, or by almost two-thirds in three-quarters of a century. Similar patterns may be noted for both gross and net reproduction rates.[18]

All these measures show truly revolutionary changes in fertility during the industrialization era in England and Wales. But these are all period measures; they relate to *cross-sections of a population* at a given time. Another perspective focuses on *groups of women* either at birth or at marriage and traces these "cohorts" through their respective reproductive periods. Fortunately, data on the fertility patterns of marriage cohorts in England and Wales are available from the mid-nineteenth century, from which we can examine the family size of women who were married in the 1860's compared to the family size of women marrying in the 1930's. The average family size of women in England and Wales who were married between 1861 and 1869 was over six children (6.2); family size declines to less than four children among the women marrying between 1900 and 1909, and to slightly more than two children for the cohorts marrying between 1935 and 1939.

This evidence sheds light not only on changes in average family size but also in the relative frequency of families of different sizes. For our purposes we may contrast two marriage cohorts: women marrying in the 1870's to women marrying in 1925. Of all the women who were married between 1870 and 1879, fully one-third had eight or more children and 11.5 per cent had eleven or more children. In sharp contrast, only 2.2 per cent of women married in 1925 had eight or more children and almost none had eleven or more children. Even more striking are the respective proportions of women who had four or more children: for the 1870–1879 marriage cohort, 71 per cent; for the 1925 marriage cohort, 19 per cent. Obviously, women in England and Wales in the 1925 marriage cohort had families of three or fewer children (81 per cent compared to 29 per cent of the 1870–1879 marriage cohorts). Indeed, over half of the 1925 marriage cohort had one or two children, a concentration in these parities over four times that of the 1870–1879 marriage cohorts. In short, by the 1925 marriage cohort, the large family of five or more children virtually disappeared and a strong behavioral preference for either the one- or two-child family was manifest. These family size patterns for the two marriage cohorts represent end points on our selected time con-

[18] Wrigley, *Population and History*, table 5–16; pp. 193–196.

tinuum, but it should be noted that the fertility transformation was uniform for all cohorts that may be identified along the continuum.[19]

This brief empirical overview of the fertility transition in England and Wales during modernization raises two broad analytic issues. First, what factors of the industrialization-modernization revolutions caused a steady, historically unparalleled decline in fertility? Are there identifiable general and specific elements in modernization processes that may be linked systematically to changing patterns of fertility? Indeed, to what extent are the factors sustaining high fertility under preindustrial conditions helpful in providing the framework for the analysis of fertility declines? A second less general but no less significant issue is the relatively low level of nineteenth-century fertility in England. High fluctuating fertility "fits" the general social fabric of premodern societies. But why wasn't fertility in 1800 in England and Wales, indeed throughout Western Europe in the nineteenth century, higher? The crude birth rate in England and Wales was less than 40 per 1,000 in 1800, much lower than the biological potential for reproduction, significantly lower than fertility levels in nineteenth-century America and Eastern Europe, and probably lower than parts of Asia, Africa, and Latin America in the late 1960's. Thus, we must determine which factors in preindustrial Western Europe were already operative in reducing birth rates below "maximum" levels and below fertility levels characteristic of other major preindustrial societies. A general theory of the fertility transition must account for fertility fluctuations and variations before and after the secular decline.

These broad issues represent complex and challenging analytic problems. Complete and satisfactory empirically based answers to some of the specific questions associated with these issues are generally lacking; also, an enormous range of societies is lumped together under categories within and between preindustrial and industrial. Yet, if we are willing to sacrifice detail for generalities and ignore some variations and exceptions to uncover overall patterns, and if we are willing to infer from fragments of evidence to add up deductively some of the missing pieces, a general mosaic may be organized that informs us of the fit between low fertility and modern social structures.

Why Fertility Declined

Industrialization, or modernization, implies major changes in all subsystems of society. Almost all these changes have been listed, in one way or another, as "determinants" of the decline in fertility. However, many specific social, economic, and cultural changes associated with the

[19] From data presented in ibid., table 5–18.

readjustment of fertility in modern societies reflect in different ways similar pressures toward reduced family size. Hence, without attempting to cover all possible factors, we may abstract general principles that in large part represent the key social processes affecting the declines in fertility and family size. Three key social processes may be identified: First, the modernization of societies implies structural differentiation, particularly the effective separation of family roles from economic, political, and social roles. In turn, the family or kinship group no longer dominates the social and economic reward system and can no longer exert pressure toward large family size goals. Second, the structure of economic institutions is changed, affecting higher standards of living, aspirations for mobility, and nonfamilial economic and social rewards. In combination with the declining pressure from kin groups for high fertility, economic changes reversed the pressure in the direction of smaller families. A third process, integral to modernization, related directly to fertility reduction, and not unrelated to these processes, involves alterations in social and personal goals and values, which are incompatible with large family size and high fertility.

To further specify these general processes more systematically, we can reexamine demographic, social-familial, economic, and cultural subsystems. If our analysis of preindustrial fertility was correct, it follows that alterations in these subsystems should help us to understand the shift to small families and low fertility.

Let us first reconsider the changing role of mortality. Although no universal pattern of mortality declines precedes falls in fertility, several relevant mortality processes are clear: First, whichever vital process begins to decrease first, the *pace* of mortality decline is swifter because mortality processes respond more directly to social and economic improvements or technological developments or both, whereas the normative structure surrounding fertility responds more slowly. Second, although under some conditions the mortality level may have not have dropped before fertility, major *fluctuations* in mortality may have decreased sufficiently to influence fertility. Third, the *long-run* consequence of mortality reduction created the potential for family size reduction without endangering group survival. Combined with the swifter pace of mortality reduction and the absence of wide national fluctuations, we may postulate that mortality reduction and consequent population growth *generated pressures for systematic fertility control*. But these demographic pressures did not operate in a social vaccum. In conjunction with familial and socioeconomic changes, demographic pressures were brought into social focus and created institutional changes in fertility. The conflict between changing living standards and aspirations for mobility was thus sharpened by the prevailing changes in demographic conditions.

At the microanalytic level, some have argued that in high mortality societies people really desired a small family but demographic pressures from high infant and child mortality required a higher number of births so that a small number of children could survive to adulthood. If this assumption is correct, it follows that when these demographic pressures were eased through mortality reduction, a trend toward convergence of desired family size and a small number of births ensued. It is difficult to accept uncritically this assumption and the reasoning behind it. First, as we have noted, nondemographic pressures may have operated to institutionalize high fertility values in premodern societies. Hence, a change in demographic pressures might not have led, in and of itself, to reevaluating high fertility norms. Second, the fall in infant mortality did not occur until well after observable declines in adult mortality and probably fifty to seventy-five years after recorded fertility declines in such countries as Sweden, France, and the United States. Third, the microdemographic argument also assumes the personal recognition of, and "rational" behavior toward, demographic processes. It seems as unreasonable to suppose that nineteenth-century man was able to recognize and interpret broad demographic processes as it is to suppose that modern man reduces his family size because of world population problems. Although not fully analogous, some evidence from contemporary underdeveloped countries describes the absence of personal recognition of mortality changes that have occurred. A study in Peru shows widespread misperception and erroneous beliefs about the existential facts of infant mortality reduction.[20] We may assume that if it takes a substantial time for demographers and social scientists to confirm trends in mortality, a fortiori nonscientists will require an equal or greater amount of time to identify accurately and certainly additional time to respond effectively to these demographic changes.

In sum, the fall in mortality, which itself was initially a consequence of social and economic changes, did not affect directly fertility changes. If there is a connection between fertility and mortality it is long-run and likely to be an indirect, rather than a causal, relationship. Mortality affected fertility through the impact of mortality changes on social institutions; at times mortality foreshadowed fertility declines in its more direct response to the same set of initial social and economic improvements, which in time affected fertility levels as well.

One of the most significant sociological features of modernization is the breakdown of the dominance and centrality of family-kin groupings.[21]

[20] See J. Mayone Stycos, "Social Class and Family Size in Peru," *American Journal of Sociology*, 70 (May 1965), pp. 651–658.

[21] This is one of the dominant themes of William Goode, *World Revolution and Family Patterns* (New York: The Free Press, 1963); cf. Chapter 4, this book.

As long as the family-kinship group held the key to economic and social rewards, its goals were primary. In modernization, functional specialization and structural differentiation occur that disengage the family from economic and social institutions and narrow its functions. The shift from extended to nuclear or conjugal family units has major repercussions for family size. The kin group in modern society can no longer either reward or withhold major rewards from its members. The number of children individual couples have are their own social and economic responsibilities, and their welfare and that of their children become primary considerations. The break between the family of orientation and the family of procreation may have been precipitated by various interacting processes, including selective migration, urbanization, and social mobility. But once the bonds that tied individuals to broader kinship groups were broken, new behavioral and value patterns became possible.

These family structural and functional changes occurred within a general socioeconomic context. The shift from agricultural to industrial structures had further repercussions on family relationships and on family size. Rising living standards, increasing economic opportunities, and, particularly, rising aspirations for social mobility conflicted with large family size norms. They were in the long run antithetical to large family size as well. In part, these social and economic changes affected family relationships and created class-generation gaps as social mobility occurred. But they exerted direct pressures toward fertility control and reduction.

The move away from family-based agricultural enterprises curtailed the productive asset of children; in turn, many children were impediments to active participation in the larger nonfamilial-based urban organizations.[22] Urban migration affected fertility by creating new conditions that enhanced favorable attitudes toward family size control. It furthered the breakdown of traditional family relationships and structures, loosened the socioeconomic controls of the extended family, and helped shake off the traditional value constraints encouraging high fertility. More than this, urbanization created a new social milieu wherein high fertility and large family size conflicted with levels of living, aspirations for mobility, and life style.

During modernization and industrialization, new values and attitudes in general were accentuated. A stress on individualism, secularism, and rationalism, hallmarks of the modern era, not only fit the specific values developed in favor of smaller families but further reinforced and encouraged its development and diffusion. The spread of achievement

22 Freedman, "The Sociology of Human Fertility," p. 50.

values in contrast to ascription resulted in direct motivations for small families.

The transformation of societies undergoing modernization and in- dustrialization touches onto every facet of human social organization. To note the impact of all these changes on fertility control and reduction would neglect the specific mechanisms by which fertility patterns are directly transformed. From the numerous changes tied to modernization and industrialization we have isolated three major, direct, interrelated, and perhaps necessary and sufficient conditions for the transition from high to low fertility: (1) the shift from kinship dominance to an emphasis on the nuclear family; (2) improved living standards and rising aspira- tions for social mobility; and (3) changing emphasis from ascription to achievement; from traditionalism to secularism; and general values and goals emphasizing individualism and rationalism. No analysis of mod- ernization is complete without considering these broad transformations; nor can any explanation of the fertility revolution fail to include these sociocultural forces as integral elements.

COMPARATIVE FERTILITY TRANSITIONS: THE LESSONS OF ENGLAND AND FRANCE

The relationship between modernization, particularly its industrial- ization component, and fertility is neither automatic nor mechanical. Rather the implications of the "industrialization-modernization" complex for social institutional and social structural changes and alterations in the cultural-ideological system must be identified in the search for the determinants of fertility reduction and control. The problem of assuming an automatic relationship between the rise of industry and the decline of fertility or, in general, the inadequacies of the mechanistic approach to historical changes in fertility control may be illustrated clearly by specific comparative evidence. Indeed, two complex questions must be resolved before any explanation of fertility processes in comparative- historical perspective can be accepted. First, if industrialization is, along with correlative social and cultural changes, important as a key element in reducing fertility, it should follow that the fertility of countries that have led industrialization should have declined first. Hence, in view of England's obvious lead in industrialization, how do we account for the fact that the historical decline in Western fertility did *not* begin in En- gland but declined earlier in several other less-industrialized European countries? As we reviewed earlier, fertility began to fall systematically in England around the 1870's, at least half a century after the Industrial

Revolution had brought about a major transformation in the English economy.[23]

Second, why is France always considered an "exception" to fertility declines in Western nations following industrialization? A general decline in fertility in France may be observed in the last several decades of the eighteenth century, seventy to one hundred years before any other European country; fertility began to fall before major industrial changes had occurred in France and when the pace of industrial growth was substantially below that of England. Whereas in England crude birth rates in the 1870's were still around 36 per 1,000 (somewhat higher than in Sweden whose birth rates began a smooth decline around 1850 and had fallen to 31 per 1,000 by the 1870's), the birth rate in France was less than 26 per 1,000 during the 1871–1880 decade.[24] The fact that French fertility declined before major industrialization, setting the pace for other more industrialized countries, plus the fact that fertility in England started to decline well after industrialization gained momentum, lagging behind European countries that were less industrialized, demands explanation. These cases of fertility transition force us to revise any simple notion of a one-to-one relationship between industrialization and fertility decline; moreover, their interpretation will sharpen and specify the critical factors involved in fertility control. Complex issues are involved in any analysis of fertility patterns in England and France. Thoroughly investigating all the specifics of these two cases would require a painstakingly detailed social history of both countries; rather, we must identify several key elements that seem in large part to account for these findings and that also shed light on general analytic issues.

England's "Delayed" Response

Only if one assumes a simple linear relationship between industrialization and fertility does it follow that the decline in fertility in England is judged as a "delayed response." [25] Because we reject any such assump-

[23] For a similar approach, see Frank Lorimer, *Culture and Human Fertility* (Paris: UNESCO, 1954), pp. 206–217.

[24] For a comparison of England and Sweden, see Dov Friedlander, "Demographic Responses and Population Change," pp. 359–381. On France, see Joseph Spengler, *France Faces Depopulation* (Durham, N.C.: Duke University Press, 1938); more recent background material may be found in several essays in *Population in History*, ed. D. Glass and D. Eversley (Chicago: Aldine, 1965), chaps. 18–21; A. Coale, "The Decline of Fertility in Europe from the French Revolution to World War II," in *Fertility and Family Planning: A World View*, ed. S. J. Behrman et al. (Ann Arbor: University of Michigan Press, 1969), pp. 3–24.

[25] Lorimer (*Culture and Human Fertility*, p. 211), for example, argues that the "late origin" of the decline of fertility in England "suggest[s] the influence of forces of a general character in English society, generated by advances in commerce, indus-

tion on theoretical and empirical grounds, it is more reasonable to re-phrase our inquiry: What were the social conditions underlying the early stages of industrialization in England that militated against a decline in fertility? Three essential and interrelated social conditions in early nine-teenth-century England that combined to retain preindustrial fertility levels were (1) the relationship between the growth of industry and family-kinship structure in the early stage of industrialization; (2) the pauperization of the industrial-urban proletariat; and (3) the relief of population strain in rural England as a result of heavy rural-urban migration. In the initial stages of industrialization, these three social conditions stymied the development of conflict between large family size on one hand and living standards and rising aspirations on the other, which would have resulted, and subsequently did result, in systematic fertility reduction.

Let us review briefly these three conditions. First, and foremost, was the particular relationship between industry and family-kinship structure in the early stages of English industrialization. We pointed out earlier that in the long run industrialization brought about structural differentiation which resulted in separating family roles from the economic system. However, in the early period of English industrial devel-opment, probably up until the mid-nineteenth century, domestic indus-tries, where the entire family worked, or factories, where children worked along with their parents, fostered the maintenance of traditional relation-ships within the family; in part the larger family continued to be eco-nomically profitable.[26] It was only around the 1840's that urban-industrial changes began to affect traditional family-economic roles sufficiently to create the conflict between levels of living and aspirations for a better life.

The retention of the traditional economic and educational roles within British working class families militated against alterations in fertility control. It is not surprising therefore that available research shows a *positive* correlation between employing children and fertility in England before 1850. Child labor may thus have exerted a positive in-

---

try, and education, tending toward restriction of fertility, *but long held in check by counterforces* tending to sustain a rather high level of fertility" (*Culture and Human Fertility*, p. 211, italics added). It seems unnecessary to postulate that industrializa-tion always brings fertility reduction unless "counterforces" check its decline. Rather, industrialization relates to fertility only under given circumstances.

[26] On the relationship between family structure and early industrialization in England, see Neil J. Smelser, *Social Change in the Industrial Revolution* (Chicago: University of Chicago Press, 1959); Smelser, *Essays in Sociological Explanation* (En-glewood Cliffs, N.J.: Prentice-Hall, 1968), chap. 4; William Goode, *World Revolu-tion and Family Patterns* (New York: The Free Press, 1963), pp. 50–51.

fluence on maintaining fertility levels because the structure of relationships within the family remained largely intact.[27] Interestingly, this
positive relationship between child labor and fertility holds *only up
to the 1850's.* When family roles became more specialized and differentiated structurally from economic and other roles, the social and economic price of having large families became prohibitive. As long as the
family retained its economic role and internal family relationships
continued undisturbed by industrial changes, the pressures toward family limitations — pressures brought about by rising aspirations engendered
by economic growth — were minimal. Moreover, these pressures, resulting from the alteration in traditional family roles, began to take on
fertility significance among the new generation beginning in the mid-
1870's. This generation experienced the full impact of structural differentiation, segregating family from economic roles.

A second major factor relates to the economic and social conditions
in urban England during the first half of the nineteenth century. Lorimer
points out that as a result of economic technology, industrial workers
were pauperized, working long hours, along with their children, for low
wages.[28] Along with the depressing influence of crowded and unsanitary
slums, the unskilled industrial workers developed no real basis for widespread aspirations toward improvement in the conditions of their lives,
one component of which would have included family size reduction. In
Chapter 5 we reviewed the high mortality rates found in urban England,
which also indicate the lack of demographic pressure for reducing
family size. Moreover, despite the improvement in overall economic
growth as a result of industrialization, wealth in England was concentrated in the hands of the few.[29] The majority of urban working class
England probably did not feel the improvement in living standards
until the 1860's or 1870's. Hence, the lack of actual improvements in living
standards combined with the absence of a base for rising aspirations
conspired to retain constant high fertility in the early decades of the
English Industrial Revolution. Moreover, only those who have experienced rising real incomes and the social and economic benefits that
such personal economic increases bring could be sensitive to the disadvantages of a large family size. Thus it was only the generation *after*
average real incomes moved decisively upward (in England in the 1870's
and 1880's; in other areas around 1850) that began to deliberately restrict the size of their families.[30]

[27] See the study by D. V. Glass cited in Lorimer, *Culture and Human Fertility*,
p. 210.
[28] *Culture and Human Fertility*, pp. 214–277.
[29] Ibid., p. 217.
[30] Wrigley, *Population and History*, p. 191.

Nor should we fail to note that the improvement in living standards throughout the nineteenth century was threatened temporarily by the serious depression of the 1870's. As Banks notes, the great depression brought "an atmosphere of uneasiness and insecurity into a world which had grown accustomed to thinking in terms of an ever-ascending march of Victorian progress and prosperity as an eternal, immutable law." [31] The economic depression thus brought into sharp focus the need for family size control to avoid reductions in living standards.

A third interrelated condition was the large-scale urban migration in England during the early stages of industrial development.[32] Although rural birth rates in England were substantially higher than urban birth rates between 1800 and 1880 and rural death rates were below urban death rates for the same period, the rural English population increased minimally while the urban population increased over ten-fold from 1800 to 1880. Thus, almost all of the natural increase resulting from the excess of births over deaths in rural England migrated outward toward the industrial areas. This pattern obviously contributed to the swelling of the unskilled urban proletariat; it also resulted in the fact that the rural English population did not face the pressure from high fertility. In contrast, for example, it has been argued that the lack of rapid industrialization in Sweden did not provide the necessary conditions for heavy rural-to-urban migration during the nineteenth century and, hence, compared to England rural birth rates in Sweden declined more rapidly, thereby affecting overall birth rates.[33]

In sum, the nature of English industrialization in the early stages was in no way incompatible with the retention of high fertility. The dispossessed farm population living in impoverished urban areas were able to retain their traditional family relations and sustain their general indifference to fertility control. Indeed, it might be argued that fertility in England remained high not *despite* early industrialization but rather *because* of it. Fertility began to decline only after industrialization improved the lot of the worker and segregated family roles outside the economic sphere. England's fertility history clearly indicates that industrialization does not result automatically in fertility control. Moreover, it suggests that at least in England, and perhaps elsewhere, three important prerequisites for family size reduction must be considered: (1)

[31] J. A. Banks, *Prosperity and Parenthood* (London: Routledge and Kegan Paul, 1954), p. 12.

[32] For this general idea and evidence, see Friedlander, "Demographic Responses and Population Change," pp. 360–362 and pp. 371–373. See also Dov Friedlander, "The Role of Migration in the Process of Demographic Change" (paper presented to the General Assembly, International Union for the Scientific Study of Population, London, 1969).

[33] Friedlander, "Demographic Responses and Population Change," pp. 375–377.

structural separation of family from economic roles; (2) increase in the living standard to some point where family size conflicts with rising aspirations, perhaps where a feeling of relative deprivation is engendered; and (3) the role of alternative responses — particularly out-migration — to demographic pressure in lieu of family size reduction.

The "Early" Decline in French Fertility

Fertility declines in France during the late eighteenth century were set into motion by changes in noneconomic social and cultural institutions.

The general decline in French fertility, a hundred years before a comparable trend may be discerned in England and the first such continuous national decline recorded in the modern era, was almost wholly a function of a fall in marital fertility. Although age at marriage was relatively high in France in the late eighteenth century as was the proportion never married, the pattern was not atypical of other Western European populations; nor were there any discernible shifts in these patterns upward or downward in late eighteenth- and early nineteenth-century France.[34] The probable mechanism for the early fertility reduction in France was *coitus interruptus*, a method used later in the nineteenth century throughout the rest of Europe and that may have been used as well during crises in preindustrial European communities. Also, abortion was probably more widespread in France than in England.[35] Whatever the "intermediate" mechanisms, fertility reduction in France was a result of factors influencing the decisions of married couples; the "rationalization" of fertility control in France at an earlier period in her demographic history makes France stand apart from other European countries. Moreover, family limitation in France during the late eighteenth and nineteenth centuries was widespread among populations whose lives had been changed very little, if at all, by the Industrial Revolution.

The reasons for the early decline in marital fertility in France are still far from clear. Nevertheless, social, economic, demographic, and cultural conditions in late eighteenth-century France show striking parallels to the mid-nineteenth-century English conditions. Specifically, let

[34] See Lorimer, *Culture and Human Fertility*, pp. 111–112; and Glass and Eversley (eds.), *Population in History*, chaps. 18 and 19.

[35] Wrigley, *Population and History*, pp. 124, 181; David Glass, "Population Growth and Population Policy," in *Public Health and Population Change*, ed. M. Sheps and J. C. Ridley (Pittsburgh: University of Pittsburgh Press, 1965), pp. 16–17, fn. 29.

us examine the pattern of family structure, distribution of economic changes, and the alternatives to fertility change in France in the late eighteenth and early nineteenth centuries as we did for nineteenth-century England.

The coincidence of the decline of fertility in France and the French Revolution is hardly fortuitous. Of particular significance was the tie of the French peasants to the land. Even before the French Revolution, half the arable land in France was owned by peasants, a condition unknown elsewhere in Europe,[36] which, in part, was the result of the common pre-Revolution practice of subdividing land equally among heirs rather than by primogeniture.[37] The Napoleonic *Code Civil* formally recognized joint heirship and legitimated its spread among the entire population. Hence, with the Revolution, an even larger number of peasants became landowners and the last vestiges of feudalism were replaced by the exceptional phenomenon within Europe, "peasant proprietorship." [38]

Some have argued that small proprietors in France had a powerful incentive to reduce family size to keep their landholdings intact and prevent the subdivision of their property among too many heirs.[39] Others have argued that property division promoted higher fertility through earlier and more universal marriages, and the single heir system (primogeniture) retarded population growth.[40] In general, children did not marry in Europe before establishing homes. Thus, the equal division of property might have enabled all the children to marry, whereas the single heir system condemned many to celibacy. Although the evidence is far from complete, and it is difficult to generalize, at least for France subdivision would have more likely led to reduced family size. The division of land resulted in reduced individual landholding; given the lack of outlets or desires for mobility off the land and the potential for reduced standards of living without family size reduction, powerful incentives for family size control would be operative. Moreover, apart from any inherent association between different types of inheritance patterns and fertility, it is likely that the promulgation of a uniform code of equal inheritance reflected growing changes in traditional family

[36] Alexis de Tocqueville, *The Old Regime and the French Revolution* (Garden City, N.Y.: Doubleday, 1955), p. 24.

[37] See Wesley Camp, *Marriage and Family in France since the Revolution* (New York: Bookman Associates, 1961), p. 117.

[38] A. M. Carr-Saunders, *World Population* (Oxford, Eng.: Clarendon Press, 1963), chap. 9.

[39] See, for example, the arguments by Le Play cited in Wrigley, *Population and History*, p. 190.

[40] See H. J. Habakuk, "Family Structure and Economic Change in Nineteenth-Century Europe," *Journal of Economic History*, 15 (1955), pp. 1–12.

structure.[41] The kinship-family relationships engendered by equal inheritance were different than those generated by primogeniture. Furthermore, the increased emphasis on equal division of family property in France must not be viewed in isolation from other social and cultural conditions leading to the Revolution. Indeed, inheritance patterns may be viewed as an *indication* of the general revolt against authority and dogma of all kinds. The spirit of individualism and rationalism permeating French society, resulting in the Revolution and progressing with it, may be reflected in the equality of relationships among inheritors, which may have "fit" in with the new social and economic aspirations among many peasants.

Such aspirations emerging from the challenge to traditional authority and from the emphasis on individual rights were complemented by important economic changes. In contrast to nineteenth-century England, wealth was not concentrated but disbursed more evenly throughout late eighteenth- and early nineteenth-century French society. The new aspirations were not limited to small segments of the population or to one class, and the opportunities for commerce and mechanical production stimulated small ventures that allowed for "a vigorous social mobility." [42] Although the increase in economic opportunities are important facilitating factors, such changes were in an "objective" sense gradual and modest. Economic growth gained more momentum in the nineteenth century and does not appear to have been more pronounced in eighteenth-century France than in other European countries so as to account for the earlier response in family size control.[43] It was exceptional that this economic growth coincided with the revolution in ideas, both of which were widespread rather than localized. For example, educational progress in France, although not accounting for the early reduction in fertility, probably was also less localized and less concentrated among the upper social classes than in England. Again, not the objective conditions of educational reforms but the spirit behind those reforms aroused the new aspirations for mobility. The spread of educational opportunities and the rising interest in child development may have, in turn, further restructured family relationships.[44]

These changes in aspirations are reflected in the demographic picture. Scattered evidence suggests that with the last great famine in France in the first decade of the eighteenth century, mortality levels, at

[41] See Lorimer, *Culture and Human Fertility,* p. 213. This inheritance pattern should of course be contrasted to the enclosure system in England and the consolidation of landholdings. See J. D. Chambers, "Three Essays on the Population and Economy of the Midlands," in *Population in History,* ed. Glass and Eversley.

[42] Lorimer, *Culture and Human Fertility,* p. 216.

[43] Ibid.

[44] Ibid., p. 213.

least toward the mid-1700's began to fall.[45] At a minimum, sharp fluctuations subsided. A more important demographic feature was the lack of rural-to-urban migration.[46] Both because of the slow industrialization in the cities and because of inheritance patterns, surplus population in rural areas was not released in large numbers to the cities. The rural masses had to choose between maintaining high fertility and reducing their living standards or reducing family size and maintaining or increasing their living standards. It was not surprising, given the spirit of the times, that fertility reduction was selected. The absence of heavy urban migration in France did not result in major impoverishment as in urban England, which might otherwise have militated against fertility control. Indeed, some evidence points to lower fertility in rural areas than in urban areas within France.[47] It is also likely that the practice of birth control within marriage documented for the French upper classes during the eighteenth century, and perhaps earlier, served as a model for the rural masses when the situation of conflict between standards of living and rising aspirations presented itself toward the end of the eighteenth century.[48]

In sum, it seems reasonable to argue that the early decline in fertility in France before major industrialization was not the result of legal changes in inheritance but rather of the *spirit* behind these legal changes; it was not the dramatic changes in economic growth but rather the *nature* of its distribution; it was not the objective demographic conditions of mortality reduction and geographic stability but the *implications* of these processes within the social and economic structure of French society. More than anything else the French Revolution symbolized and further enhanced a revolution in ideas and aspirations. It implied a challenge toward traditional authority — class and family — and emphasized rationalism and individualism. Combined with widespread opportunities and improvements in French agricultural society, rural peasant proprietors, forced in large part to remain on the land, were challenged to reduce family size or suffer a reduction in living standards. The precedent of controlling family size within marriage, set

[45] See Louis Henry, "The Population of France in the Eighteenth Century," in *Population in History*, ed. Glass and Eversley, p. 448.

[46] See Friedlander, "Demographic Responses and Population Change," p. 363; cf. Dudley Kirk, "Population and Population Trends in Modern France," in *Population Movements in Modern European History*, ed. H. Moller (New York: Macmillan, 1964); also Lorimer, *Culture and Human Fertility*, p. 215.

[47] See E. Wrigley, *Industrial Growth and Population Change* (Cambridge, Eng.: Cambridge University Press, 1961), p. 128; cf. J. D. Chambers, "Three Essays on the Population and Economy of the Midlands," in *Population in History*, ed. Glass and Eversley, p. 133.

[48] Henry, "The Population of France in the Eighteenth Century," p. 452.

both by upper class models and perhaps by their own prior experiences during crises periods, fit their new social, economic, and cultural situation better than either greater delayed marriage or increases in non-marriage.

The comparative-historical analysis of fertility patterns in England and France has been much condensed and oversimplified. Nevertheless, our brief review points to several important considerations that, in conjunction with our more general analysis, sharpen our understanding of the relationship between modernization and fertility. First, it is clear on both theoretical and empirical grounds, that fertility reduction does not result automatically and mechanically from the shift to industry from agriculture. It is likely that some forms of industrialization do not result in fertility declines. If the relationship between industrialization and fertility is mediated through social institutional and social structural changes, then it follows that such changes may be brought about by social processes not necessarily tied to industrial development. Thus, the second major point is that large-scale industrialization is not a necessary precondition for the fertility transition.[49] Combined, these two propositions — that industrialization does not in and of itself result in fertility declines and that industrialization is not a necessary prerequisite for reductions in fertility — direct our attention once again to changes in family-kinship structure, economic improvements, and cultural alterations, which are required for the fertility transition.

In general, the evolution of family size reduction and fertility control depends on whether the socioeconomic situation in which families find themselves is threatened by large family size *and* when there are no other more socially attractive responses to that situation. The pressures toward family size reduction are brought about directly through the breakup of kinship domination, improvements in standards of living, and rising aspirations for socioeconomic mobility. Some conditions — urbanization, industrial development, labor force participation of women, stabilization and reduction in mortality levels, education, among others — may bring about these institutional and structural changes, thereby generating pressures indirectly toward family size control. But they may not necessarily bring about these institutional changes. If urbanization reflects the relocation of kin groupings and does not disengage effectively kin control and power, if industrial development does not result in rising aspirations for mobility, if labor force participation of women does not provide alternative sources of prestige and status to women and does not result in releasing women from male or kinship domina-

---

[49] In slightly different form these propositions are discussed in Lorimer, *Culture and Human Fertility*, p. 217.

tion, if educational advances are focused on specialized socioeconomic groups and not dispersed more widely throughout all segments of the population, if mortality reduction is brought about through medical and technological diffusion without changes in living standards, then it is likely that these specific changes will not result in the necessary pressures engendering fertility reduction.

On the other hand, changes in family-kinship relationships, improvements in living standards, and aspirations for socioeconomic mobility may be generated by other specific changes. Effective rural land redistribution, emphasis on equal family rights and obligations, breakdown of traditional class, caste, and racial barriers to socioeconomic mobility, among others, are "functional equivalents" for the onset of structural and institutional changes resulting in fertility reduction.

Clearly, fertility declines can come about via a variety of mechanisms. Family size control is affected by marriage patterns, "mortality" practices — infanticide, abortion rates, as well as deliberate contraceptive measures. A functional equivalent to these overall mechanisms is migration, internal and external, which reduces local community population size and, through its possible effect on age structure, which may affect societal fertility rates. Hence, when socioeconomic pressures on family size through institutional and structural changes occur and movement out is either not feasible or inconsistent with socioeconomic conditions, then numerous alternative fertility control mechanisms may be selected to cope with these pressures.

FERTILITY VARIATION AND FLUCTUATION

Why were fertility rates *before* the secular decline lower in England and Wales than the biological maximum, and lower than comparable rates in late eighteenth- and nineteenth-century America and Eastern Europe, and some Asian, African, and Latin American countries in the mid-twentieth century? In England and Wales, indeed throughout Western Europe, a "unique" pattern developed: late age at marriage and relatively high rates of celibacy.[50] Hajnal argues that such a European marriage pattern existed in Western Europe at least two centuries prior to World War II, and obviously affected the size of individual families by reducing the quantity of exposure to reproduction and, in turn, the overall fertility rates of societies. When the pattern emerged is not known precisely, nor are the reasons for its specific emergence in Western Europe clear. It may have developed from the property system

[50] J. Hajnal, "European Marriage Patterns in Perspective," in *Population in History*, ed. Glass and Eversley, pp. 101–143.

associated with primogeniture, and may be related to general norms associated with requirements of land ownership or other visible means of family support as a prerequisite for marriage. The nature of kinship structure and organization appears critical for age patterns at marriage. Some have hypothesized that the complex of ideas on sex and marriage and their communication were significantly different in Western and Eastern Europe and, combined with other nonideological factors, help to explain the emergence of the Western marriage-family pattern.[51] Others have noted the importance of laws restricting marriage to protect communities against the growth of the population on relief or charity.[52] Still others have tied changing marriage patterns to economic fluctuations and constraints.[53] Although the origin of this unique pattern is open to speculation, the importance of fertility variations and fluctuations *before* the secular decline in fertility is indisputable.

This secular decline has been shown to result from social change in the behavior of millions of couples responding to alterations in social structural conditions. The general modernization of societies, and its implications for the transformation of social institutions or subsystems — family, economic, cultural, demographic, has involved as an integral change declines in family size and the "rationalization" of fertility behavior. In a general way, high fertility "fits" the fabric of societal organization under premodern conditions, whereas low fertility fits the social conditions of modern societies. Nevertheless, it is more accurate empirically to postulate *that in premodern societies fertility fluctuates around high levels and that in modern societies fertility fluctuates around low levels.*

At first glance it may appear that emphasizing "fluctuation" in the fertility patterns of societies is not very important. Perhaps the fluctuations in fertility are related to particularistic norms about the appropriate mechanisms that control fertility which developed within some societies for reasons that have little to do with conscious or rational fertility control. Hence, fluctuations and variations in fertility may have little or no theoretical importance, and analyzing them may undermine the significance of overall fertility declines. By ignoring variations in fertility under preindustrial conditions — variations over time, between and within countries — analysis can focus on the "break" in fertility patterns that modernization brings.

[51] On the role of kinship institutions, see Davis and Blake, "Social Structure and Fertility," pp. 215–218; on ideological factors, see John T. Noonan, Jr., "Intellectual and Demographic History," *Daedalus,* 97 (Spring 1968), pp. 479–482.

[52] See John Knodel, "Law, Marriage and Illegitimacy in Nineteenth-Century Germany," *Population Studies,* 20 (March 1967), pp. 279–294.

[53] Etienne Van De Walle, "Marriage and Marital Fertility," *Daedalus,* 97 (Spring 1968), pp. 486–501.

This view does injustice to the empirical facts and often results in an incomplete, perhaps misguided, theoretical analysis. It may also lead to types of fertility policy considerations that are misdirected.[54] On closer inspection, variation and fluctuation in fertility within premodern and modern societies must be considered indispensable to understanding the complexities of overall fertility analysis. Any general theory of fertility changes during modernization must account for fluctuations in fertility "before" its secular decline and "after" its transition, in addition to explaining the overall trends.

Premodern Fertility Fluctuations

The historical reconstruction of a small English parish, Colyton,[55] provides data on family size, age at marriage, and life expectancy at birth from 1560 to 1837. During this period, as might be expected from our previous analysis, overall fertility was high (in terms of both average family size and age specific marital fertility rates), as was mortality; age at first marriage was rather late for both men and women (but not out of line with the Western European model). But far more interesting are the striking fluctuations over time. During these three centuries, family size varied by over two children, age at first marriage among women fluctuated by over five years, and life expectancy at birth ranged from thirty-seven to forty-three years. These fluctuations are in no way "minor." A close inspection of the evidence suggests that from 1560 to 1646 marital fertility was high, with many families of six or more children. Indeed, among women who married before age thirty and survived through the reproductive period, a majority had six or more children. However, from 1647 to 1769 average family size dropped to between 4.2 and 4.4 children and only about 20 per cent of the families had six or more children. During this period, indirect evidence points to the practice of some form of family limitation within marriage. Comparing the period 1720–1769 with the period 1560–1646, the average age at first marriage for men and women was identical; average family size declined from 6.4 during the earlier period to 4.4. From about 1770 to 1837 family size readjusted to an average of six children.

A second point in the Colyton evidence is both the overall late age at marriage and its fluctuation over time during this period. Until the middle of the seventeenth century men and women married at an average age of twenty-seven years, obviously after a considerable amount of the

[54] See pp. 175–181, this book.
[55] This analysis is based on data presented in Wrigley, *Population and History*, tables 3–5 and 3–6, pp. 87–91.

potential reproductive span had elapsed. During the period when marital fertility fell, age at marriage rose among women to age thirty, and subsequently declined to age twenty-five in the period 1770–1837. Hence, whatever happened in Colyton to put the "squeeze" on its population between 1647 and 1769, it seems evident that the response or adjustment was later marriage and greater fertility control within marriage.

A final point, and perhaps not the least significant, is the relationship between these fertility and marriage fluctuations and changes in mortality. During the approximate time that fertility was falling, mortality levels had increased. Both fertility and mortality returned to their sixteenth-century levels before the end of the eighteenth century. The nature of the connection between fertility and mortality is not clear. Although fertility remained relatively steady between 1647 and 1769, mortality levels declined between the 1625–1699 and 1700–1774 periods. The fluctuations in both demographic processes, however, can hardly be considered fortuitous.

Another way of reviewing fluctuation and variation in preindustrial fertility is comparing fertility differences within countries *before* the onset of a secular decline. Data on rural-urban fertility differences in Sweden and England *before* noticeable secular fertility trends are instructive.[56] In Sweden, overall fertility began an uninterrupted decline up to the modern period from around 1850. However, in the century preceding any decrease in fertility — or any decrease in urban or rural fertility — crude birth rates were consistently higher in rural areas than in urban areas. In 1750, the crude birth rate in rural Sweden was 36 per 1,000, around 10 per cent higher than urban birth rates. The patterns for England show even greater urban-rural fertility discrepancies. In 1800, England had urban birth rates of 31 per 1,000, and rural rates of 40 per 1,000. Between 1800 and 1870, before any recognizable trend toward reduced fertility, rural fertility remained steady at around 40 per 1,000, although urban birth rates went below 30 per 1,000 between 1830 and 1850, increasing to 32–33 per 1,000 between 1860 and 1870. Clearly, one cannot view the higher levels of rural fertility as any "lag."

Crude birth rates do not allow any inference about the possible role of fertility control *within* marriage. Some evidence available on marital fertility in Sweden in rural and urban areas before the decline in fertility is revealing.[57] Data on marital fertility differentials and trends point unmistakably to significant rural-urban differentials in marital fertility before the secular decline and suggest an overall similarity in

[56] See data presented in Friedlander, "Demographic Responses and Population Change," tables 4 and 5, pp. 372–374.
[57] See data and discussion in Gösta Carlsson, "The Decline of Fertility: Innovation or Adjustment Process," *Population Studies,* 20 (November 1966), pp. 149–174.

the timing of the onset of fertility declines in Stockholm, other urban areas, and rural areas. Although fertility began to fall in these areas at about the same time, the fertility differential by area was retained and somewhat widened as the *pace* of change was quicker in Stockholm. The Swedish evidence on marital fertility thus points strongly to the possibility of fertility control within marriage in urban Stockholm before the decline in fertility throughout Sweden began, and to the fact that the subsequent decline in fertility in all areas began about the same time. Hence, differences between areas reflect differences in the initial level of fertility and are less reflective of differences in the time of the onset of fertility declines. A similar process may be located in Germany, England, the United States, Japan, and Spain.[58]

A third piece of evidence relates to the comparative levels of fertility among "preindustrial" nations. Although all these nations share relatively high levels of fertility, it does not follow that all preindustrial nations had similar fertility levels. Nor does it follow that fertility (actual reproductive behavior) and fecundity (potential reproductive capacity) converged among preindustrial populations. On the contrary: a substantial body of evidence points conclusively to fertility levels significantly below biological reproductive capacity and to important variations in fertility levels.[59] For example, crude birth rates for the white population of the United States between 1800 and 1850 has been estimated at between 50 and 55 per 1,000,[60] substantially higher than for Western European countries in the eighteenth and nineteenth centuries, which in turn show lower birth rates than Eastern European countries. (Indeed, the high 1800–1850 birth rates estimated for the United States population are higher than rates in most countries that are currently nonindustrialized.)

All populations prior to any systematic or continuous fall in fertility, i.e., all premodern nations, exhibit lower fertility than fecundity, and

---

[58] On England and Germany, see ibid., p. 153; on the United States, see Wilson Grabill et al., *The Fertility of American Women* (New York: Wiley, 1958), pp. 15–19; on Japan, see Irene Taeuber, *The Population of Japan* (Princeton: Princeton University Press, 1958), p. 244; Irene Taeuber, "Continuities in the Declining Fertility of the Japanese," *Milbank Memorial Fund Quarterly*, 38 (July 1960), pp. 264–283; on Spain, see Massimo Livi Bacci, "Fertility and Nuptuality Changes in Spain from Late 18th to the Early 20th Century: Part I," *Population Studies*, 22 (March 1968), pp. 83–102. The same may also be true of fertility variation within currently underdeveloped areas, i.e., fertility differentials may not be indicators of a "transitional" stage or represent a fertility "lag" but may be longstanding adjustments. See Frederick Shorter, "Information on Fertility, Mortality, and Population Growth in Turkey," *Population Index*, 34 (January–March 1968), p. 14.

[59] See Freedman, "The Sociology of Human Fertility, pp. 48–53.

[60] Y. Yasuba, *Birth Rate of the White Population in the United States, 1800–1860* (Baltimore: Johns Hopkins University Press, 1962), pp. 96–100.

their birth rates fluctuate over time and differ from nation to nation. In large part, these patterns reflect differences in age at marriage, propensity to marry, population structure (age and sex composition), and frequency of sterility and pregnancy wastage engendered by general conditions of morbidity. In addition, there is some reason to postulate differential utilization of contraception within marriage, or differential deliberate family size control, *among* preindustrial populations as well as variation over time *within* preindustrial populations.[61]

What do these bits of evidence on the fluctuations and variations in preindustrial fertility suggest about the relationship between modernization and fertility? In general terms, the evidence points to greater historical continuity in fertility patterns than is sometimes portrayed. The control and rationalization of fertility that was the overall result of modernization processes did not represent a *complete* break from the premodern period. The decline in fertility must be viewed less in terms of something new and unprecedented and more in terms of general response and adjustment to social conditions generated by modernization. In this sense, fertility reduction is an adjustment process rather than innovative, and it is fruitful to describe modern demographic history in terms of "change and response." [62]

More specifically, the decline in fertility has often been viewed, explicitly or implicitly, as a result of the spreading knowledge and utilization of birth control. Birth control, particularly within marriage, is accordingly considered to be a new and recent innovation, especially in its widespread usage. Moreover, because the *spread* of contraceptive knowledge is stressed, it follows that there is a "trickle-down" effect from urban to rural areas, from upper to lower classes, and from industrial to agricultural populations. The evidence, admittedly weak but nevertheless substantial, suggests that such a view does not fit in with all the facts. The information is rather persuasive that at various times, and in different populations, fertility control within and outside of marriage existed before any secular decline in fertility and that differentials may not be signs of a "lag" but rather of long-standing responses to differential social and economic conditions. It thus seems theoretically and empirically more accurate to posit that the decline in fertility represents an adjustment to a new set of social, demographic, and economic forces. The secular decline does not so much represent the final phase in which fertility control was not practiced, but rather should be regarded as

----

[61] On this point, see, E. A. Wrigley, "Family Limitation in Pre-Industrial England," *Economic History Review*, 2nd ser., 19:1 (1966), pp. 104–105.

[62] This is essentially one of the overall themes of Carlsson, "The Decline of Fertility: Innovation or Adjustment Process," and Davis, "The Theory of Change and Response in Modern Demographic History."

reflecting a shift in the fertility targets of controlling parents. Nor was fertility control within marriage the only possible or the only actual response to these new ideals. During social institutional and structural changes, persons caught in the "squeeze" of demographic pressure from falling or steady mortality on one hand, and from the conflict between rising living standards and mobility aspirations on the other, responded in many different ways to reduce fertility. Thus, the responses generated by these broad changes were "multiphasic." The new ideals of controlled fertility are neither absolutely new or an innovation of modernization; however, these new ideals of fertility are more strongly held and more consistently practiced in modern society.[63]

Furthermore, two processes by which modernization results in lowered fertility levels are distinct.[64] First, modernization implies shifting people into social categories that have long been associated with lower fertility. For example, the moves from rural to urban areas, from farmer to laborer categories, and from lower to middle class, all associated with modernization processes, redistribute a population into categories that are characteristically prone to lower fertility. Not, of course, that there is any magic in the recomposition of populations. Rather, the argument suggests that in modernization processes, rural, lower-class farmers retain high fertility and urban, middle-class workers retain lower fertility. As persons are redistributed into new roles, identified by social categories, they accept or adopt the family size goals of these new roles. In short, fertility transition is a product of the new socio-economic and residential composition of society engendered by modernization.

A second approach suggests that development and modernization affect all social groups in terms of redefining and reevaluating responses and adjustments. Thus, all groups participate in the onset of fertility declines — although perhaps starting at different initial levels and proceeding at different paces.

Most weight in demographic literature is placed on the former approach, at least with respect to the onset or initial stages of the fertility transition. In the long run, both processes are at work. However, some evidence suggests that both processes are operative in the initial stages as well, and it is likely that the second alternative — that all groups respond to new societal changes — should be emphasized. The rural-urban evidence from England and Sweden has been reviewed. In addition, in Japan, fertility declined in all groups and in the long run was reduced further by the altered residence and socioeconomic structures following

[63] Carlsson, "The Decline of Fertility," p. 172.
[64] See the discussion in Friedlander, "Demographic Responses and Population Change," pp. 359–365.

industrialization and modernization.[65] Data on family size by marriage cohorts and socioeconomic groups in Great Britain suggest a similar pattern. Sharp socioeconomic differentials in family size may be observed among those marrying in the late nineteenth century, but within each socioeconomic category family size becomes smaller in a consistent pattern over time. In the 1890–1899 marriage cohort, laborers had an average family size of five children; at the other end of the scale professionals had an average family size of less than three children. Although both socioeconomic categories retained their "extreme" family size position through the 1925 marriage cohort, family size had declined among laborers to three children and among professionals to 1.7 children.[66]

If fertility levels in any society represent an adjustment mechanism to broad societal conditions, then fertility patterns cannot be thought of as "fully" controlled or uncontrolled. There is no ending or starting point but a continuous adjustment to social conditions. High fertility in general was an adjustment to the societal conditions of preindustrial populations, just as generally low fertility is an adjustment to changed and different societal conditions in the modern world.

Fertility Fluctuation
in the Modern Phase

In the overview of the fertility decline, data for England and Wales from the 1800's to around 1940 were summarized. The choice of the nineteenth century should now be clear; the end point of the continuous fertility decline, 1940, needs some clarification. Although both period and cohort measures reveal consistent fertility declines up to around 1940, such is not the case since then. In particular, changes and fluctuations in period fertility measures may not necessarily reflect family size changes as much as fluctuations in family formation and child spacing.

By the 1936–1940 period crude birth rates in England and Wales had fallen to less than 15 per 1,000, the general fertility rate stood at 61 per 1,000 women 15 to 44 years old and the marital fertility rate was at 107 per 1,000 married women in the reproductive ages.[67] All three period measures showed similar patterns and approximate equivalent proportional declines from the 1870's. However, during the war years (1941 to 1945) crude birth rates and general fertility rates increased although marital fertility continued to fall. All three measures show an

[65] Taeuber, *The Population of Japan*, p. 270.
[66] Data from Wrigley, *Population and History*, pp. 186–187, table 5–13.
[67] Data for England and Wales were adapted from Wrigley, *Population and History*, tables 5–15 and 5–17.

increase in the immediate postwar era (1946–1950), a decline (1951–1955), and an increase again during the early 1960's. If we turn to marriage cohorts we discover that the long-term, uninterrupted fall in *family size*, observed from the 1861–1869 cohort, reached its lowest point among those marrying in the 1935–1939 period. *Estimates* for subsequent marriage cohorts (some of which have not completed childbearing, and thus require some assumptions and guesswork) indicate a continuous rise in average family size. The 1955–1959 marriage cohort is estimated to have a completed family size of 2.6, larger than any marriage cohort after 1915–1919 (which had an average family size of 2.46). This pattern in general characterized most Western European as well as North American countries at least with respect to the "baby boom" following World War II.[68] Crude birth rates increased in Canada and the United States from the 1940–1944 period through 1959; in Canada from 23 per 1,000 (1940–1944) to 28 per 1,000 (1955–1959) and in the United States from 20 per 1,000 (1940–1944) to 25 per 1,000 (1955–1959). However, from 1960 through 1967, Canada and the United States have experienced a continuous fall in their crude birth rates, from 27 per 1,000 in 1960 to less than 19 per 1,000 in 1967 in Canada, and from 24 per 1,000 to less than 18 per 1,000 during the same eight-year period in the United States.[69] Although birth-rate fluctuations after the "baby boom" have been in different directions among industrialized nations, absolute levels of fertility appear to converge among these countries.

These illustrations of post-World War II fluctuations in the fertility patterns of "industrialized" countries require some analytic comment. In particular, are fluctuations in aggregate fertility levels based on cross-sectional indicators reflective of "real" fluctuations in cohort family size? Second, what significance do these fluctuations have for our general analysis of fertility decline? In short, what are the implications of these patterns for understanding fertility in the modern era?[70]

It must be clear from the outset that the birth rate is *crude*. It may be, and empirically has been, "distorted" by changes in the age distribu-

[68] See D. V. Glass, "Fertility Trends in Europe since the Second World War," *Population Studies*, 22 (March 1968), pp. 103–146.

[69] See, for example, Wrigley, *Population and History*, table 6–12; Norman Ryder, "The Time Series of Fertility in the United States" (paper presented to the International Union for the Scientific Study of Population, London, 1969); J. Henripin, "Evolution de la Fecondite au Canada Depuis la Derniere Guerre Mondiale" (paper presented to the International Union for the Scientific Study of Population, London, 1969).

[70] Several significant demographic questions are excluded here, particularly those which focus exclusively on the formal demographic mechanisms connecting period and cohort measures and which attempt to disentangle period fertility measures from the effects of population structure or from the influence of intermediate variables.

tion of populations and changing patterns of family formation. For example, the crude birth rate during the 1930's in the United States was around 18 per 1,000. But a favorable age distribution inherited from previous fertility schedules "saved" the crude birth rate from even lower rates. Had the age distribution of the 1960's in the United States prevailed during the 1930's, crude birth rates would have been as low as 14 per 1,000. Similarly, the results of fertility performance during the 1930's distorted age distributions during the 1950's, so much so that, had the age distribution of the 1930's prevailed during the 1950's, crude birth rates would have been 32 per 1,000 rather than 25 per 1,000. Thus, given fluctuations in age distributions, the crude birth rate may be distorted one way or the other.[71]

In a similar way, crude birth rates are affected by marital distributions. *In part,* fluctuations in the crude birth rates in England and Wales from the 1930's to the 1960's reflect important changes in age at marriage and the proportion marrying. Between 1931 and 1963, for example, the proportion ever married increased, while age at marriage decreased. The proportion of women never married by ages 45 to 49 in 1931 was 17 per cent compared to 9 per cent in 1963. More significant were changes in the proportion married at younger ages. In 1963, 32 per cent of the males and 59 per cent of the females 20 to 24 years old were married in England and Wales compared to 14 per cent and 26 per cent, respectively in 1931. Among those aged 25 to 29 in 1963, 72 per cent of the males and 86 per cent of the females were married while the respective proportions in 1931 were 53 and 59 per cent.[72]

Of course, some period measures of fertility "control" for age and marital status. However, these measures may be affected by changes in the tempo of fertility, including the onset of childbearing and the spacing between children, as well as changes in average family size and the parity components of that average.

In the United States as well as in Europe, a significant part of the period fertility fluctuations reflect changes in the tempo of family building. Cohorts of women during the depression and war years postponed the onset of childbearing and spaced their children for longer birth intervals than postwar cohorts. Moreover, the postwar rise in American fertility was not in any way a return to the large family patterns of the early twentieth century. Real (cohort) changes in average family size in large part reflect an extraordinary increase in the number of women with

[71] These and other issues are reviewed in Ryder, "The Time Series of Fertility in the United States."

[72] Glass, "Fertility Trends in Europe since the Second World War," p. 806, table 3. On age at marriage in England and Wales, 1911–1964, see Wrigley, *Population and History,* table 6–10.

at least a second birth (55 per cent in the 1930's compared to 85 per cent in the 1960's) concomitant with a reduction in the proportion of women with four or more births. As Ryder notes, "the postwar reproductive renaissance has been predominantly an extension of the small-family franchise to embrace practically all women capable of having two children." [73] In short, although the *average* family size has increased slightly among post-World War II cohorts, the components of that "average" point to decreasing childless and one-child families as well as decreases in the larger family of four or more children. Although recent cohorts of women have yet to complete their childbearing, it is likely that the large family syndrome belongs to a past era and not to the modern period. European data on changing parity distributions within marriage point to identical conclusions.[74]

The implications of these fertility fluctuations in the modern era are clear. Period fertility rates can often be poor indications of cohort changes. The interpretation of period fertility fluctuations in terms of changing "fads and fashions" of family size ideals and reproductive behavior is absurd methodologically, empirically, and theoretically.[75] It is more reasonable and accurate to postulate that, under conditions of effective fertility control, fluctuations in the timing of marriage, the onset of childbearing, and the spacing between children are to be expected. Hence, variation in period fertility rates around low levels is the modern parallel to preindustrial fertility fluctuations and variations around high levels. But the variation in average family size among modern populations will be considerably less than fluctuations in period fertility. The conditions of the modern era conspire against any return to the large family. Whereas the quantity and tempo of cohort fertility are contingent on social, economic, and political forces, which themselves are not predictable in a precise way, the range of variation in fertility is much narrower.

However, fertility control in the modern era implies more than the *prevalence* of direct family size limitation; it connotes the *effectiveness* of control as well. A growing body of evidence in the United States and Europe indicates inefficiencies in the control of birth spacing and planning but to a much lesser extent in the control of ultimate family size. Thus, the extension of efficient contraceptive technology may result in a closer "fit" between family size desires and actual reproductive behavior. It may also place greater control over spacing, the tempo of childbear-

---

[73] Ryder, "The Time Series of Fertility in the United States," p. 3.
[74] See Glass, "Fertility Trends in Europe since the Second World War."
[75] On this point, see Ryder, "The Time Series of Fertility in the United States"; Judith Blake, "Family Size in the 1960's — A Baffling Fad?" *Eugenics Quarterly*, 14 (March 1967), pp. 60–74.

ing, in the power of individual couples. Whether family size desires are closer to two or to three children is difficult to determine directly. But we can expect that the number of "accidental" pregnancies will be reduced with the development and utilization of more efficient contraception. As long as the socioeconomic conditions of the modern era result in small family size desires, there is no reason to suspect large fluctuations in actual family size. On the other hand, the tempo of childbearing will become increasingly sensitive to short-run changes in socioeconomic conditions.

The focus of fertility research will probably become more directed to the demographic analysis of fluctuation in period fertility rates, to the sociodemographic analysis of family formation and the tempo of childbearing, and to the patterns of fertility differentials among subgroupings within society. Perhaps the major research in fertility will focus on the nonmodern countries whose preindustrial fertility levels, combined with "postindustrial" mortality, generate severe social, economic, political, and demographic problems.

FERTILITY PATTERNS AND PROSPECTS IN UNDERDEVELOPED NATIONS

In sharp contrast to post-World War II mortality changes in underdeveloped areas, fertility patterns in most of Africa, Latin America, and Asia have exhibited no discernible shift toward lower levels. Indeed, sustained high fertility, combined with relatively low or falling mortality and no significant international migrations, has resulted in population growth in underdeveloped nations and its associated social, economic, and political problems. Fertility levels in many underdeveloped countries in the 1960's and 1970's parallel preindustrial European patterns; the near universality of marriage and the early ages at marriage in most currently underdeveloped nations raise fertility to levels higher than eighteenth- or nineteenth-century Western Europe. A brief overview of fertility patterns around the world in the 1960's is instructive.[76]

For Africa as a whole in the late 1960's, crude birth rates have been estimated at 46 per 1,000; for Asia, 38 per 1,000; for Latin America, 39 per 1,000; for Europe, the Soviet Union, Japan, North America, and Oceania, crude birth rates fluctuate around 18 per 1,000. To be sure, variation in fertility levels may be observed within these heterogeneous continents. Nevertheless, the overall remarkable fact is that, exclusive of Japan and Argentina, the fertility rates among the larger countries of

[76] Data presented here have been abstracted from Population Reference Bureau, *1969 World Population Data Sheet* (April 1969). The original source for most, but not all the data, is United Nations, *Demographic Yearbook*, 1967.

Asia, Africa, and Latin America fluctuate around high levels. Within Africa, covering about 10 per cent of the world's total population, no country of 5 million persons or more has a crude birth rate below 40 per 1,000. Turkey, Iraq, India, Iran, Pakistan, Burma, Indonesia, the Philippines, Thailand, and South Korea with a combined total population of just under *1 billion* persons, have crude birth rates ranging between 52 per 1,000 (Pakistan) and only as low as 41 per 1,000 (South Korea). Similarly, eighteen out of twenty-five Latin American countries, representing over 80 per cent of the total Latin American population, have crude birth rates starting at 38 per 1,000 all the way up to 50 per 1,000. The major large country omitted from these underdeveloped areas is China, where elementary demographic information is not available. With a probable population of 800 million (plus or minus 100 million), representing one-fifth to one-fourth of the world's total, crude birth rates are probably close to double that of the major industrialized countries.

Not only has fertility remained fairly steady, with few concrete behavioral signs of decline, some evidence suggests significant, although perhaps short-run, increases in fertility levels among underdeveloped nations. In several Latin American countries age-standardized birth rates increased over 10 per cent from 1940 to 1959.[77] Ironically, these fertility increases probably reflect the improved morbidity and mortality conditions in Latin America. Upward trends in fertility following declining mortality have also been noted for British Guiana, Jamaica, Trinidad, and Tobago, among others.[78] An interesting case of this pattern is Mauritius. Crude birth rates before 1947 were relatively high and fluctuated between 30 and 40 per 1,000. We have noted in Chapter 5 the dramatic increase in life expectancy following malaria control and improvements in public health facilities within Mauritius. At the same time the death rate plummeted downward, fertility increased, so that by 1952 crude birth rates had reached 50 per 1,000. This fertility increase was so large that improvements in birth registration procedures cannot be the sole or major factor involved.[79]

[77] See, for example, O. A. Collver, *Birth Rates in Latin America* (California: International Population and Urban Research, 1965), pp. 27–28. Also, J. R. Rele, *Fertility Analysis through Extension of Stable Population Concepts,* Institute of International Studies, Population Monograph Series no. 2 (Berkeley: University of California, 1967).

[78] United Nations, Population Bulletin no. 7 (1963), p. 6; see also J. M. Stycos, *Human Fertility in Latin America: Sociological Perspectives* (Ithaca, N.Y.: Cornell University Press, 1968), chap. 14; J. M. Stycos and K. Back, *The Control of Human Fertility in Jamaica* (Ithaca, N.Y.: Cornell University Press, 1964); Judith Blake, *Family Structure in Jamaica* (New York: The Free Press, 1961).

[79] Cited in P. O. Olusanya, "Modernisation and the Level of Fertility in Western Nigeria" (paper presented to the General Assembly, International Union for the Scientific Study of Population, London, 1969).

Fertility increase following mortality reduction or stabilization is not peculiar to contemporary underdeveloped nations. Historical evidence points convincingly in the same direction for numerous industrialized nations. Improvements in mortality may affect fertility directly through its relationship to improved health conditions for mothers and young children, and through reductions in subfecundity and infertility. In some countries, the reduction in mortality may affect marriage patterns and thereby relate to fertility indirectly.[80]

The evidence from crude birth rates in developing countries, as well as from more refined fertility measures, indicates sustained high or increased fertility levels in most of the underdeveloped world. The question confronting social scientists, as well as shapers and makers of social, economic, political, and population policies, is, What are the prospects for fertility reduction? No one really knows. "Prophecy" is a dangerous business as the demographic Isaiahs of the 1930's, who predicted an incipient fertility decline for industrialized nations in the 1940's, will most readily admit. Nevertheless, we may identify some general principles that flow from the relationship between modernization and fertility. These principles are neither specific guidelines for policy nor immutable laws of population processes. They are best viewed as background information about the general conditions affecting fertility changes. We should be able to identify the nature of fertility changes that may occur and eliminate those that probably will not occur.

The Role of the Polity

In our considerations of the various social institutions and subsystems of society that shaped the pattern of fertility decline in the modernization process, one outstanding omission was the role of political institutions. In a general way, fertility reductions in currently industrialized nations have taken place, with some notable exceptions, without the conscious, direct, and formal interference of the polity. The influence of the polity on fertility has usually been inseparable from the general social and economic revolutions. Political changes have often been underlying facilitating or impeding forces behind social and economic changes and have thus affected fertility indirectly. Most influences of the polity have been manifest in one of the following forms. First, government legislation has influenced the legality of various means of fertility control. Laws about minimum ages at marriage, mechanical and chemical contraception, and abortions have been passed in various forms

[80] See the review and citations in Freedman, "The Sociology of Human Fertility," p. 54.

in many industrialized countries. This legislation has resulted in shaping the particular mechanisms used to control fertility, maximizing or minimizing the range of individual choices. Second, governments have influenced fertility directly and indirectly through monetary incentives. Several countries have family allowance schemes tied to family size, or tax structures tied to marital status and the number of dependents. Most of these policies are directed to social welfare programs, although they may tend to reinforce or encourage larger family size. Some European welfare policies were developed when fertility levels were low following the economic depression of the 1930's and were consciously pronatalist in form. A final overlapping category of political influence includes those policies directed to social and economic goals with directly or indirectly, population goals as a secondary objective. These policies include legislation dealing with mortality and migration control along with more general social and economic programs.

Clearly, in almost all industrialized countries the polity was neither responsible for the onset nor the thrust of fertility decline. Generally, awareness of the need for a "fertility" policy came about when fertility was so low that governments felt the need to stimulate its recovery. Until recently most direct fertility programs, therefore, were pronatalist. But beginning after World War II and increasingly during the 1960's, many underdeveloped countries have taken into account population factors as important parts of their programs for socioeconomic development. The development of formal "family planning" programs, or at a minimum official government recognition of the role of population processes in socioeconomic development, adds a new dimension to prospects for fertility reduction. It is not our task to evaluate the efficiency or inefficiency of current programs,[81] but any forecast of the future fertility of underdeveloped areas must reckon with this development. Nevertheless, two points about the role of the polity in fertility reduction must be clear. First, recognizing the importance of reduced fertility for socioeconomic development does not necessarily lead individual couples to control their family size. Secondly, whatever role the polity may play reducing fertility levels, it must do so by altering the socioeconomic levels and aspirations of persons so that large family size will be viewed as antithetical to improvements in sociopersonal goals. Hence, an effective

---

[81] For critical reviews, see Kingsley Davis, "Population Policy: Will Current Programs Succeed?" *Science*, 158 (November 10, 1967), pp. 730–739; Judith Blake, "Demographic Science and the Redirection of Population Policy," in *Public Health and Population Change*, ed. Sheps and Ridley, pp. 41–69; for an overall view of family planning programs, see Bernard Berelson, "National Family Planning Programs: Where We Stand," in *Fertility and Family Planning: A World View*, ed. S. J. Behrman et al.; B. Berelson, "Beyond Family Planning," *Studies in Family Planning*, 38 (February 1969), pp. 1–16.

population policy must be integral to effective social and economic policies. Although the polity may facilitate more rapid fertility reduction and may set into motion general social changes to inaugurate fertility declines, it must do so by social institutional changes. Political institutions are best viewed as facilitating or impeding units in the shaping of socioeconomic changes that directly affect fertility. Of course, this does not refer to dictatorial or totalitarian regimes that may, and have, affected fertility, positively and negatively, through military and other political pressures. Governments may "force" fertility downward through "compulsory" sterilization, abortion, infanticide, and celibacy. We are not concerned in this section with such programs but rather with the ways in which governments can affect the fertility attitudes and behavior of couples through specific population programs or through general socioeconomic and familial reorganization.

Technological Progress

The progress made in efficient contraceptive technology raises two usual arguments: The first draws an analogy between current high fertility levels in underdeveloped countries with the pre-World War II high mortality in the same areas. In extreme form the mortality analogy posits that just as mortality levels were reduced by importing Western public health and medical technology, so fertility will be reduced swiftly with the development of efficient, safe, and acceptable contraceptive technological breakthroughs. Fertility reduction therefore depends on how fast the "cure" (efficient contraceptives) can be developed and distributed to eliminate the "cancer" of high fertility. Bogue argues that "the plague of high fertility is no more insuperable than was malaria or other infectious diseases that now are all but forgotten. The timetable for the eradication of runaway population growth is about the same as for the conquest of these other diseases." [82]

The analogy between fertility and mortality is false and misleading. Fertility is not a disease nor is contraceptive technology a cure. Fertility represents an adjustment to socioeconomic conditions and kinship organization that cannot be sprayed away or inoculated against. The normative structure surrounding fertility suggests unmistakably that unless couples are motivated to desire smaller families, all the contraceptive "cures" will be social and technological quackery. The evidence on the

---

[82] Donald Bogue, *Principles of Demography* (New York: Wiley, 1969), p. 827; for an analogy between fertility control through contraceptive technology and tuberculosis control through drugs and vaccines, see Nusret H. Fisek, "Problems in Starting a Program," in *Family Planning and Population Programs,* ed. B. Berelson et al. (Chicago: University of Chicago Press, 1966), p. 304.

lower family size desires in many diverse underdeveloped areas is not fully convincing. It is likely that to the majority of women in these areas questions on family size desires have little or no meaning. Responding in terms of a specific number of children rather than "God's will" or "fate" may indicate nothing more than wishful thinking or second-guessing.[83] However, to the extent that significant sectors in underdeveloped areas are already searching for means to attain newly acquired family size goals, the distribution of efficient contraceptives will speed fertility reduction.

The second technological analogy is based on a false premise. It is often posited that the birth rate decline in European countries was the direct result of the development of modern technological methods of contraception. Hence, it would follow that "technology" is the answer to high fertility in underdeveloped countries. Notestein and others have argued after reviewing the decline in fertility in industrialized nations:

> A good case can, therefore, be made for the view that the invention of better birth control methods was a critical factor in the onset of the fertility decline . . . it has been fully demonstrated . . . that the major factor in the reduction of birth rates was the rapid spread and growing effectiveness of contraceptive practice, together with some increase in abortion.[84]

But it is clear that technology was one of the *means* of fertility reduction but not its *cause*. As we argued earlier, the decline in fertility represented less a break from the past in response to new technology than it was a readjustment of millions of couples to new socioeconomic and family pressures. Technological development of efficient contraceptive materials may facilitate a greater "fit" between fertility behavior and fertility desires but probably will not affect those desires directly. In underdeveloped areas, technology can only help those who are motivated already to reduce their family size.

Simplistic analogies with mortality declines and misplaced emphasis on technological factors fail to reckon with the social nature and complexities of fertility processes. Fertility operates within a social institutional context, and unless that context is changed major alterations in

[83] Berelson reviews family planning programs in "National Family Planning Programs: Where We Stand"; cf. Stycos, *Human Fertility in Latin America,* chap. 10; on the general neglect of the motivation element in family planning programs, see Davis, "Population Policy: Will Current Programs Succeed?" pp. 733–734.

[84] Frank Notestein et al., "The Problem of Population Control," in *The Population Dilemma,* ed. P. Hauser (Englewood Cliffs, N.J.: Prentice-Hall, 1963), pp. 127–128. They subsequently qualify their statement by adding that the failure of birth rates to fall in underdeveloped areas of the world "clearly turns less on lack of effective means than on the absence of strong motivation" (p. 128).

fertility behavior are not likely. What can organized units of society do to set into motion those changes necessary for fertility declines in underdeveloped areas to begin? How may we best utilize technological developments to help shape the thrust of fertility reduction? The social changes necessary for fertility reduction may be abstracted from the historical experiences of currently industrialized fertility controlling countries. Although the mechanisms that may bring about these necessary changes vary and the particular means to control fertility are numerous, general principles of fertility reduction are not likely to differ in the future than in the past. Hence, we turn to history to learn the lessons of these general principles but not to predict the specifics of timing, pace, or mechanism. In contrast to the ahistorical and antihistorical demographers of the future,[85] it is our premise that without a knowledge of the past, demographic incursions into the future are meaningless. It is equally naive to assume that the future will repeat exactly the past. But history can yield some general principles that should make our projections sounder.

The Lessons of History

What lessons for the future may be abstracted from the historical connection between modernization and fertility? The examination of overall fertility trends and the investigation of comparative case studies suggested that three major social changes are necessary for fertility reduction: (1) differentiation of kinship structures from other social institutions and functional specialization of family roles; (2) changes in living standards; and (3) aspirations and possibilities for social mobility. All three changes are integral elements of modernization; but they are not the only elements of modernization nor are the paths to these processes only through industrialization. It is thus insufficient and unsatisfactory to argue that unless the full processes of modernization or industrialization occur, fertility will remain high; that argument neither isolates the specifics of modernization critical to fertility reduction nor provides any alternative for underdeveloped areas to lower their fertility without duplicating all the social processes associated with long-run modernization. The argument presented throughout this chapter suggests that as long as the rewards within society are governed by the goals and desires of the extended family, as long as women have no alternative social and economic roles outside of childbearing and childrearing, as long as there are no direct social and economic rewards for smaller families through opportunities for higher standards of living, and as long as society provides no outlets or no justification for sociopersonal aspira-

[85] Cf. the antihistorical bias of Bogue, *Principles of Demography*, p. 829.

tions, real changes in fertility behavior and attitudes are not likely to become manifest. Nevertheless, fertility reduction in underdeveloped areas, when it occurs, will not follow the pattern of the currently industrialized nations in its specifics. Because some fertility transitions serve as "models" precludes exact historical repetition. Hence, linear extrapolations from the Western experience to other nations will surely be in error. Technological progress in developing and distributing efficient contraception will speed the pace of fertility transitions, once there are attitude-sets and motivations for smaller families. The active encouragement of governments and related organized units will no doubt play a role in the pattern, pace, and style of future fertility reductions. But that role will be to shape in various ways the pace of changes in family structure and economic systems, which in turn mold the fertility attitudes and behavior of couples. The lesson of history is clear: unless the social situation is so altered that having a large family conflicts with other sociopersonal goals which are defined as more important, family size will not be reduced.

The first step toward lower fertility levels is obviously to provide efficient contraceptives for those who already have formed new goals of family size, which undoubtedly will quicken the pace of fertility reduction. This task, however complex and difficult, can in no way accomplish the much more pressing and intricate problem of reorienting family size goals around lower levels, which has three basic policies or strategies. The first posits the "naturalistic" argument that, briefly, fertility values and behavior will change in natural response to socioeconomic changes. Thus, socioeconomic policies should be emphasized that will have as an indirect, natural by-product reduced family size goals and lower fertility behavior. Although the logic of the naturalistic (sometime Marxist) position is impeccable, the outcome of such a policy in practice would be to deny the legitimate, independent, and serious problems surrounding high fertility levels that may only get worse if nothing is done. Moreover, such a "nonpolicy" neglects the role and responsibilities of political and other social organizations to speed up fertility reduction. The naturalistic argument correctly recognizes that socioeconomic changes must occur before fertility will fall; what is misleading is that nothing particular would be done. It is not convincing to argue that socioeconomic changes will automatically reduce high fertility because high fertility often stymies those very socioeconomic changes.

A second policy denies the need for social changes as a prerequisite for motivating new fertility goals and instead focuses on the intermediate mechanisms of fertility control. The argument [86] in short is that the lack

---

[86] This section and the subsequent proposal have been adapted from the convincing arguments by Davis, "Population Policy: Will Current Programs Succeed?" as well as other articles by him cited throughout this chapter. See also Blake, "Demographic Science and the Redirection of Population Policy."

of contraceptive utilization in underdeveloped areas of the world is a function of the unacceptability of specific birth control devices or is due to ignorance. The problem of motivation is therefore to develop acceptable contraceptives or to employ a mass-communication approach to eliminate family-planning ignorance. Motivation toward small family-size goals is achieved through specific family-planning education and through distributing the latest, most acceptable, contraceptive techniques. This strategy and all its accoutrements is largely in fashion with family-planning agencies around the world, but as Davis suggests it misjudges or ignores the "power and complexity of social life." Although the technological-mass communications strategy has a certain simplistic appeal, it fails to recognize the *social* nature of fertility goals and behavior. Once it is recognized that fertility is bound up with complex socially motivated behavior, that it is part of an overall system of human social relationships, and hence is tied to social and personal interests of individuals, "it would be apparent that the social structure and economy must be changed before a deliberate reduction in the birth rate can be achieved." [87]

A more realistic but more difficult motivational policy is based on the premise that social institutional changes must occur before fertility goals are affected. The argument does not deny the need to assist those who already are searching for contraceptive means, nor does it ignore the power of technology and specific education for those who may be influenced. It does argue that emphasizing these techniques to the exclusion of fundamental efforts toward socioeconomic reorganization is shortsighted. Fertility policies should suggest which parts of social life might be more successfully altered to have an antinatalist consequence. If our analysis of the decline in fertility among Western nations was correct, if the same general reasons for high fertility in preindustrial European nations apply to currently underdeveloped countries, and if the general principles affecting past changes in human fertility are guidelines for the future, then it follows that motivation for smaller family size goals flows directly and only through the breakdown of kinship dominance, the creation of alternative roles and statuses for women outside the family, general increases in standards of living, and aspirations for socioeconomic mobility. Hence, governments and public and private organizations who want to guide populations toward lower fertility goals must introduce socioeconomic changes that will result in the conflict between large family size and socioeconomic goals.

What specific mechanisms will bring about the desired socioeco-

[87] Davis, "Population Policy: Will Current Programs Succeed?" p. 733. See also Freedman, "Worldwide Fertility Trends," p. 6.

nomic change and kinship reorganization, and, hence, new fertility goals? Will universal general education, or universal literacy, or the participation of women in nonfamilial social and economic activities, or improved agricultural productivity, or land redistribution, or a dozen other possibilities? We do not know; this requires serious and skillful research yet to be undertaken. Whatever specific process or combination is found to be the key in establishing new family size goals and lower fertility, it will operate through the breakdown of kinship dominance, improvements in living standards, and mobility aspirations. It is hardly likely that there is one process or one combination of processes. Parallel to historical-comparative evidence on fertility transitions, we should expect that a variety of combined processes will bring about the same shift in family and economic systems and result in new family behavior and values. Nor should we forget that reduced family size is only a means to a qualitatively improved life for the society and for the family. No fertility policy that would endanger the improved quality of life could be justified as an "effective" means to reorient family-size goals.

We have used historical-comparative analyses to suggest that the transition from high to low fertility represented a social revolution of enormous proportions for human society. To start and affect the course of that transition in the underdeveloped two-thirds of the world requires a socioeconomic revolution of equal or greater magnitude than anything that has been observed in world history. It will also require a revolutionary vision to appreciate the enormity and complexity of the task.

Chapter Seven

MIGRATION AND
SOCIOECONOMIC MODERNIZATION

\

In any attempt to locate the junctures of population processes and social, economic, political, and cultural change, we need to sketch a general picture of the nature of population processes before and after social changes occur. Most important, it is necessary to isolate the critical aspects of change processes to identify the mechanisms that link social and demographic systems. Thus, to analyze systematically the interrelationships between socioeconomic modernization and migration, a basis for historical comparisons must be established first; that is, the general outline of migration in traditional societies must be traced. Furthermore, those aspects of traditional social structure that constrain or facilitate migration should be identified. From this vantage point, comparisons to migration in modern societies allow for the identification of specific social processes that are integral to modernization and that most clearly are associated with migration changes.

As noted in Chapter 3, migration, in contrast to fertility and mortality, is not a uniform process and therefore there are greater complexities in its analysis. Thus, as an alternative to the broad sweep of analyzing and summarizing highlights from many countries, we will use one area — African migration — to *illustrate* more general patterns, although many other illustrations might have served our analytic objectives equally well. This analysis will be treated as both a case study and as an illustration of the general changes in migration that result from alterations in the social structure. Hence, the migration of Africans, of necessity, will be examined in historical and comparative contexts.

Often when African migrations are analyzed, it is convenient to treat the material as unique in two senses: African societies have experienced a different form of colonialization; consequently, the migration patterns that may have resulted from colonialization may have few parallels in the experience of most Western countries. Also, African migration studies are unique in the ahistorical perspective: that is, colonial and postcolonial migrations have been viewed as discontinuous from precolonial movements. Some research based on static, cross-sectional surveys or census materials implicitly assumes that contemporary migrations in Africa are new phenomena not linked systematically with historical patterns. To some extent, every case study is unique because social and demographic processes are intimately tied to the specifics of culture, social organization, and ecology. The fact that no two societies are alike in every respect and that migration patterns are equally diverse does not preclude sharing general social and demographic features by many societies. Nor can contemporary social and demographic processes be viewed in an historical vacuum. We have noted in previous chapters the continuities as well as the transformations in fertility and mortality. Indeed, the past and present are linked in such a way that the present cannot be comprehended fully without considering what happened before. The same is true in projecting from the past and present to the future. One fascination of studying African migrations rests with the attempt to convert the "unique" into the illustrative.

To understand general processes of change, including migration, historical and comparative analyses must be attempted. We will weave together the historical antecedents of contemporary African migrations to identify the specific effects of European colonialism and subsequent African nationalism, and, in addition, indicate the striking parallels between the determinants and consequences of African migrations and migrations that have taken place in other countries. Although colonialization and industrialization are by no means identical, and the specifics of African migrations are different from migrations in other countries, the analytic task will be to locate the unique as well as the parallels.

Africa is by no criteria homogeneous. No matter which feature of African society is examined — whether political systems, cultural values, social structure and institutions, economic development, or general ecology — diversity and complexity are the rule. This heterogeneity presents analytic problems for generalization; the absence of complete and reliable historical information and the general unevenness in the quality and coverage of available materials further complicate the problem. This is no less true of research on African migrations, and perhaps more so. Nevertheless, a fairly consistent picture of migration patterns in Africa, and particularly in West Africa, may be pieced together.

PRECOLONIAL AFRICAN MIGRATIONS: AN ILLUSTRATION OF MIGRATION IN TRADITIONAL SOCIETIES

Some general features of precolonial African migrations parallel what might be expected of migration patterns in preindustrial areas in general. Although we will be dealing with a long period of history, and with diverse types of migration, it is convenient analytically to categorize these movements as "traditional." [1] Traditional societies are commonly portrayed as self-sufficient, all-encompassing communities that meet the needs of their constituents fully and completely. They have also been described as rigid, uniform social systems characterized by few changes that take a long time to emerge. Reward and prestige are deeply entrenched in the social order and allow for little social class mobility. In short, traditional societies have come to be viewed as static and stable in terms of both social and geographic mobility.

In contrast to this simplified picture of traditional societies, social and cultural change are the outstanding features of modern societies. Modern societies are dynamic, characterized by rapid social change, social mobility, and high rates of geographic mobility. Both portraits are clearly extreme oversimplifications; at best they are ideal-types. It is more accurate to describe traditional societies in terms of *relative stability* and modern societies in terms of *relative mobility*. It seems reasonable to argue that few total societies have ever been totally closed either with respect to social or geographic mobility. The question is one of degree and of kind: the relative closure or relative stability of traditional society when compared to modern societies and the types of migration that characterize traditional in contrast to modern societies. The study of African migrations from the precolonial era through independence is no exception.

Some overall identifying features of migration in traditional societies, in general, and in precolonial Africa, in particular, require analysis. First, whereas migration is not exclusively a phenomenon of industrialized societies or of colonial or postcolonial Africa, the extent of

---

[1] It is difficult to categorize the heterogeneous migrations of "traditional" societies. For our general argument the "traditional" concept is more attractive. For example, Petersen uses the term "primitive migration" to denote nomadic wandering caused by "ecological" pressure. In addition to the derogatory overtones of the term "primitive," it should be noted that nomadic wandering is only one type of migration within traditional societies. Moreover, nomadic wandering may be "caused" by pressures other than "ecological" and may be identified in nontraditional societies as well. See Chapter 3, this book. Cf. William Petersen, "A General Typology of Migration," *American Sociological Review*, 23 (June 1958), pp. 256–265; William Petersen, *Population* (New York: Macmillan, 1969), chaps. 8, 10.

migration in traditional societies tends to be relatively small. Hence, at the macrolevel, migration is not a pervasive societal characteristic in traditional societies. Second, migrations in traditional societies generally involve movements of shorter distances and between relatively more homogeneous areas. Traditional migrations are commonly of two types: *group movements,* including nomadic wanderings of tribes or small bands, or pastoral movements, often seasonal, conditioned by the need to find pasture and water for stock; or *idiosyncratic movements* of individuals.[2] As a consequence, traditional migrations are generally unsystematic and uniformities in distance and direction moved are difficult to establish. Most important, the total impact of migration on traditional communities is minimal.

Yet, one should not conclude that migration in traditional societies involved only the movement of single, deviant, or alienated persons, or that nomadic and pastoral movements were erratic. Whereas the evidence from both preindustrial Western countries and precolonial Africa points to the diversity and heterogeneity of migrations, at the same time general directionality in migratory flows may be discerned. Thus, generalizations about the sex selectivity of migration or the composition of migration streams in traditional societies are difficult to establish. Some traditional migrations were male dominated and individualistic; others were selective of females and represented family movements; still others consisted of the resettlement of whole tribes, nomadic wanderings for subsistence, and the institutionalized migration of trading communities.

The relatively low rates of migration in traditional societies, its heterogeneity and unsystematic nature, raise several analytic questions. First, what were the general reasons for the migration that took place? Second, what impact did such migration have for the structure and function of traditional societies, and what consequences did it have for migrants and their families? Third, and most important, why was migration so limited?

The heterogeneity of migrations in traditional societies suggests, at the very minimum, that the reasons for moving and the determinants of traditional migration were also diverse. A substantial amount of traditional migration was a result of political factors. Lombard argues that in Africa "the majority of traditional migrations, whether internal or 'intertribal,' were political in nature."[3] To be sure, some movements were

---

[2] In East Central Africa traditional migration has been described as "mostly individual affairs." See Albert Trouwborst, "Kinship and Geographical Mobility in Burundi (East Central Africa)," in *Kinship and Geographical Mobility,* ed. Ralph Piddington (Leiden, The Netherlands: E. J. Brill, 1965), p. 170.

[3] Quoted in Immanuel Wallerstein, "Migration in West Africa: Political Perspective," in *Urbanization and Migration in West Africa,* ed. Hilda Kuper (Los Angeles: University of California Press, 1965), p. 149.

specific mechanisms for the exercise of political power through war and conquests. But when political structures were weak or ill-defined, there were peaceful movements in search of better land opportunities. The search for better land is tied in with ecological pressure associated with what has been called the nomadic wanderings of "primitive" communities, or more broadly, movements in response to man's inability to cope with the natural forces of his environment.[4] Indeed, the traditional answer to poor farming conditions in Africa has been the migration of whole farming communities.[5] Interrelated with political, economic, and ecological factors, social factors associated with exogamous rules may be noted. For various reasons, related in part to the incest taboo, the numerical balance of males and females, and, in part, the attempts to build political, social, and tribal alliances between small communities, exogamous marriage patterns were pervasive among neighboring traditional communities.[6] Exogamy patterns involved the exchange movements of men and women between communities and represented the early forms of "marriage migrations" so prevalent in contemporary societies.[7] Along with nomadic and pastoral groups, constant mobility was institutionalized in trading communities. All these precipitants of migration argue for treating some migration within and between traditional societies as natural, if not inevitable. Some migrants may have been deviants or outcasts, although the extent of such movement or the priority among the more general factors are indeterminate.

Using these general features and causes of migration in traditional societies, it is not difficult to suggest some general consequences of traditional migrations. Because of the small amount of movement, it is probably correct to assume that the total society was not transformed or changed by migration, either in areas of origin or destination. This is surely the case with idiosyncratic movements; group movements of nomads or of communities were institutionalized and would not involve any major impact. This is not to argue that no changes resulted from traditional movements. Some changes may have resulted from intergroup contacts and from adjustments to new environments, especially in towns or cities, but such changes were slow. Indeed, whatever the consequences of migration in traditional societies, they were neither abrupt nor radical.

    [4] Ibid., pp. 148–149; Petersen, "A General Typology of Migration."
    [5] See, for example, J. C. Caldwell and C. Okonjo (eds.), *The Population of Tropical Africa* (New York: Columbia University Press, 1968), p. 20; I. Nzimiro, "A Study of Mobility Among the Ibos of Southern Nigeria," and A. Trouwborst, "Kinship and Geographical Mobility in Burundi (East Central Africa)," both in *Kinship and Geographical Mobility*, ed. Piddington.
    [6] Cf. Trouwborst, "Kinship and Geographical Mobility in Burundi," p. 170.
    [7] See Chapter 3, this book.

One type of change that resulted from wars, conquests, political alliances, trading, and exogamy associated with migration was the merging of small groups, tribes, and communities into larger and stronger communities.[8] Migration that was part of trading between communities and later with the urban-industrial world, or that was part of the search for different or better living conditions, led to the establishment of some early towns and cities. The extent of city building and ethnic heterogeneity that resulted from migration is not always clear, although migration played an integral role.[9] Perhaps, the most important consequence of traditional migration was the foundation it laid for subsequent dramatic changes associated with political, social, economic, and cultural processes.

One of the most intriguing questions about migration in traditional societies is, Why was there so little? Theoretically, to understand mobility, we have to tackle the problem of *nonmobility*. In the present context, the question is: What were the constraints for overall stability in traditional societies? Indeed, if we are to show that social, economic, political, and cultural changes associated with colonialism in Africa, or industrialization in Western countries, accelerated the tempo of migration and reshaped its character, we must know what specific features of colonialism and industrialization are linked to migration via the social structure. To unravel the causal mechanisms, we must isolate how colonialism and industrialism affected the social structure of traditional societies in such a way as to lessen the constraints operating to minimize movement.

The most important constraint on migration in precolonial Africa, and in traditional societies in general, relates to the system of status and reward. The political and social structures of traditional societies were inflexible in the sense that those who had wealth, or vigor, or initiative to leave their own society, could not secure a status as good or better in an area of destination than in their own area of origin. Hence, movers had lower status in general than nonmovers. Loyalty to community appears to have outweighed existing pressures to migrate. Thus, a decision to move in traditional societies might have met with strong social opposition and, in turn, material disadvantages.[10]

Of course, the question is why should this have been the case. The whole character of traditional societies militated against large-scale geographic mobility. In general, traditional societies are characterized by a

[8] Cf. Wallerstein, "Migration in West Africa: Political Perspectives."

[9] See Joseph Greenberg, "Urbanism, Migration and Language," in *Urbanization and Migration in West Africa*, ed. Kuper, p. 50.

[10] See the discussion in Wallerstein, "Migration in West Africa: Political Perspectives," p. 149 and p. 196, fn. 6.

type of social integration or solidarity that tied the individual into a system of kinship, political loyalty, and economic dependence conspiring against large-scale movements. In turn, attaining status and prestige through ascription, the distribution of rewards through kin associations, loyalty to local chiefs, and the nature of socialization, fostered community or, more specifically, tribal and kinship identification, all of which impeded migration from one community to another and prevented the acceptance of "strangers" from outside.

In a sense, other impeding factors were important: linguistic barriers, lack of roads and other ecological obstacles, lack of knowledge about other social and economic opportunities, relative homogeneity of other nearby areas (i.e., a lack of striking economic differentiation), relative isolation, and so on. Nevertheless, people were relatively stable in traditional communities because almost every feature of social life focused inward toward the community, and no real competition from other sources counteracted these pressures. The social base of kinship, the economic base of subsistence agriculture, the political base of loyalty to the chief, and, consequently, the societal feature of general social integration of individuals within the community, compounded with a denial to strangers the prestige, rights, and rewards associated with personal achievement, overwhelmingly argued against migration of any large scale. Indeed, these patterns of relative stability became institutionalized into the cultural system of traditional societies. People in traditional societies were relatively nonmobile not because they valued stability. Rather, the norms associated with kinship, loyalty, rewards, prestige, etc., were institutionalized and formalized, and these norms favored stability. Thus, in part, idiosyncratic movements from one community to another were viewed as some sort of breakdown of these generally held values. It is not surprising, therefore, that the types of movements characterizing traditional societies were either part of the institutionalized framework of the group — war, political conquest, trading, nomadism, marriage, pastoralism — or were idiosyncratic. The only hospitable environment for migrants was the city, where some "traditional" rules were not strictly enforced.

Thus, relative stability was an integral part of the social fabric of traditional societies, whether precolonial Africa or preindustrial Western societies. Societies with little structural differentiation and strong kinship ties that dominate activities within societies are not likely to be characterized by heavy migration. When migration does occur in traditional societies it will more likely be the movement of the whole group rather than the systematic or regular movements of individuals or families. It follows from this argument that when the social fabric changes, alterations in the type and tempo of migration might be expected. However, migration relates to social processes as both determinant and consequence. Hence, not only will a change in the structure of society alter migration patterns, but over time changes in migration may alter the social structure and engender further movements. As a result of the interdependence of migration and social processes, the specific causal sequence is impossible to identify. Colonialization and industrialization affected migration by changing the social structure, thereby affecting migration indirectly, and as well by altering directly the tempo and character of migration, which, in turn, changed the social structure. Indeed, no matter what the starting point for social and economic change, migration appears to be affected: social change leads to migration, which leads to further social change, which, in turn, affects migration, and so on: a classic pattern of an interdependent relationship.

COLONIALISM AND AFRICAN MIGRATIONS

With the advent of colonialism in Africa, the patterns of traditional society changed and migration patterns were transformed. The specific features of colonialism that altered the character of movement and increased the tempo of migration must, however, be viewed in the context of precolonial migration patterns. Although colonialism set into motion changes that transformed African migrations, several preexisting migration patterns were accelerated and accentuated rather than developed *de novo*.

One of the most fundamental changes caused by colonialism was economic, which had three specific effects on migration. First, colonial policy involved the direct recruitment of laborers to work in mines, or in cocoa plantations, or in towns and urban areas. Second, the imposition of taxes by colonial powers forced Africans to change from subsistence farming to cash-paying jobs. The general change from a subsistence to a cash economy directly affected the need to migrate. Some also moved to avoid paying taxes. Third, the general expansion of trade and production in the colonial period demanded manpower, a mobile labor force, and the maintenance of civil order over wide areas, all requiring migration. These economic changes imposed by colonialism affected urban-town areas as well as rural-village areas. In part, colonialism led to the creation of urban-town centers to centralize and organize trade, communication, and administration.[11] The demand for jobs in these new urban areas in combination with the changing economic base in rural areas paved the way for heavy migratory flows.

[11] Ibid., pp. 151–152; William Goode, *World Revolution and Family Patterns* (New York: The Free Press, 1963), p. 171; Immanuel Wallerstein, *Africa* (New York: Vintage, 1961).

Skinner argues that labor migration among the Mossi does not differ fundamentally from that found in other parts of Africa.[12] Migrant Mossi men of Upper Volta went to the mines, plantations, and urban-industrial complexes because of the need to pay taxes imposed by the French colonists. But in contrast to other groups, the Mossi showed no hesitation to migrate for work because in the precolonial era trading journeys were institutionalized, especially for tribal chiefs. Thus, even after the French modified labor recruitment and subsequently abolished it, the pattern continued, because labor movements in general had become fully entrenched in the social structure. Whereas the thrust of migration among the Mossi was the need to earn wages to pay taxes, the process evolved smoothly from "forced" to voluntary movement. Therefore, migration can be viewed as one mechanism whereby Mossi people have adjusted to some aspects of a rapidly changing social system. Similarly, in East Africa the impetus for contemporary short-term and long-distance migration in search of employment is generally agreed to have come from the colonial imposition of taxes at the turn of the century.[13]

Other influences relate to political changes during the colonial era. As noted, the development of an administrative colonial network to replace the traditional system resulted in centralization that engendered migration. But more important, the colonial system eroded the traditional tribal authority relationships within the rural villages. The replacement, substitution, and, in part, juxtaposition of traditional authority with political allegiances to colonialists (and later to the nation-state) considerably loosened the bonds that held the population to the rural village system. In the towns and cities, authority did not flow from the tribal hierarchical system; in the villages, elders lost some of their political and social control.[14] These changes had a major impact on the migratory potential of rural persons. Moreover, as in most cases of the exercise and imposition of outside political power, some migrants were "refugees" or persons moving to escape political authority.

These economic and political changes in turn altered the nature of social control. Traditionally, social control was kinship dominated because rewards — social, economic, and political — were based less on achievement and more on ascription. Under colonialism, not only was authority to be shared, but social control based on withholding rewards or prestige could not be met effectively by the local kinship group. The

[12] Elliot Skinner, "Labor Migration Among the Mossi of the Upper Volta," in *Urbanization and Migration in West Africa,* ed. Kuper, pp. 82–84.

[13] Aidan Southall, "The Demographic and Social Effects of Migration on the Populations of East Africa," *Proceedings of the World Population Conference,* Belgrade, 1965, vol. 4 (New York, 1967), pp. 235–238.

[14] Wallerstein, "Migration in West Africa: Political Perspectives," pp. 149–150.

sanctions of traditional communities were diffused; achievement began to substitute for ascription; universalism was emphasized rather than particularism. Members of the younger generation could therefore find new roles and did not need to accept the authority of the older generation. The new job opportunities were not under the control of either tribal or family elders and thus the new system altered traditional patterns of role bargaining.[15]

Parallel to political, economic, and social changes, colonialism reduced some ecological barriers that had impeded movements in traditional Africa. Administrative requirements, the general increase in production and trade, urbanization and centralization, the exercise of political authority, and tax collecting necessitated developing transportation facilities, communication networks, roads, and services. Improvements in the infrastructure paved the way for additional migration in response to new jobs in road construction and in providing related services.[16] The rural-to-urban migrations and urbanization in Sierra Leone, for example, were facilitated not only by the evolution of commercial agriculture, the development of mining (since 1930), and the establishment of administrative centers, but also by the creation of the railway (1895–1915), and more recent road networks.[17] In a general way, removing some ecological barriers made it possible for remote areas to be tied together. Nevertheless, improved roads and transportation strengthened migratory tendencies that had existed, and were the products of the general social and political transformation in Africa. Ecological and technological changes were consistent with the more general social, economic, and political changes and at times were "intermediate" factors encouraging migration. In this sense ecological factors may be thought of facilitating or impeding, but not determining, migration.

As part of these general processes, new attitudes and values began to emerge. It is not that Africans began to value mobility under colonial rule. Rather, their newly acquired economic, political, and social values had as an essential component geographic movement. To obtain their newly created needs, migration was necessary, even if it was temporary.

The total impact of these various specific changes drastically altered migration patterns, directly and indirectly. The specific changes in the economy, polity, kinship system, culture, and ecology of Africa not

[15] Goode, *World Revolution and Family Patterns*, p. 171.

[16] Wallerstein, "Migration in West Africa: Political Perspectives," pp. 149–150; Caldwell estimates, for example, that 60,000 Ghanaians earn their income by providing transportation. J. C. Caldwell, "Migration and Urbanization," in *A Study of Contemporary Ghana*, vol. 2, *Some Aspects of Social Structure*, ed. Walter Birmingham et al. (London: George Allen and Unwin, 1961), p. 111.

[17] John Clarke, "Population Distribution in Sierra Leone," in *The Population of Tropical Africa*, ed. Caldwell and Okonjo, p. 275.

only interacted with another but also, in their total impact, added up to more than the sum of specific changes in the various spheres of society. Basic societal alterations emerged from these specific changes and had profound consequences for migration patterns. First, structural differentiation began to emerge. The economy and polity were effectively separated from kinship dominance; power became diffused; and economic heterogeneity, demanding a more fluid labor supply, encouraging occupational specialization and providing opportunity differentials, emerged and became accentuated. Another major societal change involved the changing relationships among individuals and between individuals and society. The change from particularism toward universalism in relationships among men, and from ascription toward achievement in terms of rewards and prestige, reflect this general societal change. Social integration shifted from a dependence on a traditional system to a general interdependence of social parts — in Durkheimian terms, a shift from mechanical toward organic solidarity. It is not that rural areas are integrated fully and urban areas lack integration, or that traditional societies are integrated and modern societies are not. Rather, African society under colonialism was integrated around a different matrix of relationships than precolonial African communities. Social relationships that involved kin in rural villages were replaced by association networks in urban areas and were altered within rural areas as well.[18]

Two additional general principles of migratory process emerge clearly from the colonial era. First, migration tended to gain momentum over time, that is, the movement of persons tended to begin small and subsequently increases in size. The normative acceptance of migration and of migrants increased and became institutionalized. Second, migration led to social changes (as in the breakdown of authority) which, in turn, further accelerated migration. As people moved and returned home, information and knowledge of opportunities were conveyed; some migrants in towns sent for their families. Moreover, potential migrants may have been less hesitant to move when others had smoothed the way first. The need for an innovative or adventurous spirit declines with the amount and thrust of migration that has already taken place. The widening network of migration during the colonial period enlarged the political, economic, social, and cultural perspectives of many people. The existing local system could not remain unchanged after such movements, which, in turn, affected additional migration. Thus, changes in the rural economy, initiated by colonialism and accelerated by migration, created new additional pressures for migration; the traditional political power of

[18] Cf. Peter Gutkind, "African Urbanism, Mobility and the Social Network," in *Kinship and Geographical Mobility,* ed. Piddington, p. 51.

tribal chiefs in rural villages not only held less sway over migrants who returned, but was less threatening to the stable rural population.[19]

The economic, political, social, cultural, and societal changes accompanying colonialism therefore had an enormous impact on migration in Africa, and vice versa. The most dramatic way of describing these overall changes is to note the *conspicuousness* of migration during the colonial era, and subsequently. One impressive consequence of colonialism, at the societal level, was the conversion of migration from the idiosyncratic to the general. Migration during the colonial era became for the first time a conspicuous and pervasive feature of African society. In short, colonialism systematized, integrated, and institutionalized migration as an integral part of the social order.

If colonialism sharply increased the amount of migration, how did it affect the type of migration? To be sure, some types of migration were curtailed. Although, in the main, colonialism encouraged directly and indirectly substantial movements of population in Africa, some restraints were imposed, as in the arbitrary national boundaries superimposed on areas considered by the local population as parts of a whole. For example, between 1900 and 1960 the colonial powers of British West Africa, Portuguese Guinea, and French areas, as well as independent Liberia, made international frontiers rigid. Each colonial power developed lines of communication and transportation as well as currency systems within its own area and, thus, the economy of West Africa was not integrated as a whole. Fees and customs for crossing these international borders intimidated potential migrants and lengthened the stay of those who made the crossing. Freezing land ownership may have also impeded the movement of some within a family and, in conjunction with administrative regulations, surely affected rates of return migration.[20] The boundaries of African colonies at times were drawn to suit the political conveniences of the European colonists without regard to the social organization or culture of African tribes, ethnic groups, or kingdoms. The most dramatic example of this arbitrariness is the way the British delimited Nigeria to include the Yorubas and the Ibos and the civil war that ensued.[21] In terms of migration, establishing boundaries by colonial rulers often divided families and ethnic groups between two colonial powers. Thus, some movers who may be regarded "officially" as international

[19] Cf. Wallerstein, "Migration in West Africa: Political Perspectives," pp. 153–154.

[20] Ibid., pp. 150–151; cf. Elizabeth Colson, "Migration in Africa: Trends and Possibilities," in *Population in Africa*, ed. Frank Lorimer and Mark Karp (Boston: Boston University Press, 1960).

[21] Discussed briefly in Robert Blauner, "Internal Colonialism and Ghetto Revolt," *Social Problems*, 16 (Spring 1969), p. 400.

migrants may merely be following accustomed routes of travel before the fixing of national boundaries.[22] However, some have argued that despite superimposed frontiers and the subsequent hardening of boundaries following independence, little evidence indicates that "international" migration of unskilled labor has been appreciably reduced.[23]

Colonialism also terminated or curtailed other precolonial migration patterns. Moves occasioned by war and conquest among local tribes were minimized as well as general movements associated with conditions of political and social instability.[24] In lieu of war-related migrations, the colonial administration provided safeguards and guarantees for general peaceful migration. The introduction of land tenure contracts and freezing land ownership militated against migration for conquest.[25] The pattern of rural-to-rural migration in traditional Africa appears to have been reduced with the accelerated flow from rural to urban areas or to towns, as well as to mining areas and cocoa plantations.

Even though migrations during the colonial period were large and of different types, they do not represent such drastic breaks with the past as might appear. Although moves in the twentieth century differ in quantity and quality, preexisting conditions continue to exert influence. For example, routes and destination of migrations display the persistence of pre-European patterns.[26] Even the persistence of seasonal and temporary migration so accentuated during the colonial period followed common patterns of traditional precolonial Africa. Thus, precolonial migration and colonial movements display continuity; colonialism accelerated the pace of past movements and accentuated various forms. The total pattern, however, resulted in the drastic transformation of African society.

Although in West Africa, indigenous cities of considerable size predate the colonial period, large-scale urbanization in most of sub-Saharan Africa is a modern phenomena associated with colonialism. Most African cities grew out of Western contact and have arisen *de novo* or from

---

[22] See D. K. Ghansah and A. F. Aryee, "The Demographic and Social Effects of Migration in Ghana," *Proceedings of the World Population Conference*, Belgrade, 1965, vol. 4 (New York, 1967), pp. 199–201.

[23] See, for example, Elliot Berg, "The Economics of the Migrant Labor System," in *Urbanization and Migration in West Africa*, ed. Kuper, p. 162.

[24] R. M. Prothero, "Migration in Tropical Africa," in *The Population of Tropical Africa*, ed. Caldwell and Okonjo, p. 252; Trouwborst, "Kinship and Geographical Mobility in Burundi," pp. 166–182.

[25] Wallerstein, "Migration in West Africa: Political Perspective," pp. 150–151; Colson, "Migration in Africa: Trends and Possibilities"; Caldwell, "Migration and Urbanization," p. 111.

[26] Cf. Colson, "Migration in Africa: Trends and Possibilities"; Greenberg, "Urbanism, Migration and Language," pp. 50–51; Jean Rouch, "Migrations Au Ghana (Gold Coast)," *Journal de la Societe des Africanistes*, 27:1–2 (1956), pp. 33–196.

villages and small towns. Thus, whereas towns existed in nineteenth-century East and West Africa, for much of tropical Africa towns began to develop only with the arrival of territorial administrations and the penetration of commerce.[27]

With political independence in the late 1950's and through the 1960's nationalism replaced colonialism as the dominant societal process relating to African migrations. It is too early to gauge the possible long-run consequences of nationalism vis-a-vis migration. Nevertheless, most colonial migration patterns have become institutionalized and continue unabated in the postcolonial era. Some evidence, which will be examined in the ensuing section, shows that temporary migration is slowly becoming more permanent. As African economies became more industrialized, the intensity and permanence of migration will increase. One thing is clear: there is no trend toward a return to tribal authority or traditionalism and the associated migration processes. In this sense, colonialism laid the foundation for nationalism and was congruent with the types of social, economic, political, and cultural changes associated with modernization.[28] The impact of these changes on migration, the acceleration of social changes through migration, and the influence of migration on subsequent migration all indicate an expected increase and intensification of migration as integral to contemporary African society.

This relates to migration in general, but especially internal migration. Nationalism and the development of independent nation-states in Africa continued the tradition started during the colonial period of establishing more rigorous frontiers symbolizing political entities. International migration may have been impeded by these rigid borders between states. In addition, attempts to establish economic integration within states and political factors often create difficulties for international migrants. For example, limiting voting rights only to native populations and "permanent" immigrants is one new type of pressure to cut down migration across frontier areas. Migrants who move from one state to another are no longer merely of different tribes or ethnic groups but now are of different nationalities. Although independence often led to pressures to cut down on migration across frontier areas, some international migration between Africa and the rest of the world, particularly of elites, increased.[29]

Up to this point, we have considered some very general features of

---

[27] J. C. Caldwell, "Introduction," in *The Population of Tropical Africa*, ed. Caldwell and Okonjo, p. 22; for the role of British colonialism in introducing urbanism in East Africa, see Norton Ginsburg, "Urban Geography and 'Non-Western' Areas," in *The Study of Urbanization*, ed. Philip Hauser and Leo Schnore (New York: Wiley, 1965), pp. 312–315.

[28] Wallerstein, "Migration in West Africa: Political Perspective," p. 157.

[29] Ibid., pp. 157–159.

migration in Africa and the specific impact of social, economic, and political changes associated with colonialism. But we have revealed little about the migration process itself. For example, we need to know how much movement is taking place, of what kind and in what directions; who moves and why; who remains in the rural areas and why; and what consequences are engendered by contemporary migration. Although we cannot present definitive answers to all these questions, or for all areas within Africa, we can examine some migration processes and consequences for selected areas. Particular, but not exclusive, attention will focus on Ghana, because relatively reliable survey and census materials for the 1960's are available. In the discussion of the specifics of migration process, the material should be viewed in terms of general *patterns* rather than *specific* statistical items.[30]

THE MIGRATION PROCESS IN AFRICA

Extent of Migration

How extensive was the migration process? We are not able to provide a quick and easy answer, but a feeling for the extent and amount of migration may be obtained in various ways. First, the growth of urban centers (defined here as centers of 5,000 or more inhabitants) indicates that part of urban increase which may be attributed to *net* in-movement. Urban growth is a crude way of examining migration because it would, at best, represent a conservative estimate, particularly in Africa, because a significant amount of movement is temporary, seasonal, and return migration. In addition, rural movements are omitted and the total amount of movement is significantly larger than net migration estimates. Nevertheless, in the absence of reliable, direct, and specific data on movements, urban growth is a useful approximation.

After World War I and the establishment of contemporary boundaries, urban growth in Ghana increased from 180,000 in 1921 to over a half million by 1948. In the ensuing twelve years, to 1960, the urban population trebled again to over one and one-half million. The proportion of total urban population of Ghana increased from 8 per cent in 1921 to 23 per cent in 1960. Although the total population of Ghana trebled from 1921 to 1960, the urban sector multiplied nine times. Be-

---

[30] As one illustration of the problems involved, we may note that the 1960 census of Ghana is considered to be one of the best in Africa and a model for other African states. Yet, age misstatements are enormous. For example, eight times as many people are listed at age sixty as at age sixty-one. For a general discussion, see J. C. Caldwell, "Population: General Characteristics," in *A Study of Contemporary Ghana*, vol. 2, ed. Walter Birmingham et al., pp. 27–28 and chap. 1.

tween 1948 and 1960, the population in Ghana increased 64 per cent
from 4 million to 6.7 million; the urban sector of Accra more than
doubled during the same time period, from 222,000 to 492,000.[31]

This excess urban growth has been the result of both internal and
external movements. Estimates are that about one-third of the migrants
is "international" and about one-fifth of the urban population is of foreign origin. Foreign origin in Ghana is used to describe persons whose
fathers or grandfathers (in matrilineal societies, mothers and grandmoth-
ers) come from another African country. This appears somewhat justifiable in West Africa where international migration is largely temporary
and tribal-community ties to countries of origin are maintained.[32] Of the
increase in the urban population of one million persons between 1948 to
1960, at least 40 per cent has been attributed to internal migrants and
their natural increase, and close to 30 per cent to net migration alone.
This internal rural-to-urban migration reduced the population increase in
rural areas by one-fifth to one-quarter.[33]

These net flow estimates obscure the great interchange of movements. For example, Northern Ghana in 1960 contained 41,000 residents
who had migrated from areas farther north, whereas 116,000 persons
originating from Northern Ghana were living in Southern Ghana. Hence,
although at least 157,000 persons had moved in and out of Northern
Ghana, the areas lost a net of 75,000 persons. In terms of annual international migratory flows, estimates indicate that migration into and out
of Ghana exceeds 300,000 persons in each direction. Since 1957, the annual rate of migration to Ghana has been about 5 per cent per year and
increasing.[34] In Ghana, as in the United States at the end of the nineteenth century and indeed other countries with substantial foreign immigration, the magnitude of net international movements has forced the
pace of urbanization.

Another way to obtain a feeling for the extent of migration is to
examine labor force data. It is difficult to estimate the proportion of the
total paid employed labor force in Africa accounted for by migrants,
broadly defined. The character of some of the migration, temporary and

[31] J. C. Caldwell, "Determinants of Rural-Urban Migration in Ghana," *Population Studies,* 22 (November 1968), p. 361; *Ghana Census, 1960,* vol. 1 (Accra: Government Printing, 1963–1964), p. xxii.

[32] Caldwell, "Population: General Characteristics," p. 25.

[33] Caldwell, "Determinants of Rural-Urban Migration in Ghana," pp. 361–362.

[34] Caldwell, "Introduction," in *The Population of Tropical Africa,* ed. Caldwell
and Okonjo, p. 20; Caldwell, "Migration and Urbanization"; see also B. Gil, "Immigration into Ghana and Its Contribution in Skill," *Proceedings of the World
Population Conference,* Belgrade, 1965, vol. 4 (New York, 1967), pp. 202–206;
Ghansah and Aryee, "The Demographic and Social Effects of Migration in Ghana,"
pp. 200–201.

seasonal, the lack of clear-cut definitions of "paid, employed labor force," and the general absence of reliable data militate against accuracy beyond guesswork. The total labor force in paid employment in West Africa has been estimated at about 2 million. Berg suggests that almost all those in paid agricultural employment and perhaps half of those in nonagricultural employment are temporary migrants; overall, it is likely that more than half of all those who work for remuneration are migrants.[35]

In Ghana it is a common saying that "any village in Ghana without a Nigerian trader is not a complete village." [36] According to the 1960 Ghana census, this saying has some basis in reality. The proportion non-Ghanaian males employed in specific occupations was 67 per cent in diamond mining, 60 per cent in petty trading, 52 per cent in personal services, 44 per cent in mining and quarrying, 40 per cent in domestic services, and 20 per cent in cocoa farming. Yet of the total employed males, non-Ghanaians accounted for less than 15 per cent, but they formed 22 per cent of the unemployed males.[37]

In 1956, half of Nyasaland (East Africa) wage earners were employed outside that territory, mainly in Southern and Northern Rhodesia. In Southern Rhodesia, half the wage earners were immigrants, whereas in South Africa in the late 1950's, fully two out of every three Africans employed in mining industries came from other territories.[38]

A third indicator of the extent of migration is the view from major sending countries. Again, the amount of migration is equally impressive. Balima speaks of the thousands of citizens from Upper Volta who voluntarily migrate to Ghana and the Republic of the Ivory Coast on a *daily basis*. Somewhere between 300,000 and 400,000 emigrants from Upper Volta are in Ghana and 200,000 to 250,000 are in the Ivory Coast.[39] Mossi workers from Upper Volta constitute the majority of the 50,000 workers officially recruited each year to work on the coffee and cocoa plantations of the Ivory Coast, and anywhere between 50,000 and 100,000 Mossi workers migrate annually to Ghana.

Direct but often crude census information provides additional insight into the extent of migration. An examination of interprovincial migration in Kenya, with a base population of around 10 million, calculated by place of birth, reveals the great interchange of populations. The total number of in-migrants of all provinces in Kenya was around

[35] Berg, "The Economics of the Migrant Labor System," pp. 161–162.
[36] Ghansah and Aryee, "The Demographic and Social Effects of Migration in Ghana," p. 199.
[37] Ibid., pp. 199–200, table 1.
[38] H. W. Singer, "Demographic Factors in Subsaharan Economic Development," in *Economic Transition in Africa*, ed. Melville Herskovits and Mitchell Horwitz (Evanston, Ill.: Northwestern University Press, 1964), pp. 242, 255, table 11.2.
[39] Skinner, "Labor Migration Among the Mossi of the Upper Volta," p. 61.

605,000 with about 590,000 out-migrants. Some areas, particularly higher per capita income areas, gained a net flow of migrants (e.g., Nairobi extraprovincial district), while others of lower per capita income lost population (e.g., central province).[40]

All these indicators of the extent of migration confirm the general impression that migration is a conspicuous and pervasive phenomenon in present-day Africa. Although some workers return to their rural tribal areas and not all migrate to urban areas, African urban centers are growing at a faster rate than rural areas, and in large part, migration is responsible. Permanent urbanization, along with conspicuous migration, of a substantial and increasing part of the African population is now a continent-wide phenomenon.

Distance and Direction

In general, for both external and internal movements, the shorter the distance, the greater the likelihood of migration. This general rule is no less true for African migrations. For example, most immigration to Ghana has been over short distances. Only about one in a thousand migrants to Ghana come from outside West Africa; two out of every three international migrants originate from adjoining countries. Over 80 per cent of the migrants to Ghana come from Togo, Upper Volta, and Nigeria. The first two have common borders with Ghana. Migrants from Nigeria to Ghana cross two intervening countries but this exception may be explained by the relatively short distance from Southwest Nigeria to Southeast Ghana. More important, Nigeria has a large population base from which migrants may be drawn, and is the nearest ex-British colony to Ghana. The common use of English as a national language in both countries, their common history, and administrative similarities stemming from common colonial backgrounds, lead the potential migrant to feel that he is not moving into a completely foreign or hostile environment. Finally, contemporary migration patterns from Nigeria to Ghana are continuous with established and institutionalized movements during the colonial era.[41]

The distance principle operates for internal movements in Ghana as well. The greater the distance between the rural area and the town, the

[40] Calculated from S. H. Ominde, "Some Aspects of Population Movements in Kenya," in *The Population of Tropical Africa*, ed. Caldwell and Okonjo, p. 265, tables 3 and 4. The 1960 census of Ghana showed that 42 per cent of the population was born in localities other than the one in which they were enumerated. See Prothero, "Migration in Tropical Africa," p. 256, table 1. For other measures from scattered census reports, see Prothero, pp. 255–261.

[41] Caldwell, "Population: General Characteristics," p. 26; Caldwell, "Migration and Urbanization," p. 114.

lower the probabilities of migration. This inverse relationship reflects (1) the greater costs of transportation associated with greater distance; (2) the greater extent of isolation from relatives in towns as distance increases; (3) the lower rates of diffusion of knowledge from towns to villages; and (4) with increasing distance, the society and economy of the village become more traditional and less affected by changes occurring in towns.[42] Hence, the relationship between distance and migration is very much tied to the entire process of social change that generates migration.

The same argument applies with equal force to directionality. Two interrelated patterns may be observed: (village) rural to (town) urban mobility and movements from poorer to richer areas. Both are integral interrelated patterns in social and economic change. General movements to Ghana, as well as to other African states, are from relatively poor areas, which is true for internal movements from village to town. As Caldwell notes, much of the population movement within Ghana is still directed to cocoa farms and gold mines, but the towns have become increasingly important destinations for both internal and external migrants. Thus, although migration between rural areas is still the predominant pattern in tropical Africa, the most significant migration is the movement into towns. The streams of migration that were once largely rural in destination and in origin have been increasingly diverted to towns and urban areas. Because much of the economic development has been concentrated in towns, the demands for labor often cannot be met by the local supply; increasingly this demand is met by rural migrants.[43]

Indeed, as we noted, one of the most significant and portentous developments in contemporary Ghana is the swelling of town populations as a result of rural migration. Because the larger the town, the lower the proportion of the labor force engaged in agriculture, rural-uban moves become entwined in the general processes of social and economic modernization. Rather than being areas of large-scale industry, most towns are chiefly commercial and service centers. The direction of rural-to-urban migration within Ghana is thus determined by previous settlement patterns and general economic development within the country.[44]

International migration into Ghana, which becomes differentiated significantly from internal movements with increasing nationalism, may

[42] For example, the proportion educated decreases with distance from towns. See Caldwell, "Determinants of Rural-Urban Migration in Ghana," pp. 374–375. For similar findings in East Africa, see Southall, "The Demographic and Social Effects of Migration on the Populations of East Africa," pp. 235–238.

[43] Caldwell, "Migration and Urbanization," p. 125; Caldwell, "Determinants of Rural-Urban Migration in Ghana," p. 362; Prothero, "Migration in Tropical Africa," p. 252.

[44] Caldwell, "Migration and Urbanization," pp. 125–135.

also be viewed as one form of rural-to-urban migration. About 70 per cent of the immigrants to South Ghana come from rural villages. When the decision to move and obtain a job is made, the question of where to move is made in terms of a Ghanaian town just as well as to one in their own country. Therefore, internal and external migration represents movement between rural areas, and the trend toward rural-to-town mobility is significant. The growing industrialization of the Southern areas of Ghana, and their need for laborers, has shaped the movement from the poor and crowded Northern areas.[45]

Indeed "the society and economy of Southern Ghana is in many ways an African counterpart to the countries of overseas European settlement. To each, people came from other areas of similar culture for their personal economic betterment." [46] The crowded areas of the upper region of Ghana may eventually serve as a pool of labor hungry industries in the South, as Southern Italy's population was for factories of Northern Italy.[47] Similarly, just as immigration from Europe to the United States in the nineteenth century was in part a rural-to-urban move, responding to early industrialization, so are internal and external moves to Ghana. Moreover, migration patterns are in transition in Africa. Despite the social, political, and economic significance of village and rural to town and urban moves, several other directionality patterns exist.[48]

Two additional features of migration processes, not unrelated to directionality, are important. The first is the seasonal and temporary character of African migration; the second is the process of chain migration. The tensions created, on the one hand, by the existence of strong family, kinship, and tribal ties characteristic of a society in transition combined with an institutionalized system of migration established during the colonial period, on the other hand, may be resolved in several ways. First, migration away from home may be temporary; second, migrants may move with their families or move alone at first, subsequently followed by families; third, migrants who move alone and do not return and do not send for their families may send money or gifts back to village areas; finally, migrants may be assisted in various ways in the urban area by relatives and fellow tribesmen.

Characteristically, labor markets in West Africa have been dominated by migrant workers shuttling between villages and employment sites. For example, among Mossi migrants of Upper Volta most stay away regard-

[45] Ibid., pp. 117–120.
[46] Caldwell, "Population: General Characteristics," p. 26.
[47] Caldwell, "Migration and Urbanization," p. 121.
[48] For a discussion of movements rural-rural, rural-urban, urban-rural as well as seasonal (six months), temporary (up to two years) and permanent moves, see Prothero, "Migration in Tropical Africa," pp. 252–255.

less of work (and most work is farm labor) for five to six months coinciding with the dry season at home. According to Skinner, only about 20 per cent do not return at the end of the season.[49] A somewhat different picture emerges from migration to Ghana, where we must separate international from internal migration and desires and intentions from actual return movements.

Among international migrants to Ghana, most intend to return eventually to their country of origin. Only one out of eighteen immigrants intend to remain in Ghana. But intention does not correlate perfectly with reality. Caldwell suggests that a large proportion fail to return home. Perhaps some do not return because of the expense of the return trip or because their social and economic ties have multiplied within Ghana. Hence, although most immigrants feel that they should return home, at least for periodic visits, the majority have never managed to make a single return visit.[50] The nearly universal determination by immigrants to return home is no less characteristic of internal migrants. However, most movers from rural Ghana areas to Ghana towns fulfill their intentions.[51]

Migration in Ghana has always had a seasonal component, but not all migration is seasonal. In the Southern areas of Ghana where jobs are plentiful, people move not only because of a desire for some cash income, but also because of a desire for *higher* incomes. These migrants tend to be longer term settlers, although again most express the desire to return home.[52] Formerly, most migrants from Northern Ghana returned home for planting; married men usually migrated alone and sent for their families on finding a steady job. The present tendency is toward longer term migration, although the expressed intention among migrants is still to return home eventually.[53] Obviously, the normative ties to place of birth are still quite strong and even for more permanent migrants total severance is too painful. Although, within Ghana, movement is often circular — from village to town and back to village — net rural-to-urban

---

[49] Skinner, "Labor Migration Among the Mossi of the Upper Volta," p. 68; see also Berg, "The Economics of the Migrant Labor System," p. 160.

[50] Caldwell, "Migration and Urbanization," p. 118. Along with such permanence is more equal sex ratios, suggesting that for international migrants, moves at least over time are of families (p. 115). In his survey of Nigerian and Togolese migrants in Ghana, Caldwell finds that 94 per cent stated that they had intended to return to their homelands, but a majority had lived in Ghana for more than ten years ("Population: General Characteristics," p. 25).

[51] See Caldwell, "Determinants of Rural-Urban Migration in Ghana," p. 377. Gil points out that 80 per cent of the migrants in Ghana stay less than one year at a time ("Immigration into Ghana and Its Contribution in Skill," pp. 202–206).

[52] Caldwell, "Migration and Urbanization," pp. 111–112.

[53] T. E. Hilton, "Population Growth and Distribution in the Upper Region of Ghana," in *The Population of Tropical Africa,* ed. Caldwell and Okonjo, p. 287.

movement has been large. Caldwell predicts an increase in long-term internal migration, greater family movement, and a general decline in seasonal migration within Ghana.[54] Similarly, studies in East Africa point to the increase in urban growth and rural-to-urban migration for the period following colonialism and projections are made for more permanent migration in the future.[55]

Permanent movements from village to towns in Ghana are frequently chain migrations and exhibit some efficiency and strains of that process. About 75 per cent of rural migrants indicate that help from friends and relatives is given; half received help from friends and relatives in housing and feeding, and one-fifth received assistance in their search for a job. Three-fifths had to borrow money, most from relatives, to make the trip from the village. On arrival in a town, 40 per cent stay at first with relatives and one-fourth more stay with friends from the same district. One in twelve, having neither relatives nor friends, goes to that part of town where fellow district migrants reside. Only one-fifth of the rural-urban migrants search immediately on their own for a room or a house.[56] The permanent migration from outside Ghana to Ghana exhibits similar characteristics. The majority of immigrants from Togo and Upper Volta to Ghana settle among their relatives and ethnic groups. Four out of every five international migrants to Ghana made their original journey on their own but of those who arrived alone, half have sent for relatives.[57]

In addition, the migrants who remain in Ghana towns maintain contact with tribe and family by sending home gifts and money. These remittances do not appear to be a transient phase of migrant life: over four-fifths of urban migrants claim that they send money to the village even after long absences. The flow of cash and goods back to distant villages, as well as heavy rates of return migration, are obvious mechanisms for rural social and economic change, as well as for strengthening ties between town and village populations.[58]

Seasonal and temporary movements, chain migration, and the retention of contacts with the village even among permanent migrants are important both in predicting the future course of migration in Africa and in analyzing the consequences of migration. At this point, it is important to stress that not all international migration is permanent nor is all internal movement temporary. The patterns that may be observed suggest

[54] Caldwell, "Migration and Urbanization," pp. 135–144.
[55] Gutkind, "African Urbanism, Mobility and the Social Network," pp. 49–51.
[56] Caldwell, "Migration and Urbanization," pp. 141–142.
[57] Ghansah and Aryee, "The Demographic and Social Effects of Migration in Ghana," p. 200; Caldwell, "Migration and Urbanization," p. 117.
[58] Caldwell, "Migration and Urbanization," pp. 141–147. See also Caldwell, "Introduction," in *The Population of Tropical Africa,* ed. Caldwell and Okonjo, p. 25.

that with time, and, in turn, greater economic development, permanent migration will become the dominant pattern of movement in Africa. Nevertheless, some have pointed out that stabilizing the work force under African conditions would require a large expenditure on social services, housing, and support for the worker's family. In conjunction with the difficulties of restructuring urban areas, few workers may be willing to abandon their place in traditional villages or give up land rights. Thus, Berg suggests that until basic economic changes occur in Africa, the pattern of temporary migration will persist.[59]

Differentials and Determinants

No description of migration processes is complete without some notion about who moves and who stays. Although we will focus more fully and systematically on the general question of differential migration in Chapter 11, a brief description of the characteristics of movers and nonmovers in Africa is of analytic importance for understanding the relationship between socioeconomic modernization and migration. Again, studies of differential migration in Ghana will be highlighted.

Because of the temporariness of migration and the economic factors associated with why people move, it is not surprising that young males predominate among movers. As in most migrations, young adults are heavily concentrated in the rural-to-urban migration in Ghana. When a person is no longer dependent on the older generation and when he is in a position to decide with some independence where he wants to live and how he is to be employed, he is most likely to migrate. Nor should we neglect to note the direct recruitment of the young for jobs. The predominance of the young among internal migrants within Ghana is parallel to age differentials in international migrations to Ghana. For example, in a survey of migrants to Ghana from Togo and Nigeria, less than one-eighth arrived after age thirty, and over 40 per cent were less than twenty years of age.[60]

The general tendency in Africa is for males to migrate more than females. For example, most migrants in Sierra Leone are males who form substantial majorities in those areas experiencing inward migration. The 1963 census revealed that the diamond-mining area in eastern Sierra Leone had a total excess of 46,000 males. In several towns of diamond-

[59] Berg, "The Economics of the Migrant Labor System," pp. 174–175.

[60] Caldwell, "Determinants of Rural-Urban Migration in Ghana," p. 376; cf. Gil, "Immigration into Ghana and Its Contribution in Skill," pp. 202–206. Caldwell, "Migration and Urbanization," p. 116, table 3.2; Skinner, "Labor Migration Among the Mossi of the Upper Volta," p. 162.

mining areas, there were less than 500 females per 1,000 males.[61] In part, excess male migration rates reflect the greater independence of males, the temporariness of migration, and the type of economic opportunity available (as well as recruitment practices) in towns, mines, and cocoa plantations, which are male dominated. Although fewer women migrate, those who do are more likely to stay longer. One African study suggests that a higher proportion of female than male migrants intended to settle permanently.[62] In Ghana, although more males migrate than females, survey data point to the rapid reduction of the sex differential in rural-to-urban migration, an additional indication of trends toward more permanent migration. Similarly, survey and census data in Nigeria show a trend toward sex equalization in heavy migrant areas, increases in female migration, and a high proportion of married migrant households.[63]

The propensity to migrate increases steadily with family size. In Ghana, males who had ever migrated rose steadily from 33 per cent among those with one male sibling to 50 per cent among those with five or more male siblings.[64] Part of this no doubt reflects chain migration, partly the increased pressure on subsistence in rural areas for those in larger families, and in part the lesser family constraints on sons moving when other sons remain at home. Perhaps those in larger families are relatively more deprived, economically and socially, than those in smaller families, and thus respond more readily to these pressures through migration.

Ghanaians are aware of the strong link between education and out-migration from rural areas. In Caldwell's survey one of the most common responses to the question why a certain person stayed in the rural areas was that he had no schooling; to the question of why another person had gone to the town the response usually was that he had been to school. These attitudinal responses are no mere fantasy. Objective information suggests that of the males and females who had no schooling, less than one-fourth migrated from rural to urban areas, whereas two-thirds of the males and over six out of ten of the females with secondary or university

---

[61] Clarke, "Population Distribution in Sierra Leone," pp. 275–276; similar higher rates of male migration have been recorded for East Africa. See Ominde, "Some Aspects of Population Movements in Kenya," p. 268, table 5.

[62] Cited in Goode, *World Revolution and Family Patterns*, p. 185; see also Michael Banton, *West African City* (London: Oxford University Press, 1957), p. 217; A. I. Richards, *Economic Development and Tribal Change* (Cambridge, Eng.: Cambridge University Press, 1953), pp. 265–267.

[63] Caldwell, "Determinants of Rural-Urban Migration in Ghana," p. 368; C. N. Ejiogu, "African Rural-Urban Migrants in the Main Migrant Areas of the Lagos Federal Territory," in *The Population of Tropical Africa*, ed. Caldwell and Okonjo, pp. 323–329.

[64] Caldwell, "Determinants of Rural-Urban Migration in Ghana," p. 371.

schooling had migrated.[65] Education and occupation obviously have a close relationship; without education or training, obtaining a good job is highly unlikely. Both education and occupation are related to income and wealth. It is not surprising, therefore, to find that a disproportionate fraction of the conspicuously wealthier households were migrants. Twice as many of those found in "above average" households planned to move to urban areas compared to those found in "below average" households.[66] Indeed, taken together, these factors suggest the importance of the economic motive for migration and how migration potential is tied to wealth and education. Caldwell finds that "pull" factors in the minds of people are the most important reasons given for moves, and Skinner notes that the Mossi from the Upper Volta place so much emphasis on the economic motive for labor migration that none states they have gone to the Gold or Ivory Coast for any other reason.[67] However, the likelihood of pull factors operating to induce migration is contingent on the financial ability to move and the knowledge of opportunities elsewhere. Consequently, migration in modern Africa is similar to present-day European migration in that it is mostly "unorganized," and is usually carried out for economic reasons. But we should not overlook the possible rural pressures, demographic and social, encouraging migration in Africa. The key to understanding the direct relationship between education and migration in Africa rests with the meaning of education as compared to wealth and the importance of both with respect to knowledge of urban opportunities. In turn, these opportunities are related to the nature of chain migration and the interaction between relatives in urban areas and the village community.

There is a very strong association between the presence of some rural household members in the towns of Ghana and the likelihood of other members of the household visiting the town on a temporary basis. Often this serves as a prelude to migration. In short, chain migration is an important mechanism in rural-to-urban migration in Ghana.[68] However, chain migration does not account for why migration gets started in the first place or who starts it. Part of the initiation of migration is brought about by the fact that some households come to regard themselves as migrant households; these are "better-off" households that may have part of their income coming from urban areas and that provide

---

[65] Ibid., pp. 369–371; the direct relationship between education and migration has also been found for Nigeria. See Ejiogu, "African Rural-Urban Migrants . . . ," pp. 326–327.

[66] Caldwell, "Determinants of Rural-Urban Migration in Ghana," pp. 366–367.

[67] Caldwell, "Migration and Urbanization," p. 138; Skinner, "Labor Migration Among the Mossi of the Upper Volta," p. 66.

[68] Caldwell, "Determinants of Rural-Urban Migration in Ghana," p. 367, table 3.

higher levels of education for their children. In turn, households become defined as wealthier when their standard of living is raised with town money. Hence, chain migration.[69] Moreover, it seems likely, in conjunction with other differentials in African migration and with comparative materials on migration processes, that education and wealth may reveal the greater feeling of "relative deprivation" among selected subgroups within a society. Those who have begun to taste the advantages of education and cash income may no longer be able to satiate their social, economic, and political appetites in the rural-traditional areas. Hence, it is not unexpected that those subgroups who may feel relatively deprived may have the greatest probabilities for mobility.

We may deduce from this description that a list of characteristics of villagers who do not move would include older persons, less educated, poorly informed, poorer persons, those living at greater distances from urban or town areas, and those who do not have relatives or friends in towns. Moreover, when these characteristics are taken together it seems clear that the more closely integrated a person is within the village, economically, politically, socially, and culturally — that is, the more someone has to lose by moving — the less likely he is to move. It is interesting to note in this connection that two out of every three persons who stayed in the village explained this by saying that they had a farm or had been occupationally successful in the village; one out of every six had some strong political or familial tie within the village.[70]

THE IMPLICATIONS
OF AFRICAN MIGRATIONS

The preceding sections have emphasized the role of migration as a response to social, political, economic, and cultural changes in Africa and the nature of the migration process itself. Although for analytic purposes migration may be viewed as a dependent variable in the examination of change, it is quite clear that migration must also be viewed as an independent variable affecting change processes. Given a pattern of population movement, what social, political, economic, and cultural consequences ensue?

Just as the transformation of African society has converted idiosyncratic movement into a conspicuous pervasive phenomenon, so has migration restructured African society. As Caldwell notes in connection with Ghana: "Migration has profoundly affected Ghana, and its extent is a reflection of the depth of the economic and social changes which

[69] Ibid., p. 375.
[70] Caldwell, "Migration and Urbanization," p. 139.

have occurred during this century. It, in its turn, is an agent of further change." [71] Thus, to round out relationships between socioeconomic changes and migration, we must examine selective consequences of migration in Africa.

Demographic Consequences

One primary demographic consequence of migration has been in population redistribution, particularly urbanization. It has already been noted that about two-thirds of urban growth in Ghana is a function of internal and external migration. Moreover, because of the selectivity of migration, persons with certain characteristics are more concentrated in towns in contrast to rural village areas. However, the high rates of natural increase in rural areas and the high rates of return migration reduce the equilibrium function of migration; in short, the siphoning of excess rural population through mobility to urban areas has been less than dramatic.[72]

Little direct information on the consequences of migration for mortality seems to be available. One would expect that the selective migration from village areas of young adults might alter the age structure of the rural area to increase areal mortality rates. The extent of such changes in age structure of both rural and urban areas is not clear, particularly with the high fertility rates in both areas, which generally result in a heavy concentration of persons in the very young ages. It is also indeterminate whether the mortality level of migrants has been affected in any way. However, some available data suggest a marked urban-rural differential in mortality in tropical African countries; in some countries the crude death rate in urban areas is around one-half the crude death rate in rural areas. Part of this may reflect the younger age structure of towns resulting from in-migration. But it may also be assumed that the large towns are healthier because of improvements in public health measures and increases in physicians and hospitals as well as in the general standard of living. For example, in Northern Ghana, males have more favorable mortality rates than females, contrary to what is generally the case in most other countries. Hilton argues that most adult males in Northern Ghana have participated in seasonal migration, thus spending a considerable part of their adult years in Southern Ghana, where health facilities and a more favorable environment prevail. Women, on the other hand, remain in the North during the

[71] Caldwell, "Population Change," in *A Study of Contemporary Ghana*, ed. Birmingham et al., p. 112.
[72] Caldwell, "Determinants of Rural-Urban Migration in Ghana," pp. 376–377.

dry season and suffer from periods of recurrent hunger.[73] In addition, rural-urban migration may be selective of healthier persons.

A major factor related to variation in fertility levels in Ghana is the sex balance controlled by selective migration. The percentage of females living for considerable periods of time without a husband is accentuated in areas of low income and high out-migration of married males. In those areas, fertility is relatively low. Hence, although it is easy to show a relationship between regional income and fertility, it is also misleading. Caldwell suggests the possibility that with a rise in the standard of living and subsequent family migration, fertility may increase.[74]

Among the economically better-off in towns, the status of women and of children is changing and families are worried about the expenditures required for large families. Although the question of family size is discussed in towns, there is no evidence that desires for family size reduction have occurred. In rural areas of Ghana, the large family is still very much admired. But large families are advantageous economically only in predominantly subsistence farming areas of the North and not in the cash economy areas of the South. With the spread of the cash economy and pressures to educate children for urban occupations, along with continued economic development and social modernization associated with urban areas, the conditions appear ripe to result in increased pressures for smaller families.[75]

Economic Growth

The migrant labor system in West Africa represents an "efficient" adaptation to an economic environment. Historically, migration has permitted West Africa to enjoy more rapid economic growth than otherwise might have been possible. Berg argues that labor migration has been an economic benefit to labor exporting villages as well as to recipient areas.[76] Nevertheless, others have argued that temporary migration makes labor productivity lower than it would be if the same labor force were permanent; it prevents establishing a permanent industrial labor

[73] Caldwell, "Introduction," *The Population of Tropical Africa*, ed. Caldwell and Okonjo, p. 11; Hilton, "Population Growth and Distribution in the Upper Region of Ghana," p. 289.

[74] Caldwell, "Population Change," p. 97. This is similar to the argument that demographers have made about the likelihood of increased fertility in the early stages of industrialization or modernization where standards of living increase or in general where mortality declines. In the long run others have argued that declines in mortality may result in decreases in fertility. Cf. Chapter 6, this book.

[75] Caldwell, "Population Prospects and Policy," in *A Study of Contemporary Ghana*, ed. Birmingham et al., pp. 161–162. Cf. Chapter 6, this book.

[76] Berg, "The Economics of the Migrant Labor System," p. 160.

force, prevents the acquisition of skills and labor organization, and may lead to social problems in towns and mining areas where males from different ethnic groups are thrown together.[77]

Seasonal migration among the Mossi has affected the agricultural practices of Mossi in rural villages, the types of crops they produce, and work patterns. Seasonal migration has resulted in the discontinuance in large part of family farming; collective farming needs every male hand. Moreover, attitudes toward farming have changed from farming for subsistence to farming for profit. As a result, many Mossi migrants who return give up agricultural pursuits. Some turn to local trade, whereas others resort to trading enterprises between the home community and the area of destination, Ghana. Thus, labor migration has changed the economic and material life of the Mossi, but it is not clear whether it has resulted in any substantial increases in the standard of living.[78]

Migration strengthens the economic infrastructure through the need to develop roads and transportation facilities. The cash economy has spread to rural areas as a result of the interchanges of population between rural and urban sectors of Ghana and other African countries. Migration may prove critical in encouraging and stimulating industrialization processes in the larger towns, particularly the development of heavy industry. Rather than serving as a response to rapid industrialization and the need for an urban labor supply, migration in Africa may stimulate industrialization and generate economic development. Thus, not only are rural areas changing because of the links to urban areas but urban values and structure are also changing because the urban centers are tied to the outside world.[79]

Sociopolitical Changes

Examining the economic consequences of migration in Africa without taking into account some short- and long-run social and political consequences would be oversimplification. Despite the apparent economic advantages of labor migration, seasonal movements may generate social and political problems. Such temporary migration means

[77] Singer, "Demographic Factors in Subsaharan Economic Development," p. 242.

[78] Skinner, "Labor Migration Among the Mossi of the Upper Volta," pp. 69–72; see also Elliot Skinner, "Labor Migration and Its Relationship to Socio-Cultural Change in Mossi Society," in *Social Change,* ed. Immanuel Wallerstein (New York: Wiley, 1966). However, Caldwell argues that town earnings in Ghana indeed have increased the rural standard of living ("Determinants of Rural-Urban Migration in Ghana," p. 377).

[79] Caldwell, "Migration and Urbanization," pp. 120, 144.

/ *urban problems in U.S.*

disrupting agricultural production and authority structure in rural areas. In urban areas, it means establishing a permanent unskilled labor force, and a young, male, potentially violent population. For society as a whole it may mean unemployment and group tensions. One tension associated with migration is the alterations it engenders in authority, family, and kinship relationships. For example, migration has altered traditional marriage patterns among the Mossi, and migrants are no longer beholden to elders who formerly controlled all lineage resources. Urbanization and migration tend to undermine the control of the younger generation exercised by parents because of the separation factor. The absence of the father in those cases where migration is heavily male selective has an obvious affect on wives, family discipline and authority, and family relationships. Where women migrate and settle in the same number as males, they become much more independent when compared to village women.[80]

The general diffusion of social and economic changes from town to village brought about by rural-to-urban movement and large-scale return migration has generally meant continuation of strong links between towns and villages. In one sense, these village-town ties and the tensions generated thereby raise the question of how migrants "assimilate" in urban areas and how they are received when they return to the rural community. Skinner details the mediating role of expatriate Mossi chiefs in areas of destination as forces that maintain effective ties between the migrant and his homeland. In destination areas, Mossi males do not come into close contact with the local population, and do not learn the language or customs. Even in mining areas, some mines are worked solely by Mossi migrants who retain traditional attitudes and values.[81] Similarly, Banton argues that the changes brought about by migration into cities cannot be explained without taking into account the patterns of "group alignment," perceived by immigrants and affected by the structure of the larger political, economic, and social system. He argues that immigrants are absorbed into the urban system of Freetown in West Africa not by individual changes in line with the melting-pot conception of assimilation but through membership in a local group of people drawn from tribal sources.[82] Similar pluralistic processes of migrant adjustments in urban areas have characterized racial and ethnic patterns in the United States, as well as in other areas.

[80] See Skinner, "Labor Migration Among the Mossi of the Upper Volta," p. 73. For a general discussion of the impact of colonialism on urbanization in Africa and in turn on the African family, see Goode, *World Revolution and Family Patterns,* pp. 186–187 and chap. 4; Banton, *West African City,* p. 217.

[81] Skinner, "Labor Migration Among the Mossi of the Upper Volta," pp. 76–77.

[82] Michael Banton, "Social Alignment and Identity in a West African City," in *Urbanization and Migration in West Africa,* ed. Kuper, pp. 146–147.

Nevertheless, African residents in towns are not merely transplanted rural residents who seek a conscious modification of rural ideas and habits suitable under new conditions. Rather, even where "tribalism" prevails in urban areas, it is part of the urban process, and may be considered an adaptive mechanism.[83] In urban areas, very few Africans drop their associations with tribal areas completely. Hence, tribal modes of behavior coexist with urban social relations. Thus, international migrants do not merge imperceptibly into traditional Ghanaian society and do not usually expect to do so. Ethnic associations that abound in many African urban towns thus serve as agents of resocialization, fitting new migrants into their new milieu.[84]

We noted earlier that migration was selective in terms of education and occupation. Migration has thus led to the concentration in urban areas of persons with jobs associated with particular strata. Class and ethnicity often become interrelated. In the economic competitive situation of the town, migrants form "ethno-professional" communities or become what Wallerstein calls "supertribalized" for protection and advancement.[85] Developing class consciousness in urban areas is less divisive than might appear, and such patterns may be consistent with the transformation from the traditional tribal framework to the "modern" loyalties associated with nationalism. The notion of tribalism in urban areas, or social group alignment, or supertribalization, is not unprecedented. For example, in the United States, *Landsmannschaften* did not function as a long-term segregating influence; rather it eased the acculturation and absorption of foreign immigrants to urban areas at the turn of the twentieth century.[86] Thus, extended kinship is not necessarily incompatible with African urban society nor does African mobility invariably weaken *all* traditional kinship and group ties. Although political, economic, social, and cultural factors associated with migration weaken kin bonds in many ways, they also bind kin together, particularly be-

[83] See, for example, Peter Gutkind, "African Urban Family Life and the Urban System," *Journal of Asian and African Studies,* 1 (January 1966), pp. 35–42; Paul Meadows and Ephraim Mizruchi (eds.), "Introduction," *Urbanism, Urbanization, and Change: Comparative Perspectives* (Reading, Mass.: Addison-Wesley, 1969); Kenneth Little, "The Role of Voluntary Associations in West African Urbanization," *American Anthropologist,* 59 (August 1957), pp. 579–596.

[84] See J. Clyde Mitchell, "Urbanization, Detribalization, Stabilization and Urban Commitment in Southern Africa," in *Urbanism, Urbanization and Change,* ed. Meadows and Mizruchi, p. 472; Caldwell, "Population: General Characteristics," p. 26; Nzimiro, "A Study of Mobility Among the Ibos of Southern Nigeria," p. 128.

[85] Wallerstein, "Migration in West Africa: Political Perspective," p. 155.

[86] Gutkind, "African Urban Family Life and the Urban System"; Little, "The Role of Voluntary Associations in West African Urbanization," pp. 579–596.

cause men have to rely on kinsmen for assistance in dealing with their transformed social network.[87]

It is likely that the particular changes in areas of origin of large scale seasonal migration may be less dramatic or at least more subtle when compared to more permanent migration. Skinner argues that the seasonal movements of the Mossi from the Upper Volta are legitimated by family and friends by according the Mossi immigrant prestige and status. Nevertheless, migration is too common in Mossi society for the return migrant to occupy the center stage very long. As time passes, migrants are fully reabsorbed into the life of the community. They become, in time, indistinguishable from Mossi men who have not been away and from those who plan to migrate the following year.[88] Yet, on the other hand, migration brings new ideas particularly for children born in towns, who may return with their parents at some point to the village. To these urban-born children, village life constitutes a frame of reference that is new, different, and foreign to their experiences.[89]

One factor that shapes the complexity of African societies is the large number of diverse languages spoken. Earlier we noted that linguistic barriers may have impeded migration during the precolonial period. In the colonial and postcolonial periods, linguistic and corollary ethnic-tribal heterogeneity presents difficulties in establishing community identity and general acculturation in urban centers. In part, linguistic differences shape the ethnic diversity in cities and the need for migrants to join local tribal segments. Hence, language diversity becomes one mechanism for social isolation, segregation, and potential tension-related phenomena. The African pattern is an accentuated form of parallel processes observed in the United States at the turn of the twentieth century following heavy immigration. But in Africa the pattern is accentuated not only because of the greater number of linguistic differences but also because of the absence of any "host" language as English was to immigrants to the United States, or as in the linguistic equilibrium established in Switzerland.[90]

The most elemental problem of migration is in language and communication with employers and others with whom the migrant interacts.

[87] Gutkind, "African Urbanism, Mobility and the Social Network," pp. 48–60; Trouwborst, "Kinship and Geographical Mobility in Burundi (East Central Africa)," pp. 166–182.

[88] Skinner, "Labor Migration Among the Mossi of the Upper Volta," p. 69.

[89] Wallerstein, "Migration in West Africa: Political Perspective," p. 157.

[90] On the linguistic equilibrium, see the articles by Kurt Mayer, "The Impact of Postwar Immigration on the Demographic and Social Structure of Switzerland," *Demography*, 3:1 (1966), pp. 68–89; "Migration, Cultural Tensions and Foreign Relations: Switzerland," *Journal of Conflict Resolution* (June 1967), pp. 139–152.

Language is not only a means of communication but is the single most important criterion of group identification and social identity expressed in language loyalty. Although tension creating, the diverseness of ethnic groups speaking many languages may mean, in time, a greater social acceptance of other African migrants.[91]

In sum, the consequences of migration stem indirectly from general processes of social and economic change of which migration is a part, as well as directly from the migration process itself. We may be able analytically to disaggregate these components, but in reality they are much more complex. African society is in a stage of transition from traditional to modern. The pace of that change has been accelerated by external forces and internal dynamics. We may slice cross-sections of Africa and examine change over distinct time periods. But change processes are continuous rather than discrete. The changes brought about by general social, economic, cultural, and political processes and by the specifics of migration have thrust African society into the modern world. It is premature to evaluate and analyze fully the results of African migration patterns when the processes of change have not yet crystallized. Caldwell notes that despite widespread poverty in the Black Africa of legend and of modern nationalism, the pace of social change is startling and staggering.[92] Some Africans have experienced the transformation of their society in a way that no European witnessed in his lifetime. The pace, newness, and heterogeneity of these dramatic changes require that analyses remain tentative and sketchy.

SOME COMPARATIVE OBSERVATIONS

The analysis of migration in African society from the precolonial period through nationalism and independence illustrates the general relationship between social and economic modernization and migration. However, although the common response to colonialization, industrialization, and modernization (or more generally social, economic, political, and cultural change) has been geographic mobility, the *specific* nature and character of that response have varied widely. Countries in various stages of social, political, and economic growth have received substantial numbers of immigrants. The United States, Germany, and France were areas of heavy immigration in their early phases of industrialization, whereas Switzerland has experienced a large inflow of

[91] Greenberg, "Urbanism, Migration and Language," p. 51 ff.; cf. Caldwell, "Migration and Urbanization," p. 118.
[92] See his "Introduction" to *The Population of Tropical Africa*, ed. Caldwell and Okonjo, p. 3.

migrant workers from Italy as a response to postwar economic growth and labor demands.[93] Other countries have experienced heavy emigration as a relief from rural population increase or from the inability of their urban areas to accommodate rural migrants economically or socially. Ireland, England, and Sweden at various times are examples.[94] During social and economic change most countries have undergone urbanization, a substantial part of which has been the flow from rural areas, but the extent of such movement has varied enormously. Other countries have experienced emigration at an early stage of economic growth and subsequently a heavy rate of return migration, for example, Puerto Rico.[95] To be sure, modernized and modernizing countries have had some combination of these migration patterns, as well as others, and often experience different patterns over time as the pace and level of social and economic change fluctuate. Nevertheless, despite the heterogeneity of migration responses to social and economic modernization, one process is beyond dispute: an integral part of modernization and industrialization has been accelerated geographic mobility. The study of African migrations may illustrate the general migration response to social and economic change but not the specific form of that response.

Although industrialization and socioeconomic modernization cannot occur without migration, the reverse may not necessarily be true: migration may occur without signs of industrialization and social modernization. In Africa, as well as other underdeveloped countries, migration at times is a response to imposed external pressures or pressures on rural agricultural subsistence due to rural population increases. Although some changes in both the rural and urban populations have occurred, migration has been less an adjustment-equilibrium mechanism for rural areas because of high rates of rural natural increase. The general difficulties associated with rural-to-urban migration are compounded in many areas by the slow pace of economic development, which, in part, has not kept pace with the rural inflow to urban areas and the natural increase of urban populations.

[93] See Ernest Rubin, "The Demography of Immigration to the United States," *The Annals of the American Academy of Political and Social Science*, 367 (September 1966), pp. 15–22; see also the discussion and sources cited in United Nations, *The Determinants and Consequences of Population Trends* (New York, 1953), pp. 100–106; on Switzerland, see footnote 90 above.

[94] See Brinley Thomas, *Migration and Economic Growth: A Study of Great Britain and the United States* (Cambridge, Eng.: Cambridge University Press, 1954); Alva Myrdal, *Nation and Family* (Cambridge, Mass.: MIT Press, 1968), pp. 17–21; United Nations, *Determinants and Consequences of Population Trends*, pp. 100–106.

[95] Jose Alvarez, *Return Migration to Puerto Rico*, Institute of International Studies, Population Monograph Series no. 1 (Berkeley: University of California, 1967).

This general argument has significant parallels to the theory relating fertility to modernization processes outlined in Chapter 6. We suggested that in the modernization of Europe, North America, and Japan, a common response had been the reduction of fertility. But it was a multiphasic response and adjustment; the particular mechanisms of fertility decline varied with the specifics of the social, economic, political, and cultural situation. Moreover, whereas industrialization and modernization have as integral correlative processes mortality and fertility control, the reverse does not necessarily hold: mortality reduction, and to a lesser extent fertility declines, may occur without industrialization and modernization. This same theoretical principle applies to migration as well.

Historical changes in African migrations, the causal nexus of migration changes, and the processes and consequences of migration in Africa pose several comparative questions. What insights into the general relationship between migration and social, economic, political, and cultural change may be obtained by analyzing African migrations? What migration processes may be observed in Africa that parallel the experience of other nations?

Socioeconomic Modernization and Migration

Social and economic modernization in Africa, as well as in other countries, implies some basic changes in the organization of society. To detail and specify these changes requires a dynamic framework of analysis. Precolonial or preindustrial traditional societies are generally characterized by relative stability. It is not surprising to find this characteristic in harmony with the basic features of "traditional" social organization: the systems of status, kinship, economy, polity, and culture. The dominance of kinship ascriptive systems, which were primary in our fertility analysis, take on additional relevance for studying migration. The lack of structural differentiation and the dependence of individuals on community and kin constrain any large-scale movement. Indeed, the movements that occur in traditional society are those which are institutionalized into the political system (war, conquests), economic system (search for better land), social-kinship system (exogamy), or are of "deviant" individuals.

Colonialism in Africa and industrialization processes in other areas are forces of change in the basic fabric of traditional social organization. Colonialism affected migration directly through labor recruitment but drastically altered the fabric of African society and as a by-product loosened the constraints minimizing mobility. The alteration of the economic system through taxation and economic expansion and the general shift from a subsistence to cash economy fostered migration. In turn, economic changes, engendered by external political control and exploitation, altered further the political and social systems through the need for centralized administrative bureaucracies, replacement of tribal authority, reduction in kinship control, and placement of the young in new role-bargain relationships. Consequently, different values emerged: achievement rather than ascription, universalism rather than particularism. The structural differentiation that ensued from colonialism thus altered the relationships among individuals and relationships between individuals and their communities.

These same basic social changes that characterized Africa during the colonial period are not very different from the basic changes associated with industrialization. This does not mean that both processes are identical. Rather, colonialization and industrialization imply the general restructuring of society in which migration patterns played an integral role. The specifics of migration vary and depend on the starting point, the pace of change, and the interaction among social subsystems. The general result has been increased geographic mobility. Indeed, just as relative stability is integral to the social fabric of traditional society, so it is clear that relative mobility is integral to the changes generated by the major social revolutions associated with colonialization and industrialization.

Comparative Migration Processes

Although the specific migration processes in Africa when taken together are unique, some dominant processes of movement have precedence in other areas of the world. The uniqueness is both in the total combination of processes and in the accentuated form in which selected processes are manifest within Africa. Indeed, no more revealing evidence on the relationship between socioeconomic changes and migration processes in comparative context may be cited than the parallels between African and non-African migration, some of which have already been noted in the general discussion.

1. One dominant feature of African migration is its temporariness and concomitant high rates of return movement. Although this migration pattern is accentuated within Africa, it has many parallels. For example, it is estimated that perhaps a third of the European immigrants to the United States in the mid-nineteenth and twentieth centuries returned to their country of origin. Comparable remigration rates have been noted for other areas that received heavy migrations from Europe, for example, Brazil, Argentina, and Canada. More than half the migrants

to Argentina returned to Europe and over six out of every ten migrants to Venezuela between 1950 and 1955 reemigrated. Similar patterns characterize the Puerto Rican exchanges with the United States, as well as other international exchanges.[96]

2. Another feature of migration in Africa, not unrelated to remigration, is the extent of labor, seasonal, and repeat migration. Again, these are not unique African patterns. For example, repeat migration has been found to be an important characteristic of American and Danish internal migration.[97] In the early part of the twentieth century about 10 per cent of the Italians entering the United States had been there before.[98] In addition to the seasonal Mexican farm workers in California and seasonal agricultural workers in New England, some European migrants to the United States also have been seasonal migrants, hiring themselves out on alternative shores of the ocean. For example, historical records reveal the pattern of seasonal migration among English house painters who pursued their trade in the United States during the spring, worked in Scotland for the summer, and returned home in the autumn. Other forms of seasonal migration within Europe in the early twentieth century and in the post-World War II era have been documented.[99]

3. The trend in Africa appears to be in the direction of longer-term, permanent migration to urban towns. The general extent of "urbanization" is low in Africa compared to almost every other area of the world. But the patterns point to a more rapid increase as migratory flows accelerate and as industrialization proceeds. Although the pace is different, the pattern is similar.

[96] See Frank Thistlethwaite, "Migration from Europe Overseas in the Nineteenth and Twentieth Centuries," in *Population Movements in Modern European History,* ed. Herbert Moller (New York: Macmillan, 1964), pp. 75–76; Arthur H. Neiva, "International Migrations Affecting Latin America," *Milbank Memorial Fund Quarterly,* 43 (October 1965), pt. 2, pp. 125–128; Alvarez, *Return Migration to Puerto Rico;* Clarence Senior, *The Puerto Ricans* (Chicago: Quadrangle, 1961), chap. 1; Anthony Richmond, *Post-War Immigrants in Canada* (Toronto: University of Toronto Press, 1967); K. V. Pankhurst, "Migration Between Canada and the United States," *The Annals of the American Academy of Political and Social Science,* 367 (September 1966), pp. 53–62; R. T. Appleyard, "The Return Movement of United Kingdom Migrants from Australia," *Population Studies,* 15 (March 1962), pp. 214–225.

[97] See the series of articles by Sidney Goldstein: "Repeated Migration as a Factor in High Mobility Rates," *American Sociological Review,* 10 (October 1954), pp. 536–541; "The Extent of Repeated Migration: An Analysis Based on the Danish Population Register," *Journal of the American Statistical Association,* 59 (December 1964), pp. 1121–1132; *Patterns of Mobility, 1910–50* (Philadelphia: University of Pennsylvania Press, 1958).

[98] Thistlethwaite, "Migration from Europe Overseas in the 19th and 20th Centuries," p. 77.

[99] Ibid., pp. 77–78; see also articles by Kurt Mayer cited in footnote 90 above.

4. The importance of the economic motive in both internal and external migration is well established.[100] It is no less true for Africa. Nevertheless, we have specified the mechanism that ties the economic motive to the social structure, particularly the role of knowledge of "opportunities," the relationship to education, and the pattern of chain migration. In addition, the general concepts of relative deprivation and social integration were isolated as determinants for selective movements. We will discuss in Chapter 11 the generality of these determinants.

5. The extent of chain migration in Africa is well documented. Many studies of internal and external migration in other countries have pointed to the significance of chain migration as an essential feature of most large-scale movements.[101] As Davison suggests for West Indian migrants to Great Britain:

> The more people who go, the more they encourage others to go. There are districts in the West Indies today where there are more people away in Britain than there are at home. Those who remain feel left out and depart to join their families and friends. It is clear that this momentum is likely to be self-perpetrating.[102]

The same description might have been written about migration within Africa.

6. The general pattern of assimilation or more generally the consequences of migration might have been predicted for Africa from general studies and vice versa. The assumptions associated with the inevitability of migrant assimilation are not only challenged by African data but by other research that has focused on pluralistic societies.[103] The general consequences of migration in Africa for rural and urban areas and for the migrants themselves are unique only in their extent but not in their form.

7. African and non-African migrations have many other parallels

---

[100] See United Nations, *Determinants and Consequences of Population Trends*, chap. 6.

[101] See, for example, John S. and Beatrice D. MacDonald, "Chain Migration, Ethnic Neighborhood Formation and Social Networks," *Milbank Memorial Fund Quarterly*, 42 (January 1964), pp. 82–97; Alvarez, *Return Migration to Puerto Rico;* Donald Bogue and K. C. Zachariah, "Urbanization and Migration in India," in *India's Urban Future*, ed. Roy Turner (Berkeley: University of California Press, 1962), p. 42; Petersen, "A General Typology of Migration."

[102] R. B. Davison, *West Indian Migrants*, Institute of Race Relations (London: Oxford University Press, 1962), p. 8; cf. Alvarez, *Return Migration to Puerto Rico*, p. 6.

[103] See, for example, Milton Gordon, *Assimilation in American Life* (New York: Oxford University Press, 1964); Judah Matras, *Social Change in Israel* (Chicago: Aldine, 1965); Shmuel Eisenstadt, *The Absorption of Immigrants* (Glencoe, Ill.: The Free Press, 1955); Shmuel Eisenstadt, *Israeli Society* (New York: Basic Books, 1968).

as well as differences. The relationship between language diversity and migration processes, patterns of institutionalized migration processes, and the relationship between nationalism and the development of rigid boundaries are among the issues raised by African migration patterns that require more systematic research. Parallels do not imply similarity; they do suggest the potential for abstracting from the unique to uncover general principles of migration processes.

Part
3

Social Differentiation
and Population Processes

Chapter Eight

SOCIAL DIFFERENTIALS IN DEMOGRAPHIC PROCESSES

In any analysis of human society, the scientist is confronted with the methodological dilemma of emphasizing its overall unity and relative homogeneity or its internal complexity, variegation, and heterogeneity. When the focus is on total societies — communities, nations, groups of nations, or broad geographic regions — the form of inquiry is referred to as *societal analysis*. When the units chosen for analysis are smaller than a total society — subgroups, subcultures, subcommunities, or subpopulations — and differences between subunits are compared, the methodological strategy is called *differential analysis*. Both approaches rest on assumptions regarding the most fruitful means to uncover the nature of social processes. Underlying societal analysis is the implicit, often overlooked, assumption that internal variations within societies are less significant conceptually and empirically than heterogeneity between societies or changes in total societies over time. Furthermore, the analysis of total societies rests on a postulate that the individuals and groups that form the mosaic called society share a sufficient commonality to permit historical and comparative research. Thus, generalizing to total societies combined with assumptions about the most rewarding ways to locate the determinants of social structure and social change processes results in treating the total society as the basic unit of analysis.

In contrast, differential analysis emphasizes the heterogeneity of total societies and concentrates on variations within societal units. It argues that the influence of critical analytic variables on social processes may be identified and isolated more successfully by examining group variations within societies. When subgroups within the same society are

compared and specific differences are isolated and contrasted, we gain
the analytic advantage that these subgroups share common factors because overall societal features are "controlled." However, it is incorrect
to equate societal analysis with comparative and historical research and
argue, as is often implied in the literature, that the analysis of differentials is cross-sectional, static, and culture-bound. Historical and comparative perspectives may be utilized within the framework of differential
analysis as well: social groups may be compared over time and between
different societies. Nevertheless, differential analysis adds to historical
and comparative perspectives a third option not possible within societal
analysis: social processes may be compared at the same point in time,
within the same society, among different subgroups, subcultures, and
subpopulations. Differential analysis, therefore, allows for "time" and
"society" to be controlled, whereas societal analysis, which is neither
historical nor comparative, i.e., when it is cross-sectional, is descriptive
rather than analytic. Often, as a result, differential analysis is the only
possible methodological strategy when the evidence available is limited
to a cross-sectional snapshot of social processes. Finally, the usual units
used for differential analysis are social categories or subgroups, rather
than the total society. However, because total societies are in fact composed of smaller social units, inferences about the structure and functions
of whole societies may be made by analyzing how the parts interrelate to
form the whole. Similarly, an understanding of the workings of social
process among subunits may be extracted and generalized to cover the
operative mechanisms of social process in whole societies. In population
analysis, the cumulative social characteristics of total societies are usually
treated under the rubric *population composition,* within which *population structure,* age and sex composition, is an integral and essential
component.

The analytic choice between an emphasis on total societies or an
emphasis on differentials within societies is in large part tied to theoretical and methodological issues associated with the units and levels of
analysis.[1] In addition, the complexity of society and the nature and extent of its internal heterogeneity are important empirical considerations
in deciding whether societal or differential analysis is to be accentuated.
Although some types of analytic questions may be investigated with
either societal or differential analysis, other problems are best treated
within only one perspective. In an overall view of the social scientific
enterprise the distinction between the two types of analytic foci is artificial. Despite differences in approach, societal and differential analyses
are viewed most accurately not as competing or alternative perspectives

[1] See the discussion in Chapter 2, this book.

but rather as complementary and supplementary frameworks that together reinforce and strengthen the generality of observations obtained
within only one framework. The best of classical sociological literature,
particularly Weber and Durkheim, treats societal and differential analyses as mutually supporting methodological strategies.[2]

In Part 2 we investigated the general societal transformations
linked to mortality, fertility, and migration processes. These broad
changes, particularly connections between modernization and population
processes in comparative and historical perspectives, provide us a better
comprehension of the interrelationships and interconnections between
social and demographic systems. In the next several chapters our attention shifts to another side of the analytic coin — the analysis of demographic heterogeneity within societies. Although we will not be concerned directly with the specific problem of differential demographic
responses to modernization, our analysis of selected social differentials
in demographic processes is consistent with the general conclusions
derived from our societal analysis of population processes. Together
these two methodological strategies provide us with a comprehensive
portrait of the dynamic interplay between population and social systems.

THE CONTEXTS
OF DIFFERENTIAL ANALYSIS

Before we illustrate in detail the sociological approach to the study
of social differentials in mortality, fertility, and migration processes, a
general and logically prior set of issues must be clarified: What are the
analytic goals and objectives of differential demographic analysis? In
what theoretical contexts may we best appreciate the empirical findings
of differential mortality, fertility, and migration research? In short, what
types of analytic demographic questions will differential analysis help us
solve?

For some analysts the rationale for studying differentials in demographic processes has already been suggested: heterogeneity within societies exists and therefore must be studied. Empirically, we may observe
systematically or casually that not every woman gives birth to children,
and, of those that do, some have larger families than others; not everyone
migrates and some move greater distances and more often than others;
although everyone dies, some die at younger ages than others and from
different causes. Also, these individual demographic observations often

---

[2] See the comments on this point and specific illustrations in Neil Smelser,
Essays in Sociological Explanation (Englewood Cliffs, N.J.: Prentice-Hall, 1968), pp.
69–75.

appear to have a patterned regularity at the group level: for example, the rich seem to live longer than the poor; Catholics tend to have larger families than Protestants; young adults are more migratory than older persons. Because socially patterned variations occur in demographic behavior and processes, the population specialist must identify the forms and account for the patterns of these variations.

Beyond the justification of studying differential demographic patterns because they exist, we need to inquire further into the ways in which analyses of demographic differentials are conceptualized and utilized in research. It is instructive to clarify theoretical and methodological notions of relevance and significance implicit in demographic research on social differentials.

Social Differentials as Determinants

One main objective of any scientific analysis — societal or differential, comparative, historical, or cross-sectional — is to identify the determinants or causal factors involved. In a demographic context, the goal is to obtain insights into the determinants of population processes. The ways in which societal demographic analysis may be utilized toward this objective have been demonstrated in the preceding chapters. Analyzing social differentials in demographic processes has a similar objective: One way to locate the social factors that are important in determining variations and changes in population processes is to examine subgroup differences in these processes. The direct role of differential analysis in locating the determinants of population processes may be understood by briefly examining a critical differential for demographic analysis; age. Age factors are direct determinants of fertility, mortality, and migration, at macro- and microlevels of analyses; age is a complex variable connoting biological as well as social and cultural meaning.

First, age sets biological limitations on reproductive behavior. Obviously, most women are able to conceive and give birth only within rather restricted age categories. Moreover, fecundity varies within the reproductive age span, being greater at the younger end of the span. Within the biological limitations imposed on reproduction by age, age has important sociocultural meaning related to reproductive performance. One apparent mechanism by which age affects fertility directly relates to variation in the age of entry into sexual unions.[3] In most societies, where reproduction takes place largely in legitimate, socially sanc-

---

[3] See the discussion of age of entry into sexual unions as an intermediate variable in Kingsley Davis and Judith Blake, "Social Structure and Fertility: An Analytic Framework," *Economic Development and Cultural Change*, 4 (April 1956), pp. 211–218.

tioned, family units, age of entry into sexual unions as it relates to fertility behavior is more or less equivalent to age at marriage, broadly defined to include consensual unions. Because age at marriage is circumscribed culturally and socially, age factors become direct determinants of fertility behavior linking social structure and demographic process. At the macrolevel of analysis, the reproductive potential of a society or subsociety and its actual fertility level is determined, in part, by the age distribution of its female population and sociocultural forces that shape variations in age at marriage and the proportions marrying.

Age is related to mortality in similar ways. Variation in death rates among age groups partly reflects the biological inevitability of death. Death rates are always higher among the youngest and oldest age groups of a society than among persons in the "middle" years, irrespective of the level of mortality or extent of its control. However, differential mortality by age, under conditions of relative "control" or "noncontrol," often reflects sociocultural factors affecting the quantity of deaths at various ages. In this sense, infant mortality differentials reflect both biological components and sociocultural dimensions that are age related. Such forms of mortality as infanticide, parricide, and suicide are socially significant and age related. Societies or subunits within societies that are composed disproportionately of older persons will be characterized by differential death rates when compared to societies or subunits composed largely of young adults. Populations composed mainly of groups that do not reproduce and that are subject to higher mortality risks, i.e., infants and older people, will, all other things being equal, have lower birth rates and higher death rates. One major determinant of differential mortality rates of suburban areas and retirement communities is obviously their differential age structures.

Age as a migration determinant does not operate in large part through its biological implications but rather through its social meaning. As we shall examine in detail in Chapter 11, the relationship between age and migration is strong and pervasive. Age factors determine the extent of mobility largely because age defines life-cycle stages and is interrelated with sociocultural community ties. Hence, age differentials in mobility may be viewed as indicators of social attachments and community integration. In turn, the age structure of a society or of subgroups within society is an important determinant of overall mobility rates. Because the age structure of a population has clear-cut relationships with economic and family systems, which, in turn, are major determinants of migration levels, analyzing age differentials in migration connects these social subsystems to demographic processes.

The key role played by age structure and distribution as a determinant of population processes and the fact that age structure is itself a product of the balance of past demographic events provide the demographer with the ingredients to construct formal population models based on the dynamic interplay of population processes and structure. Furthermore, analyses of the age composition of societies permit the reconstruction of demographic rates and the projection of demographic trends, when the assumption of *ceteris paribus* is made.

In a related but distinctly separate way differential analysis may be viewed as assisting *indirectly* in the search for the determinants of demographic processes. Once social differences in fertility, mortality, and migration are isolated, we can ascribe other social characteristics of those categories or groupings as determinants of demographic processes. In simple form, we may argue that better educated persons have been characterized by lower fertility; hence, one determinant of fertility levels is educational attainment. Young, newly married couples are more likely to be mobile; therefore, age and marital status determine migratory potential. Infant mortality is lower in urban industrial groupings; thus, urbanization and industrialization are determinants of reduced mortality.

At times, we may not be satisfied with this type of mechanistic inference, although the literature on differential population processes abounds with such "explanations." Often we shall need to go beyond the mere ascription of social characteristics as determinants to raise more difficult questions. What is it about the particular characteristic that relates to population processes? What are the values, attitudes, and life style which social characteristics connote that underlie the formal relationship? What is it about education that leads to lower fertility? What are the connotations of age and marital status that result in its relationship to migration? What are the features of urban-industrial life that influence infant death rates? Surely education, age, marital status, place of residence, type of economy, and other social, economic, political, and cultural characteristics have no magical qualities that result in their interrelationship with demographic variables. Hence, in using differential analysis to isolate the determinants of population processes, we must go beyond the mechanical correlations to identify the complex matrix of values and life styles that the social differentials reflect. These values and life styles are the underlying causes of social differentials in demographic processes.

Differentials and Diffusion Processes

Evolving from the consideration of social differentials as direct and indirect determinants of demographic processes is the use of differential analysis as guidelines in projecting future patterns. In an attempt to assess theoretically future demographic trends or extrapolate empirically present patterns into the future, social differentials in fertility, mortality, and migration provide us with clues about the greater susceptibility to demographic change among social groupings. Those social groupings that may be identified as the forerunners of demographic change are sources of potential diffusion to other groupings, particularly if the subgroup represents the direction in which the entire society is moving. If, for example, the more educated limit their family size, plan and control the timing of their reproduction, then as total units become more educated, as societies or subgroupings within societies raise their educational level, similar patterns of motivation for family-size control and planning will evolve and lower overall fertility or lower fertility for these specific groups will emerge. If urbanized, industrialized segments of a population are characterized by greater geographic mobility, then as societies become more urbanized and industrialized, geographic mobility will increase. Similarly, if infant mortality rates are inversely related to income, then as overall income increases, infant mortality should decrease.

Moreover, subgroups that have led in demographic changes may also serve as *models* of diffusion. The education level of societies or subgroups may not be changing but the matrix of values associated with reduced fertility may diffuse to the less educated sectors of a society in "imitation" of the fertility behavior and attitudes of the elite models. Once geographic mobility begins among those who are most involved in urban-industrial processes, the pattern may filter down to other segments of society. Similarly, once the underlying causes of reduced infant mortality among higher income groups are understood, technological, medical, and health services may be diffused to lower income groups.

Projecting future trends, either with the social recomposition model (i.e., as a larger number of persons enter into categories which have been in the forefront of population changes, the level of change of the society will accelerate) or with the diffusion model (i.e., as the social change process filters down to other groups of society, demographic change will be imitated), is a direct objective of differential analysis and one major context within which social differentials are analyzed. Although such inferences have often turned out to be incorrect empirically, it is not the inconsistency of the reasoning that needs remedying but the mechanistic analogies that have often been made, the inadequate number of variables that have been included, and the failure to recognize the complexities of sociodemographic changes.

It should be clear that when empirical extrapolations from the past and present to the future are made, knowledge of heterogeneity and variation in demographic processes within aggregate units is indispensable. Indeed, the number of differentials that are entered into extrapolation equations has a strong positive correlation to the probable accuracy of those extrapolations. For example, refined fertility projections and extrapolations, partly based on expected family size, must include variations by socioeconomic status, race, religion, etc.[4]

Controlling Differentials

Up to this point we have considered social differentials as "operative variables," that is, social variables that are known or thought to affect demographic processes and are allowed to vary to measure that effect. But social differentials are also *parameters,* that is, determinants that are known or thought to affect demographic processes but are made or assumed not to vary.[5] In some intergroup and international comparisons, we may be interested in comparing the effects of certain variables on population processes and, hence, are forced to control the effects of other variables that are important overall but which nevertheless are not of direct analytic concern.

This process of "control" operates in two ways, depending on the unit of analysis. If the total society is analyzed, we may contrast and compare the fertility, mortality, or migration patterns between two countries. But we know that these population processes are affected directly by such compositional differences as age, sex, marital distributions, and various socioeconomic factors. Hence, if we want to compare differences in population processes we must utilize statistical measures that exclude the effects of significant compositional differences that are generally relevant but irrelevant to the problem under investigation. We have already shown how this is done in our analysis of total societies.

If the analysis unit is social group comparisons within countries, the logic remains the same. For example, let us hypothesize a relationship between religious preference and fertility.[6] To test this hypothesized relationship, we may find data showing that religious groups have different fertility patterns. But we also know that social class affects fertility and that religious groups have different social class compositions. Thus, to refine our analysis of religion and fertility, we need to eliminate or control the influence of these variables. Our problem now becomes, Is the relationship between religion and fertility solely a function of the

[4] See, for example, Ronald Freedman et al., *Family Planning, Sterility and Population Growth* (New York: McGraw-Hill, 1959); Pascal Whelpton et al., *Fertility and Family Planning in the United States* (Princeton: Princeton University Press, 1966).

[5] For this distinction, see the discussion in Smelser, *Essays in Sociological Explanation,* pp. 16–20.

[6] This relationship is elaborated in Chapter 10, this book.

different social class concentrations of religious groups? Or, put in another way, does the relationship between religion and fertility operate at all social class levels or within social class categories? Of course, other social characteristics of religious groups must be controlled or eliminated to conclude that religion per se and not some "intervening" variable is critical in fertility variation. Moreover, we could have posed the problem in reverse: What is the relationship between social class and fertility controlling for religious differences? Nevertheless, some variables that affect the dependent process under investigation will be treated as operative variables, whereas others will be viewed as parameters. The failure to "control" for intervening variables may lead to misdirected conclusions. A classic sociological illustration of this failure is in Max Weber's use of statistics on the types of school attended by Protestants and Catholics, in Baden. From the overrepresentation of Protestants in certain types of schools, Weber draws the conclusion about the "spiritual peculiarities" of Protestantism and Catholicism. However, Weber failed to account for areal differences. The overall correlation hinges on the fact that in the towns with a larger Protestant majority (in a country otherwise Catholic), there were more Protestants than Catholics in secondary schools. If the religious denomination of students had been compared *controlling* for differential population composition within school districts, the proportion of Catholics and Protestants in secondary schools would have been identical.[7]

Cumulative Differentials and Population Composition

Differential analysis is also important at the macrodemographic level, especially for questions of population composition. Two major areas of macrodemographic research have been based on differential analysis: analysis of the proportional representation of social segments within a society, and limitations set by population composition on social structure and social institutions.

The first type of macrolevel inquiry derived from differential analysis is directed to differential growth rates of subgroupings within total societies. As a direct consequence of differential fertility, mortality, and/or migration patterns, subgroups within society exhibit different growth rates and, hence, affect the general social composition of society, particularly when social group differentials are large. For example,

[7] See Max Weber, *The Protestant Ethic and the Spirit of Capitalism,* trans. Talcott Parsons (New York: Scribner's, 1958), pp. 188–189; on this specific point, see Kurt Samuelson, *Religion and Economic Action* (New York: Harper Torchbook, 1961), pp. 138–142.

higher fertility among the black population of Rhodesia, all other things being equal, will result in higher rates of black population growth and a growing proportion of black population in the total Rhodesian society. Differential growth rates of selected segments of society and the consequences of differential growth for the sociodemographic composition of society have been important themes in some classic research on differential fertility. These themes continue to underlie population eugenics and, in particular, the alarm expressed about the higher fertility among the poor, less educated, lower class, low I.Q. segments and its implications for the social composition of society. Differential growth rates of the less advantaged have often been one of the latent themes of the Malthusian argument. Perhaps it is not such a great leap from the context of examining the social composition implications of differential fertility to the question of the changing composition of world population. The argument has been made in various forms that the proportional representation of "Western" countries of the world total population is declining as the poorer, less educated, underdeveloped areas of Asia, Africa, and Latin America grow rapidly. Both arguments employ the same general pattern of logic and are derived from parallel types of differential analysis.

Usually, social differentials in fertility and mortality are not large enough to affect dramatically population composition. Of greater significance are the consequences of differential rates of internal and international migration for the sociodemographic composition of societies. Differential or selective migration is of key importance in population composition when the analysis unit is smaller than the total nation. Research on the redistribution of the black population of the United States from the South to nonsouthern areas and from rural to urban centers is often placed in the context of changing population compositions in areas of origin and destination. Similarly, large-scale immigration from diverse areas of the world or from areas distinct socially and culturally from the receiving country obviously affects the sociodemographic composition of nations. Differential compositional changes as a result of immigration patterns have been the underlying research theme of some studies in differential international migration, often geared to affecting government policies restricting free immigration or placing national or social quotas. The question of the relative proportion of selected segments of populations has been in recent times at the foundation of political conflict: the relative proportion of the "coloured" immigrants to Britain, the size of the Italian segment of the Swiss population, the sharp differential growth rates of Arab and Jewish sectors in Israel, and the growth differentials of white and black segments in white-dominated African nations illustrate the types of issues that emerge from differential demographic analysis and the contexts within which such research is placed. In short, immigration differentials are of central importance in the study of pluralistic societies and of assimilation-acculturation; internal migration differentials are critical in research on the social composition of urban areas and the adjustment-integration of migrants within countries; and general population growth differentials are significant in the changing sociodemographic composition of whole societies.

A second macrolevel inquiry based on differential analysis examines the relationship between the social composition of society and its social institutions and structure.[8] Each social institution of a society presupposes a particular population composition. The sociodemographic characteristics of a population limit the number and types of social institutions and structures that have the potential to emerge within society at any point in time. Hence, population composition places limitations on the institutional structures of whole societies. For example, the nature and character of the labor force structure of a society are limited by the distribution of population in various age categories. A society with a high proportion of young adults and children, as a result of high fertility or selective in-migration or both, will have a different labor force structure than a society composed largely of older persons. Similarly, the number of marriages that can potentially occur in any time period is fixed by the number of eligible persons who can marry. Whether the number of professors in a given population will find academic appointments depends on many social, economic, political, cultural, and personal factors, but the number of professors within a society limits the rate of expansion of educational facilities that depend on their services. These illustrations, among others, indicate how analyzing differentials within society informs us of the compositional restraints on social institutions and social structure.

Because the sociodemographic composition of society is affected by its differential demographic history on the one hand and affects the institutional social structure on the other, it may be argued that the analysis of population composition is a central mechanism for studying the junctures of social and demographic processes. Age, as we have noted earlier, has a clear relationship to each demographic component. But age is also related to social, economic, political, and cultural institutions. Hence, analyzing the determinants and consequences of age structure links demographic processes to social institutions and social structures. Age structure and distribution have been considered of key importance in demographic analysis; they are also a central feature of social structure.

[8] This argument and its development are based on Amos Hawley, "Population Composition," *The Study of Population,* ed. Philip Hauser and O. D. Duncan (Chicago: University of Chicago Press, 1958), pp. 378–380.

Just as age groupings (and sex) are fundamental categories in population research, so they are basic social categories that define the relationship of individuals to society and its culture. Age and sex structures have been called the living record of a nation's population history and have been referred to as "the building blocks of the society." [9] Consequently, investigating age and sex differentials in population processes provides the opportunity to relate basic social processes and demographic systems.

Demographic Differentials as Social Process

Differential analysis is also addressed to the issue of how we can improve our understanding of society or social groups within society through population studies. In part, it may be argued that demographic analysis in general is relevant to the study of social structure and social process, and therefore any analysis that contributes to the clarification and explication of population processes will contribute indirectly to the understanding of social systems. But another valid argument and one of direct significance for the sociological analysis of demographic phenomena emphasizes the contribution of differential fertility, mortality, and migration research for understanding social differentiation within society.

Fertility, mortality, and migration represent patterns of social behavior, social process, and are life-style indicators. Hence, one way to understand how social groups within society differ from one another is to examine differential demographic processes. The orientation of this approach is not on demographic processes as dependent variables but on the subunit per se, and population elements are viewed as integral parts of the social makeup of that subunit. For example, social class groupings vary widely on a large number of items — social behavior, norms, values, life styles. They also vary in their demographic patterns. Thus, differential demographic patterns by social class may be added to the list of social factors that distinguish one class from another. Because fertility, mortality, and migration differentials by social class in part result from broader, more general social class differences, demographic variation may serve as indicators of these broader social processes. Equally important, differential fertility, mortality, and migration affect the fluidity of the class structure and generational replacement in

[9] On the demographic importance of age composition, see United Nations, *The Determinants and Consequences of Population Trends* (New York, 1953), chap. 7. The quotation has been attributed to Ralph Linton by Harry Alpert, "Sociology: Its Present Interests," in *The Behavioral Sciences Today*, ed. Bernard Berelson (New York: Harper Torchbook, 1963), p. 58. On the sociology of age structure, see Chapter 11, this book.

social class categories. Thus, the justification of studying social differentials in demographic processes, according to this line of argument, rests in the merits of discerning the extent of subgroup variation by means of differences in reproduction, mobility, and death. At the macrolevel, differential analysis should provide insight into the fundamental nature of such processes as stratification, household composition, and family structure.

Two important points emerge from this view. First, analysis of differential population processes is important sociologically because it reveals significant aspects of group behavior, social process, and life styles. Because births, deaths, and movement are fundamental and integral elements of social group life in human society, variation in these phenomena should inform us about the subgroups under investigation. It should also provide clues to the basic structure of general social processes. Second, to comprehend demographic processes and their variations, we must integrate analyses of subgroup differentials in population processes with other social characteristics, norms, values, and life styles of subgroups. In this sense, differential analysis in population studies adds another critical juncture to the relationship between sociological and demographic processes. Indeed, when all the contexts and objectives of differential analysis in population processes are taken together it becomes clear that just as societal analysis ties together the sociology and demography of total societies, so differential analysis links the study of social groups to the nature of demographic heterogeneity within societies.

TYPES OF DIFFERENTIALS

The contexts and objectives of differential analysis significantly parallel the arguments used for societal analysis. The differences between these methodological strategies are essentially in the unit chosen for research. But which subgroupings within society are to be examined? In societal analysis, the units selected for investigation — societies, nations, groups of nations, geographic regions — are self-defining. The number of such units, defined historically and comparatively, is relatively circumscribed and limited. However, internal heterogeneity within societies has no self-defining quality nor any imposed upper limit. Hence, the relevant groupings in the differential analysis of population processes must be defined and clarified.

When the social scientist systematically studies social differentials in population processes, he usually focuses on *selected* differentials but not all possible differences. Often the demographer defines "relevant" differentials in fertility, mortality, and migration as those available in the administrative records of censuses or vital statistics systems. Thus, a "relevant" social characteristic for demographic analysis depends "on whether it is capable of being identified and recorded accurately by those who collect the data used by demographers." [10] Similarly, although recognizing that many characteristics differentiate individuals but not all are necessarily relevant, Hawley reduces the question of relevance to "those characteristics of individuals which are enumerable by non-professional personnel employing census procedures. Accessibility to observations, in other words, is an important determinant of what is sub-sumed under composition." [11] Petersen argues tautologically that "a relevant characteristic of a population can be defined as one that exhibits a significant differential pattern with respect to demographic rates" or "a population datum is relevant if either demographic or social rates differ by this variable." [12]

We are not, at this point, concerned with those characteristics collected or included by census or vital statistics agencies but rather *why* these characteristics are collected; we are interested not only in those differentials that have been related in past research to demographic processes, but rather in which differentials *should* be related and *why*. We need not necessarily restrict our research to analyzing the easily observable differentiators but include as well subtle social-psychological variables that *may* have relevance for demographic theory and research.

Intuitively, we might expect studies of fertility to investigate differentials by skin color but not by hair or eye color, despite the relative ease of observation of all three variables. Religious preference might be thought to be an important factor in mortality differentiation but probably not voting preference. Migration patterns will likely be related to age and sex but not to artistic abilities or height. Thus, the study of differentials in fertility, mortality, and migration selects the "differentials" to be examined; that selectivity is not based on the simplified dichotomy of biological versus nonbiological traits, or of ascribed versus achieved status, or on the basis of the ease of observation and enumeration, or the inclusion of *all* social, psychological, and cultural differences.

It would not serve our general objectives to list some major relevant characteristics that should be involved in studying social differentials in population processes or in examining population composition. Any such list usually does not exhaust all potential relevant characteristics; nor could items listed be mutually exclusive. Hence, such lists as

[10] Warren Thompson and David Lewis, *Population Problems*, 5th ed. (New York: McGraw-Hill, 1965), p. 58.

[11] Hawley, "Population Composition," p. 361.

[12] William Petersen, *Population* (New York: Macmillan, 1961), p. 69; also from the second edition, 1969, p. 92.

have been prepared by demographers from time to time may *illustrate* the types of characteristics that, under some conditions, are relevant, but usually are not very instructive or informative. Rather, we need to indicate briefly the underlying criteria of relevance for social characteristics, i.e., why some physical characteristics are important while others are not; why some biological characteristics are more relevant to demographic research than others; why some achieved and ascribed social characteristics are of greater significance for some research problems and not others.

Two tests of relevance for studying social differentials in population processes seem indispensable: First, does the characteristic, or attitude, or value have social and cultural meaning? Second, is there theoretical justification for relating the differentiator to a particular demographic process?

Age and sex are critical factors in social and demographic processes simply because these biological characteristics are invested with social and cultural meaning. Hair and eye color are not. There is age grading in societies and sex role differentiation. The differentiation "race" based on skin color has little if anything to do with biological factors associated with race but rather with its social and cultural significance. Moreover, a nonbiological ascribed characteristic such as place of birth has relevance only when place of birth (country, province, state, city, neighborhood, etc.) has social and cultural meaning. It may not make much difference vis-a-vis fertility and mortality processes whether someone living in California was born in Montana or in Idaho, but it *may* be significant whether he was born in Mississippi or Massachusetts because these states generally reflect different social, economic, cultural, and political milieu. For migration research, on the other hand, distinctions between Montana and Idaho as states of birth may be significant. Hence, it is often not the social, personal, and cultural characteristic that has independent significance for sociodemographic analysis, but rather it is the meaning attached to the characteristic, the possible socioeconomic or cultural environment it may reflect, and the specifics of the analytic problem under investigation. Therefore, the first test of relevance of a characteristic or trait is whether it connotes social or cultural meaning.

A second test is to determine whether the particular relationship between the trait or characteristic and the particular population process under scrutiny is *theoretically* relevant. Contraceptive usage and fecundity may have clear theoretical importance for fertility analysis but no manifest relevance for migration or mortality research. Citizenship may have clear sociopolitical meaning, but there may be no theoretical justification for linking it to fertility. Whether one majors in the social or natural sciences in college is an important variable in determining career choice and perhaps subsequent migration patterns. But it may not be very significant to relate that variable to mortality or fertility. On the other hand, direct theoretical links between a particular variable and a specific population process may not be clear, but they may have indirect connections. For example, contraceptive usage *may* connote variation in family formation and family size, and, in turn, family formation and size may be connected to migration. One's major in college *may* be a rough indicator of differential tension and psychological pressure, which may be linked to heart disease or suicide potential and, hence, indirectly to mortality. Citizenship *may* differentiate natives and foreigners, which, in turn, may be related to acculturation and assimilation with direct meaning for fertility. When specific connections between social variables and population processes are made, the theoretical justification for such connections must be clarified. This process of finding theoretical links between social differentiators and population elements may uncover that the differentiator per se is theoretically relevant, or that it is to be utilized as an indicator of some other process, or indeed that the linkage has no justification.

Most reviews of differentials in mortality, fertility, and migration cover a large number of subgroup differences, often superficially, treating each variable independently. A more fruitful strategy is to select one major differential and to explore in depth the connections between it and related variables. The choice of a particular differential is secondary to the goal of illustrating the style and complexity of the sociological approach to differential analysis.

Chapter Nine

THE SOCIAL INEQUALITY
OF DEATH

Social inequality is a discernible feature of all known human societies. The forms, scope, and functions of inequality vary considerably from one society to another and, over time, may change as societies evolve. Yet there is a nagging temptation to locate universal elements of social structure that generate inequality. Because social inequality is so central a component of social life, social scientists have long recognized the significance of exploring its various manifestations and the need to investigate the conditions under which its manifold forms emerge. Indeed, the scientific analysis of inequality is a fundamental concern of sociological inquiry, around which have been constructed elaborate theories, methodologies, and empirical research. The ubiquity of social inequality directs attention to the connections between inequality and human behavior, attitudes, and values; to the consequences of inequality for the nature and character of human societies; and to the relationships within societies of subgroups characterized by inequality.[1]

In any investigation into the nature of social inequality, it is important to bear in mind the distinction between social differentiation and social stratification. Social differentiation refers to the ordering of social positions in a hierarchy of evaluation. In all societies, in conjunction with some division of labor, a process of ranking and evaluating the importance of different roles and functions occurs. Hence, at any one point in time we may observe inequality as it relates to subgroups that

[1] Melvin Tumin, *Social Stratification: The Forms and Functions of Inequality* (Englewood Cliffs, N.J.: Prentice-Hall, 1967), p. v.

occupy differentially valued positions within society. In a more dynamic perspective, collectivities or subgroups may continue to occupy the same ranked positions through several generations. When social positions are inherited, differentiation evolves into stratification.[2]

The ranking of positions, whether at one point in time or inherited over time, involves developing within society differential life styles and life chances. "Life style" covers a wide range of factors, among which are included economic and occupational class factors, status-prestige components, and elements of power, influence, and authority. "Life chances" may be viewed in the narrow sense of length of life or may be broadened to include health and general welfare. Indeed, it may be argued that life chances are the consequences of life style in the sense that the quantity of life and the physical quality of life are in large part shaped by the social and economic quality of life.

No matter whether we focus on social differentiation or social stratification, on life styles or on life chances, our concern as scientists of human society is centered, explicitly or implicitly, on social, economic, and political inequalities that exist. As Tumin notes:

> The study of the sources, patterns and consequences of social inequalities has been a dominant pursuit of sociologists and is likely to continue to enjoy widespread attention so long as inequalities persist, and so long as they are consequential for the life chances and life-patterns of the different strata that make up any society.[3]

In this chapter, we will explore inequalities in life chances in the narrow sense of differential mortality. To be sure, death is only part of the broader life-chances concept, but it is an observable, measurable, and dramatic sign of social inequality. Mortality variation among subgroups within society is one consequence of economic, social, and political inequality. Inequality in life and inequality in death are interrelated: persons born wealthy have differential access to education, and in turn subsequent differential occupational opportunities and income, which are linked to differential health and welfare and ultimately length of life. Viewing the process in reverse, we may argue that life styles and socioeconomic environments of persons in different social strata are revealed or indicated by differential mortality. In simple terms, one way to examine the manifestation of inequality is to isolate the dramatic and visible signs of inequality resulting from differential life styles: death and illness. Life chances, in contrast to life styles, are much more de-

---

[2] Kurt B. Mayer, *Class and Society* (New York: Random House, 1955), chap. 1; Kurt B. Mayer, "The Changing Shape of the American Class Structure," *Social Research,* 30 (Winter 1963), pp. 458–468; Walter Buckley, "Social Stratification and Social Differentiation," *American Sociological Review,* 23 (August 1958), pp. 369–375.

[3] Tumin, *Social Stratification,* p. 11.

termined by what at first glance appear to be involuntary and impersonal social forces; but such a view is deceiving.

The determinants of differential mortality among subgroupings within societies are social; hence, an investigation into patterns of death is instructive for the general analysis of social inequality. In short, mortality variation within and between societies is significant for sociological inquiry not only because mortality is an analytic component of population processes that, in turn, may be interrelated with social processes, but also because mortality, as an independent process, may be viewed as a consequence, correlate, and indicator of social inequality. Empirically, mortality is higher in the underdeveloped, "have-not" countries compared to the industrialized, "have" countries; enormous mortality declines have characterized the evolutionary changes accompanying industrialization and modernization. International comparisons and historical trends of mortality largely reflect the inequality of social and economic development and changes in the general standard and level of living. Historical and comparative mortality patterns using the nation as the analysis unit have been explored in Chapter 5. In this chapter the focus is on differential mortality among subgroups within society as a means to explore one manifestation of social inequality.

Life chances are influenced directly by the location of persons in the economic class structure or by one's racial or ethnic characteristic, where racial-ethnic systems overlap with the stratification system. Persons in similar economic or class positions share, in general, similar opportunities and life chances. Indeed, the social inequality of death is not so much a recent phenomenon as it is a recently recognized process. Social scientists recognize today as forms of inequality social patterns that were accepted only a few years ago — not because these were deemed just, but simply because they were still unidentified.[4] This applies with equal weight to mortality, although, in addition, mortality has rarely been conceptualized as a sensitive indicator of social inequality. Differential mortality analyses abound in the demographic literature, but in most investigations the relationships are presented mechanistically without regard to theoretical considerations.

RACIAL INEQUALITY
IN THE UNITED STATES

The inequality of death has many faces in the United States, as in other societies. Mortality differences may be observed between men and women, young and old, farmers and urbanites, college educated and

[4] Otis D. Duncan, "Discrimination Against Negroes," *The Annals of the American Academy of Political and Social Sciences*, 371 (May 1967), p. 86.

high school dropouts, professionals and laborers, rich and poor, and other categories of social differentiation. In the United States, one major social fact of inequality is race, often bisecting social class and residential differentiation. Despite the Emancipation Proclamation over a century ago and numerous Supreme Court rulings and legislation dealing with "equality" of opportunity in education, jobs, housing, and the like, racial inequities not only persist in American society but in many spheres have widened. The two decades following World War II may be viewed as a period of progress for the Negro vis-a-vis his own social conditions — health, education, welfare. Paradoxically, despite major social changes, the position of the Negro *relative* to the majority white community has not substantially improved. Both Negroes and whites have increased their standards of living, but the gap between the two has narrowed little.[5] We have to distinguish, therefore, between "absolute" and "relative" inequality and deprivation. Some pockets of "absolute" deprivation among Negroes remain in southern rural areas and in the urban slums. Compared to the overall social, economic, and political conditions of Negroes before World War II the sharp decline in absolute inequality must be recognized. The vast majority of Negroes suffer from a more subtle and less understood malady — relative deprivation. The relative social, economic, and political position of Negroes compared to whites has changed little and, due to its nature, may have widened precisely because things have improved. In our context, it is not that mortality among Negroes has remained high; to the contrary, major mortality declines have occurred. Nevertheless, mortality among whites has declined more rapidly; hence, the relative gap between white and Negro populations has increased. In short, relative inequality in death has increased despite declines in the absolute levels of mortality.

A fundamental conclusion of the controversial 1965 Moynihan report on the Negro family was that "the circumstances of the Negro American community in recent years have probably been getting *worse, not better*. . . . The gap between the Negro and most other groups in American society is widening."[6] Similarly, the report of the United States Riot Commission in 1968 reached this basic interpretation of the evidence: "Our nation is moving toward two societies, one black, one white — separate and unequal."[7] The picture of racial inequality in the

[5] See, for example, Donald Bogue and Reynolds Farley, "Population Growth, Problems and Trends in the United States," *American Journal of Public Health*, 56, pt. 2 (January 1966), pp. 85–93.

[6] See the report and surrounding social and political controversy in Lee Rainwater and William Yancey (eds.), *The Moynihan Report and the Politics of Controversy* (Cambridge, Mass.: MIT Press, 1967). (Quotation from p. 43.)

[7] U.S. Riot Commission Report, *Report of the National Advisory Commission on Civil Disorders* (New York: Bantam Books, 1968), p. 1.

United States painstakingly sketched by that commission has brought public attention to some very real consequences of racial inequality and its underlying causes. The cumulative effects of the handicaps Negroes encounter at every step in their lives produce a series of unequal opportunities that can only be understood as a vicious cycle.[8] Indeed, the consequence of this life style results in serious disadvantages in life chances.

Mortality differences by race are the outward and visible signs of underlying social problems and measure the ultimate effects of differences in the manner, style, and level of living characteristic of the white and Negro populations. The differential ability of human beings to survive, which reflects in large part social and cultural rather than biological elements, is the net effects of factors associated with the differences in how members of various groups live in society.[9] The Riot Commission notes that the conditions of life in black ghettos are so strikingly different from those to which most whites are accustomed — especially the middle-class majority — that it is important to describe and gauge the effects of these conditions on the lives of the people involved.[10] Thus, whether we view mortality as an *indicator* of inequality, or a *correlate* of inequality, or a *consequence* of inequality, one conclusion is inescapable: differences between whites and blacks in life chances are fundamentally social, economic, political, and cultural and illustrate dramatically the broader racial inequalities pervasive in American society. Racial inequality in death is a function of racial inequalities in life.

We will utilize the white-nonwhite categorization of the American population, despite its scientific absurdity, because it is utilized by vital statistics and census publications in the United States. For most analytic purposes, nonwhite patterns refer essentially to Negroes. Nationally, Negroes comprise 92 per cent of the nonwhite category (approximately 22 to 25 million population in the 1960's); the remaining include one-half million Indians, 450,000 Japanese-Americans, 237,000 Chinese-Americans, 176,000 Filipinos, and 218,000 "others."[11] Although Negroes are the overwhelming majority of the heterogeneous nonwhite category, when they are separated they exhibit even higher mortality rates than the total nonwhite population. Therefore, whereas the absolute rates to be

[8] Peter M. Blau and Otis D. Duncan, *The American Occupational Structure* (New York: Wiley, 1967), p. 204.

[9] Albert J. Mayer and Philip Hauser, "Class Differentials in Expectation of Life at Birth," *La Revue de l'Institut International de Statistique,* 18 (1950), pp. 197–200.

[10] U.S. Riot Commission Report, pp. 266–269.

[11] Helen C. Chase, "White–Non-White Mortality Differentials in the United States," *Health, Education, and Welfare Indicators* (June 1965), pp. 27–38.

presented are underestimates of Negro-white mortality differentials, the *pattern* of Negro-white mortality differences is very similar to the pattern of the more ambiguous categorization of deaths by nonwhite and white.[12]

In the United States, regardless of the measure utilized and as far back as the data extend, mortality has been consistently higher for the nonwhite population than for the white population. In reviewing racial differentials in mortality, several measures of mortality will be utilized. Our objective is not to examine critically mortality measures in a technical sense nor to present all such measures. Rather, we need to show the inadequacy and incompleteness of selected measures of death, particularly with respect to the question of changes in the mortality gap between the two populations.

Crude and Age-Specific Death Rates

The simplest and weakest summary measure of mortality is appropriately called the crude death rate: the number of deaths per 1,000 population. In 1900, the crude death rate for the white population in the United States was 17 per 1,000 population; for nonwhites, the rate was 25 per 1,000. Sixty-three years later the crude death rate discrepancy between whites and nonwhites declined from a 47 per cent difference to a 6 per cent difference — 9.5 per 1,000 for whites and 10.1 per 1,000 for nonwhites.[13] From these data, we might draw the conclusion that the initial wide gap between white and nonwhite mortality that existed at the beginning of the twentieth century has been largely eliminated as mortality for both populations has decreased substantially. However, a more careful look at age-specific death rates shows that such a conclusion would be erroneous.

Because crude death rates are affected by mortality at specific ages and by the age distributions of populations, it is necessary to control for age or examine specific types of mortality that take age factors into account. Crude death rates are therefore poor comparative measures for determining the extent of mortality declines between populations because the Negro population has always been younger than the white population, with a concomitant smaller percentage at the upper age categories where mortality is obviously higher. Thus, the crude death rate tends to understate the relative excess of Negro mortality. For example, a vital statistics study in 1957 noted that crude death rates

[12] Evelyn M. Kitagawa, "Race Differentials in Mortality in the United States, 1960 (corrected and uncorrected)" (paper presented at the annual meetings of the Population Association of America, Boston, 1968).

[13] Chase, "White–Non-White Mortality Differentials in the United States," p. 28.

were 11 per cent higher among Negroes when compared to whites, whereas age-adjusted death rates were fully 50 per cent higher.[14]

Indeed, when one examines detailed age-specific death rates, it becomes clear that the mortality gap between whites and nonwhites has *widened* in recent years. Between 1900 and 1963 the mortality difference between whites and nonwhites for the major span of adult life (25 to 74 years of age) has increased. Although age specific mortality for both populations has decreased overall, the declines have been greater for whites despite their initial lower levels. Among whites, 25 to 34 years of age, mortality declined 84 per cent from 1900 to 1963 (8.1 to 1.3 per 1,000), whereas among nonwhites in the same age group the decline was 74 per cent, from 12.1 to 3.2 per 1,000.[15] Thus, in 1900, the nonwhite death rate among those from 25 to 34 years of age was one and one-half times the white rate; in 1963 the nonwhite rate in the same age group was two and one-half times the white death rate.

Life Expectancy

A better known complex summary measure of mortality is life expectancy at birth, which represents the average number of years that members of the life table cohort (hypothetical) may expect to live at the time of birth. In other words, it is the average age at death of the life table population. The twentieth century has witnessed a significant increase in life expectancy which, on the average, has added about 23 years to the life of each newborn infant in the United States: in 1900, life expectancy at birth in the United States was 47 years, by the mid-1960's it had increased to 70 years. Life expectancy throughout this century has been invariably shorter for nonwhites. In 1900, life expectancy at birth was 48 years for whites and only 33 years for nonwhites; in the mid-1960's, life expectancy at birth was 71 years for whites and 64 years for nonwhites. Even in the prime working ages, life expectancy is significantly lower for nonwhites when compared to whites. In 1966, nonwhite persons age 25 could expect to live 11 per cent fewer more years than whites.[16]

Although this mortality measure, as the crude rates, shows a narrowing of the mortality gap between whites and nonwhites, the trend

---

[14] Cited in Richard F. Tomasson, "Patterns in Negro-White Differential Mortality, 1930–1957," *Milbank Memorial Fund Quarterly*, 38 (October 1960), p. 363.

[15] Chase, "White–Non-White Mortality Differentials in the United States," p. 29. Petersen, on the basis of crude death rates and life expectancy, concludes erroneously that Negro mortality has fallen faster than whites. See William Petersen, *Population*, 2nd ed. (New York: Macmillan, 1969), pp. 554–555.

[16] Chase, pp. 30–31; *Vital Statistics of the United States*, vol. 2, sect. 5 (1966).

comparison is not very reliable. The 1900 life table values, and the age-specific rates upon which it is calculated, are based on only ten states and the District of Columbia, and are no doubt a poor reflection of the entire population. This is particularly true for the nonwhite population because the death registration states covered the urban Northeast and excluded the majority of the nonwhite population in the rural South. Only 5 per cent of all nonwhites were included in the death registration area of 1900 and only 12 per cent by 1910. By 1920, thirty-four states were covered, which included two-thirds of total nonwhite population.[17] Moreover, because life expectancy at birth is a cumulative average by age, it is a less sensitive measure of mortality in our context.

Two measures of mortality that are generally considered to be the most revealing reflections of social and economic conditions and to changes in these conditions over time are: (1) maternal mortality (deaths to women as a result of pregnancy and childbearing), and (2) infant mortality (deaths to infants in their first year of life). Infant mortality may be subdivided into (a) neonatal mortality (deaths to infants in the first twenty-eight days of life), and (b) postneonatal mortality (deaths to infants from the first to the twelfth month of life). Neonatal mortality largely depends on factors associated with congenital malformations, prematurity, birth accidents, and general physiological and biological causes. Postneonatal mortality is the most sensitive single indicator of environmental, social, and economic situations, standards of nutrition, and general factors that can be improved by advances in public health, education, and general social and economic development.[18] Unfortunately, the available quantity and quality of information do not always allow for the separation of these two components.

Maternal Mortality

Deaths to women as a result of pregnancy and childbirth have been sharply reduced in the United States over the past half century, as they have been in every other developed, industrialized country. The maternal mortality rate in the United States is not at an irreducible minimum or the lowest in the world. For example, it is over 50 per cent higher than the rate for Sweden, for 1963 to 1965.[19] Since 1915, maternal mortality

[17] M. Gover, "A Survey of Negro Mortality," *Journal of Negro Education*, 18 (Summer 1949), p. 215; Tomasson, "Patterns of Negro-White Differential Mortality, 1930–1957," p. 363.

[18] United Nations, *Demographic Yearbook* (1966), p. 3.

[19] The maternal mortality rate in the United States from 1963 to 1965 was 34 per 100,000 live births compared to 20 per 100,000 live births in Sweden. At least ten other countries reported lower maternal mortality rates than the United States. A significant part of this higher rate is a function of excess maternal mortality among

has declined by over 90 per cent in the United States. But, as with other mortality measures, nonwhites have had, and continue to have, higher maternal mortality rates than whites. Although the rate has declined substantially in both populations, the relative gap between whites and nonwhites has increased. From 1915 to World War II, the nonwhite maternal mortality rate was slightly less than twice as high as the rate for the white population. Since 1955, nonwhites have had a maternal mortality rate four times as high as the white rate; in 1965, the rate for whites was 21 per 100,000 live births, for nonwhites it was 84 per 100,000 live births. Indeed, the 1965 rate of maternal deaths for nonwhite women in the United States lags behind comparable rates for white women by a *quarter of a century*.[20]

In several states, maternal death rates among nonwhites exceed 125 per 100,000 live births, or fully six times the total white rate. These states include New York, West Virginia, South Carolina, Kentucky, Alabama, and Mississippi. (This is true of Utah and Alaska but the proportion of Negro nonwhites in these states is much smaller than the national total.) In almost half the states where maternal death rates are available, maternal mortality among nonwhites exceeds 100 per 100,000 live births. The range of the maternal death rate among nonwhites is tremendous, reflecting social, economic, and environmental conditions rather than biological factors; the highest recorded rate is 166 per 100,000 live births (West Virginia), the lowest is 20 per 100,000 live births (Minnesota). The range for whites is much smaller with none exceeding 50 per 100,000 live births. Ironically, in the capital of the United States, the District of Columbia, the discrepancy between whites and Negroes is most pronounced: the rate of maternal deaths among Negroes is over fifteen times as high as that among whites! [21]

Infant Mortality

The second mortality measure most often utilized to reflect social, economic, and environmental conditions is the infant mortality rate. Again, nonwhites since the first decades of the twentieth century, when data first became available, have had higher infant mortality rates than whites. From 1915 to 1919, nonwhites had an infant mortality rate of 150 per 1,000 live births compared to 93 per 1,000 live births among whites.

nonwhites. Only three countries (Sweden, Norway, and Denmark) had lower rates than the white population of the United States. See Metropolitan Life Insurance Co., *Statistical Bulletin*, 49 (December 1968), pp. 2–5, table 2.

[20] Mary McCarthy, *Infant, Fetal and Maternal Mortality: U.S. 1963*, National Center for Health Statistics, ser. 20, no. 3 (September 1966).

[21] Ibid., p. 59.

The infant mortality discrepancy between whites and nonwhites increased by the 1960's to a ratio of 2 : 1 in favor of whites, again despite sharp declines for both populations. The 1964 infant mortality rate for nonwhite children has not been recorded for white infants since 1941.[22] The nonwhite infant mortaliy rate in the 1960's in the United States is typical of rates recorded for Southern and Eastern European countries and exceeds the rate characterizing such developing countries as Jamaica, Taiwan, Singapore, Puerto Rico, Trinidad, and Tobago.[23] Hence, although infant mortality has been reduced to one-fourth its World War I level in the United States, gains have been unevenly distributed among whites and nonwhites.

When the infant mortality rate is subdivided into neonatal and postneonatal mortality, the inequality between whites and nonwhites in social and economic conditions can be seen most dramatically. The neonatal rate for nonwhites has remained steady at about one and one-half times higher than whites. The postneonatal rate gap has increased from less than twice as high for nonwhites in the early decades of the twentieth century to three times as high in 1965.[24] The identical pattern may be observed when comparisons are made between 1940 and 1965, or between the 1949–1951 and the 1959–1961 periods. Although white-nonwhite differences in neonatal mortality have widened slightly during these periods, they have not widened nearly so much as postneonatal mortality differences, as a larger percentage of nonwhite babies are taken home to hazardous environmental situations. For example, the infant, neonatal, and postneonatal mortality rates for whites declined in the 1949–1951 to 1959–1961 decade by 16, 12, and 26 per cent, respectively; for nonwhites the decline was 7, 3, and 11 per cent, respectively. Thus, the percentage excess of nonwhite infant mortality compared to whites increased in this ten-year period from 68 to 86 per cent; in neonatal mortality from 43 to 56 per cent; and in postneonatal mortality, the excess rose from 133 to 180 per cent.[25]

Similar to variation by states in maternal mortality, infant mortality among whites (1963) ranged from 18 per 1,000 live births (Utah) to 28

[22] Ibid.; Chase, "White–Non-White Mortality Differentials in the United States"; Eleanor Hunt and Earl Huyck, "Mortality of White and Non-White Infants in Major U.S. Cities," *Health, Education, and Welfare Indicators* (January 1966), pp. 1–18.

[23] United Nations, *Demographic Yearbook* (1966), p. 2.

[24] Chase, "White–Non-White Mortality Differentials in the United States," p. 30.

[25] See Sam Shapiro et al., *Infant and Perinatal Mortality in the U.S.*, National Center for Health Statistics, ser. 3, no. 4 (October 1965); U.S. Riot Commission Report, p. 270; Earl E. Huyck, "White–Non-White Differentials: Overview and Implications," *Demography*, 3:2 (1966), pp. 548–565.

per 1,000 live births (Nevada); the range for nonwhite infants was substantially greater — from 21 per 1,000 live births (Oregon) to 58 per 1,000
live births (Mississippi). Because of poverty, isolation, poor medical
services, and discrimination, Indians in Arizona had an infant mortality
rate of 62.4 per 1,000 live births.[26] Inequality in death, as in life, is the
consistent and persistent, visible and dramatic consequence of the convergence of class and racial-ethnic systems infused with prejudice and
discrimination.

The Context of Inequality

To what can we attribute the sustained higher mortality of nonwhites and the increasing discrepancies between whites and nonwhite
mortality? No doubt, the excess mortality of nonwhites is a multifaceted
and complex problem. Included among factors that must be considered
are (1) biological and hereditary factors; (2) distribution and availability
of medical facilities and health services; (3) socioeconomic factors that
affect the utilization of available medical and health services; (4) personal motivation to achieve a positive state of health; and (5) general
environmental and life-style factors associated with the concentration of
nonwhites in the lower social classes, in poor housing, and in racial
ghettos.[27] Quite obviously, we cannot isolate empirically each of these
factors for analytic purposes not only because they are difficult to
measure but also because the requisite information is not available. We
can obtain some indicators of these factors to get a feeling for their
relative importance.

Before proceeding with some empirical tests of these contributing
and interrelated factors that account for the excess mortality among
nonwhites, we must first ascertain whether the data upon which the
previous analysis was constructed are accurate. Surely we know that
there is underrecording of Negro births and deaths in vital statistics
systems and underenumeration of Negro population in census data. The
extent of such underrepresentation and the potential extent of error have
not been calculated. However, no one can argue that the very real and
significant mortality discrepancies are artifacts solely of data inaccuracies.
But we may inquire whether the *increased* discrepancy is a function of
improved data collection. We have no reliable answer. Nevertheless,
according to analysts and collection agency personnel, the increasing
mortality gap between whites and nonwhites despite general declines in

[26] McCarthy, *Infant, Fetal and Maternal Mortality: U.S., 1963*, pp. 3–4.
[27] Cf. Chase, "White–Non-White Mortality Differentials in the United States,"
p. 36.

both populations is indeed real. For example, it has been argued that the increased mortality gap appears *even after allowances are made for deficiencies in birth and death registration* that were greater at the beginning of the twentieth century and greater among the nonwhite segment.[28]

Let us therefore assume that the mortality excess of Negroes is real and examine some contributing factors. Turning first to biological differences and heredity factors, we must admit that information is limited, and as social scientists we are biased in emphasizing the social, economic, cultural, and environmental dimensions. Nevertheless, some convincing evidence suggests that biological factors, even though they may be operative, are clearly not primary or the most important in the overall picture. This is the unmistakable implication of the tremendous variation by states in nonwhite mortality rates reported earlier, as well as the implication of the declines noted and the social class variation to be discussed.

Another way of looking at the biological component is to examine selected causes of death among nonwhites — particularly those causes of death that are "preventable." Over the years, mortality among the nonwhite population has been consistently higher for most causes of death. But the highest ratios are for tuberculosis, influenza, pneumonia, and homicides, which are in excess of 2 to 1 unfavorable to nonwhites, and are all related to socioeconomic, environmental, ghetto conditions. Tuberculosis, among communicable diseases, is over four times higher as a cause of death for nonwhites (1963) compared to whites, as is syphilis.[29] Looking at infant mortality by cause for the ten largest cities in the United States, excess infant mortality among nonwhites is highest for those causes listed as "accidents," clearly a nonbiological factor! [30] Health conditions also indicate the minimum role biological factors play in the excess mortality of nonwhites.

The next group of factors relates to health utilization, availability of medical and health facilities, and interrelated morbidity factors. If we are able to view inequality in life chances in terms of end-product consequences — mortality, we should also be able to identify inequality in the health conditions of the living — morbidity. As we will show later, poor health and low income are highly correlated. Not only do low-income persons have high levels of illness but fewer receive health services. About 30 per cent of all families with incomes below $2,000 a year suffer

[28] Ibid., p. 31.

[29] Ibid., pp. 31–35; Huyck, "White–Non-White Differentials: Overview and Implications."

[30] Hunt and Huyck, "Mortality of White and Non-White Infants in Major U.S. Cities."

chronic health conditions compared to less than 8 per cent of families
with incomes of $7,000 a year or more; however, nine out of ten high-
income families have health insurance benefits compared to only 34 per
cent of low-income families.[31] These health factors are aggravated for
the Negro population for two reasons. First, and most simply, the proportion of persons in the United States who are poor is three and one-half
times as high among Negroes as among whites (41 per cent compared to
12 per cent in 1966).[32] Because the lowest income group contains a much
larger proportion of nonwhite families, the overall discrepancy in medical
care is significant. Thus, it is not surprising that overall morbidity conditions among Negroes are so much worse on the average than among
whites.

A second more complex fact emerges from the evidence on the
poorer health conditions in the ghetto: *Negroes with incomes similar to
whites spend less on medical services and visit medical specialists less
often.* In the under $3,000-a-year income class, the percentage of family
expenditure spent for medical care (1960–1961) is twice as great among
whites than nonwhites; even among the population with incomes of
$7,500 a year and over, the proportion of family expenditure spent for
medical care among whites is one and one-half times that of nonwhites.
Similar evidence is available for health expenditures per person, per year.
Among low-income persons, total medical expenses per person, per year,
were twice as high among whites than among nonwhites; among high-
income persons ($10,000 a year and over) the total nonwhite medical
expenditure was less than three-fourths of the total white medical expenditure.[33] Together these data indicate that nonwhite families in the
lower income group spent less than half as much per person on medical
services as white families with similar incomes. The lower medical expenditure may be attributed to several factors. Negro households are
larger and require as a result larger amounts of nonmedical expenses for
each household, leaving less money for meeting needed medical care.
Thus, even if the amount spent for medical care *per household* is the
same for whites and nonwhites, the amount *per person* will be, on the
average, lower for nonwhites.

Moreover, some evidence documents that Negroes pay more for
basic necessities than comparable income groups among whites. Finally,
medical and doctor facilities are less conveniently located and are less
available to nonwhites than to most whites. The environmental, sanitation, and neighborhood conditions characteristic of a significant propor-

[31] U.S. Riot Commission Report, pp. 269–270.
[32] Ibid., p. 270.
[33] Ibid., p. 271.

tion of urban Negroes are additional factors.[34] In sum, the inequality of the races in the United States, whatever its origin, whatever causes it to persist, manifests itself in morbidity as well as in mortality differentiation. Indeed, poorer morbidity conditions may be viewed as intermediate links between poorer mortality conditions on the one hand, and poorer socioeconomic, environmental conditions on the other.

Under the general heading of socioeconomic and environmental conditions determining the excess mortality of nonwhites, we are able to consider two general questions. First, are differences between the mortality of whites and nonwhites a function of the differential concentration of these populations in urban, rural, metropolitan, and nonmetropolitan areas? Second, is excess mortality among nonwhites a function of the concentration of nonwhites among the poor?

The rapid urbanization of American Negroes in the post-World War II era, both relative to their urbanization before this period and relative to the urban concentration of whites, may be thought of as contributing to the increasing excess mortality among nonwhites. Moreover, the concentration of urban Negroes in the central core of urban areas and the social class selectivity among whites in the out-migration from urban centers also may contribute to the increased excess mortality. Again, we are unable to estimate precisely the importance of these factors. Some insight may be obtained by examining infant mortality *within* relatively homogeneous residential areas.[35] Data on infant mortality for the total United States (1960–1962) show an excess mortality among non-whites of 85 per cent. In urban areas the excess is 75 per cent, in rural areas 109 per cent or over twice as high; in metropolitan counties the excess is 76 per cent, in nonmetropolitan counties the excess is 96 per cent.

In general, excess nonwhite infant mortality is slightly lower in larger cities with populations of over a half million and in urban areas. Thus, the increased discrepancy between white and nonwhite infant mortality cannot be attributed in large part to the growing concentration of nonwhites in areas that have lower mortality rates. Moreover, the differences between whites and nonwhites *within* all areas are substantial. In sum, differential residential concentrations of the two populations do not account for their differential mortality rates. Interestingly, excess neonatal mortality does not vary much by residence (the range of non-white excess mortality is between 48 per cent for nonmetropolitan

[34] Ibid.
[35] See tables presented in Chase, "White–Non-White Mortality Differentials in the United States."

counties to 59 per cent in metropolitan counties). However, postneonatal mortality, the component of infant mortality that reflects socioeconomic, environmental conditions, ranges from an excess nonwhite rate of 262 per cent in rural areas to 95 per cent in cities of 500,000 or over. Nevertheless, even the lowest discrepancy in postneonatal mortality controlling for area of residence is about twice as high among nonwhites when compared to whites.

The final factor, which underlies some factors already considered, is socioeconomic status. As we will see in a subsequent section, socioeconomic status has long been a key and significant differentiator of mortality in the United States as well as in other countries. The question here is whether the difference between the mortality of whites and nonwhites can be explained by the concentration of nonwhites among the poor and lower social classes. We must point out that little direct reliable information is available as evidence, but some fragments of information seem to add up to a uniform and consistent argument.

First, we know that higher rates of infant mortality are concentrated in deprived socioeconomic areas and deprived social-ethnic populations. Second, if we rank racial-ethnic populations by socioeconomic indicators, the rank will be identical to a ranking on mortality. Kitagawa argues [36] that income may account for some differences noted between Negroes, Japanese, and white life expectancy rates. Using life expectancy at birth and family income (1959–1961) the rankings of Negro, white, and Japanese were identical. Third, the range in mortality by socioeconomic status is as great or greater than the range by white-nonwhite. For example, in New York State from 1950 to 1952 (exclusive of New York City), the range of neonatal mortality by occupation was 14.1 to 22.8 per 1,000 live births, and postneonatal mortality by occupation ranged from 3.5 to 9.6 per 1,000. The respective ratios of highest to lowest occupation was 1.6 and 2.7 for neonatal and postneonatal mortality. In the same area (1950–1954), the excess nonwhite neonatal mortality ratio was 1.5 and postneonatal mortality excess ratio was 2.5.[37] Thus, the range by occupation was as great or greater than that by race.

Finally, ecological studies have consistently revealed the tremen-

[36] Kitagawa, "Race Differentials in Mortality in the United States, 1960"; longitudinal studies in Detroit suggest that the *instability* of income, not just the actual level of income, is an important correlate of fetal loss. See Ronald Freedman, et al., "Social Correlates of Fetal Mortality," *Milbank Memorial Fund Quarterly*, 44 (July 1966), pt. I, p. 337.

[37] Occupation differential from Helen Chase, *International Comparison of Perinatal and Infant Mortality*, National Center for Health Statistics, ser. 3, no. 6 (March 1967), pp. 67–68; racial differentials from Chase, "White–Non-White Mortality Differentials in the United States."

dous reduction in the discrepancy between white and nonwhite infant mortality when socioeconomic area is controlled. A 1950 Chicago study showed that differences in socioeconomic levels between whites and non-whites accounted for almost all their differences in mortality. Overall infant mortality was 40 to 60 per cent higher than white rates alone. When differences in socioeconomic status (area) were held constant, infant mortality for nonwhite females was the same as white females, and for males, the 60 per cent excess of nonwhite infant mortality was reduced to 13 per cent.[38] Census tract data in Syracuse, New York, support these findings. The research concludes that Negro and native-white populations have similar neonatal mortality rates when socioeconomic status is held constant. Although neonatal mortality is less susceptible to environmental conditions, the study notes that neonatal mortality varies inversely with the income level of neighborhoods.[39] Finally, a study of Baltimore, Maryland, grouped census tracts by median rental (1960) and correlated infant mortality rates (1963) of whites and nonwhites. In the total Baltimore area the infant mortality of nonwhites was 61 per cent higher than whites. However, in the lowest economic area, based on rental value, the excess nonwhite infant mortality was reduced to 17 per cent. The infant mortality of whites and nonwhites improved as the areal location improves.[40]

Admittedly, the evidence is weak. But the direction is unmistakable: socioeconomic factors, however crudely measured, account for a substantial part of the inequality of death between the races. It seems reasonable to hypothesize that if information on white and nonwhite mortality by class measures and residence were available on an individual basis, most, if not all, the excess nonwhite mortality rates would be eliminated when these factors were controlled.

INEQUALITY IN SOUTH AFRICA

Often the evidence on racial differences in life chances is viewed solely in an American context. In some respects the higher mortality of Negroes is a uniquely American dilemma, especially as it conflicts with

[38] Cited in Hunt and Huyck, "Mortality of White and Non-White Infants in Major U.S. Cities"; cf. Evelyn Kitagawa and Philip Hauser, "Trends in Differential Fertility and Mortality in a Metropolis," in *Contributions to Urban Sociology*, ed. E. W. Burgess and D. J. Bogue (Chicago: University of Chicago Press, 1964); Mayer and Hauser, "Class Differentials in Expectation of Life at Birth."

[39] Charles V. Willie and William B. Rothney, "Racial, Ethnic and Income Factors in the Epidemiology of Neonatal Mortality," *American Sociological Review*, 27 (August 1962), pp. 522–526.

[40] Cited in Hunt and Huyck, "Mortality of White and Non-White Infants in Major U.S. Cities," p. 13.

egalitarian norms. We should, however, keep in mind that racial inequality in the United States is by no means unprecedented or extreme. Rather, the pattern of racial inequality and its consequences for differential life chances is pervasive in many societies where racial and class systems are intertwined; the United States is but one illustration.

South African society represents an extreme pattern wherein the stratification and racial systems are clearly interrelated. Racial segregation — in residential, marital, occupational, and every other sphere of social, economic, and political activity — pervades South Africa and is inherently unequal. Race is by far the most important criterion of status in South Africa, and it is the only principle of stratification that permeates the entire social structure. As van den Berghe notes:

> The most salient idiosyncrasy of South Africa is, of course, its racial syndrome. . . . Whatever thread one picks up in the social fabric of the country, one ends up with "race." Race, in the social as opposed to the biological sense, is a special criterion of ascription based on human phenotypes. Physical characteristics have no intrinsic significance; they only become relevant as they are seized upon in a given society as criteria of group definition, and as pegs on which to hang prejudice and discrimination.[41]

Although van den Berghe notes the parallels between South Africa and the southern states of the United States at the height of the Jim Crow era (between 1890 and 1920), he points out that South Africa represents an extreme case in terms of the persistence and thoroughness with which the system of racial inequality is maintained.[42] Given this system of racial stratification, it is not surprising that mortality is significantly and dramatically higher among the deprived segments. United Nations data subdivide South Africa into colored, white, and Asiatics. An examination of various mortality indices reveals that, regardless of the measure, whites have significantly lower mortality than the colored population and Asiatics occupy an intermediate position. Indeed, white mortality patterns are quite similar to the low levels characteristic of Western European countries, whereas mortality levels of the colored population are comparable to some of the most underdeveloped countries of the world, and Asiatics may be categorized in the "transitional" position. That these three groups live in the *same country*, reveals dramatically the social inequality of death.

[41] Pierre van den Berghe, *South Africa: A Study in Conflict* (Berkeley: University of California Press, 1967), p. 266.
[42] Ibid.

The information on mortality in South Africa compiled by the United Nations yields the following summary profile: [43]

1. The crude death rate (number of deaths per 1,000 population) in 1966 was 15 per 1,000 among the colored population compared to 9 per 1,000 whites.

2. Life expectancy at birth (1950 to 1952) among white males was sixty-four years — twenty years longer on the average than colored males and nine years longer than Asiatics. Among females the discrepancy between these social groupings was greater. Moreover, the life expectancy disparity between whites and colored exists even at ages twenty and twenty-five: the colored population at these ages can expect ten years less of additional life than whites. These same patterns have been observed with data for the 1960's.[44]

3. Deaths to females as a result of childbearing (maternal mortality) was almost five times higher among the colored population compared to the white population and over twice as high among the colored female population than among the Asiatic female population.

4. Infant mortality in 1965 among the colored population was 136 per 1,000 live births, over four and one-half times the white infant mortality rate and over twice the Asiatic mortality rate. Indeed, in the twenty years to 1965, infant mortality among the colored population changed little, although among whites the rate of infant deaths declined by 22 per cent and among Asiatics by 25 per cent.

5. The time components of infant mortality (neonatal and post-neonatal) show that, in 1962, the excess mortality among colored infants increases as socioenvironmental conditions play a more important determining role. Although mortality in the first week of life is about the same for the white and colored population, the mortality rate from the first to the fifth month is eight times greater among the colored population than among whites, and for the latter half of the first year of life, the mortality rate of colored infants is over twelve times the white rate. In all instances, Asiatic mortality is in an intermediate position between the white and colored rates.

Similar patterns of differential mortality by race have been observed for other African nations where the white population discriminates systematically against the nonwhites. In Southern Rhodesia (1960's), the crude death rate of the "African" population was estimated at 26 per

[43] Derived from United Nations, *Demographic Yearbook,* 1966, tables 14, 15, 17, 20, and 21, and data limitation discussion, pp. 29–30.

[44] Ranjan Som, "Mortality Levels in Africa" (paper presented to the General Assembly, International Union for the Scientific Study of Population, London, 1969), table 1.

1,000, four times the rate of the white population; expectation of life at birth was twice as high among whites compared to Africans. In 1964, the colored population of Namibia (the former territory of Southwest Africa, now administered by the South African government) had a crude death rate of 15 per 1,000 and an infant mortality rate of 111 per 1,000 births; the crude death rate for the white population of Namibia was 7 per 1,000 and the infant mortality rate was 39 per 1,000 births.[45]

Although the overall mortality patterns of South African society (and other racially segregated African nations) show the inequality of life chances for racial and ethnic populations, the United Nations data are less than complete and historical patterns cannot be identified fully. Although the conclusion that racial inequality in life chances is inescapable, we do not know whether the discrepancy between the races is narrowing, increasing, or unchanging. A detailed study of Cape Town, where data are more complete for a longer period of time, confirms the general excess mortality of the colored population and, in addition, sheds some light on patterns of changing mortality discrepancies.[46] The population of Cape Town may be subdivided into whites (Europeans); colored (former slaves who share language, religion, and general culture with whites differentiated only by their poverty); natives or Bantu (most of whom are migrant laborers — for most United Nations data compilations the Bantu are excluded); and Asiatics (mainly recent in-migrants from India). The non-Europeans, of which the colored are the largest proportion — over 80 per cent in 1951 — are worse off economically than Europeans in such socioeconomic dimensions as housing, nutrition, occupation, education, etc.[47]

As with South African society as a whole, mortality rates show marked racial differentiation in Cape Town. The overall crude death rate for whites in Cape Town at the turn of the twentieth century was 14 per 1,000 population declining to 9.5 by the mid-1950's. The crude death rate for non-Europeans fell even more sharply from 32 per 1,000 (1911–1920) to 14 per 1,000 (1950–1954). Part of this apparent decline is a function of the changing age distribution of the two populations. Thus, when we examine infant deaths, the more sensitive socioeconomic indicator, a growing gap between Europeans and non-Europeans is evident. In the first two decades of the twentieth century, 9 per cent of the babies born to Europeans died in their first year of life; by the mid-

[45] Ibid.

[46] The data on Cape Town have been derived from Harry T. Phillips, "An Inter-Racial Study in Social Conditions and Infant Mortality in Cape Town," *Milbank Memorial Fund Quarterly,* 35 (January 1957), pp. 7–28.

[47] For a detailed discussion of these subpopulations, see van den Berghe, *South Africa,* and Phillips, "An Inter-Racial Study. . . ."

1950's, less than 3 per cent of the European infants died during their first year. Infant mortality among non-Europeans steadily declined as well during this period, although not as sharply: from 26 per cent to 11 per cent. Thus, in the early decades of the twentieth century the non-European infant mortality rate was three times as high as the European infant mortality rate, and by the 1950's the mortality gap widened and the infant mortality rate of non-Europeans was four times that of Europeans in Cape Town. In other words, European infant mortality, despite its lower initial level, decreased more rapidly than infant mortality rates of the non-Europeans. Indeed, the percentage of non-European babies who survived their first year of life in 1948–1949 was the same as the percentage of European babies surviving *forty years earlier.*

When the "non-Europeans" are subdivided, the extreme inequality of the natives (Bantu) in Cape Town is dramatically apparent. For every 1,000 births (1950–1953) among the natives, 225 die in their first year of life, a rate twice as high as the non-European total and almost ten times the infant mortality rate of Europeans. Moreover, the infant mortality rate of the Bantu in Cape Town is over two and one-half times the European rate of the 1913–1918 period.

It is significant that the comparative mortality of infants between their first and second year of life show greater discrepancies between racial groups than mortality during the first year of life. In twenty years (to 1946–1951), the death rate per 1,000 infants one to two years of age declined 80 per cent among Europeans, 43 per cent for non-Europeans. The disparity between Europeans and non-Europeans in deaths to infants one to two years of age (1926–1931), was five to one in favor of the Europeans. By the 1946–1951 period this discrepancy, which mainly reflects socioeconomic, environment, public health, and nutrition differentials, increased to a fantastic fifteen to one!

Phillips notes that, in terms of formal public policy, medical and health services are provided free to all citizens of Cape Town if they are unable to afford private medical and health services.[48] In practice, however, it has been far more difficult for non-Europeans to obtain such services, nor are such services of uniformly high quality. In addition, social and economic conditions, indeed the stratification system as a whole, are inextricably intertwined with the racial and ethnic divisions of Cape Town.

The evidence on inequality of death between racial and ethnic populations in South Africa, and in the United States as well, cannot be interpreted by innate biological factors. Throughout, we have pointed to social and economic conditions and in general social class factors that

[48] Phillips, ibid.

affect life chances. To pursue this inquiry, we now turn to a more detailed review of the information available on the trends and comparative
levels of social class differentials in mortality. Two questions are of
direct concern: (1) What are the differences in mortality by social class
in various countries? (2) Have mortality discrepancies increased between
the highest and lowest social classes over time to parallel the increase in
excess mortality noted between the races in the United States and South
Africa?

SOCIOECONOMIC STATUS AND MORTALITY

On April 14, 1912, the maiden voyage of the Titanic met with
disaster. However, not all the passengers died at sea. The official casualty
lists revealed that only 4 first-class female passengers (3 voluntarily chose
to stay on the sinking ship) of 143 were lost; among second-class passengers, 15 of 93 females drowned; among third-class female passengers,
81 out of 179 died.[49] The social class selectivity among females on the
Titanic — from 3 per cent to 45 per cent who died — dramatically illustrates the general inequality in death associated with social class levels.

The unequal distribution of death for various social classes has
been observed regularly since the turn of the twentieth century. Sir
Arthur Newsholme wrote in 1910 about England that "no fact is better
established than that the death rate, and especially the death rate among
children, is high in inverse proportion to the social status of the population." In a review of infant mortality conditions in the United States
during the first quarter of this century, Woodbury notes that low socioeconomic status, particularly low-income earnings, is the "primary cause"
of excess mortality.[50]

Let us review briefly the relationship between social class and
mortality for several European countries, where data have been more
accurate and more readily available for a longer period of time, and for
the United States. The countries to be considered include Scotland, England and Wales, the Netherlands, Denmark, the United States, and one
underdeveloped country, Chile.

In Scotland, infant and fetal mortality rates for all social classes
(defined by father's occupation) have declined over the last three
decades, but the mortality differential between the lowest and highest

[49] Cited in Aaron Antonovsky, "Social Class, Life Expectancy and Overall
Mortality," *Milbank Memorial Fund Quarterly*, 45 (April 1967), pt. I, p. 31.
[50] Both Newsholme and Woodbury are cited in Edward G. Stockwell, "Infant
Mortality and Socio-Economic Status: A Changing Relationship," *Milbank Memorial
Fund Quarterly*, 40 (January 1962), pp. 102–103.

social class has widened. In 1939, the fetal death rate of the lowest occupation class was one and one-quarter times as high as that of the highest occupational class grouping; in 1963, it was two and one-third times as high. Similarly, in 1939, the highest social class had a neonatal mortality rate of 30 per 1,000 live births, whereas the lowest social class had a neonatal mortality rate of 40 per 1,000 live births; in 1963, the gap widened with the highest social class having a neonatal mortality rate of 9.5, and the lowest social class a rate of 22.3. Moreover, the gap between these two class extremes was most evident in the postneonatal period, where socioeconomic environmental conditions clearly outweigh biological factors. In 1939, postneonatal deaths in the lowest occupational class were six times that of the highest occupational class, whereas in 1963, the differential more than doubled, and postneonatal death rates were more than thirteen times as great among the lowest than among the highest social classes.[51]

Since 1911, British statistics have repeatedly shown this same inverse relationship between parental social class (father's occupation) and infant mortality. Although significant declines in infant mortality *within* each social class during the first half of the twentieth century have been reported, the relative differences *between* classes have not decreased.[52] The gap is indeed large: mortality among infants born into families of unskilled laborers is two and one-half times that of infants born into families of professionals and rates of infant deaths among the lowest class lag thirty years behind infant death rates among the highest class.[53] This has occurred in Britain and Scotland even when medical care is readily available to the entire population and where maternity hospital accommodations are ample. Moreover, some evidence shows that the steep mortality gradient from the highest to the lowest occupational class has widened in England and Wales, as in Scotland, precisely

[51] The data for Scotland are based on a report by Dr. Charlotte Douglas reviewed in U.S. Department of Health, Education and Welfare, *Report of the International Conference on the Perinatal and Infant Mortality Problem of the U.S.*, National Center for Health Statistics, ser. 4, no. 3 (June 1966), p. 3. (Similar findings are cited for France and Hungary.) Although Dr. Douglas notes the difficulty in understanding the widening class differential in infant mortality in Scotland, she suggests that nutrition, housing, economic conditions, and general life styles conspire to produce the class gap.

[52] See the summary by Dr. Katherine M. Hirst, in ibid., pp. 4–5; Cf. K. Hirst et al., *Infant and Perinatal Mortality in England and Wales*, National Center for Health Statistics, ser. 3, no. 12 (November 1968), pp. 31–32; Chase, *International Comparison of Perinatal and Infant Mortality*, p. 67.

[53] See R. K. Kelsall, *Population* (London: Longmans, Green, 1967), pp. 47–50; for earlier reports, see R. M. Titmuss, *Birth, Poverty and Wealth* (London: H. Hamilton Medical Books, 1943); J. N. Morris and J. A. Heady, "Social and Biological Factors in Infant Mortality," *Lancet*, 268 (March 1955), pp. 554–560; and several studies cited in Kelsall, *Population*, p. 98.

during the same period when the gap between the incomes of these class extremes has decreased.

The Danish evidence reveals the same pattern of considerable mortality differences from one occupation group to another. In a 1967 report, data derived in 1954–1955 show that two and one-half times as many children of "domestic workers" (lowest occupational rank) died in their first year of life when compared to the children of self-employed persons in professional services.[54] The widening of class inequalities in life chances, particularly between the highest and lowest social classes, has also been observed for Denmark.

The Netherlands data provide an interesting confirmation of the persistence of inequality in death rates between social classes. Infant mortality in the Netherlands (15 per 1,000 live births in 1964) is one of the lowest recorded in the world (second only to Sweden) and probably one of the lowest recorded in world history. After World War II, the Netherlands became one of the Western European welfare states characterized by social security for the great masses, moderate wages increasing with the living standard, relatively little unemployment, and no real poverty. Yet, despite the fact that infant loss has reached low levels, the classic rule still prevails: unfavorable social conditions increase perinatal and postnatal mortality. Mortality is lowest in the highest social class and increases more or less progressively with decreases in social class. Data for 1961–1962 show a wide mortality range by social class in the Netherlands. Neonatal and postneonatal mortality among children with parents in the highest occupational class was about 20 per cent below the averages for the country as a whole, whereas in the lowest occupational class, the mortality rates were 10 per cent above the national average. The influence of father's occupation on infant mortality is unmistakable. Infant mortality in the lowest social class shows a lag of about seven years in reaching the level attained by the highest social class. The lag would be even greater if the highest income group included in the highest occupational class were compared with the lowest income group in the lowest occupational class. The decline in infant mortality has been fairly uniform for all occupational groups and, at least over the last decade, no appreciable increase in the gap between the highest and lowest class has been observed.[55]

[54] P. C. Matthiessen et al., *Infant and Perinatal Mortality in Denmark*, National Center for Health Statistics, ser. 3, no. 9 (November 1967), pp. 15–16, and tables S and 12, p. 55. The same pattern was observed in earlier years.

[55] Data on the Netherlands were derived from J. H. de Haas-Posthuma and J. H. de Haas, *Infant Loss in the Netherlands*, National Center for Health Statistics, ser. 3, no. 11, pp. 16–24 and table 11. Social class differences in mortality remain practically the same when adjustment is made for parity and age of mother. See ibid., p. 32.

Most European data available on social class differences in general mortality are based on the occupation of father. For overall mortality, it is difficult to separate deaths associated with the "risks" or hazards of various occupations from deaths due to the social and economic implications of life styles associated with occupational class. But, the data on infant mortality classified by the occupation of father unmistakably reflect life style and social class factors. In addition, information in England on social class differentials in mortality of women classified by the occupation of their husbands show the same mortality gradient by social class. In these cases, the relationship found could only be a function of differential social and economic life styles indicated by occupational groupings.[56]

Comparable data on socioeconomic class differences in mortality are unavailable for the United States. The several community, ecological studies (ranking census tracts by some measure of socioeconomic status and correlating census tract mortality measures), direct studies for New York State and California, and preliminary national estimates based on death record–census matching of 1960 have all noted the inverse relationship of social class indicators and mortality. These findings, based on various methodologies, gain in reliability not only because of the consistency of results but because of the overall similarity with the European evidence, which is based on more accurate data for a longer period of time. Several United States studies illustrate similar findings using the three methodologies cited.

First, one of the most carefully executed ecological-correlation studies, of Providence, Rhode Island, found infant mortality to be less a sensitive indicator of socioeconomic status as it was in the past. However, when neonatal mortality was separated from postneonatal mortality, i.e., where the major causes of death are farther removed from the physiological processes of gestation and birth, the findings point clearly to an inverse relationship between postneonatal mortality and socioeconomic status.[57]

In a 1961–1963 special study of health problems associated with poverty in New York City, sixteen poverty areas were identified by low income and high frequency of social problems. In 1961–1963, infant mortality in New York City was 26 per 1,000 live births, but in the sixteen poverty areas the rate was 35 per 1,000. The maternal mortality rate for the sixteen poverty areas was almost 2½ times that of the rest of New York City. When health districts were grouped by housing quality in New York City, districts with poor housing had an infant mortality

[56] Cf. Harold Dorn, "Mortality" in *The Study of Population*, ed. Philip Hauser and Otis D. Duncan (Chicago: University of Chicago Press, 1959).

[57] Stockwell, "Infant Mortality and Socio-Economic Status," pp. 101–111.

rate over twice that of districts with good housing and a maternal mortality rate almost four times as high.[58]

Studies of upstate New York, for the 1950–1952 period, reaffirm the inverse relationship between level of father's occupation and infant deaths. Neonatal mortality ranged from 14 per 1,000 births among the children of professionals to 20 per 1,000 among the children of laborers; postneonatal mortality (28 days to 11 months per 1,000 survivors to 28 days among births) ranged from 3.5 to 3.7 among professionals and managers to 9.6 among nonfarm laborers.[59]

Finally, carefully matched death and census records (350,000) in the United States resulted in the following estimates of mortality (twenty-five years of age and older) by years of school completed and family income.[60]

1. Among white males with no schooling, mortality was about 10 per cent higher than among the college educated; among females mortality was about 50 per cent higher among those with no schooling than among those with some college education. The inverse gradient characterizes both sexes and most age groups.

2. Among white males with family incomes below $2,000 a year, mortality was over 50 per cent higher than among males with incomes $10,000 a year or more; among females mortality was slightly less than 50 per cent greater among those with the lowest family incomes than among those with the highest family incomes.

3. A strong inverse relationship between mortality and level of educational attainment was found for the 1960 nonwhite population. Among nonwhite males, from 25 to 64 years of age, mortality was 31 per cent higher for those with less than five years of schooling when compared to males with some high school or college education. Poorly educated nonwhite females from 25 to 64 years of age had mortality rates 70 per cent higher than better educated nonwhite females.

Health can be measured not only by length of life but also by positive elements of good health. Information from the United States National Health Survey clearly confirms the generally accepted positive

[58] Hunt and Huyck, "Mortality of White and Non-White Infants in Major U.S. Cities."

[59] Chase, *International Comparison of Perinatal and Infant Mortality*, pp. 67–68.

[60] Evelyn Kitagawa and Philip Hauser, "Education Differentials in Mortality by Cause of Death, United States, 1960," *Demography*, 5:1 (1968), pp. 318–353; Evelyn Kitagawa, "Social and Economic Differentials in Mortality in the United States, 1960" (paper presented to the General Assembly, International Union for the Scientific Study of Population, London, 1969).

264 Social Differentiation and Population Processes

relationship between poor health and low income.[61] People in families with a total income of less than $2,000 a year (in 1961) had twenty-nine restricted days of activities per year, per person; for those with family incomes of $2,000 to $4,000 a year, disability days dropped to eighteen, and in families with incomes of $4,000 a year and over the number was thirteen. To some extent income may be low because of greater illness just as illness may be low because of higher incomes — but it is clear that the two misfortunes exist together.

The National Health Survey in the United States further reveals that lower income persons, despite their increased level of illness and greater need for health care, receive fewer health services than people with higher incomes. Information gathered between 1963 and 1964 shows that 59 per cent with family incomes below $2,000 a year consulted a physician at least once during the preceding year, compared with 66 per cent of those with annual incomes between $4,000 and $7,000 a year and 73 per cent of those with annual incomes of $10,000 a year. Finally, twice as many of those with higher incomes ($7,000 a year or more) avail themselves of medical specialists when compared to those with the lowest income status (below $2,000 a year).

In sum, the evidence from several European countries and the United States points consistently to the social inequality of death for members of different social strata. Some evidence, by no means universal or documented fully, also indicates an increased mortality discrepancy between the highest and lowest classes since World War II, paralleling the findings for racial mortality differentials in the United States and South Africa. Sufficient materials are not yet available to account for these increased mortality discrepancies, if they do in fact exist. Two points of conjecture are worthy of intense and rigorous testing. First, social class mobility may result in the movement out of the lower classes of persons who are healthier and more motivated to achieve a positive state of health. In the process, the lower classes, over time, may become composed of social and physical "rejects," whose mortality patterns may be consequently higher. This selective upward mobility may have increased after World War II, and, in part, may account for increased discrepancies between the lowest and higher classes. A second possibility relates to processes of urbanization and changing environmental densities since the end of World War II. The increasing urbanization of the lower classes, especially Negroes, as a result of rural-to-urban and interurban mobility, and the increasing concentration of urban residents among the poor in substandard housing and deprived social environments, may have

[61] Data from the National Health Survey have been presented in Forrest E. Linder, "The Health of the American People," *Scientific American*, 214 (June 1966), pp. 21–29.

increased mortality rates between classes and races. Although static areal measures show lower mortality rates in overall urban areas, more refined measures that subdivide urban areas into homogeneous socioeconomic sections are needed. A contributing and interrelated factor beyond the changing social-environmental situation of millions of poor persons relates to the differential availability of health and medical facilities and services and, more significantly perhaps, differential motivation to utilize services when they are available. Whether these motivational elements have changed in the last decades requires careful research. These suggestions for research may illuminate the specific problem of the social inequality of death, its persistence and increase, and in the process may suggest alternative solutions for diminishing such inequalities.

ARE MORTALITY DIFFERENTIALS "TRANSITIONAL"?

The pattern of class mortality differences, in general, and race mortality differences, in particular, have often been viewed as temporary or "transitional" phenomena. The argument runs as follows: In a high mortality society, large mortality differences between social strata are not likely. Similarly, where mortality is relatively low, and social, economic, and welfare planning is pervasive, social class differentials in mortality diminish sharply. In short, it is assumed that the pattern of mortality differences between social classes is curvilinear when viewed historically. Under extreme conditions of mortality control or noncontrol, little class inequality in death exists.[62] This position assumes that before mortality began its long descent in preindustrial Europe there were small class differences in mortality; as the "demographic transition" from uncontrolled to controlled deaths occurred, class mortality differentials widened only to diminish as death control became extensive.

Little direct evidence is available to support or reject critical parts of this argument. But there are sufficient grounds to be somewhat skeptical of the view that class mortality differentials are "transitional." First, the evidence reviewed in this chapter points convincingly to the retention and, in many instances, widening of the social class gradient in mortality in selected European nations. Despite the dramatic mortality declines within social classes accompanying industrialization, social and economic modernization, and health and welfare planning, no country has eliminated class mortality differences and few have been successful in reducing mortality discrepancies. A second feature of the "transi-

---

[62] See Antonovsky, "Social Class, Life Expectancy and Overall Mortality," pp. 32–33, 68.

tional" argument may also be challenged, i.e., the argument that few class differences in mortality existed in preindustrial Europe. Attempts at reconstructing preindustrial population dynamics suggest that mortality decreased as social class increased. For example, Wrigley argues that part of the population model of preindustrial Europe should include class mortality differentials:

> To be wealthy is to be well fed even in times of general dearth. . . . Expectation of life was probably normally better among the upper ranks of society than among the lower. The former could not escape easily in serious epidemic outbreaks (except by flight, and even then their wealth was a notable advantage), but they were largely cushioned from the shock of harvest failure and famine prices which caused the death of so many less fortunate men and women. Moreover a well-fed man is less likely to succumb to infection than a man weakened by short commons over many months. Therefore as a gross generalization it would be true that mortality rose at each step down the social hierarchy.[63]

This conclusion is rather persuasive, although the evidence upon which it is based is partly conjecture and less rigorous than could be desired.

Some weight is given to this argument by examining social class differentials in mortality in currently developing areas. If class mortality differentials are minimal when mortality is uncontrolled (or high), we should expect small mortality differences between the classes in underdeveloped countries. But data available from at least one underdeveloped area (Chile, 1959) suggest that even under conditions of relatively high mortality, social class inequalities in death are obtained.[64] Infant mortality in Chile is about five times the rate of the United States and about seven times the rate of the Netherlands. Postneonatal mortality in Chile is fully ten times that of the United States — 77.0 versus 7.4 per 1,000 live births. We need not review here the underdeveloped economy of Chile but only note that a large part of the working classes is unable to solve its subsistence problem.

The evidence for Chile points clearly to the existence of social class differences in mortality. Rural provinces of low income have infant mortality rates 75 per cent higher than the mortality of the largest urban area, Santiago. In some provinces with little or no medical care, infant

---

[63] E. A. Wrigley, *Population and History* (London: Weidenfeld and Nicolson, World University Library, 1969), p. 102. Others have argued that an inverse relationship between social class and mortality characterized parts of ancient Rome. See, for example, John Durand, "Mortality Estimates from Roman Tombstone Inscriptions," *American Journal of Sociology*, 65 (January 1960), p. 366.

[64] The data are reported in Hugo Behm et al., *Recent Mortality Trends in Chile*, National Center for Health Statistics, ser. 3, no. 2 (April 1964), pp. 17–19.

mortality reaches levels of 150 to 200 per 1,000 live births. The mortality rates of three social classes in Chile confirm this ecological evidence. Infant mortality among the middle classes is about half the rate of the working classes *holding constant medical care.* When compared to working classes with no medical care, the middle classes (with medical care) have one-third the infant mortality rate. As with developed countries, the relationship between social class and infant mortality in Chile is most pronounced in the postneonatal phase. Postneonatal mortality among the middle class with medical care is 36 per 1,000 live births; among working classes with medical care, 74 per 1,000 live births; and among the working classes with no medical care 108 children one to eleven months old die out of every 1,000 births. This is in addition to the 49 out of every 1,000 lower class children less than one month old who die. Consequently, even though medical care is provided, substantial mortality differentiation exists between middle and working classes, and the differential is pronounced with those mortality measures that most clearly reflect socioeconomic conditions, i.e., the postneonatal mortality rate. Chilean evidence does not confirm that class mortality differentials existed in preindustrial areas because mortality in Chile has already declined. But it does suggest that even under conditions of relatively high mortality, the inequality of death by social class exists.

Antonovsky's summary of some thirty or more studies on the relationship between social class and overall mortality in various countries over an extended period, as well as the material presented in this chapter, provides no basis for rejecting the inferences that may be drawn from the figures of the *Titanic* disaster. Despite the multiplicity of methods and indices utilized, and despite cross-national comparisons, "the inescapable conclusion is that class influences one's chance of staying alive. Almost without exception, the evidence shows that classes differ on mortality rates." [65] Of the studies that he found showing little or no relationship between social class and overall mortality, two are dismissed by classification procedures that minimized mortality differences. The only study where data strongly contradict the link between class and mortality is for Amsterdam from 1947 to 1952. Those data, for a population with about the lowest death rate ever recorded, suggest to Antonovsky the hypothesis that as the overall death rate is lowered, class differentials similarly decline.

The more comprehensive evidence presented earlier on the infant mortality rate in the Netherlands does not confirm his hypothesis. However, it may very well be that infant mortality, particularly the postneonatal component which is most sensitive to environmental, socio-

[65] Antonovsky, "Social Class, Life Expectancy and Overall Mortality," p. 66.

economic conditions, is a more revealing indicator and correlate of social class than is overall mortality. Antonovsky does note that despite an overall decline in mortality for all social classes, the closing of the gap between the social classes, a trend of the earlier decades of the twentieth century, has been checked, if not halted. Although a clear class gradient has become blurred, Antonovsky suggests that

> what seems to be beyond question is that whatever the index used and whatever the number of classes considered, almost always a lowest class appears with substantially higher mortality rates. Moreover, the (mortality) differential between it and other classes evidently has not diminished over recent decades.[66]

We might add that substantial evidence reviewed previously shows a widening class differential in infant mortality. His comprehensive review of overall mortality by social class in England and Wales in the twentieth century indicates that mortality differentials between the middle and upper levels (among whom mortality rates differed little even in earlier years) have more or less disappeared, and that the lowest class still has strikingly worse life chances than the rest of the population. This finding may be generalized to other developed, and probably underdeveloped, countries as well.

    In conclusion, the temporary or transitional character of class mortality differentials may be challenged on three grounds: First, from evidence showing the retention and often the widening of class differences in mortality in the post-World War II period, we must conclude that even the most advanced countries have not successfully eliminated class inequalities in death. Second, although the preindustrial period is still shrouded in demographic mystery, it is as reasonable to hypothesize small or no class mortality differentials as it is to hypothesize the reverse. It seems that on balance there were class mortality differences, although the extent of such differences is not clear and no doubt varied between communities and fluctuated over time. Third, evidence from Chile, a currently underdeveloped country with relatively high mortality, indicates class differences in mortality even under conditions of moderate death control. These arguments point to the complexity of the issues involved and the enormous problems associated with empirical confirmation or rejection. The theory of curvilinearity in the relationship between social class and mortality in historical perspective is much too oversimplified either to represent the complexity of demographic history or as to use for projecting future patterns.

    An additional argument against the notion that class inequalities in death are transitional is based on our general conceptualization of the

[66] Ibid., p. 67.

meaning of social class differences in mortality. We have argued that mortality patterns are significant indicators of social inequalities that exist in society, be they class or racial-ethnic inequalities. It follows that as long as such inequalities in life exist (including differential life styles, differential access to and availability of general social and economic goods, as well as specific health and medical services, differential motivation for utilizing services and general health care, and differential social, economic, and health environments), social inequalities in death are inevitable. It is not appropriate here to discuss whether inequalities in life are necessary and integral features of human society. But inequalities clearly exist in reality and have existed for a long period of human history; as long as inequality continues to characterize human societies, it will be reflected in the ultimate symbol of such inequalities, death.

Chapter Ten

RELIGION, MINORITY GROUP STATUS, AND FERTILITY

Sociological inquiry stresses the significance of religion as an object of scientific investigation, as a major determinant of social processes, and as a social institution interrelated with other institutional systems of society. Emile Durkheim's analysis of the interrelationships between religious systems and social order and social disorganization, and Max Weber's comparative studies of religious values and social-economic systems, particularly the role of the Protestant Ethic in the development of capitalism, are among the classic sociological treatises.[1] Religion is important in analyzing social systems and as a differentiator of social processes because religion is the most common although not the only manifestation of value orientations. The social scientist usually treats religion as encompassing an institutionalized system of symbols, beliefs, values, and practices focused on questions of ultimate meaning.[2]

Contrary to what might have been expected, religion has remained a vigorous and influential institution in modern, secularized, economically developed, educated, industrialized societies. Its influence extends to the very core of social behavior, attitudes, and values so much so that

[1] See, for example, Emile Durkheim, *The Elementary Forms of the Religious Life,* trans. John W. Swain (New York: Collier, 1961); Émile Durkheim, *Suicide,* trans. John A. Spaulding and George Simpson (Glencoe, Ill.: The Free Press, 1951), pp. 152–170; Max Weber, *The Protestant Ethic and the Spirit of Capitalism,* trans. Talcott Parsons (New York: Scribner's, 1958); Max Weber, *Sociology of Religion,* trans. Ephraim Fischoff (Boston: Beacon Press, 1963).

[2] Cf. Charles Y. Glock and Rodney Stark, *Religion and Society in Tension* (Chicago: Rand McNally, 1965), chap. 1, especially p. 4.

religious group membership in the United States has been connected empirically to such diverse factors as voting behavior, social mobility, strength of family ties, levels of income, delinquency, amount of education, attitudes toward the welfare state, freedom of speech, racial integration, occupations, among many others.[3]

Often religion and religious institutions are conceptualized solely in terms of church doctrines, rites, customs, and general theology. Although religion is considered to have a pervasive influence in structurally undifferentiated preindustrial or preliterate communities, in modern, structurally differentiated societies, a narrow functional role is associated with religion and religious institutions. However, nothing could be farther from a complete picture of the impact of religion on the social organization of modern societies. Religious groups not only bear religious norms in the narrow sense but carry complex subcultures relevant to all phases of human life. Religion and religious affiliation in modern society connote a wide range of social and cultural values, attitudes, and life styles. As Lenski observes:

> The subculture of a socio-religious group represents the accumulated solutions of the group to the whole range of problems which group members deal with *both in the association and in the subcommunity*. Thus, while many problems of a political or economic character may not concern the association, they may be of great concern to group members and be seriously discussed in the primary groups which constitute the subcommunity. . . . *To the degree that such primary groups form segregated communications networks limited to the adherents of the same faith, they facilitate the development and transmission of distinctive political and economic norms.*[4]

Therefore, religion and in turn religious differentials encompass both the specific religious normative structure of the religious group and, often more importantly, the social, economic, and political values and life styles of the membership of religious subcommunities. From this broader sociological perspective, one would certainly expect religious groups to differ from each other not only in beliefs, doctrines, rites, and religious

[3] See the findings reported in Gerhard Lenski, *The Religious Factor* (New York: Doubleday, Anchor Books, 1961); Will Herberg, *Protestant–Catholic–Jew* (New York: Doubleday, Anchor Books, 1956); Sidney Goldstein and Calvin Goldscheider, *Jewish Americans* (Englewood Cliffs, N.J.: Prentice-Hall, 1968); Sidney Goldstein, "Socioeconomic Differentials Among Religious Groups in the United States," *American Journal of Sociology*, 74 (May 1969), pp. 612–631; Calvin Goldscheider and Jon E. Simpson, "Religious Affiliation and Juvenile Delinquency," *Sociological Inquiry*, 37 (Spring 1967), pp. 297–310.

[4] Lenski, *The Religious Factor,* pp. 335–336.

custom but in a much wider range of matters relating to the most mundane and "secular" aspects of daily life. Thus, Lenski's central finding is:

> Religion in various ways is constantly influencing the daily lives of
> the masses of men and women in the modern American metropolis.
> More than that: through its impact on individuals, religion makes
> an impact on all the other institutional systems of the community
> these individuals staff. Hence the influence of religion operates at
> the social level as well as at the personal level.[5]

Thus, membership in religious subcommunities should have a significant relationship to demographic processes, particularly when fertility,
mortality, and migration are conceptualized as social behavior, social
process, and social indicators. In the United States, some systematic
evidence is available for religious differentials in migration (e.g., the
differential immigration to the United States of religious ethnic groups
and differential levels of urbanization) and mortality (e.g., differential
suicide and general mortality by religion), but social scientists have
rarely examined these relationships. However, growing evidence has
accumulated about the role of religion as a differentiator of fertility
patterns.

PREVALENT HYPOTHESES

Two basic hypotheses inform most explanations of religious subgroup differentiation of fertility patterns. First, the "particularized
theology" proposition states that the impact of religion on fertility behavior and attitudes operates with *particular* church doctrine or religious
ideology on birth control, contraceptive usage, and norms of family
size. In terms of the general scheme presented earlier,[6] religion, religious orientations, and religious institutions are parts of social organization that influence fertility by *religious ideological norms regarding
family size and birth control,* which in turn affect the "intermediate"
variables, which in turn shape fertility levels. According to this proposition, if religious group A has higher fertility than religious group B,
higher fertility is a function of the particular religious doctrines of
religious group A about birth control and family size ideals.

Second, the "characteristics" proposition hypothesizes that the distinct fertility of religious subgroups merely reflects a matrix of social,
demographic, and economic attributes that characterizes the religious
subgroup. Religious group identification or affiliation is treated as an

[5] Ibid., p. 320.
[6] See Chapters 2 and 6, this book.

indicator of social class (educational attainment, occupational distribution, and income level), degree of urban concentration and rural experience, and social mobility patterns. Accordingly, religious group membership *per se* is not significant but rather the social, demographic, and economic characteristics that religious group membership connotes determine fertility levels, trends, and differentials within religious groups. Moreover, it is argued, when the social, demographic, and economic characteristics of religious groups are similar — through standardization and statistical controls or at some time in the future — differences in their fertility behavior should be eliminated. Thus, fertility differences between religious groups that may exist at one point in time are considered temporary phenomena representing a social or cultural lag, which is often manifest in social and economic backwardness or deprivation.

These two propositions should not be viewed as mutually exclusive, independent, or contradictory. Very often the "particularized theology" and "characteristics" hypotheses are part of a general approach to interpreting the relationship of religion and fertility. The argument often combines elements of both propositions: If two religious groups do not have explicit or identifiable religious ideologies about birth control or ideal family size, any fertility differences between these religious groups must result from a matrix of social, demographic, and economic characteristics; or, in another form, if fertility differences between religious groups persist after controlling for differential social, demographic, and economic characteristics, the explanation of residual fertility differentiation must rest with a particularized religious ideology on birth control and family size.

The first combined proposition has almost always been used to interpret Jewish fertility. Because Jews have no explicit, identifiable, and commonly shared religious ideology about birth control and contraceptive usage, any difference in the fertility patterns of Jews and non-Jews must be simply a function of the peculiar social class and residential characteristics of Jews. The second combined proposition is often applied to Catholic–non-Catholic fertility differentials. Because fertility differences between Catholics and non-Catholics are not diminished when social, demographic, and economic characteristics are controlled, the explanation of the unique Catholic fertility pattern rests largely with the particular ideology of the Catholic church about birth control and ideal family size.

These propositions, either as independent hypotheses or in combination, involve two theoretical fallacies: first, religion, religious affiliation, and religious institutions have no independent vitality in influencing behavior and attitudes in modern societies; second, the influence of religion, if any, is functionally specific to the process under investigation. The first fallacy results in the characteristics interpretation, the second in the particularized theology proposition. Although both theoretical fallacies have been discarded in the sociological analysis of religion, demographic studies of religion and fertility persist in retaining, often implicitly, the essential features of these propositions. We must summarize and evaluate critically the literature relating to religious differentials in fertility and examine how the empirical materials have been explained. Essentially, we want to ascertain whether there is empirical support for the hypothesis that fertility differences between religious groupings are indistinguishable when social, demographic, and economic characteristics are standardized and controlled. If fertility differences persist, the task will be to determine the role of particular religious ideologies in accounting for the residual fertility differences. If the particularized theology proposition is not sound, empirically as well as theoretically, we will explore an alternative theory that posits that the relationship between religion and fertility is one illustration of the more general relationship between religion and social action. Flowing from the sociological analysis of religion, it may be argued that religious subgroupings, based on affiliation and identification, constitute distinct subcommunities and subcultures; thus, differential fertility patterns by religion may best be viewed as reflecting the *total* social organization of these subcommunities and subcultures. With respect to the earlier discussion of the determinants of fertility, our view is that religion *interacts* with other aspects of social organization of the subcommunity and subculture, and it is through the total content of that social organization, of which the particular theology is but one part and often not the most significant, that fertility patterns are affected.

Decennial censuses of the United States have never included a question on religious preference or affiliation nor do birth records include information on religion.[7] The heavy reliance of demographers on "official" data sources has, in the past, precluded a focus on religion as a differentiator of demographic processes. Indeed, no national American data are available on the relationship between religion and migration or religion and mortality, and only since the mid-1950's has national information on religion and fertility been collected. Unfortunately, availability of published records has often dictated to population experts not only research foci but also notions of relevance.

Most evidence on religious differentials in fertility is limited to sample survey research. The first major study containing information on religion and fertility was the Indianapolis study of the late 1930's and

[7] For a comprehensive review, see Goldstein, "Socioeconomic Differentials Among Religious Groups in the United States."

early 1940's.[8] Although the detailed survey was limited among other things to Protestants, the preliminary household sample, used to screen eligible Protestant couples, contained some information on Catholics and Jews as well as Protestants. Parenthetically, it is significant to note that the focus on Protestant fertility was based precisely on the recognition that religion was an important differentiator of American fertility patterns. However, two underlying assumptions of the Indianapolis study, later shown to be incorrect empirically, guided the selective focus on Protestants. First, flowing out of nineteenth-century positivism was the assumption that religion does not have a pervasive influence on social behavior, values, and attitudes in modern industrialized society; second, it was assumed that non-Protestant fertility patterns represented a social or cultural "lag" that, as acculturation occurred, would catch up to or follow the Protestant model. One objective of the study was, therefore, to isolate the group that would foreshadow future fertility patterns of the total American population, i.e., Protestant, educated, native-born whites in a "typical" American city. The study focused on this particular subpopulation because "it was believed that this group was setting the fertility pattern to which other population groups would eventually conform." [9] The notion that fertility patterns of religious subpopulations differ from each other merely because of different social and economic characteristics continues to inform "explanations" of religious and other subgroup differentials in fertility. The empirical indefensibility of this "characteristics" hypothesis will be discussed in a later section.

The major fertility studies emphasizing religious differentials have been the Growth of American Families (GAF) studies of 1955, 1960, and 1965 (in 1965 it was called the National Fertility Survey) [10] and the

[8] Pascal K. Whelpton and Clyde V. Kiser (eds.), *Social and Psychological Factors Affecting Fertility*, 5 vols. (New York: Milbank Memorial Fund, 1946–1958).

[9] Clyde V. Kiser, "Aims, Methods and Some Results of the Indianapolis Study," *Report of the Proceedings of the Fifth International Conference on Planned Parenthood* (Tokyo, Japan, October 1955), p. 98.

[10] See Ronald Freedman, Pascal K. Whelpton, and Arthur Campbell, *Family Planning, Sterility and Population Growth* (New York: McGraw-Hill, 1959); Pascal K. Whelpton, Arthur Campbell, and John Patterson, *Fertility and Family Planning in the United States* (Princeton: Princeton University Press, 1966); the 1965 study has not been published in full as of this writing. Selected reports are contained in Norman Ryder and Charles Westoff, "The Trend of Expected Parity in the United States: 1955, 1960, 1965," *Population Index*, 30 (April–June 1967), pp. 153–168; also by Ryder and Westoff, "Recent Trends in Attitudes Toward Fertility Control and the Practice of Contraception in the United States," in *Fertility and Family Planning: A World View* (Ann Arbor, Mich.: University of Michigan Press, 1969); "United States: Methods of Fertility Control, 1955, 1960 and 1965," *Studies in Family Planning*, no. 17 (New York: The Population Council, February 1967); "The United States: The Pill and the Birth Rate," *Studies in Family Planning*, no. 20 (New York: The Population Council, June 1967); "Use of Oral Contraceptives in the United States, 1965," *Science*, 153 (September 9, 1966), pp. 1199–1205.

longitudinal Princeton fertility surveys.[11] Other studies available have either focused on limited areas of fertility, or local populations, or on one religious group.[12] Surveys in the United States in the 1920's and earlier were based on clinically obtained samples or special area studies. These earlier attempts have been overshadowed by the more recent and systematic work, and will be referred to only incidentally in the discussion that follows.

RELIGION AND FERTILITY: OVERALL PATTERNS

The evidence almost without exception indicates the following major finding about differences in the fertility levels among Protestants, Catholics, and Jews in the United States: *Catholics have the highest fertility of the three groups, Jews have the lowest, and Protestants occupy an intermediate position.* This relationship has been observed with every measure of fertility and almost every fertility-related variable. Catholics have a larger completed family size; a larger proportion use the least efficient contraceptive methods, expect and desire larger families, and consider as ideal larger families; a larger proportion have an "unplanned" pregnancy, and, in general, have shorter intervals between births. Jews have smaller families; marry at later ages; practice contraception more efficiently using the most efficient birth control methods; expect, desire, and consider as ideal smaller families; have fewer unplanned pregnancies; are more likely to plan the number and spacing of all their children; and, as a result, have longer birth intervals. Protestants generally may be located in between these two models. The Catholic and Jewish models are extremes only in a relative sense: the majority of all members of these religious subcommunities desire, expect, consider as ideal, and have two to four children.[13]

---

[11] Charles Westoff et al., *Family Growth in Metropolitan America* (Princeton: Princeton University Press, 1961); Charles Westoff et al., *The Third Child* (Princeton: Princeton University Press, 1963).

[12] See, e.g., Paul Glick, "Intermarriage and Fertility Patterns Among Persons in Major Religious Groups," *Eugenic Quarterly,* 7 (March 1960), pp. 31–38; Judith Blake, "The Americanization of Catholic Reproductive Ideals," *Population Studies,* 20 (July 1966), pp. 27–43; Calvin Goldscheider, "Fertility of the Jews," *Demography,* 4:1 (1967), pp. 196–209; Charles Westoff and Raymond Potvin, *College Women and Fertility Values* (Princeton: Princeton University Press, 1967); for a comprehensive bibliography of materials up to the early 1960's, see Ronald Freedman, "The Sociology of Human Fertility," *Current Sociology,* 10/11 (1961–1962); for a more current list, particularly for Catholic–non-Catholic fertility differentials, see Gavin Jones and Dorothy Nortman, "Roman Catholic Fertility and Family Planning: A Comparative Review of the Research Literature," *Studies in Family Planning,* no. 34 (New York: The Population Council, October 1968).

[13] See Whelpton, Campbell, and Patterson, *Fertility and Family Planning in the*

This pattern of differential fertility among the three religious groupings is not a new or temporary phenomena: scattered evidence suggests that these fertility differences extend back at least to the late nineteenth and early twentieth centuries in the United States. Although many traditional social and economic differentials in fertility have narrowed — for example, education, occupation, income, and residence — some evidence suggests a widening of fertility differences between Catholics and non-Catholics, particularly since World War II.[14] Moreover, the pattern of religious differentials in fertility is not a unique feature of American society. Various studies show that beginning around the middle of the nineteenth century in Western Europe, for the first thirty years of the twentieth century in Eastern Europe, and for most contemporary European and North American countries where Jews continue to live, lower Jewish fertility is the rule.[15] The cross-national pattern for Catholics is equally clear, and higher Catholic fertility has been observed in almost every "developed" country where data are available.[16]

The consistency of findings regarding differences in fertility among Protestants, Catholics, and Jews, historically and comparatively, demands explanation. If we argue in general that examining differentials in fertility helps to isolate the general determinants of fertility,[17] then it follows that insight into the determinants of Protestant, Catholic, and Jewish fertility may be obtained by investigating and analyzing social and economic differences *within* each of the three subpopulations. In addition, to isolate the particular role religious affiliation plays as a determinant of fertility and to test the "characteristics" hypothesis discussed earlier, we must "control" for such major intervening factors as socioeconomic status and residence. Moreover, we must examine the subgroups within each religious grouping that are more identified and

---

United States, pp. 71–72; Ronald Freedman, "American Studies of Family Planning and Fertility: A Review of Major Trends and Issues," in *Research in Family Planning,* ed. Clyde Kiser (Princeton: Princeton University Press, 1962), p. 216, and sources cited therein.

[14] Whelpton, Campbell, and Patterson, *Fertility and Family Planning in the United States,* p. 123; Ryder and Westoff, "The Trend of Expected Parity in the United States," pp. 164–166.

[15] See Goldscheider, "Fertility of the Jews," and the sources cited therein; see also the *Proceedings of the Fifth World Congress of Jewish Studies,* Demographic Section (Jerusalem, 1969). An interesting pattern of lower fertility among Jews in Italy starting in the eighteenth century is discussed in Sergio Della Pergola, "La Popolazione Ebraica d'Italia: Caratteristiche demografiche, economiche e Sociali," *Genus* 24 (1968), pp. 135–175.

[16] See the comprehensive review in Jones and Nortman, "Roman Catholic Fertility and Family Planning," especially table 1.2, p. 4.

[17] Cf. Chapter 8, this book.

committed to the norms and values of the religious group, i.e., we need to analyze the relationship of religiosity and fertility. This is particularly important in testing the particularized theology hypothesis.

The first and logically prior step before *analyzing* differentials within each of the religious groups is to *control* for differentials. Are fertility differences between Catholics, Protestants, and Jews merely the consequence of the differential social and economic characteristics of these subpopulations? A review of the relevant materials suggests that this question must be forthrightly answered in the negative. Except for some minor qualifications, which will be discussed later, the conclusion of every major empirical study has been that controlling for almost every social and economic characteristic, fertility differences between Protestant, Catholic, and Jewish couples remain. In other words, controlling for race, urban or metropolitan residence, education, occupation, income, and other socioeconomic measures, Catholics retain higher levels of fertility, Jews retain the lowest levels, and Protestants have an intermediate position. Thus, it cannot be argued that religious differentials in fertility reflect only differential concentrations of these subgroups in socioeconomic or residence categories. The characteristics hypothesis not only fails to admit to the vitality of religious group membership in modern societies but also may be clearly dismissed as inadequate on the basis of empirical evidence now available.

SUBGROUP DIFFERENTIALS

Although the literature is unanimous in pointing to the general differences in fertility between Protestants, Catholics, and Jews, findings with respect to differentials *within* these subgroupings are not altogether consistent. Some contradictions in the literature reflect changes over time in these relationships, the problems of sampling error, and the use of nonrepresentative samples.

Socioeconomic Status

The relationship between socioeconomic status and fertility appears to change during industrialization and modernization. In preindustrial Europe, it seems that fertility was positively associated with socioeconomic status.[18] The historical evidence is not altogether without exception, and analogies with the oft-noted direct relationship between

[18] Cf. Kingsley Davis, "Some Demographic Aspects of Poverty in America," in *Poverty in America,* ed. Margaret Gordon (San Francisco: Chandler, 1965), pp. 300–301, fn. 1; E. A. Wrigley, *Population and History* (London: Weidenfeld and Nicolson, World University Library, 1969), pp. 101–102, 185 ff.

fertility and socioeconomic status among present-day underdeveloped societies are fraught with difficulties. Nevertheless, the upper classes in European society were more susceptible to birth control practices as industrialization began, and, at least since the nineteenth century, have been characterized by lower fertility than persons in the lower classes. As industrialization and modernization proceeded, lower fertility values, norms, knowledge, and motivation about family planning diffused from the upper to the lower positions in society, particularly with the emergence of a large middle class and with the growth of individual opportunity for social mobility. In advanced stages of modernization, some convergence of the social class difference in fertility occurs with the reduction of lower class fertility and slight increases in fertility among the middle and upper classes.

Thus, sociologists and demographers have reached two related conclusions about the changing relationship of socioeconomic status to the fertility patterns of American couples. First, socioeconomic groupings have become more uniform in their fertility behavior, and class fertility differences are in the process of further contraction. Second, as a result of this convergence and contraction there has been a partial reversal of the inverse relationship of education, occupation, and income to fertility.[19] These changes, observed since World War II, have been explained by two opposite trends: (1) the rise in the fertility of groups with higher status and the changing desires of these groups for slightly larger families; and (2) the decline in fertility of groups of lower status with their increasingly extensive and successful use of contraception.[20] Some demographers have predicted the disappearance of the social class differential in fertility patterns of developed countries,[21] and others suggest that future social class differences may again, as in preindustrial times, relate directly rather than inversely to fertility.[22]

---

[19] For evidence on the contraction of socioeconomic differentials in American fertility, see the GAF and Princeton studies (cited in fns. 10 and 11); and Wilson Grabill, Clyde V. Kiser, and Pascal K. Whelpton, *The Fertility of American Women* (New York: Wiley, 1958), pp. 173–184; Clyde V. Kiser, "Differential Fertility in the United States," in *Demographic and Economic Change in Developed Countries* (Princeton, N.J.: 1960), National Bureau of Economic Research, pp. 77–112; Charles Westoff, "Differential Fertility in the United States: 1900–1952," *American Sociological Review*, 19 (October 1954), pp. 549–561; Clyde Kiser et al., *Trends and Variations in Fertility in the United States* (Cambridge: Harvard University Press, 1968), pp. 147–207.

[20] Freedman, Whelpton, and Campbell, *Family Planning, Sterility and Population Growth*, p. 318; Westoff et al., *The Third Child*, p. 129.

[21] E.g., Dennis Wrong, "Trends in Class Fertility in Western Nations," *Canadian Journal of Economics and Political Science*, 24 (May 1958), pp. 216–229.

[22] E.g., Westoff, "Differential Fertility in the United States: 1900–1952," p. 561; Clyde V. Kiser, "Educational Differentials in Fertility in Relation to the Demo-

More important in the present context is the speculation that part of the contraction of social class differences in fertility may be due to different relationships between socioeconomic status and fertility for Protestants and Catholics, and the widening religious differences in fertility. Results of the Princeton fertility study show that, regardless of the measure of socioeconomic status, fertility was inversely associated with socioeconomic status of Protestants and directly related to the socioeconomic status of Catholics. Thus, the authors of the Princeton fertility study suggest that the traditional inverse relationship between fertility and socioeconomic status in the United States may be primarily an association among the Protestant population.[23] Similar findings are reflected in the Growth of American Families study of 1955 and 1960. Data from the 1955 GAF national survey indicated that family size expectations — minimum, most likely, and maximum — were lower for college- than grade school-educated Protestants, although for the Catholic population, fertility expectations were higher for the college-educated segment than for the noncollege-educated segment.[24] The 1960 GAF study confirms these findings for fertility expectations. Although there was a definite inverse relationship of wife's education and family size expectations for the Protestant group, college-educated Catholic women expected significantly larger families than Catholic women who attended high school.[25] In general, among Catholics the relationship of social class and fertility appears U-shaped, i.e., higher and lower status groupings tend to have higher fertility than the middle classes.[26]

The number of cases included in the major fertility studies is too small for detailed analysis of socioeconomic variation within the Jewish population. However, specialized studies of Jews have suggested that higher status American Jews have larger families than lower status American Jews.[27] This finding is consistent with the evidence from the major fertility studies, which shows that among couples who completely plan

---

graphic Transition" (paper presented to the General Assembly, International Union for the Scientific Study of Population, London, 1969). Cf. Judith Blake, "Are Babies Consumer Durables?" *Population Studies*, 22 (March 1968), pp. 3–25.

[23] Westoff et al., *The Third Child*, pp. 111–129.

[24] Freedman, Whelpton, and Campbell, *Family Planning, Sterility and Population Growth*, p. 289, fig. 9–2.

[25] Whelpton, Campbell, and Patterson, *Fertility and Family Planning in the United States*, p. 124.

[26] Ibid., chap. 3; Jones and Nortman, "Roman Catholic Fertility and Family Planning," p. 5.

[27] Calvin Goldscheider, "Socio-Economic Status and Jewish Fertility," *Jewish Journal of Sociology*, 7 (December 1965), pp. 221–237; Sidney Goldstein, "Completed and Expected Fertility in an American Jewish Community," *Proceedings of the Fifth World Congress of Jewish Studies*, Demographic Section (Jerusalem, 1969).

their families, there tends to be a direct rather than an inverse relationship to socioeconomic status.[28]

In sum, the information available suggests a positive relationship between socioeconomic status and fertility among couples who rationally plan their families. Moreover, data on Protestants and Jews indicate a trend toward convergence and homogeneity in the fertility patterns of socioeconomic groupings within these populations. The contraction of socioeconomic differentials may result from the widespread rationality with which most contemporary Jews and a significant proportion of Protestants plan their families, the absence of rapid upper mobility characteristic of earlier cohorts, the greater homogeneity of contemporary Protestant and Jewish social structures, and the growing concentration of Jewish and Protestant populations among the college trained and in white-collar occupations.[29]

Residence

Urbanization in the Western world has long been identified with social changes that have brought about declines in fertility. In some Western countries, the rural-urban fertility differential extends back to the seventeenth century. Family limitation and fertility control appear to have originated in cities and, as a result of rural-urban migration and urban-rural cultural diffusion, the rural population has experienced fertility declines as well.[30] The convergence of rural and urban fertility has taken place when metropolitan areas were expanding and distinctive fertility patterns developed in suburban areas. The general pattern is that suburban populations are characterized by larger families than urban populations.

However, the evidence available on suburbanization and fertility among Protestants, Catholics, and Jews is not clear. The 1955 GAF study concluded that Protestant and Catholic wives in the suburbs of the twelve largest cities expected slightly more births than wives in central cities. Although patterns of residential differences in fertility were the same for Protestants and Catholics, differences were greater among Protestants. In smaller metropolitan areas, no statistically significant differences in the fertility expectations of Protestant and Catholic city residents when compared to Protestant and Catholic suburban residents

---

[28] Whelpton and Kiser (eds.), *Social and Psychological Factors Affecting Fertility*, vol. 2, p. 389; Whelpton et al., *Fertility and Family Planning in the United States*, pp. 240–242; Westoff et al., *The Third Child*, p. 118.

[29] Cf. Goldstein and Goldscheider, *Jewish Americans*; Goldstein, "Socioeconomic Differentials. . . ."

[30] United Nations, *The Determinants and Consequences of Population Trends* (New York, 1953), pp. 78–86.

were found.[31] The Princeton study found that Catholic fertility was not at all associated with residence, whereas, among Protestants, higher fertility characterized central city residents.[32] The 1960 GAF study does not specifically deal with fertility in the suburbs but suggests a narrowing of all residence related associations with fertility.

It may be argued that suburban areas represent the advanced stages of urbanism and that religious differences would decrease. This pattern may be the result of the greater acculturation of Catholics who move to the suburbs, i.e., suburban selectivity, or may reflect the particular pronatalist social forces operative in suburban areas. An analysis of the relationship between suburbanization and fertility in six metropolitan areas suggests that Protestant-Catholic fertility differences are still found in the central cities. However, fertility differences between Protestants and Catholics largely tend to disappear among suburban residents. This convergence of fertility behavior in the suburbs is the result of the combined effects of higher fertility among Protestant suburban residents when compared to central-city Protestants, although suburban Catholics tend to have fewer children than those who live in the city.[33]

The pattern of suburbanization and Jewish fertility is less clear. Some evidence shows that suburban Jews are much more acculturated than Jews in central cities and that the suburbs are selective of Jews with plans for larger families.[34] Thus, one might hypothesize greater fertility convergence among the three religious groups in the suburbs or, at the very least, a greater fertility homogeneity among Protestants, Catholics, and Jews in the suburbs than in urban areas.

Religiosity

If religion is related to fertility as the evidence suggests, it is all too easy to view the relationship as a consequence of particularized theology rather than as an integral part of the social makeup of religious subgroups. Although Lenski notes that socioreligious groups are subcommunities involving more than differences in theology, he places family size differences among religious groups in the narrow context of

[31] Freedman, Whelpton, and Campbell, *Family Planning, Sterility and Population Growth*, pp. 309–313.

[32] Westoff et al., *Family Growth in Metropolitan America*, pp. 263–281; Westoff et al., *The Third Child*, pp. 157–182, 241–242.

[33] This argument and the analysis of data in support of it are presented in detail in Basil Zimmer and Calvin Goldscheider, "A Further Look at Catholic Fertility," *Demography*, 3:2 (1966), pp. 462–469.

[34] For a more extensive discussion, see Goldstein and Goldscheider, *Jewish Americans*, pp. 125–126.

norms with respect to family size and contraception rather than taking into account the broader implications of religious group identification and membership.

> The Catholic church has opposed the use of many of the more efficient means of contraception as immoral and has encouraged the view that large families are pleasing to God. On the other hand, the Protestant churches have increasingly taken the position that there is nothing immoral in the use of modern methods of contraception, and the *failure* to limit family size can be immoral if parents continue to have children when they are unable to provide properly for the spiritual and physical needs of those they already have. The problem is to determine how far these different viewpoints affect actual practice.[35]

The problem, however, is to examine not only the effects of various church doctrines on fertility but to determine the broader implication of religious group affiliation and concomitant norms and values for fertility.

The "particularized theology" school argues that if the relationship of religion and fertility reflects religion per se, as the controls for socioeconomic status, residence, and a host of other variables suggest, then it follows that the degree of devoutness or involvement in *religious activities* would be of signal importance.[36] The role of religious ideological factors takes the form of the specific doctrines of the Catholic church on birth control and ideal family size or, in the case of Protestants and Jews, the preachings on "social responsibility in parenthood." [37]

Theoretically, as noted earlier, this interpretation of religion and fertility is incomplete precisely because it fails to treat socioreligious groups as subcommunities and narrows its focus on particular fertility-related theology. Empirically, replies to questions on a whole series of religiosity indices in the GAF and Princeton studies suggest that *no* significant or consistent relationship exists between religiosity, religious commitment, or ritual observances and Protestant fertility. Only when religiosity among Protestants reveals a *matrix* of values associated with fundamentalism is there any theoretical or empirical support for such a correlation.[38] Catholics appear to have a positive association of religiosity measures and fertility — the more religious (or better, the more identified and committed to the church subculture and subcommunity)

[35] Lenski, *The Religious Factor*, p. 236.

[36] Whelpton, Campbell, and Patterson, *Fertility and Family Planning in the United States*, p. 82.

[37] See Westoff et al., *Family Growth in Metropolitan America*, pp. 196–198.

[38] See, for example, Gordon F. De Jong, "Religious Fundamentalism, Socio-Economic Status and Fertility Attitudes in the Southern Appalachians," *Demography*, 2 (1965), pp. 540–548.

the higher the fertility. Indeed, part of the positive association of socio-economic status and the fertility of Catholics reflects this religiosity factor.

The official religious position on birth control or family size among Jews is unclear; even among Jewish fundamentalists, where the stand against birth control may be clearer, Jewish couples are seldom aware of the position taken. Moreover, American Jews have no central religious authority or central religious organization. It would therefore be unwarranted to expect Jewish fertility differentials to be related to religious ideological factors that are in large part unknown and inoperative on the personal level. The evidence, however, suggests that religious differentials in fertility appear within the Jewish group: Orthodox, Conservative, and Reform Jews (religious to secular) have different fertility patterns. Nevertheless, when social class and generation differences among these religious subdivisions within the Jewish population are controlled, differences in the fertility of those identifying with these religious denominations disappear. Thus, few fertility differences exist within the Jewish group that cannot be explained by social class or generation status factors. Other data on a wide range of religiosity variables show little relationship to fertility among Jews and *religion* conceptualized narrowly in terms of ritual practices, and religiosity plays a minor role in determining Jewish fertility behavior.[39]

Thus, although religious ideological factors *may* play a part in determining higher Catholic fertility, no such interpretation can be regarded as sound for Protestants or Jews. Yet how are differentials in fertility by religious groupings explained if the social characteristics hypothesis is inadequate and if the particularized theology hypothesis at best accounts for higher Catholic fertility. Because we are concerned with *consistency of explanation* as well as with adequacy and accuracy of explanation, the particularized theology argument loses its potency even as a potential explanation of Catholic fertility.

FERTILITY OF MINORITY GROUPS

The combined propositions of the characteristics argument and the particularized theology approach fail to account for the empirical evidence available. We are thus left with fertility differences between religious groups that require a coherent sociological interpretation.

[39] Calvin Goldscheider, "Ideological Factors in Jewish Fertility Differentials," *Jewish Journal of Sociology*, 7 (June 1965), pp. 92–105; see also Bernard Lazerwitz, "Jewish Identification and Jewish Fertility in the Chicago Jewish Community," *Proceedings of the Fifth World Congress of Jewish Studies*, Demographic Section (Jerusalem, 1969).

Protestants

If we treat the Protestant population as the "standard" or the "model" from which Jewish and Catholic fertility deviate, our task is reduced to interpreting why Jews have lower fertility and why Catholics have higher fertility. With respect to the Protestant model we may note that the particularized theology argument is less than cogent. Although members of Protestant denominations differ in fertility behavior and attitudes, such variation reflects more of the total social organization and life styles of the denominations rather than religious theology *per se*. Religious fundamentalism among Protestant denominations is highly correlated with "social fundamentalism." Social class and residence factors, which are indicators of life style, are the key internal differentiators of American Protestant fertility. If religious ideology determines fertility levels of Protestants, the causal mechanism is intimately linked up with social, demographic, and economic factors.

Jews [40]

As previously indicated, the evidence from census materials and sample surveys consistently points to the lower fertility of Jews, which has been usually interpreted as the consequence of the social and economic characteristics of the Jewish population. The authors of the GAF studies suggest that the long urban experience of Jews and their concentration among the educated, professionals, and middle class result in lower fertility when compared to Protestants or Catholics.[41] Similarly, Thomlinson argues that lower fertility rates of Jews "may be explained by their concentration in cities, their higher occupational standing, their higher educational achievement, and their liberal attitudes toward contraception." [42] Petersen states that "the small family size of Jews derives from their concentration in cities, especially in those urban occupations that are always associated with low fertility." [43] Rosenthal dismisses

[40] The remainder of this chapter represents in large part a revision of Calvin Goldscheider and Peter Uhlenberg, "Minority Group Status and Fertility," *American Journal of Sociology*, 74 (January 1969), pp. 361–372.

[41] Ronald Freedman, Pascal Whelpton, and John Smit, "Socio-Economic Factors in Religious Differentials in Fertility," *American Sociological Review*, 26 (August 1961), pp. 608–614; Freedman et al., *Family Planning, Sterility and Population Growth*, p. 104; Whelpton et al., *Fertility and Family Planning in the United States*, pp. 72–73.

[42] Ralph Thomlinson, *Population Dynamics* (New York: Random House, 1965), p. 179.

[43] William Petersen, *Population* (New York: Macmillan, 1961), p. 223. In the 1969 revised edition of this widely used text, Petersen maintains a similar position with respect to Jews, and indeed, more or less accepts the "characteristics" hypothe-

the theory that minority group status exerts an independent effect on Jewish fertility: "The religio-cultural complex called Jewishness is not, as has often been theorized, a major factor in the Jewish fertility rate." [44]

Obviously, the concentration of Jews among the urban, middle-class population and among the college-educated professionals accounts, *in part,* for their lower fertility. Nevertheless, several major empirical findings about Jewish fertility reveal the incompleteness of the "characteristics" explanation. As noted earlier, studies have documented the lower fertility of Jews compared to non-Jews when major social and economic characteristics have been standardized or controlled. Canadian census data reveal the lower fertility of Jews in both urban and rural areas. Indeed, older Jewish women in rural areas of Canada have lower fertility than *urban* Protestants.[45] Jews in the United States have lower fertility than Protestants or Catholics when education is controlled.[46] The Princeton fertility studies consistently show that the lower Jewish fertility behavior and attitudes are not solely a function of metropolitan residence or social class variables because, when these are jointly controlled, Jews retain lower levels of fertility when compared to Protestants or Catholics.[47]

The only contradictory evidence indicating that the social, demographic, and economic characteristics of Jews account fully for lower Jewish fertility is the widely cited precision-matching of sixty-six Jewish couples with Protestants and Catholics in the 1955 GAF study.[48] The small number of Jewish cases included in this study raises questions of sample variation, sample representativeness, and sampling error. Averages are presented rather than distributions; differences in family building and formation that directly affect fertility were not considered. However, if we grant that the matching was sound methodologically and if we disregard other evidence that dismisses the characteristics interpretation, we must still explain why matched Jewish and Protestant couples differed significantly in the proportion who planned the number and

---

sis. He states that "the effect of religion *per se* on the reproductive behavior of most persons in the West is now probably close to nil. What may seem to be a religious influence often reflects the fact that the members of any denomination are typically concentrated in a very few places in the social structure as defined by occupation, education, income, or any other of the usual indices" (p. 538).

[44] Erich Rosenthal, "Jewish Fertility in the United States," *Eugenics Quarterly,* 8 (December 1961), pp. 198–217.

[45] For documentation, see Goldscheider and Uhlenberg, "Minority Group Status and Fertility," pp. 365–366.

[46] Goldscheider, "Socio-Economic Status and Jewish Fertility," pp. 233–234.

[47] See reference in fn. 11.

[48] Freedman, Whelpton, and Smit, "Socio-Economic Factors in Religious Differentials in Fertility," pp. 608–614.

spacing of all pregnancies: 47 per cent of the Jews compared to 33 per cent of the matched Protestants.

Moreover, the evidence of lower Jewish fertility in the United States extends back to the 1880's and in European countries for at least the last seventy-five years. The social and economic characteristics of Jews at earlier points in time were those usually associated with *higher* rather than lower fertility. Hence, other factors besides the "characteristics" of Jews must be investigated to account for their lower fertility. The consistently lower fertility of Jews over time, in the United States and Western countries, and controlling for residence, social class, and other significant sociological and demographic variables, suggests that interpretations of lower Jewish fertility based solely on the characteristics of the Jewish population are inadequate.

Because lower Jewish fertility in almost all cases persists with controls for intervening variables, some have been tempted to explain residual differences as a function of the religious ideology of Jews — particularly, the notion of religious doctrines of "social responsibility in parenthood." But again, this fails to note the empirical problem of no relationship between religiosity and fertility among Jews, and fails to examine the broader qualities of the social organizational implications of Jewish group membership and identification. One distinguishing feature of Jews in Western countries over time is minority group status. Perhaps, minority group status has some significance that influences behavior in general and fertility behavior in particular.

Negroes

The evidence unanimously points to the higher fertility of Negro Americans when compared to white Americans.[49] Because Negro Americans do not constitute a religious subcommunity, the particularized theology hypothesis cannot be applied. However, the characteristics approach has been. Indeed higher Negro fertility has almost always been explained in terms of the "deprived characteristics" of the Negro population in the United States. Petersen argues that "Negroes have no culture trait that affects natality independently of their occupation or education. Race is not a cause of family size but an index of social class."

---

[49] On the higher fertility of American Negroes, see, for example, Grabill, Kiser, and Whelpton, *The Fertility of American Women*, chaps. 4–6; Anders Lunde, "White-Nonwhite Fertility Differentials in the United States," *Health, Education, and Welfare Indicators* (September 1965); Kiser et al., *Trends and Variations in Fertility in the United States;* Anders Lunde, "Recent Trends in White-Nonwhite Fertility in the United States" (paper presented to the General Assembly, International Union for the Scientific Study of Population, London, 1969).

Furthermore, he suggests, that given increasing levels of urban concentration and social mobility among Negroes, "there is good reason to expect that the differential birth rates by race will begin to converge again in the near future." [50] T. Lynn Smith states that "Because Negroes are still residents of the most rural region of the country (the South) and probably because they tend to live in the most rural sections of that region, their rate of reproduction is slightly higher than that of whites." [51] Similarly, Thomlinson suggests that "racial differences in fertility are largely explained by differences in social and cultural environment . . . [and] fertility rates by color appear likely to continue to converge." [52] The Lees, comparing Negro-white differential fertilty in 1950, point out that "the pattern of Negro fertility is remarkably similar to that of native whites. . . . The fertility of the Negro most closely approached those of native whites where the Negro has been permitted to share most freely in the general culture." [53] Regarding the future fertility of American Negroes they suggest "the higher Negro fertility can be explained in terms of differences in education and socio-economic level. When Negroes and whites are equated in these matters, no matter how roughly, Negro fertility seldom appears much higher than white and it is often lower." [54]

If these widely held ad hoc interpretations are entirely correct, it is reasonable to expect similar fertility among Negroes and whites when educational level and region of residence are controlled. The evidence, however, consistently indicates that this is not the case. United States census data of 1960 show that urban nonwhites (over 90 per cent of whom are Negro) with at least four years of high school education have *lower* rather than similar fertility when compared to whites. The fertility difference is substantial: Among urban college graduates, family size of nonwhites is 20 to 25 per cent smaller than whites, and family size among urban residents who have more than a college education is between 30 and 40 per cent smaller for nonwhites than whites. Moreover,

---

[50] William Petersen, *Population* (1961 ed.), pp. 226, 228. In the 1969 edition, he argues similarly that "Differentiation by race is largely an index of social class on fertility" (p. 509).

[51] T. Lynn Smith, *Fundamentals of Population Study* (Philadelphia: Lippincott, 1960), p. 322.

[52] Ralph Thomlinson, *Population Dynamics*, p. 178. In the 1960 U.S. Census monograph on fertility it is argued that a major reason for higher nonwhite fertility is that, "the characteristics generally associated with high fertility tend to characterize the nonwhite population to a greater extent than the white population." Kiser, Grabill, and Campbell, *Trends and Variations in Fertility in the United States*, p. 56.

[53] Anne and Everett Lee, "The Differential Fertility of the American Negro," *American Sociological Review*, 17 (August 1952), p. 446.

[54] Anne and Everett Lee, "The Future Fertility of the American Negro," *Social Forces*, 37 (March 1959), p. 231.

nonwhites within each educational level – from elementary school only to college graduates and above – who live in the North Central region of the United States have consistently lower fertility than whites. Even in the South, nonwhite college graduates have substantially lower fertility than college-educated whites. Patterns of lower fertility among nonwhites, compared to whites, who are high school graduates and residing in northern regions of the United States have also been noted in analyses of 1940 and 1950 census data.[55]

Additional support for the lower rather than similar fertility level of nonwhites compared to whites when both have similar social and economic characteristics may be found in the second GAF study.[56] Although only 270 nonwhite (256 Negro) women, eighteen to thirty-nine years of age, married, living with husband, were interviewed, the results revealed the lower fertility behavior and attitudes of selected but significant subgroups within the nonwhite population. College-educated nonwhites expected 20 per cent fewer children than whites (2.4 versus 3.0) and fewer than a matched sample of whites. By the time of the study (1960) nonwhite college-educated women had fewer children than whites, even when matched very closely to whites on duration of marriage, wife's age at marriage, wife's religion, region of residence, and selected other variables. Furthermore, nonwhites of all educational levels living in the Northeast expected fewer children than the total or matched white sample. Finally, nonwhites in the Northeast and North Central regions and those with at least some high school education wanted significantly fewer children when compared to total or matched whites.

Lending weight to these findings are several local studies. Studies in Detroit in 1954 revealed that Negroes expressed significantly lower family size ideals than whites. Negroes thought the ideal number of

[55] For documentation, see Goldscheider and Uhlenberg, "Minority Group Status and Fertility," pp. 362–365. Some studies have shown the lower fertility of Negroes compared to whites at lower than high school education levels or in other areas than in Northern urban sectors, 1940 and 1950. We have isolated the high school graduate and urban-Northern segments of the Negro population: (1) to eliminate the question of possible fecundity differentials by race at lower socioeconomic status levels; (2) to eliminate the problem of rural slave background and culture; and (3) to examine subgroups within the Negro population that may foreshadow trends for the future Negro population as a whole. For evidence on Negro lower fertility in 1940, 1950, and more recent dates, see Clyde V. Kiser, "Fertility Characteristics of the Nonwhite Population in the United States," *Bulletin de l'Institut International de Statistique,* 36:2 (1958), pp. 296–304; Clyde V. Kiser, "Fertility Trends and Differentials Among Nonwhites in the United States," *Milbank Memorial Fund Quarterly,* 36 (April 1958), pp. 149–179; "New Patterns in U.S. Fertility," *Population Bulletin,* 20 (September 1964), pp. 136–138; Peter D. Uhlenberg, "Negro Fertility Patterns in the United States," *Berkeley Journal of Sociology,* 11 (1966), pp. 54–65.

[56] Whelpton, Campbell, and Patterson, *Fertility and Family Planning in the United States,* chap. 9.

children should average 2.3 compared to 3.1 expressed by whites. This differential was the largest found between any major strata, including religion and social class, and the ideal family size expressed by Negroes was the lowest obtained for any subgroup in their 1952 or 1954 samples. Furthermore, 40 per cent of persons stating an ideal family size of less than two children were Negroes, although Negroes comprised only 14 per cent of the population.[57] Similar findings were obtained in more recent studies of Negroes in Chicago: ideal family size was lower among Negroes compared to whites for the total Chicago sample as well as when education, income, and occupation were controlled; the proportion approving family limitation was *greater* among Negroes.[58]

Although data on family size "ideals," "norms," and "desires" are not necessarily the basis for predicting actual reproductive behavior, family size is not likely to exceed "ideals" or "desires" among those segments of the Negro community that plan their families and use effective means of contraception (i.e., college-educated, middle-class, urban Negroes). Moreover, even if fertility norms and behavior are not perfectly correlated, why do Negroes express a lower ideal family size, want fewer children, and approve family limitation in larger proportions than whites?

Taken together, the available information suggests that other factors independent of social and economic characteristics depress the fertility behavior and attitudes of selected segments of the Negro population below white levels. Just as explaining Jewish fertility in terms of socioeconomic characteristics is inadequate, explaining Negro fertility in terms of the characteristics of a deprived population is inadequate; it is incomplete precisely among groupings within the Negro population that are the models for the future pattern and direction of fertility of the Negro population as a whole (i.e., the educated, urban, and middle classes). The evidence indicates the probability of lower rather than similar fertility of Negroes compared to whites when and if social and economic equalization with whites occurs. It is quite clear that the fertility variations within the Negro population (from an average of over six children among Negroes in rural-farm areas of the South to an average of less than two children among college-educated Northern Negroes) and the higher total fertility of nonwhites compared to whites reflect, in large

[57] Ronald Freedman, David Goldberg, and Harry Sharp, " 'Ideals' About Family Size in the Detroit Metropolitan Area: 1954," *Milbank Memorial Fund Quarterly*, 33 (April 1955), pp. 191–193.

[58] Annie O. Blaire, "A Comparison of Negro and White Fertility Attitudes," and Elvira Mendoza, "Socio-Economic Correlates of Attitudes toward Family Size," in *Sociological Contributions to Family Planning Research*, ed. Donald J. Bogue (Chicago: Community and Family Study Center, University of Chicago Press, 1967), pp. 8, 42–50.

part, social and economic differences. Yet, the accentuation of lower fertility among subgroups within the Negro population that most closely approximate the white community must be explained by other factors.

Japanese Americans

Relatively little attention has been paid to fertility of American minority groups other than racial (Negro) or religious (Jews and Catholics). Nevertheless, United States census data on Japanese Americans further bring into question the adequacy of the characteristics interpretation of subgroup fertility. Although no direct data on the fertility of Japanese American women by social class measures are available, evidence on children "ever born" by age and residence is revealing.[59]

Japanese American women in specific age groups (20 to 39) have lower fertility than native white Americans when either the total population or the urban sectors are examined.[60] Japanese Americans living in areas of lower Japanese concentration accentuate the trend toward lower fertility. The Japanese Americans in regions outside the West are generally younger, second generation, and characterized by higher socioeconomic status than those in the West, and, hence, distance from the West may be considered an indicator of acculturation. The lower Japanese American fertility in these areas, and in urban areas in general, parallels the findings noted earlier among Jews and segments of the Negro population, and contradicts the argument that fertility levels of religious and other minority groups converge as acculturation proceeds, because fertility differences are not solely a function of "lags" in socioeconomic characteristics. Again, other factors independent of social and economic characteristics may be operating to depress Japanese American fertility below native white levels.

It may also be noted that the fertility rates of Chinese Americans in urbanized areas are also below those of native whites for the younger age groupings. Age may be viewed as a rough indicator of generation

[59] For documentation, see Goldscheider and Uhlenberg, "Minority Group Status and Fertility," pp. 366–368.

[60] Age differentiation among Japanese Americans is a sensitive indicator of generation and, in turn, acculturation. The younger second generation, Nisei, differ substantially from first-generation Japanese Americans. See Toshio Yatsushiro, "The Japanese Americans," in *American Minorities*, ed. Milton L. Barron (New York: Knopf, 1962), p. 323; Dorothy Swaine Thomas, "The Japanese Americans," in *Understanding Minority Groups*, ed. Joseph B. Gittler (New York: Wiley, 1964), pp. 84–108. On the rapid acculturation of second-generation Japanese Americans, see William Petersen, "Family Structure and Social Mobility Among Japanese Americans" (paper presented at the annual meetings of the American Sociological Association, San Francisco, August 1967); Harry Kitano, *Japanese Americans* (Englewood Cliffs, N.J.: Prentice-Hall, 1969).

status and, in turn, of acculturation. Consequently, it is particularly significant that younger Chinese Americans are characterized by lower fertility. Because the fertility information on Chinese Americans is sketchy, we can only speculate that, similar to other American minority groups, when second and third generation Americans of Chinese ethnic background acculturate and are socially mobile, their fertility levels will be lower than comparable socioeconomic status groups among native whites.

It is important at this point to indicate that the Negro and Japanese American populations, as with the Jewish population, do not have specific norms or religiocultural ideologies encouraging large families. The identification of persons with these minority communities would in no way require large family size ideals or behavior. Except for numerically insignificant sectors of the Negro (Black Muslims) and Jewish (Hasidim and some ultra-Orthodox Jews) populations, membership in these minority communities implies no religious, cultural, or social ideology that values large families nor any group norm prohibiting the use of efficient contraceptive methods.

Catholics

As noted earlier, most American demographers had assumed that the higher fertility of American Catholics represented a "cultural lag," but it is quite clear that "the distinctive Catholic pattern is not a result of low social or educational status or of recent urbanization. In fact it is most distinctive among the well-educated urban group." [61]

The evidence available on Catholic fertility irrefutably dismisses the characteristics hypothesis. However, it is not at all clear what factors interact to produce the observed Catholic–non-Catholic fertility differential. Part of the differential may be attributed to the opposition of the church to efficient methods of contraception and to the normative encouragement of the church for large families.[62] But, the higher fertility of American Catholics cannot be attributed to one specific doctrinal element, nor could one predict from Catholic doctrine the actual fertility behavior of contemporary Catholics.[63] The fertility norms and behavior

[61] Freedman, "American Studies of Family Planning and Fertility," p. 224. For a specific and early reference to Catholic fertility as a "cultural lag," see Norman Himes, *Medical History of Contraception* (Baltimore: Williams and Wilkins, 1936), p. 413.

[62] Cf. Blake, "The Americanization of Catholic Reproductive Ideals."

[63] See, for example, Thomas K. Burch and Henry J. Jacek, Jr., "Church Teaching and the Fertility of Catholic Americans: A Partial Replication" (paper presented at the Population Association of America meetings, Ohio, 1967); Freedman, *The Sociology of Human Fertility*, pp. 63–64; Kingsley Davis, "Values, Population and the Supernatural: A Critique," in *Studies in Population*, ed. George Mair (Princeton: Princeton University Press, 1949), pp. 135–139.

of Catholics accentuate the "large" family only in comparison with Protestants but, as noted earlier, within a narrow range of two to four children.

Part of the explanation of the higher fertility of subgroups within the American Catholic population (e.g., better educated, more church affiliated, or those exposed and trained in Catholic-related schools) may reflect the subtle institutionalized impact of the Catholic subcommunity and subculture rather than total conformity to the church's religious ideology about family size and contraception. Ethnic fertility differences, particularly changes within the Irish and Italian segments of the American Catholic community,[64] and other fertility differentials (such as the convergence in suburban areas) would best be treated in the larger context of minority group assimilation and acculturation. It appears from the various findings about Catholic fertility that Catholics consistently have higher fertility than Protestants but that this difference varies with the nature of church identification, which, in turn, may reflect acculturation types among Catholics.

The general and widely accepted notion that the peculiar fertility of American Catholics is a function of specific norms about family size and contraception appears superficial as well as inadequate. It is analogous to explaining the unique voting or political behavior and attitudes of Catholics in terms of *specific* church norms with respect to voting or political behavior. Rather, just as when we deal with other social behavior of Catholics we attempt to invoke the broader sociocultural complex of the Catholic situation in the United States, so it seems necessary to broaden our explanation of Catholic fertility. (Indeed, this is precisely the approach that Durkheim takes in the analysis of suicide rates by religion, where he dismisses any "particularized theology" explanation and focuses on the nature of the religious subcommunities and subcultures treated as "societies.") [65] The distinctions between the fertility of Irish and Italian Catholics is therefore less in terms of specific commitments of these ethnic subgroups to the family size and contraceptive norms of the church, but rather to the integration of these groups into the institutionalized Catholic structure, the assimilation-acculturation patterns of the two groups, and the more general social and cultural milieu of the American Catholic subgroup.[66]

---

[64] The Princeton study, for example, found that Italian Catholic fertility was as close to Protestant fertility as to Irish Catholics. Westoff et al., *The Third Child*, pp. 103–106.

[65] Durkheim, *Suicide*, pp. 152–170.

[66] See, for example, John M. Goering, "The Structure and Process of Ethnicity: Catholic Family Size in Providence, Rhode Island," *Sociological Analysis*, 26 (Fall 1965), pp. 129–136; on the Irish and Italian sociocultural situation, see Nathan Glazer and Daniel Moynihan, *Beyond the Melting Pot* (Cambridge, Mass.: MIT Press, 1963).

THE MINORITY GROUP STATUS
HYPOTHESIS

As an alternative to the particularized theology and characteristics propositions, we propose to integrate the analysis of religious differentials in fertility with the interaction of religion and social organization. The lower fertility of Jews and segments of the Negro and Japanese American populations may be explained by the interaction of minority group status and socioeconomic status. Membership in, and identification with, a minority group that does not have a normative system encouraging large families, and that does not prohibit or discourage using efficient contraception methods, depresses fertility below majority levels. This is not to argue that a significant part, but of unknown magnitude, of the generally lower fertility of Jews and the higher fertility of most Negroes is not a direct result of the social, demographic, and economic characteristics of these groups. As Lenski notes, subcultures of every socioreligious group are always profoundly affected by the social situation of the group.[67] Subcultures of religious groups in urban situations differ from those of groups in rural agrarian areas, and the same is true for socioeconomic status and other social situational indicators. But social situational factors are only one type of determinant. What happens when the discrepancies in social characteristics are eliminated and no longer operate to differentiate fertility behavior and attitudes? In general, the residual lower fertility of minority groups may result from the insecurities associated with minority group status.

Yet, if this is the case, aren't Catholics a minority group, and isn't Catholic fertility, in general, higher than non-Catholics? In attempting to answer this, Lincoln Day shows that, among developed countries, the fertility of Catholics in countries where they constitute a distinguishable *minority* of the population exceeds that of Catholics where they constitute a majority. He concludes that Catholic pro-natalism serves to increase fertility only in situations in which Catholics define themselves as members of a group constituting a socially important minority.[68] Thus, if minority group integration and identification (which is a natural rather than a temporary phenomena in a structurally pluralistic society) imply greater commitments to a religious ideology or sociocultural norm encouraging large families or restricting contraception usage, then minority group status will enhance the differential between minority and majority

[67] Lenski, *The Religious Factor,* p. 336.
[68] Lincoln Day, "Natality and Ethnocentrism: Some Relationships Suggested by an Analysis of Catholic-Protestant Differentials," *Population Studies,* 22 (March 1968), pp. 27–50.

groups through higher minority fertility. Differences within the Catholic community reflect in part the degree of minority group integration, i.e., receptivity to the norms governing Catholic identification.[69]

The isolation of minority group status as an independent factor in fertility is only a starting point. The significant, yet unresolved issues are how and under what conditions minority group status depresses fertility and what dimensions of minority group identification affect fertility. Some tentative generalizations emerge from our review of the fertility of racial (Negroes), religious (Jews and Catholics), and nationality (Japanese Americans) groups in the United States. These generalizations require rigorous testing but are presented here as insights derived from the available evidence.

First, as a general principle, Protestant, Jewish, Catholic, Negro, and Japanese American fertility must be treated within a broader context of other social behavior characterizing these subgroups. Minority group status and fertility may very well be a special case of the general relationship of minority group status and social behavior. Because these minority groups have experienced social and cultural changes of various velocities at different points in their American history, minority group status and fertility must be considered within a dynamic framework of sociocultural change. Hence, the relationship of minority group status and fertility operates within the particularized, but changing, social situation of minority groups.

Second, a key element in the relationship of minority group status and fertility is the degree of, and desire for, acculturation. These degrees and desires do not necessarily imply structural integration or total assimilation. Rather, the combination of cultural and behavioral convergences with the majority and structural separation may produce the insecurities of minority group status.[70] Advancing up the educational and other social and economic scales appears to be harder for minority group

[69] Cf. Lincoln Day, "Fertility Differentials Among Catholics in Australia," *Milbank Memorial Fund Quarterly*, 42 (April 1964), pp. 57–83; F. Van Heek, "Roman Catholicism and Fertility in the Netherlands: Demographic Aspects of Minority Status," *Population Studies*, 10 (November 1956), pp. 125–138; Lincoln Day, "Catholic Teaching and Catholic Fertility" (paper presented at the United Nations World Population Conference, Belgrade, Yugoslavia, September, 1965, B.2/V/E/202); Thomas K. Burch, "The Fertility of North American Catholics: A Comparative Overview," *Demography*, 3 (Spring 1966), pp. 174–187.

[70] The literature on "marginality" suggests that persons in this position frequently are characterized by insecurity, strong self-consciousness, and rationality in behavior. See Arnold Green, "A Re-Examination of the Marginal Man Concept," *Social Forces*, 26 (December 1947), pp. 161–171; Aaron Antonovsky, "Toward a Refinement of the 'Marginal Man' Concept," *Social Forces*, 35 (October 1956), pp. 57–62; Alan Kerckhoff and Thomas McCormick, "Marginal Status and Marginal Personality," *Social Forces*, 34 (October 1955), pp. 48–53.

members. As minority group persons enter more generally in competition with the majority community, they may tend to counteract some of their disadvantages by deferring or limiting childbearing.[71] If the desire for acculturation is not an integral part of the social situation of the minority group, members of minority groups often become concerned with group preservation and quantitative strength. This appears to be true of such diverse groups as Black Muslims, Hasidim, and Hutterites. Resistance to assimilation tends to enforce the persistence of traditional patterns of family life conducive to high fertility despite technical and economic conditions that might otherwise lead to lower fertility.[72]

Third, within the context of acculturation, the social and economic characteristics of minority groups are critically important. The relationship between minority group status and fertility does not operate at all socioeconomic levels. On one hand, equalization of social and economic characteristics implies, at a minimum, similar access and knowledge regarding birth control methods and similar social and economic motivations and social pressures for their effective use. On the other hand, the dynamic aspect of minority group acculturation implies that real or perceived opportunity for social mobility may substitute for equivalent social characteristics. Thus, achievement values must be present for minority group members to translate the "goals" of social mobility for themselves and their children into "means" that include family size limitation. The desire to improve and achieve within an acculturation situation implies greater deferred gratification than in members of the majority group who do not suffer the disadvantages and ambiguities of minority status.

Finally, the "deviant" Catholic fertility pattern, i.e., higher rather than lower fertility in the acculturation process, suggests that specific norms regarding family size and birth control must be considered. Obviously, identification with a minority group characterized by large family size norms and doctrinal prohibitions against the use of efficient contraceptive methods may raise rather than lower fertility. The distinction between changes in the fertility of Irish and Italian Catholics reflects, in

[71] For the recognition of the possible role of minority group status in Negro fertility, see Lee and Lee, "The Future Fertility of the American Negro," p. 231; on Catholic fertility and minority group status, see Burch and Jacek, "Church Teaching and the Fertility of Catholic Americans"; and references cited in fn. 69; on Jewish fertility, see Lee and Lee, "The Future Fertility of the American Negro," p. 231; on United States," in *Jewish People, Past and Present*, vol. 2 (New York: Central Yiddish Culture Organization, 1949); Charles F. Westoff, "The Social-Psychological Structure of Fertility," *International Population Conference* (Vienna, 1959), pp. 361–362.

[72] See the discussion of the Amish in Pennsylvania and the Mormons in Utah by Frank Lorimer, *Culture and Human Fertility* (New York: UNESCO, 1954), p. 184.

part, the differential acculturation of the two groups in conjunction with their differential integration and identification with the church. Furthermore, although specific family size and contraception norms are significant, the broader sociocultural situation of Catholics must be considered, particularly when comparative, cross-national studies are examined. The most important generalization that emerges from a comparative examination of Catholic fertility is that "the fertility, ideal family size, and contraceptive practice of Catholics across the world depend on the milieu in which they live more than on doctrine as such. . . . Catholics in developed countries are closer to non-Catholics in the same countries than they are to Catholics in underdeveloped countries." [73]

As a general hypothesis we would argue that the insecurities of minority group membership operate to depress fertility below majority levels when (1) acculturation of minority group members has occurred in conjunction with the desire for acculturation; (2) equalization of social and economic characteristics occurs and/or social and economic mobility is desired; (3) no pro-natalist ideology is associated with the minority group and no norm discourages the use of efficient contraceptives.

Obviously, the nature of minority group identification assumes that intragroup social contact is fostered, particularly primary group relations.[74] Indeed, the quality of minority group cohesion and integration becomes a key axis of fertility heterogeneity *within* the minority group. In this sense differentials *within* subgroups must be interpreted. The degree of minority group integration and the accentuated marginal position between acculturation and structural separation will determine the behavior patterns of minority group members, all other things considered, vis-a-vis the majority community.

The analysis of religious and other minority group fertility patterns suggests that previous explanations have been incomplete. The alternative hypothesis — that minority group status exerts an independent effect on fertility — appears consistent with the evidence. Whether the disadvantages and insecurities of minority group identification are in fact related to the fertility behavior and attitudes of minority group members should be tested directly. Moreover, we need to focus on the social and

---

[73] Jones and Nortman, "Roman Catholic Fertility and Family Planning," p. 24.

[74] It is of major significance that religious and racial groups are highly endogamous and that the close relatives and friends of most minority group members share the same religious or ethnic identity. Although members of different minority groups interact in economic and other "impersonal" spheres of activity, they frequently do not interact in primary group relations in which the shaping of values and internalization of norms occur. The more isolated and self-contained the minority community, the greater the pressure toward conformity to group norms. See Lenski, *The Religious Factor,* pp. 36–40, 320–326; Gordon, *Assimilation in American Life* (New York: Oxford University Press, 1964); Goldstein and Goldscheider, *Jewish Americans.*

psychological mechanisms that may be operating and extend the investigation to incorporate other minority populations within and outside the United States. However, our review clearly shows that the "particularized theology" and "characteristics" propositions are unsound theoretically and empirically; they are thus limited as interpretations of the relationship between religion and fertility. Only when religious identification is viewed as involving subcommunities and subcultures and only when fertility is viewed as social behavior or social process can we expect beginning solutions to the sociological understanding of the relationship between religion and fertility.

Chapter Eleven

SOCIAL INTEGRATION
AND MIGRATION

It is a common observation that not everyone migrates; some persons migrate more often than others, over longer distances and in different directions; some societies are characterized by greater population movement than others; and the distance, volume, and direction of movement fluctuate at various points in the economic, political, and social history of societies. It is equally well established that those who move are significantly different sociologically from those who do not move. Hence, one of the few generalizations that may be made about migration processes, and a universal feature of population movements, is that *migration is selective*.

The fact that migrants are not a representative cross section of the population they leave or the population to which they move has obvious implications. Essentially it suggests that movement has patterned social, economic, and demographic determinants and consequences. If those who moved had the same characteristics as those who did not move, it would be difficult to discern, explain, or predict the volume, rate, and processes of movement; only minimum social, economic, or demographic changes would occur in the areas of origin or destination as a result of movement; migrants would not face major adjustment problems nor would communities have to adjust to migrants; migration could not be linked to broader social, demographic, and economic change processes. Indeed, the selective feature of migration in general makes migration analysis sociologically relevant.

Not only are economic and social opportunities differentially dispersed within and between societies, but the demands of these opportuni-

299

ties require the movement of selected types of persons; most important, subgroupings within society differentially perceive such opportunities and differentially respond to social and economic changes by moving. Because mobility under some conditions is an integral element of social change processes — whether that change process is family formation, expansion and dissolution, or urbanization-industrialization — social categories of persons who are more involved in those processes are more prone to move than others. As Bogue notes:

> Selective migration in some form should be regarded as a necessary phenomenon of all modern, highly specialized societies. Persons with unique qualifications, training, or work histories need to be located where their activities can be used. A certain amount of reshuffling of the population is required to locate the various specialized categories of population where they are of most value and where they can best participate in the social and economic system. . . . In modern industrialized societies most migration probably is selective in some respects; in such societies migration must be selective in order to be effective.[1]

Although it may be granted that selective migration is a feature of all "free" mobility, where at least some individual choice is operative and may be particularly accentuated in modern societies, the universal characterization of migratory selectivity appears to be challenged by some types of movement, particularly forced migration. Forms of migration, especially the forced relocation of total subcommunities and nomadism, labor migration, and seasonal migration, appear, at first glance, to be predicated on the notion of nonselectivity. However, a careful examination of such movements reveals that selectivity is involved but in a different sense. The selective nature of "forced" mobility rests not with the internal characteristics of the movers as in free migration but rather with the comparison of the relocated or migratory subcommunity to the broader society of which it is a part. Subcommunities are displaced on the basis of ethnicity, or religion, or social class and, hence, differ significantly in these characteristics from the total society. Moreover, insight into the ways in which constant mobility influences other social institutions and the sociological understanding of the nature of political, economic, and social structures that displace or relocate subcommunities may be obtained only by systematic comparative analysis. If all societies were nomadic or if subcommunities were randomly rather than systematically relocated, i.e., if there were no patterns of group selectivity, we

[1] Donald Bogue, "Internal Migration," in *The Study of Population,* ed. Philip Hauser and Otis D. Duncan (Chicago: University of Chicago Press, 1959), p. 497.

would not have a basis for sociological analysis. Hence, all types of migration are selective but vary in the nature of the selective process, ranging from internal, self-selection of free migrations to external, group selectivity of forced migrations. Selectivity with respect to nomadic wanderings is found in the comparisons to either the broader stable society of which it is a part or other non-nomadic subsocieties.[2]

Given that migratory selection or differential movement is a universal feature of mobility processes, the *pattern* of selectivity varies enormously. The relationship between specific sociodemographic characteristics and migration varies with the social, economic, political, demographic, and cultural contexts of societies. The relative importance among differentiators also varies with the social organizational context of movement and the type of migration examined. The *potential* differential characteristics of migrants compared to nonmigrants are limited only by those characteristics thought to have sociological or social and psychological relevance.[3]

The proposition that migration is selective or that differentials in migration exist is but a primitive conceptual starting point. In addition, we need to know how and why migration is selective, which subgroups within societies are more prone to move and why, how differences in migratory propensity inform us about the nature of subgroups within society, about differential processes of social and cultural change, and about the structure of society as a whole. Moreover, the study of differential migration is the cornerstone for developing and constructing theories of the determinants and consequences of migration patterns. If we want to understand why people move, we must recognize that most migrants do not move for the sake of moving. Migrants are influenced by a complex set of dissatisfactions and aspirations, situations and opportunities, reflected in their social and personal histories and characteristics.

Although we might not expect clear answers to all these issues, we should expect some cumulative empirical generalizations about such differentials in migration as education, occupation, income, race, ethnicity, marital status, sex, age, etc. This expectation has simply not been fulfilled. The voluminous literature on the characteristics of migrants and nonmigrants and on the differential propensity to move among subgroups of populations yields no cumulation of findings. Only one significant,

[2] Similarly, migratory regulation by legislation, political policies, or recruiting agencies are selective of migrants. See William Petersen, *Population*, 2d ed. (New York: Macmillan, 1969), p. 262.

[3] On the types of "relevant" characteristics, see the discussion in Chapter 8, this book.

albeit negative, conclusion can be reached: Few, if any, empirical generalizations about differential migration have been made with precision and accuracy.

GENERALIZATIONS ABOUT MIGRATION DIFFERENTIALS

Those who have read, evaluated, and reviewed the migration literature have all been, without exception, frustrated in their attempts to unravel systematic migration differentials. Dorothy Thomas's classic report on migration systematized and evaluated what was known about the field in 1938. The hundreds of studies that she reviewed in search of persistent and significant characteristics differentiating migrants from nonmigrants yielded only one definitely established generalization: young adults are more mobile than older persons.[4] But even this generalization could not be stated with precision.[5] Bogue's review twenty years later of migration differentials that "always held true" was "most disappointing." He concluded that "only one migration differential seems to have systematically withstood the test — that for age." He found the following generalization "to be valid in many places and for a long period of time: Persons in their late teens, twenties and early thirties are much more mobile than younger or older persons. . . . But even this is quite variable; in some streams of migration there is a much higher proportion of older people and children than in other streams."[6] Finally, Lee's attempt in the 1960's to synthesize the characteristics of migrants in the form of testable propositions resulted in a series of hypotheses that tell us little about *specific* migration differentials. His propositions include: (1) migration is selective; (2) migrants may be positively or negatively selected and in any migration stream selection is bimodal; (3) the characteristics of migrants tend to be intermediate between the characteristics of the population at areas of origin and areas of destination. Only one specific characteristic is noted that differentiates migrants from nonmigrants, that of life cycle. Lee suggests that migration in some instances is part of the *rites de passage*, particularly marriage formation and dissolution: "Since some of these events happen at quite well defined ages, they are important in shaping the curve of age selection."[7]

Why have consistent differentials in migration not been located?

---

[4] Dorothy S. Thomas, *Research Memorandum on Migration Differentials* (New York: Social Science Research Council, 1938).

[5] Cf. Dorothy S. Thomas, "Age and Economic Differentials in Interstate Migration," *Population Index*, 24 (October 1958), pp. 313–325.

[6] Bogue, "Internal Migration," p. 504.

[7] Everett Lee, "A Theory of Migration," *Demography*, 3:1 (1966), pp. 56–57.

Because generalization is one objective of scientific analysis, and a focus of this chapter, we must examine more closely an interrelated issue: Are generalizations about migratory selectivity and differential propensities to move possible? Indeed, can we expect some reviewer in the mid-1970's to conclude once again that little is known about migration differentials except that age is important?

Data Problems

The reason most often cited for the absence of empirical generalizations about migration differentials is the lack of accurate information and the limitations of available data.[8] More so than with other areas of demographic inquiry, the census represents the primary and often the only source of information on migration. Although vital events, births and deaths, are registered continuously, few countries (Scandinavian countries, the Netherlands, Italy, and Israel are the major exceptions) register changes in residence. Given the lack of sample survey studies of migration comparable to those in fertility, migration research relies heavily on available census data, which are almost always severely limiting for accurate analysis of migratory selectivity. Two general types of census data on migration are available, direct and indirect. For example, since 1940, the United States decennial censuses have included a direct question on mobility, generally a five-year question except for 1950 when a one-year question was asked. The Current Population Survey in the United States has annually included (since 1948) a one-year question on mobility. State of birth data are available for a longer period of time but have severe limitations for differential migration research.[9] Indirect data on migration are based on isolating and excluding population changes due to fertility and mortality and attributing the residual population change to migration. Indirect migration estimates, if accurate, may be useful for differential analysis only at crude aggregate levels, where migratory streams may be interrelated with broad social and economic aggregate characteristics. Often, this will involve ecological correlations with net migration rather than a direct focus on the differential characteristics of migrants and nonmigrants.[10]

[8] Thomas, *Research Memorandum on Migration Differentials.*

[9] See Everett Lee et al., *Population Redistribution and Economic Growth, United States, 1870–1950,* vol. 1 (Philadelphia: The American Philosophical Society, 1957); Everett Lee, "Migration Differentials by State of Birth in the United States," *Proceedings of the International Population Conference: 1961,* Session 4, I (London, 1963).

[10] On the general problems of migration data in the census, see Henry Shryock, *Population Mobility Within the United States* (Chicago: Community and Family Study Center, University of Chicago Press, 1964); Everett and Ann Lee, "Internal

Because for most analytic purposes we are restricted to using direct migration data from the census, we must remember that the characteristics of migrants are obtained not before or at the time of migration, but usually *after* migration has occurred; at times, it is impossible to discern the exact time relationship between migration and the characteristic under investigation or to reconstruct whether a sequence or relationship exists. For example, suppose we want to examine the income level of migrants and nonmigrants and income changes that migration may engender (or reflect). This relationship is critical to the general notion that migrants move in response to economic opportunity in areas of destination and/or lack of economic opportunities in areas of origin. At the very least, information would be needed on the average income of migrants and nonmigrants at the area of origin *before* migration takes place and the average income of migrants at area of destination *after* the move occurred. Moreover, to examine comparative changes, i.e., what income changes resulted from migration (what would have been the income level of migrants if they had not moved), we need to include the income levels of the persons in the area of origin after (and before) the migrants left and the income level of the population at the area of destination before (and after) the in-migrants arrived. Schematically, information is needed to fill all six cells in Table 11.1.

Table 11.1. Average Income

	Time 1 (before migration)	Time 2 (after migration)
Population at area of origin	A_1	A_2
Migrants from area of origin to area of destination	B_1	B_2
Population at area of destination	C_1	C_2

To be sure, additional information and controls would have to be incorporated.[11] But at the very minimum we need to compare changes in income levels of migrants before they moved (time 1) with conditions after they moved (time 2) using the populations at origin and destina-

---

Migration Statistics for the United States," *Journal of the American Statistical Association*, 55 (December 1960), pp. 664–697; United Nations, *Measures of Internal Migration*, Manuals on Methods of Demographic Analysis, Manual VI (New York, 1970); Karl Taeuber et al., *Migration in the United States: An Analysis of Residence Histories*, Public Health Monograph no. 77 (Washington, D.C.: U.S. Government Printing Office, 1968).
[11] See the discussion of the migration system, Chapter 3, this book.

tion as the comparative populations over time. But even for this simple scheme decennial census data are totally inadequate. For example, the 1960 census obtained information on mobility by ascertaining where people lived as of April 1, 1955; income data referred to total 1959 income. Thus, for people moving during the 1955–1958 period, the income data refer to income *after* the move took place; for people moving during 1959, income data pertain to income more or less *at the time* of moving (or at least the year of moving); for people moving during 1960, income related to conditions *before* the move occurred. However, there is simply no way to differentiate these three categories of persons, or to simulate the comparative income changes of populations at origin or destination before and after mobility, as suggested by the scheme. The decennial census data are thus not fully adequate for the systematic analysis of the relationship between income and mobility.

A critical examination of Current Population Survey data, which provide information on one-year mobility and income during the year preceding the survey, reveals serious interpretation problems as well. The mobility question included asks where people lived as of the exact year (and month) preceding the survey. Change of residence between March 1963 and March 1964, for example, was identified in the March 1964 survey as a move. Income data, however, refer to the amount of income received from January to December 1963. Again, the two items of information do not relate to the same period. Income data refer to times before, during, and after mobility for various groups of movers. Whether we assume that the income information relates to conditions before or after mobility, we cannot with either assumption fill in the cells of the before-after model. Consequently, the relationship uncovered by the Current Population Survey data that intercounty and intracounty mobility rates are higher among those with lower incomes for almost all age groups [12] does not necessarily imply that people move to change their low-income status. The Current Population Survey makes the implicit assumption that the income data relate to premobility conditions. For many, perhaps the majority, the income information, however, refers to postmigration situations and, hence, if migration occurred to raise income levels, we must judge it as relatively unsuccessful. In any case, despite the theoretical importance of examining the relationship between income and mobility and notwithstanding the attractiveness of published records as sources of research data, the interaction of income and mobility cannot be discerned fully or untangled completely using decennial censuses or Current Population Survey data.

[12] U.S. Bureau of the Census, *Current Population Reports*, ser. P-20, no. 141 (September 7, 1965).

The very real problem of interpreting migration differentials under the handicap of inadequate statistics may be further illustrated with a concrete example. Many would serve; we will use Ann Miller's study of "Migration Differentials in Labor Force Participation in the United States." [13] She states:

> It has been widely assumed that a close positive relationship exists between migration status and labor force status, that is, that, by and large, people move for economic reasons and that, as a corollary, the people who move are more likely to be in the labor force than those who do not.

The data used to examine this question compare the labor force status in 1960 of interstate migrants (persons who lived in a different state in the United States in 1955 compared to 1960) with the labor status of the total American population in 1960 (labor force includes all persons who were either employed or looking for work during the census week).

Such an approach has many associated problems, among which are the limitation of confining migrants to interstate movers rather than total movers; the underestimation of interstate migrants in 1955 to 1960 due to return movement, multiple moves, movers who died or were living abroad by 1960; and no separation of migration streams (area of origins and destinations). Most serious, the study might have separated employed, unemployed, and those not in the labor force. Annual mobility data strongly indicate the higher mobility rate of the unemployed compared to the employed throughout the age distribution. This finding is indeed consistent with the economic doctrine that the equilibrium between jobs and workers tends to be maintained by the movement of workers in response to the demands of their services.[14] A special study sponsored by the Bureau of Labor Statistics shows that among workers who had reported themselves unemployed in March 1962, the percentage unemployed in March 1963 was lower among those who had not changed their county of residence.[15] However, even within the framework of Miller's study and recognizing the limitations of available data, we are unable to examine the relationship between labor force participation and migration. Census data are not designed in a way that we might know

---

[13] Ann Miller, "Migration Differentials in Labor Force Participation in the United States, 1960," *Demography*, 3:1 (1966), pp. 58–67. For a critical analysis of the problems using retrospective census data on migration and "employment," see George Masnick, "Employment Status and Retrospective and Prospective Migration in the United States," *Demography*, 5:1 (1968), pp. 79–85.

[14] See, for example, *Current Population Reports*, ser. P-20, no. 141 (1965).

[15] Samuel Saben, "Geographic Mobility and Employment Status, March 1962–March 1963," *Monthly Labor Review* (August 1964), pp. 873–892; cf. Masnick, "Employment Status and Retrospective and Prospective Migration in the United States."

the labor force conditions *at the time of migration,* and migration may have taken place any time between 1955 and 1960. Hence, we cannot establish the sequence of labor force and mobility changes.

The data Miller presents show that, controlling for age, labor force participation rates for interstate migrants (e.g., white males) are either identical with or below those for the total 1960 civilian population. For example, as of 1960, 94 per cent of the white, male, civilian, and interstate migrant populations aged 25 to 29 were in the labor force. It must be assumed that if data were available comparing these populations at the time of or before migration, the labor force pattern would be similar. But, indeed, this assumption is what is purportedly tested! The labor force participation of migrants may have gone up or down as a result of migration while the labor force participation of the total population may not have changed; the labor force participation of the total population may have increased or decreased while the labor force participation of interstate migrants may have remained the same; or the labor force participation of both migrants and nonmigrants may have changed in similar or opposite directions. These different conditions imply different associations of labor force status and mobility and therefore require different interpretations. Because the data available from census sources are unable to inform us about labor force status at the time of movement, we cannot begin to discern the relationship between labor force participation and migration; certainly no precise inference can be made about the analytic question of whether migration is a response to economic opportunity. Hence, Miller's conclusions [16] that "there is no evidence that interstate migrants are more likely to be in the labor force than the general population" when age differences are controlled, and that, among whites, "interstate migrants are somewhat less likely to be in the labor force," must remain hypotheses to be tested.

This brief, critical evaluation of Miller's study is not intended to dismiss her conclusions or to single out her research as less than definitive. Rather, our objective has been to illustrate that one obvious and powerful reason why empirically verified generalizations in the study of migration differentials are so lacking rests, in large part, with the limited data sources that have been so often utilized. The reliance on severely limited data forces research not only to be tentative rather than definitive, but impedes the cumulation of verified empirical generalizations about migration differentials. The same limitations would apply to all other characteristics that may change with residential mobility (e.g., social and economic status, marital and family status) when the

[16] Miller, "Migration Differentials in Labor Force Participation in the United States, 1960," p. 67.

characteristic measured is obtained only at areas of destination after migration occurred. These restrictions are by no means limited to United States data sources but pertain to every country that relies on census-type sources to relate retrospective mobility and current sociodemographic characteristics.

Are Generalizations Possible?

If the absence of generalizations in migration differentials stems solely from inadequate and incomplete information, we can remedy the situation by improving census or Current Population Survey data, or by conducting special sample surveys. Some have argued, however, that except for limited relationships, as between age or life cycle and migration, *further systematic differentials in migration do not exist empirically and should not be expected to exist.* In general, the argument states that migration is too complex a process, involving a wide range of types, distances, directions, reflecting an infinite number and combination of social, economic, and demographic conditions at areas of origin and destination, and a host of "personal factors," to allow for generalizations about migration selectivity. Thus, Petersen, in an effort to establish testable propositions, relates migration selectivity to various types of migration but concludes, "we know enough now to assert that migratory selection does vary considerably, and that a search for universal generalizations would be fruitless." [17] Bogue argues forcefully:

> A little reflection convinces one that the search for universal migration differentials not only is doomed to failure but also fails to appreciate the reasons for migration selectivity. . . . Migrants must be expected to reflect, in their characteristics, the social and economic changes that are taking place. Because these changes vary from place to place and from time to time, it is to be expected that the characteristics of migrants cannot remain fixed.[18]

It seems, however, that the quest for generalization is not necessarily limited to a search for immutable, "universal" laws about specific relationships between selected sociodemographic characteristics and mobility or about differential propensities among subgroups within society that are constant for all historical and comparative conditions.[19] Rather,

[17] Petersen, *Population*, p. 301.
[18] Bogue, "Internal Migration," p. 504.
[19] This error of searching for universal laws or, in more subdued terminology, general propositions, without considering the social, economic, demographic, political, and cultural contexts or without subdividing migration into types has characterized one tradition in migration research starting from Ravenstein. See Lee, "A Theory of Migration," pp. 47–57 for a discussion of Ravenstein and for Lee's attempts at proposition formation "in vacuum." Cf. Chapter 3, this book.

our objective in generalizing is to establish the dynamics of how socio-demographic characteristics are related to migration *under specific conditions*. Both arguments, which attempt to account for the absence of cumulative research in migration differentials, inadequate data, or the absence of generalizable "laws," are only partially correct. To be sure, sound, adequate, and comprehensive information is a *necessary* prerequisite for generalizing about empirical regularities in migration differentials, although by no means is it a *sufficient* condition. Furthermore, the differential characteristics of migrants and nonmigrants should be expected to vary widely depending on the type of social, economic, and demographic changes that the migration reflects, within historical and comparative contexts. Yet, these social, economic, and demographic changes are, within limits, generalizable, and no a priori justification is apparent for excluding the possibility that migratory selection follows a generalizable pattern under given restricted conditions. Migration patterns and, in turn, selective migration cannot be more complex than the broader processes of which they are a part. Because these more general social, economic, and demographic processes are generalizable, it is unreasonable to postulate that one component of them is not generalizable.

In sum, a more basic reason why the study of differential migration has not been cumulative may be the absence of theory that would provide a guide or framework for analysis and help make sense of what might otherwise remain "inscrutable" or "unmeaning" empirical findings.[20] As a first step, we must look beyond the specific differentials in migration to determine their implications and meanings. For example, what is it about age, or marital status, or sex, or socioeconomic status that relates to mobility propensity? We have to establish the meaning of these relationships within the context of social and economic changes rather than examine differentials in migration mechanically. It is as much faulty or inadequate conceptualization, the absence of theory and research directed to solving *probing*, analytic questions, as it is the lack of appropriate information or the nonexistence of general migration differentials that may be responsible for the critical absence of cumulative findings. We should not propose, or expect to develop, "laws" of selective migration in vacuum any more than we should enunciate "laws" of social, economic, political, or demographic processes. Nevertheless, we ought to be able to uncover systematic processes of migratory selection that are generalizable under given conditions.

Age is the only differential in migration consistently reported in

---

[20] On this function of theory, see Abraham Kaplan, *The Conduct of Inquiry: Methodology for Behavioral Science* (San Francisco: Chandler, 1964), p. 302. Cf. Chapter 2, this book.

the literature. We plan to illustrate how the underlying conceptualizations of the relationship between age and migration inform us about selected other differentials and indeed reveal a great deal about migration in general. Moreover, the analysis will tie together two general "theories" of migration, life cycle and economic opportunities, within a coherent sociological framework. Again, as in the two previous chapters, the objective is to illustrate the analysis of one differential among many so that we can more clearly comprehend the logic and form of the sociological analysis of demographic processes. Because the discussion relies on cumulative census findings, both decennial and Current Population Surveys, supplemented somewhat by survey data, we must bear in mind the inadequacy of these data sources, and the tentativeness of the analysis. The evidence focuses on the United States; whether broader generalization to other countries is possible must await systematic comparative research.

AGE AND MOBILITY:
THE OVERALL EVIDENCE

The proposition that younger persons are more mobile than older persons intentionally leaves open and vague three important specifics: (1) the level of mobility, (2) the specific ages of highest mobility, and (3) the relative magnitude of difference between older and younger mobility rates. These specifics should be expected to vary depending on the political, economic, and social organization of societies, and the specific type of migration examined. For example, in societies where age at marriage is late, say around age thirty, the peak age of mobility may be later than in societies where the average age at marriage is less than eighteen years. Even where age at marriage is early, mobility may peak at later ages if housing is not readily available for independent young married couples or if norms exist for joint or extended family structures in the early marriage stages. Similarly, if the pace of economic development is rapid or the level is advanced, residential mobility may peak at different ages than if economic changes were slow and minimal. The stage and level of industrialization may determine the specific ages at which migration is highest and the absolute level of mobility. The relative mobility rate differentiation between older and younger persons may be associated with housing markets, levels of industrialization, the tempo of social mobility, family structure, and mortality and health levels, among others. The type of movement also will influence these specifics of age differentiation. For example, refugee movements will have different age patterns than rural-to-urban movements, urban-to-urban migration, and frontier movements. Similarly, the relative magnitude of difference between younger and older movement will vary with the ease with which older persons can change their residences, their financial situations, and the availability of housing designed for their needs.

The generally higher mobility rates of younger persons to a considerable extent reflect two general life-cycle, age-related processes: (1) marriage and family formation, and (2) career and job mobility. To be sure, available housing, the tempo and level of the economy, the character of the polity, the level of technology, the structure of family interaction and norms, the knowledge and perception of "opportunities," and other cultural factors *facilitate* or *impede* the degree to which family formation and career mobility involve residential changes. Indeed, these and other facilitating factors shape the general level of mobility, not only the specific differential migration pattern. Yet, given a variety of political, social, economic, cultural, and demographic contexts, age remains a critical differentiator of migration. Thus, if migration and social, economic, and political processes are intertwined, why is the younger population more mobile than the older population? Young adults are in that stage of the life cycle that involves leaving their parental home, establishing a family of their own in independent household units, starting a career, entering the labor force, having children, moving within or between jobs, and so on. The different ways in which age is related to family formation and career and social mobility determine the specifics of the relationship of age and mobility. Similarly, the stabilization of the family and the career cycle where a stake in a particular job or home occurs and, in turn, the entrenchment in one's community militate against greater mobility at later ages.

Isolating these family and economic factors raises another question: Which inherent qualities of these structural relationships have a bearing on residential mobility? More generally we need to focus on the sociological meaning of age as it may relate to mobility propensity.

THE SOCIOLOGICAL MEANING OF AGE

In examining the relationship between age and mobility, we must recognize that the social and cultural significance of age groups is of prime importance. In contrast to fertility and mortality, where age factors are infused with biological relevance and importance, often setting up limiting parameters to vital processes, mobility differentials by age are not generally biologically conditioned. The significance of age categories from a sociological perspective revolves around role differentiation and structural integration.

Eisenstadt has noted that age differences are among the "most basic and crucial aspects of human life and determinants of human destiny." [21] At different age stages, different tasks are performed and different roles in relation to other members of society are defined. All societies have to cope with the problems ensuing from the gradual progression and unfolding of power and capacities associated with age changes. The transition from infancy to old age is thus subject to social and cultural definitions.

> We know of no society which does not differentiate between various ages and does not define them through the norms and values of its cultural tradition. . . . A cultural definition of an age grade or age span is always a broad definition of human potentialities and obligations at a given stage of life. It is not a prescription or expectation of a detailed role, but of general, basic role dispositions into which more specific roles may be built and to which they may be ascribed.[22]

Thus, when we examine the migration patterns of age groups we refer to the *differential dispositions* to move associated with different complex role types. Membership in an age group involves some role expectations regarding mobility, particularly as these age-related roles are intertwined with structural features of society — particularly kinship-family and economic-occupational systems. Indeed, although these subsystems function in structurally separate and differentiated ways within modern industrialized societies, age factors represent important integrating elements for the social system. As Parsons notes, age categories "constitute one of the main links of structural continuity in terms of which structures which are differentiated in other respects are articulated with each other." [23] Age categories are thus "connecting links" and "organizing points of reference" for the major structures of society.

We may therefore understand mobility differences of age groups in terms of (1) the special role dispositions associated with age changes, (2) the articulation of these roles within family-kinship structures, and (3) the articulation of these roles within occupational and economic systems. Age factors differentially integrate individuals to the family and occupational system and, in turn, function differentially as a cohesive element integrating individuals to the community. Thus, the meaning of age to migration, and in turn the meaning of family formation and career mobility, is the degree to which individuals are integrated within their communities via family and economic ties.

This conceptualization is consistent with the two general related

---

[21] S. N. Eisenstadt, *From Generation to Generation: Age Groups and Social Structure* (New York: The Free Press, 1956), p. 21.

[22] Ibid., p. 22.

[23] Talcott Parsons, "Age and Sex in the Social Structure of the United States," *American Sociological Review*, 7 (October 1942), p. 604, fn. 1.

approaches to the study of differential migration: (1) family and life cycle, and (2) career patterns and economic opportunity.[24] In the first approach, mobility patterns are integral to changes in the life cycles of individuals. Marriage formation, family expansion, family reduction, and marriage dissolution involve the movement of people. The second approach emphasizes the close relationship between social and geographic mobility. Social mobility, which includes upward, downward, or horizontal changes in social class (defined in many ways), intergenerational and intrageneration (career) mobility, often involves residence changes. The more general notion that migration is one response to economic opportunities at both macro- and microlevels of analysis also fits in with this general approach. Because both life-cycle and social mobility are age-related, we would expect the relationship between these factors and migration to vary by the specific social and economic conditions imposed by the complexities of roles associated with age. In addition, responses to economic opportunity in terms of geographic mobility will depend on the degree to which individuals are integrated within the community via family and occupation structures. Thus, conceptualizing family and career formation as determinants of mobility is significant in that these processes reflect the broader processes of community and social integration.

The higher mobility of the young is thus of social, demographic, and economic significance. The young are the most productive from both an economic and demographic point of view. They are at the beginning of productive occupational careers and the threshold of family life and parenthood. The break between the family of socialization and the family of procreation along with the so-called generation gap are of critical significance in maintaining social and cultural continuity.[25]

MOBILITY OF OLDER PERSONS

The two general arguments used to explain residential mobility in general and mobility differentials by age in particular appear to be limited when we consider the *mobility* of older persons. The life-cycle and economic-career opportunities hypotheses have often been cited as the basic causes of mobility, and indeed are often "proven" by looking at the lower mobility of older persons. Older persons are the least mobile

[24] Cf. Gerald Leslie and Arthur Richardson, "Life Cycle, Career Pattern and the Decision to Move," *American Sociological Review*, 26 (December 1961), pp. 894–902.
[25] Cf. Ronald Freedman, "Cityward Migration, Urban Ecology and Social Theory," in *Contributions to Urban Sociology*, ed. Ernest Burgess and Donald Bogue (Chicago: University of Chicago Press, 1964), p. 181.

sector of the age span precisely because they are in a stable life-cycle family position and either at the end of their occupational careers or out of the labor force. That these hypotheses are not the total explanation can be seen when we note that not all older persons are residentially stable — nor, for that matter are all younger persons mobile, or do all young adults respond equally to economic opportunity. Even among those who move as a response to economic changes or life-cycle factors the question remains, How do these processes relate to migration? We contend that life-cycle or economic job changes as such do not determine migration, but have implications for the development of community, neighborhood, and family ties. Hence, our hypothesis is that social integration and residential mobility are inversely related, and that this relationship should account not only for the greater stability of older persons and the greater mobility of young adults but also for mobility differentials within age groups. By examining of mobility within the older population, we essentially control for life-cycle and economic participation rates. Although our focus is on mobility differentials among older persons, some insight into differential stability of younger persons may be obtained.

Why Study Mobility Among Older People?

The evidence that young adults predominate among movers and the general characterization of stability among the older population often obscure and overlook equally consistent evidence showing significant movement among the older population. In the United States, approximately 10 per cent of the population fifty years of age and older annually change their place of residence; about 30 per cent move at least once over a five-year period. This level of annual mobility has remained fairly constant for over two decades (since 1948) when Current Population Survey data included a one-year retrospective mobility question. In the 1960's this mobility rate translates into a volume of well over 4 million persons over age fifty who change their place of residence *every year*.[26]

The mobility of older persons has not received much attention mainly because of their general pattern of relatively greater stability. Nevertheless, it may be instructive theoretically to examine carefully mobility patterns of the older population as a "deviant" case. First, as noted, these mobility patterns cannot be attributed fully to either life-cycle or economic reasons. Secondly, the mobility of older persons may

[26] See Calvin Goldscheider, "Differential Residential Mobility of the Older Population," *Journal of Gerontology*, 21 (January 1966), pp. 102–108.

shed light on why most older people do not move, just as the general stability of older persons informs us about why younger people move. Finally, studying residential mobility of the older population is significant in and of itself because within this social grouping we can examine many elements of differential migration, including the selective characteristics of movers and nonmovers.

Moreover, some have viewed the mobility patterns among older persons as one increasingly problematic aspect of this group and in turn for society as a whole. Although residential mobility among older people has remained *proportionally* constant since World War II, numerically the *volume* of movement has increased and may be expected to increase steadily. Because the absolute number, rather than the proportion, of the older population is increasing, if the rate remains the same, the number of older people who move can be expected to increase. Furthermore, there are reasons to anticipate an increase in the *rate* of mobility among the older population. Some evidence suggests that almost a third of the older population desire to move every year but of these only one out of four successfully carry out their plans or desires. Although younger persons are much more likely to move and plan or desire to move in a given time period, *younger people are more than twice as likely to carry out their mobility plans and desires than older people.* Thus, the difference between the actual mobility of older and younger populations is substantially greater than differences in mobility plans and desires.[27]

If certain "obstacles" or "impediments" — usually housing and money — that prevent more older people from realizing their residential mobility plans and desires are removed or made less restrictive, we may expect that a larger proportion of the older population will move. A large proportion of older persons express dissatisfaction with their present housing and neighborhoods. Perceptually as well as objectively "appropriate" housing that fits the financial, emotional, and social needs of older people is lacking.[28] This "obstacle" has been changing slowly with the development of federally and locally sponsored housing for older persons and with the construction of retirement villages, condominiums, and hotel-apartments for the aged. The second obstacle, not unrelated, is financial. The older population represents one of the largest groups among the American poor. Almost one-third of all families with annual

[27] See ibid.; cf. Calvin Goldscheider et al., "Residential Mobility of Older People," in *Patterns of Living and Housing of Middle-Aged and Older People*, U.S. Department of Health, Education and Welfare, Public Health Publication no. 1496 (Washington, D.C.: U.S. Government Printing Office, 1966), pp. 65–82.
[28] Cf. Goldscheider et al., "Residential Mobility of Older People."

income less than $3,000 in 1959 had heads of households over age sixty-five.[29] Improvements in the economic situation of older persons may lead to the greater fulfillment of their plans and desires for residential mobility. It is therefore likely that not only will more older people move in the future, but that the mobility rate among the older population may increase if housing and economic impediments are removed.

The significance of residential mobility of the older population can also be illustrated at the macrolevel of analysis. The general overall pattern of stability among older persons had led to the hypothesis that increasing age segregation of American metropolitan centers is a function of the mobility of the young to the suburbs and the stability of older persons in the central city or, more commonly, to reverse moves of older persons to the central city area. However, age concentrations in metropolitan subareas in longitudinal perspective suggest that persons of all ages appear to be moving into newer sections of metropolitan areas, but the younger population is moving at a relatively more rapid rate. The increasing differences in settlement patterns within metropolitan structures between older and younger populations do not appear to be solely a function of older population stability and younger population mobility or to the movement of older persons to long-settled central core areas. Rather, age concentrations are related to the more rapid intrametropolitan mobility of the younger population and the *relatively greater stability of the older population.*[30]

Thus, as metropolitan areas increase in population, via natural increase or in-migration, and reach a stage of urban maturation, expansion outward occurs. Although participation in this expansion process characterizes the entire metropolitan population, regardless of age, relatively greater participation typifies some subgroupings. Segments of the population that are in the expansive life-cycle stage and that are socially mobile, particularly with respect to career mobility, will be more migratory prone and will participate more readily in metropolitan expansion. The older population, representing the more stable stage of the life cycle, having completed their career mobility, coupled with the lack of appropriate housing in suburban areas and, perhaps, the lack of funds to move, are less prone to move to these newer settlement areas. Moreover, the relatively greater stability of older persons may, in addition, reflect an adjustment to their housing needs and neighborhood ties, transportation facilities, and more conveniently located medical-health services available in urban areas.

[29] Herman Miller, *Rich Man—Poor Man* (New York: Signet, 1965), pp. 78–88.
[30] For one illustration, see Calvin Goldscheider, "Intrametropolitan Redistribution of the Older Population," *Pacific Sociological Review,* 9 (Fall 1966), pp. 79–84.

Complementing these aspects of internal metropolitan expansion are the effects of intermetropolitan mobility. The greater movement of younger persons between metropolitan areas accentuates the age concentration patterns because they will more likely settle in the newer areas. These newer areas are attractive to the younger in-migrants not only because of the greater availability of services and facilities congruent with personal and family needs but also because these areas are "new," i.e., they have not developed the informal, localized neighborhood ties and character typical of urban core areas. (Of course, this sketch assumes a free market as well as free mobility and would not typify all subpopulations, particularly ethnic or racial minorities.)

Mobility Differentials
Among the Older Population

Any description of the subgroups within the older population that are more prone to move must remain tentative because of the cross-sectional, retrospective character of census materials discussed previously and because so few longitudinal survey studies have been undertaken. Nevertheless, a fairly consistent portrait of movers and nonmovers among the older population in the United States emerges from the information now available. The basic finding, using various indicators and several data sources, is that social, family, and economic stability within the older population is highly correlated with residential stability. This finding at first glance is not very startling; its significance rests with three additional consistent relationships: (1) the converse is typical of younger segments of the population — social mobility, including family formation and growth, and residential mobility are highly correlated; (2) the relationship between major sociodemographic characteristics and mobility operates in distinctly opposite directions for older compared to younger population groupings — particularly marital status and socioeconomic status; (3) the general notion that greater residential stability among the older population reflects the overall social and economic stability characteristic of this life-cycle stage.

An elaboration of the general relationship of social and residential stability among the older population, or a test of this hypothesis, requires that we carefully inspect stability indicators among older people and relate these indicators to mobility propensity. Using census, Current Population Survey, and sample survey materials, three major categories of indicators will be examined: (1) family status and household composition, which ties in with family stability and cohesion; (2) economic and social status indicators associated with economic and social ties and stability; and (3) indicators of community ties, specifically the role of previous residential mobility with current (or projected) movement.[31]

Family and Household Ties

In 1960, among males, 65 years of age and older, married with spouse present, 24 per cent changed their residence at least once over a five-year period. This mobility rate represented the *lowest* rate of residential changes of all marital status categories within the older population. In direct contrast, among males from 20 to 24 years of age, married with spouse present, 93 per cent moved within a five-year period, the *highest* mobility rate of this age segment among all marital status categories. Comparatively, almost four times as many younger males who were married moved when contrasted to older males in the same marital status category; among single males, younger persons moved only about 1½ times the rate of older persons. Within any of the marital status categories except married, spouse present — i.e., among single, separated (married spouse absent), widowed, or divorced — younger persons are less than twice as likely to move compared to older persons in a five-year period. Hence, the mobility discrepancy between younger and older populations is twice as great among those married, spouse present, than among any other marital status category. The lowest discrepancy between younger and older persons is among the divorced: 48 per cent of the divorced population 65 years of age and older moved in a five-year period compared to 72 per cent of the divorced population 20 to 24 years of age.

Current Population Survey data on one-year mobility dramatically confirm this general relationship of marital and residential stability among the aged. Single males, 18 to 24 years of age, moved about 1½ times the rate of single males age 65 and over, but the annual mobility rate of married, spouse present, younger males was almost *ten* times the mobility rate of married, spouse present, older males. Moreover, single

---

[31] The data analysis here uses census materials based on U.S. Bureau of the Census, *United States Census of Population: 1960, Subject Reports, Mobility for States and State Economic Areas,* Final Report, PC(2)-2B (Washington, D.C., 1963), table 7, pp. 16–18; Current Population Survey data were taken from U.S. Bureau of the Census, *Current Population Reports,* ser. P-20, no. 141 (September 7, 1965), and refer to mobility during March 1963 to March 1964; the survey data refer to a longitudinal mobility survey carried out in the Los Angeles metropolitan area under the direction of Georges Sabagh and Maurice D. Van Arsdol, Jr., as reported in Goldscheider, "Differential Residential Mobility of the Older Population," pp. 103–108; Goldscheider et al., "Residential Mobility of Older People," pp. 65–82. For the general design of the larger survey study, see Maurice D. Van Arsdol, Jr., et al., "Retrospective and Subsequent Metropolitan Residential Mobility," *Demography,* 5:1 (1968), pp. 249–267.

older persons are more than twice as likely to change their residence in a one-year period compared to married older persons, whereas the reverse pattern characterizes the young — married young males are three times as mobile as single young males. Again, the married among the elderly are the least mobile of all marital status categories — less than half as mobile as the nonmarried.

Viewed in another way, Current Population Survey data reveal that of all young males who did not move in a one-year period, 81 per cent were single, 17 per cent were married; of all nonmovers among the older male population, 6 per cent were single, 71 per cent were married, and 23 per cent were divorced, widowed, or separated. Furthermore, the Current Population Survey examines the contribution of "being married" to mobility rates by calculating the expected mobility of the population if the age-sex mobility rates of single persons were applied. The CPS estimates that among the young (18 to 24 years of age) the high mobility associated with early married life contributes over two-thirds to the rate of local mobility. Thus, in the age range in which most marriages occur, marriage and family formation contributes heavily to mobility; in the age range in which most marriages may be assumed to have persisted over a considerable number of years, the married state restricts mobility. Thus, the report concludes that getting married and making the necessary adjustments of the early years of marriage appreciably contribute to the mobility of young adults; the dissolution of marriages also makes an additional contribution. The annual mobility data suggest that marital status changes including formation and dissolution account for 15 to 20 per cent of the total recorded mobility.

Among the older population, the married sector is not only the most stable residentially over five- and one-year periods, but limited survey data suggest that married older persons plan and desire to move less than single, widowed, divorced, or separated older persons. Consequently, it is not solely the inability, for financial or other reasons, of married older persons to move; rather, residential stability is part of the more general life style and norms of married older persons.

Complementing the evidence on the greater stability of married persons, and an interrelated aspect of family ties and cohesion, are survey data on the relationship between the number of persons in households and mobility propensity among older persons. For both one- and two-year residential mobility, survey data reveal that the number of persons in the household is inversely related to residential mobility propensity among the older population. Members of one-person households (composed of the nonmarried) are more than twice as likely to move as are members of households with three or more persons and twice as likely to successfully carry out their plans and desires for mobility. For example, 32 per cent of older persons living alone changed their place of residence in a two-year period, compared to 20 per cent of persons living with one other individual and 14 per cent of older people in households with three or more persons. Of those in one-person households who planned or desired to move in a one-year period, 31 per cent moved; in contrast, among those living in three- or more person households who planned or desired to move, only 16 per cent moved.

Socioeconomic Status and Integration

Another category of indicators relates to the position of persons in the social and economic structure. For older people, higher levels of education and income, and to a lesser extent occupation, not only have implications for housing and life styles but may be viewed as indicators of social and community ties. The evidence suggests a general tendency toward an inverse relationship between socioeconomic status and residential mobility among older persons. Census and Current Population Survey data suggest, in general, that among those 25 and older higher educated people are more mobility prone (20 per cent of the college educated move in a one-year period compared to 14 per cent of the elementary school educated). At the middle ages the relationship between education and mobility tends to be U-shaped — both the higher and lower educated groups are more mobile. For those 65 years of age and older only minor differences in mobility by education exist but the least educated have a strong tendency to move more.

Occupation data are difficult to interpret, particularly for the older population. Nevertheless, Current Population Survey reveals that professionals and managers among the young are much more likely to move than lower occupational groupings, but among the older population, over twice as many in service occupations move than those in white-collar occupations. Income data are much clearer. Among the population 18 to 24 years of age the higher the income the higher the mobility; among the older population the reverse relationship may be found — four times as many older persons with low incomes move when compared to those with higher incomes.

The tendency toward an inverse relationship between socioeconomic status and residential mobility among the older population, gleaned from official sources, gains support from survey data. Older persons with less education, lower incomes, and who had lower status blue-collar occupations had significantly higher one- or two-year mobility rates. Again, this does not solely reflect "forced" movement, as these groups plan and desire to move much more than better educated, higher income, and white-collar occupation segments. For example, 18 per cent of the older population with an eighth-grade education or less moved in a one-year period compared to 10 per cent of those with college educations; 33 per cent of those with a sixth-grade education or less moved in a two-year period compared to 16 per cent of the college group. Over a fourth of the lower status groups planned to move and almost a third desired to move compared to about 18 per cent (plan) and 29 per cent (desire) of the higher status groups.

A significant part of the inverse relationship of socioeconomic status and residential mobility among the older population may reflect the stability associated with home ownership among the higher status groupings and, in turn, the relationship between home ownership and residential stability. Renters are about three times as mobile as home owners among middle-aged and older persons. Significantly, about 40 per cent of the renters plan or desire to move compared to 15 per cent (plan) and 26 per cent (desire) among home owners. Perhaps because of their greater experience in moving, renters are well over twice as likely to carry out their plans and desires to move.

One might expect that older nonwhites, because of their greater concentration in the lower social classes, would have higher mobility rates than whites. Limited survey data suggest, however, that older whites are twice as mobile as nonwhites. Yet, a larger proportion of older nonwhites compared to whites want to move (42 per cent versus 30 per cent). Hence, more older nonwhites want to move than whites, although older whites are more mobile; over three times as many older whites compared to nonwhites realize their mobility plans and desires. This finding suggests that despite the poor housing and neighborhood conditions of older nonwhites, mobility discrepancies reflect differential opportunity favoring the white older population.

Repeated Mobility and Social Integration

Community roots as reflected in previous mobility patterns are also indicators of social stability. In general, previous residential mobility has been found to be an important determinant of current mobility propensity.[32] Not only is repeat movement related to mobility propensity but the converse is true — those with permanent roots as evidenced by non-mobility are less likely to be mobility prone. For example, survey data in one metropolitan area reveal that of those older persons who moved during 1960–1961, 30 per cent moved again in 1961–1962, compared to 13 per cent of those who had not moved in 1960–1961. Similarly, older persons who moved three or more times during the 1950–1960 decade

[32] See Chapters 3 and 7, this book.

three times as likely to move again during 1960–1962 than those who did not move in the 1950–1960 period. For one-year mobility the findings are more dramatic: six times as many older persons moved in one-year periods if they had moved three or more times in the previous decade than if they had not moved during the previous decade. (Mobility rates were 31 per cent and 5 per cent, respectively.) About one and one-half times as many repeat movers than nonrepeat movers planned or desired to move in one-year periods. The experience of moving around has a profound effect on the success with which older persons are able to plan and carry out their mobility desires. Almost half of the older population who moved three or more times during 1950 to 1960 and who planned or wanted to move again in 1961–1962 were successful (i.e., moved), a figure three times the success rate of those who had not moved from 1950 to 1960 but who planned or desired to move in 1961–1962. (The same general pattern holds for younger age groups.)

Thus, not only is repeat mobility, in general, more characteristic of younger persons and continued stability more characteristic of older persons, but within the older population repeat movement accounts for a disproportionate share of the total mobility rate of the older population. About two-thirds of the general one-year mobility rate is a function of repeat movers.

RECAPITULATION AND IMPLICATIONS

In examining the relationship of age and mobility, we have uncovered bits of evidence that should not only account consistently for the empirical data but should be coherent with the general sociological significance of age and consistent with the general theories of life-cycle and economic career mobility. The evidence provides the following tentative summary profile: (1) young adults are more mobile than older persons; (2) within the older population, the nonmarried, one-person households, low socioeconomic status persons, renters, and repeat movers are more mobility prone (these factors are obviously highly interrelated); (3) younger persons are much more likely to plan and desire to move than are older persons, and more likely to carry out these mobility plans; (4) housing and economic factors deter a significant number of older persons who want to move from moving; (5) among younger persons, career formation, career mobility, marriage, family formation, and family expansion clearly differentiate residential mobility. The explanation of these facts of migration must be consistent theoretically, that is, we must account for greater mobility between age groups as well as for differential mobility within age groups by using the same conceptual framework.

In general, we would argue that older persons are more integrated in the community through family, friends, housing investments, social organizations, and so on and, consequently, are much more prone to be residentially stable than younger persons who do not have these same social and economic investments. An inherent characteristic of the life-cycle state that older persons reflect is the long-term development of these neighborhood, familial, economic, and social ties; therefore, they are less prone to break them by moving, and if they move it will usually be within the same general community or neighborhood. And it is precisely those persons within the older population who are without such ties (i.e., repeat movers, renters, nonmarried, and to a lesser extent lower socioeconomic groupings) who are more prone to move. The overwhelming majority of older persons develop norms of social and residential stability usually broken only in instances of social or personal disruption — e.g., widowhood, retirement, institutionalization.

The general argument that social integration and migration are inversely related among the older population may shed some theoretical light on mobility patterns in general. The general notion that younger persons move in response to economic opportunity and economic changes is only a partial explanation. Surely, as was pointed out, a significant number of younger persons move in response to career changes, social mobility, and family changes. But we still have the problem of why some young persons do not move (not everyone responds to economic "opportunity") and the question of which, among the multitude of opportunities, will be selected. It may very well be that economic changes or economic opportunity should not be viewed as leading to or determining mobility but rather should be conceptualized in terms of facilitating factors. That is, mobility among the young relates directly to the types of social, community, and familial ties that determine the extent to which responses to economic change will involve a move. In fact, in terms of distance moved, relationship to community, family, and social ties may be key factors.

As a result of the analysis of life-cycle and residential mobility, we must conclude that economic motives are best treated as part of the more general life orientations of individuals. It seems that economic opportunities, although predominant, are more facilitating in the sense of allowing persons within various life-cycle stages to respond to opportunities that require residential mobility if social ties are weak. In any case, economic factors are not primary among all age segments and probably are of less importance in mobility within communities.

Following this, we must recognize the key position that life cycle, and its indicator, age, assumes in any migration analysis, particularly the various role dispositions associated with age groups and, in turn, the meaning of age to family, economic, and social cohesion. Obviously, we cannot expect empirical or theoretical generalizations about the relation-

ship of marital status or socioeconomic status and residential mobility
without the specific life-cycle context, i.e., without examining relationships within homogeneous age groups or controlling for age. But if we
argue for theoretical consistency we should be able to apply the analysis
of social cohesion, or social integration, or social ties to migration differentials within all age groups — even when the relationships are in different directions for younger and older populations. Thus, we would argue,
for example, that among the young, being married in the early stages of
family formation, or being in the higher socioeconomic status groupings
results in higher rates of mobility precisely because the balance of ties
(job, career, community, family) favor mobility. But at later points in the
life cycle, at middle and upper age levels, available economic opportunity must be balanced against the developed local, familial, and other
economic ties. Thus, being married and developing familial ties or being
in higher socioeconomic status positions implies a stable set of integrative forces for older persons.

Although family and economic motives are perceived as most important among younger movers, the overwhelming majority of reasons
older persons give for moving are related to housing and neighborhood
dissatisfactions. In conjunction with the evidence associated with the
repeat-mover phenomenon, it may be suggested that these perceptions
must be integrated with the general life orientations of individuals who
are mobile. The lack of social, community, and family ties might indeed
engender dissatisfactions as it engenders repeat mobility; perhaps, repeat mobility implies a lack of such ties.

An interesting convergence to the social integration theory of
residential mobility has been argued indirectly by Ladinsky.[33] His
examination of five-year mobility rates of detailed occupations within
the "professional" category using 1960 United States census data suggests
that structural conditions of work and career account for variation in
mobility rates. Particularly important in the present context is the relationship of individuals to their jobs as well as the nature of the jobs
themselves. In almost all cases where job investments were high either
through heavy investments in capital equipment or the close cultivation
of clienteles, migration rates were low. On the other hand, salaried professionals with unstandardized work conditions, no state licensing, and
strong occupational communication networks had higher long-distance
migration rates. High mobility rates also characterize those salaried

[33] Jack Ladinsky, "Occupational Determinants of Geographic Mobility Among
Professional Workers," *American Sociological Review*, 32 (April 1967), pp. 257–264;
and Ladinsky, "Sources of Geographic Mobility Among Professional Workers: A Multivariate Analysis," *Demography*, 4:1 (1967), pp. 293–309.

workers in highly professional occupations who tend to move in national or regional rather than local labor markets.

Ladinsky's analysis adds work organization and career traits as important determinants in geographic mobility. In the present context, the implications of his analysis strongly suggest the importance of the relationship between job and economic-career integration as part of the differential stability of persons within, and perhaps between, occupations.

Essentially, these data all indicate the need to redirect the general analysis of migration differentials toward a broader hypothesis concerning the relationship between social cohesion and integration and social ties on one hand, and migration propensities on the other. At this point, the hypothesis seems to account, in large part, for most available evidence. The hypothesis has the advantage of theoretical consistency and, most importantly, locates migration processes within a social structural context. Ultimately, the balance of social, familial, and economic ties within the life situation of individuals or groups determines rates and types of mobility (particularly distance). And mobility decisions (and we are mainly addressing ourselves to those decisions) are not only a function of the actual social ties of persons but of the more general norms and values that determine the relative significance of each social bond. The manifestation of social integration, social cohesion, and social ties along with the norms of social integration varies within and between societies, but will have as one consequence differential mobility rates.

Finally, when evaluating the determinants of any mobility pattern — whether from an historical, comparative, or differential perspective — it is insufficient to merely test mechanically a series of independent variables. That type of analysis usually results in the compilation of isolated bits of information that tend to be inconclusive. Concluding that economic and family changes are "determinants" of mobility patterns says little about the processes of migration and nothing about the social mechanisms and conditions under which these factors operate. By examining the significance of these variables, i.e., by seeing economic and family changes as reflecting the ties that bind individuals to their communities, we address ourselves to the nature of moving processes and relate those processes to broader social processes. In this sense, economic and social determinants are facilitating conditions permitting or impeding the expression of the relationship of individuals to society by their decisions to move or stay. Hence, a general migration hypothesis, which should be tested directly rather than inferentially, is that the patterns of community, social, and personal integration of individuals within society (and the underlying norms and values that are reflected in, and shape, such ties) determine the extent to which responses to economic opportunity and family changes are expressed in terms of mobility or stability.

Select Bibliography

Excellent bibliographic guides are available for students interested in reading more of the population literature; this select bibliography is intended to be only a preliminary introduction to the vast materials in the field. The basic and most comprehensive reference source in demography is *Population Index*, published quarterly in the Office of Population Research, Princeton University, for the Population Association of America. Available since 1935, *Population Index* lists and annotates an enormous range of demographic materials and is an indispensible tool for reading and research. An excellent guide to the literature through the 1950's is contained in Hope T. Eldridge, *The Materials of Demography*, published in 1959 by the International Union for the Scientific Study of Population and the Population Association of America. Less comprehensive and more selective, but still quite useful, is *Sociological Abstracts*, published regularly since 1953.

Several journals focus almost exclusively on demographic topics. These include: *Demography* (since 1964 the official journal of the Population Association of America); *Population Studies* (published since 1947 by the Population Investigation Committee of the London School of Economics); *Population* (published since 1946, in French with brief English summaries, by the Institut National D'Études Démographiques); and short articles in *Population Index*. Other journals that regularly feature articles of interest to demographers include: *International Migration Review; Milbank Memorial Fund Quarterly; Economic Development and Cultural Change; Population Review* (India); *Journal of Marriage and the Family; Population Bulletin* (Population Reference Bureau); *Studies in Family Planning, Country Profiles,* and *Reports on Population/Family Planning* (issued by the Population Council); and *Journal of the American Statistical Association*. There are, in addition, the important sociology journals, such as: *American Sociological Review; American Journal of Sociol-*

ogy; *British Journal of Sociology; Sociology; Social Forces; Social Problems; Annals of the American Academy of Political and Social Science; Comparative Studies in History and Society.*

The United Nations' population publications are rather extensive, and the reader is referred to their regular issues of *Population Bulletin* and *Population Studies* as well as to listings in *Population Index.* The annual statistical and demographic yearbooks published by the United Nations contain demographic and sociological data compiled from sources around the world. For in-depth and more thorough demographic profiles of specific countries, there are no substitutes for the census and vital statistics reports of those countries.

The somewhat arbitrary bibliography that follows focuses on some recent books and monographs (most published within the last decade and omitting journal articles) that I think are helpful guides to further reading and research. Additional materials on specific topics may be found in the footnotes to the chapters of this book, in the materials cited above, and in the bibliographies and footnotes listed in sources below.

GENERAL REFERENCES AND TEXTS

F. Bechhofer, ed. *Population Growth and the Brain Drain* (Edinburgh: Edinburgh University Press, 1969).

Bernard Benjamin. *Demographic Analysis* (New York: Praeger, 1968).

James Beshers. *Population Processes in Social Systems* (New York: Free Press, 1967).

Donald Bogue. *Principles of Demography* (New York: Wiley, 1969).

Paul Ehrlich and Anne Ehrlich. *Population, Resources, Environment* (San Francisco: Freeman, 1970).

D. E. C. Eversley. *Social Theories of Fertility and the Malthusian Debate* (London: Oxford University Press, 1959).

Thomas Ford and Gordon De Jong, eds. *Social Demography* (Englewood Cliffs, N.J.: Prentice-Hall, 1970).

Ronald Freedman, ed. *Population: The Vital Revolution* (Garden City, N.Y.: Doubleday, 1964).

David Glass and D. E. C. Eversley, eds. *Population in History* (Chicago: Aldine, 1965).

William Goode. *World Revolution and Family Patterns* (New York: Free Press, 1963).

Philip Hauser, ed. *Population and World Politics* (New York: Free Press, 1958).

Philip Hauser, ed. *The Population Dilemma,* 2nd ed. (Englewood Cliffs, N.J.: Prentice-Hall, 1969).

Philip Hauser and Otis Duncan, eds. *The Study of Population* (Chicago: University of Chicago Press, 1959).

David Heer. *Society and Population* (Englewood Cliffs, N.J.: Prentice-Hall, 1968).

David Heer, ed. *Readings on Population* (Englewood Cliffs, N.J.: Prentice-Hall, 1968).

"Historical Population Studies." *Daedalus,* 97 (Spring 1968), pp. 353–635.

E. P. Hutchinson. *The Population Debate* (Boston: Houghton Mifflin, 1967).

Kenneth Kammeyer, ed. *Population Studies* (Chicago: Rand McNally, 1969).

Peter Laslett. *The World We Have Lost* (New York: Scribner's, 1965).
Thomas Malthus, Julian Huxley, and Frederick Osborn. *On Population: Three Essays* (New York: Mentor, 1960).
Ronald Meek, ed. *Marx and Engels on Malthus* (New York: International Publishers, 1954).
Charles Nam, ed. *Population and Society* (Boston: Houghton Mifflin, 1968).
Katherine Organski and A. F. K. Organski. *Population and World Power* (New York: Knopf, 1961).
William Petersen. *The Politics of Population* (Garden City, N.Y.: Doubleday, 1964).
William Petersen. *Population*, 2nd ed. (New York: Macmillan, 1969).
Alfred Sauvy. *Fertility and Survival* (New York: Collier, 1963).
Alfred Sauvy. *General Theory of Population* (New York: Basic Books, 1969).
T. Lynn Smith and Paul Zopf. *Demography: Principles and Methods* (Philadelphia: Davis, 1970).
Mortimer Spiegelman. *Introduction to Demography* (Cambridge, Mass.: Harvard University Press, 1968).
Ralph Thomlinson. *Demographic Problems* (Belmont, Cal.: Dickenson, 1967).
Ralph Thomlinson. *Population Dynamics* (New York: Random House, 1965).
Warren Thompson and David Lewis. *Population Problems*, 5th ed. (New York: McGraw-Hill, 1965).
United Nations. *The Determinants and Consequences of Population Trends* (New York: United Nations, 1953).
E. A. Wrigley. *Population and History* (London: Weidenfeld and Nicolson, 1969).
Dennis Wrong. *Population and Society*, 3rd ed. (New York: Random House, 1967).
Louise Young, ed. *Population in Perspective* (New York: Oxford University Press, 1968).

TECHNIQUES, METHODS, AND DATA PROBLEMS

George Barclay. *Techniques of Population Analysis* (New York: Wiley, 1958).
Bernard Benjamin. *Health and Vital Statistics* (London: George Allen and Unwin, 1968).
Judith Blake and Jerry Donovan. *Western European Censuses, 1960: An English Language Guide* (Berkeley: University of California, Institute of International Studies, Population Monograph Series, no. 8, 1970).
Nathan Keyfitz. *Introduction to the Mathematics of Population* (Reading, Mass.: Addison-Wesley, 1968).
Forrest Linder and Robert Grave. *Techniques of Vital Statistics* (Washington, D.C.: Office of Vital Statistics, 1963).
Milbank Memorial Fund. *Emerging Techniques in Population Research* (New York: Milbank Memorial Fund, 1963).
Roland Pressat. *Demographic Analysis*, trans. Judah Matras (Chicago: Aldine, 1971).

POPULATION PATTERNS IN SELECT COUNTRIES

Donald Bogue. *The Population of the United States* (New York: Free Press, 1959).
John Caldwell. *Population Growth and Family Change in Africa* (Canberra, Aust.: Australian National University Press, 1968).

John Caldwell and C. Okonjo, eds. *The Population of Tropical Africa* (New York: Columbia University Press, 1968).
Ansley Coale and Edgar Hoover. *Population Growth and Economic Development in Low-Income Countries* (Princeton: Princeton University Press, 1958).
Kingsley Davis. *The Population of India and Pakistan* (Princeton: Princeton University Press, 1951).
Lincoln Day and Alice Day. *Too Many Americans* (New York: Dell, 1964).
Reynolds Farley. *Growth of the Black Population* (Chicago: Markham, 1970).
D. V. Glass. *Population Policies and Movements in Europe,* 2nd ed. (New York: Kelley, 1967).
R. K. Kelsall. *Population* (London: Longmans, Green, 1967).
Clyde Kiser, ed. *Components of Population Change in Latin America. Milbank Memorial Fund Quarterly,* 43 (October 1965), part 2.
Frank Lorimer. *The Population of the Soviet Union* (Geneva: League of Nations, 1946).
Milbank Memorial Fund. *Population Trends in Eastern Europe, the USSR, and Mainland China* (New York: Milbank Memorial Fund, 1960).
Widjojo Nitisastro. *Population Trends in Indonesia* (Ithaca: Cornell University Press, 1970).
Daniel Price. *Changing Characteristics of the Negro Population* (Washington, D.C.: U.S. Government Printing Office, 1969).
Edward Stockwell. *Population and People* (Chicago: Quadrangle, 1968).
J. Mayone Stycos, ed. *Population Dilemma in Latin America* (Washington, D.C.: Potomac Books, 1966).
Conrad Taeuber and Irene Taeuber. *The Changing Population of the United States* (New York: Wiley, 1958).
Irene Taeuber. *The Population of Japan* (Princeton: Princeton University Press, 1958).
E. A. Wrigley, ed. *An Introduction to English Historical Demography from the Sixteenth to the Nineteenth Centuries* (London: Weidenfeld and Nicolson, 1966).

STUDIES OF MORTALITY

Eduardo Arriaga. *Mortality Decline and Its Demographic Effects in Latin America* (Berkeley: University of California, Institute of International Studies, Population Monograph Series, no. 6, 1970).
Eduardo Arriaga. *New Life Tables for Latin American Populations in the Nineteenth and Twentieth Centuries* (Berkeley: University of California, Institute of International Studies, 1968).
Bernard Benjamin. *Social and Economic Factors Affecting Mortality* (The Hague: Mouton, 1965).
Katherine Hirst et al. *Infant and Perinatal Mortality in England and Wales* (Washington, D.C.: National Center for Health Statistics, ser. 3, no. 12, 1968).
Milbank Memorial Fund. *Trends and Differentials in Mortality* (New York: Milbank Memorial Fund, 1956).
Milos Vacek. *Mortality Trends in Czechoslovakia* (Washington, D.C.: National Center for Health Statistics, ser. 3, no. 13, 1969).

STUDIES OF FERTILITY

J. A. Banks. *Prosperity and Parenthood* (London: Routledge and Kegan Paul, 1954).

J. A. Banks and Olive Banks. *Feminism and Family Planning in Victorian England* (New York: Schocken, 1964).

Bernard Berelson, ed. *Family Planning and Population Programs* (Chicago: University of Chicago Press, 1966).

Larry Bumpass and Charles Westoff. *The Later Years of Childbearing* (Princeton: Princeton University Press, 1971).

O. A. Collver. *Birth Rates in Latin America* (Berkeley: Institute of International Studies, Research Series, no. 7, 1965).

Ronald Freedman et al. *Family Planning, Sterility and Population Growth* (New York: McGraw-Hill, 1959).

Ronald Freedman and John Takeshita. *Family Planning in Taiwan* (Princeton: Princeton University Press, 1969).

Wilson Grabill et al. *The Fertility of American Women* (New York: Wiley, 1958).

Clyde Kiser, ed. *Research in Family Planning* (Princeton: Princeton University Press, 1962).

Clyde Kiser et al. *Trends and Variations in Fertility in the United States* (Cambridge, Mass.: Harvard University Press, 1968).

Lee Rainwater. *And the Poor Get Children* (Chicago: Quadrangle Books, 1960).

Lee Rainwater. *Family Design* (Chicago: Aldin, 1965).

Norman Ryder and Charles Westoff. *Reproduction in the United States: 1965* (Princeton: Princeton University Press, 1971).

J. Mayone Stycos. *Human Fertility in Latin America* (Ithaca: Cornell University Press, 1968).

J. Mayone Stycos and Kurt Back. *The Control of Human Fertility in Jamaica* (Ithaca: Cornell University Press, 1964).

H. Yuan Tien. *Social Mobility and Controlled Fertility* (New Haven: College University Press, 1965).

Charles Westoff et al. *Family Growth in Metropolitan America* (Princeton: Princeton University Press, 1961).

Charles Westoff et al. *The Third Child* (Princeton: Princeton University Press, 1963).

Charles Westoff and Raymond Potvin. *College Women and Fertility Values* (Princeton: Princeton University Press, 1967).

Pascal Whelpton et al. *Fertility and Family Planning in the United States* (Princeton: Princeton University Press, 1966).

David Yaukey. *Fertility Differences in a Modernizing Country* (Princeton: Princeton University Press, 1961).

STUDIES OF MIGRATION

José Hernández Alvarez. *Return Migration to Puerto Rico* (Berkeley: Institute of International Studies, 1967).

G. Beijer. *Rural Migrants in Urban Setting* (The Hague: Martinus Nijhoff, 1963).

Eugene Brody, ed. *Behavior in New Environments: Adaptation of Migrant Populations* (Beverley Hills, Cal.: Sage, 1969).

John Caldwell. *African Rural-Urban Migration* (Canberra, Aust.: Australian National University Press, 1969).

R. B. Davison. *West Indian Migrants* (London: Oxford University Press, 1962).

Bruce Herrick. *Urban Migration and Economic Development in Chile* (Cambridge, Mass.: M.I.T. Press, 1966).

John Jackson, ed. *Migration* (London: Cambridge University Press, 1969).

Clifford Jansen, ed. *Readings in the Sociology of Migration* (London: Pergamon, 1970).

J. Mangalam. *Human Migration: A Guide to Migration Literature in English, 1955–62* (Lexington: University of Kentucky Press, 1968).

William Petersen. *Planned Migration* (Berkeley: University of California Press, 1955).

Peter Rossi. *Why People Move* (New York: Free Press, 1955).

Judith Shuval. *Immigrants on the Threshold* (New York: Atherton, 1963).

Henry Shryock. *Population Mobility Within the United States* (Chicago: Community and Family Study Center, University of Chicago, 1964).

Index of Authors

Inkeles, Alex, 25, 45, 96

Jacek, Henry J., Jr., 292, 296
Jones, Gavin W., 87, 276, 277, 280, 297

Kaplan, Abraham, 38, 39, 47, 309
Karp, Mark, 193
Kelsall, R. K., 110, 260
Kerckhoff, Alan, 295
Kimble, George, 129
Kirk, Dudley, 159
Kiser, Clyde V., 275, 277, 279, 280, 281, 287, 288, 289
Kitagawa, Evelyn M., 244, 253, 254, 263
Kitano, Harry, 291
Knodel, John, 141, 162
Kumar, Joginder, 71
Kuper, Hilda, 185, 187, 190, 194, 211
Kuznets, Simon, 73, 95

Ladinsky, Jack, 52, 69, 324, 325
Laslett, Peter, 107, 108, 128, 130
Lazerwitz, Bernard, 284
Lee, Ann, 288, 296, 303
Lee, Everett, 36, 51, 52, 53, 60, 65, 66, 69, 70, 71, 288, 296, 302, 303, 308
Lenski, Gerhard, 271, 272, 282, 283, 294, 297
Le Play, F., 157
Leslie, Gerald, 52, 313
Lewis, David, 236
Linder, Forrest E., 264
Linton, Ralph, 234
Little, Kenneth, 212
Litwak, Eugene, 68
Livi-Bacci, Massimo, 107, 165
Lorimer, Frank, 152, 153, 154, 156, 158, 159, 160, 193, 296
Lunde, Anders, 287

McCarthy, Mary, 247, 248, 249
McCord, William, 95, 129, 130, 143
McCormick, Thomas, 295
MacDonald, Beatrice D., 219
MacDonald, John S., 219
McKeown, Thomas, 112
Mair, George, 292
Marsh, Robert, 93
Masnick, George, 306

Matras, Judah, 219
Matthiessen, P. C., 261
Mayer, Albert J., 243, 254
Mayer, Kurt B., 213, 218, 240
Mazur, Allan, 7
Mazur, D. Peter, 112
Meadows, Paul, 212
Mendoza, Elvira, 290
Merton, Robert, 7, 22, 41, 44
Metropolitan Life Insurance Company, 247
Meuvret, J., 109
Miller, Ann, 306, 307
Miller, Herman, 316
Mills, C. Wright, 31, 32
Miltenyi, K., 121
Mitchell, J. Clyde, 212
Mizruchi, Ephraim, 212
Moller, Herbert, 159, 218
Moore, Barrington, Jr., 7
Moore, Wilbert, 22, 92, 95, 97, 98
Morris, J. N., 260
Moynihan, Daniel, 293
Myrdal, Alva, 215
Myrdal, Gunnar, 115

Neiva, Arthur H., 218
Ness, Gayl D., 40
Newsholme, Sir Arthur, 259
Nisbet, Robert, 41, 44
Noonan, John T., 162
Nortman, Dorothy, 276, 277, 280, 297
Notestein, Frank, 177
Nzimiro, I., 186, 212

Okonjo, C., 186, 191, 194, 195, 199, 202, 205
Olusanya, P. O., 173
Ominde, S. H., 199, 205

Pan, Chia-Lin, 124
Pankhurst, K. V., 218
Park, Robert, 37, 61
Parsons, Talcott, 45, 270, 312
Patterson, John, 275, 276, 277, 280, 283, 289
Petersen, William, 34, 35, 36, 50, 51, 52, 63, 64, 65, 71, 108, 117, 184, 186, 219, 236, 245, 285, 286, 287, 288, 291, 301, 308
Phillips, Harry T., 257, 258

Index of Subjects

abortion, 138, 142, 144, 161
acculturation, 291, 295–297
Africa, 53, 63, 71, 72, 89, 116, 119, 120, 129, 133, 147, 161, 172, 173, 182–220, 232, 256 (*see also specific countries*)
age: as biological and cultural variable, 226, 227; errors in reporting, 196; fertility and, 48–49, 226–227; at marriage, 145, 156, 161–164, 227; migration and, 204, 207, 302–303, 310–325; mortality and, 121–122, 227; population and, 227–228, 233–234; sociological meaning of, 311–313
aged, migration of, 313–325
agriculture: in England and Wales, 154–155; in France, 157–159
Agriville, 15–19
Alabama, 247
Alaska, 247
Amish, 296
Amsterdam, 267
Angola, 120
Arab, 232
Argentina, 90, 121, 172, 217, 218
Arizona, 249
Asia, 90, 92, 116, 133, 147, 161, 172, 173, 232, 255–257 (*see also specific countries*)

assimilation, migration and, 56, 210–214, 219 (*see also* acculturation)
Atlantic Ocean, 70
Aubagne, 109
Australia, 116

baby boom, 42, 169–171
Baltimore, 254
Bantu, 257–258
Barbados, 118
birth control, 166–167, 171; Catholics, 283, 292–293; Jews, 284, 285–287; Protestants, 283, 285
birth rate, crude, 145, 152, 169–170, 174
births (*see* fertility)
Black Muslims, 292, 296
Bolivia, 121
Boston, 62
Brazil, 217
British Guiana, 173
Brittany, 108
Burma, 173

California, 218, 237, 262
Canada, 89, 118, 119, 169, 217, 286
Cape Town, 257
Catholic (-s, -ism), 92, 226, 231, 273, 275–278, 280–286, 291–297; birth

339